EVIDENCE: PRINCIPLES, POLICY AND PRACTICE

GREENS CONCISE SCOTS LAW

EVIDENCE: PRINCIPLES, POLICY AND PRACTICE

SECOND EDITION

By

Fiona Raitt, LLB, PHD, SOLICITOR
Professor of Law at the University of Dundee

with

Eamon H. Keane, LLB (HONS), DIP LP
(trainee solicitor)

First published 2008

Published in 2013 by W. Green & Son Limited
21 Alva Street
Edinburgh EH2 4PS

Typeset by YHT Ltd, Hillingdon
Printed in Great Britain by CPI Antony Rowe.

No natural forests were destroyed to make this product;
only farmed timber was used and replanted.

A CIP catalogue record of this book is available from the British Library.

ISBN 978-0-414-01832-7

Thomson Reuters and the Thomson Reuters logo are trademarks of
Thomson Reuters.

PREFACE

The first edition of this book was published in 2008 and since then the pace of change in Scots law has, if anything, increased. Although change is often driven by the Scottish Government agenda—two major justice Bills are going through Parliament at the date of publication—these also reflect reforms inspired and shaped by a diverse group of institutions, including the European Parliament, the judiciary in Scotland, the UK Supreme Court and the European Court of Human Rights, as well as the Scottish Law Commission and the academy.

Recent reforms to the civil court structures, as well as those being ushered in to the criminal justice system following the decision in *Cadder v HM Advocate*, have created intense periods of critical reflection in the on-going search for reforms that at least retain, if not improve, the quality of justice dispensed to citizens. While some might be weary or suspicious of change, the very process of reflection and re-evaluation of our legal system is a healthy indicator of a well-functioning democracy. As a nation we remain attuned to our tradition of engagement with the rapid developments in the global environment affecting law and legal practice, which we instinctively know we must embrace if we are to have a legal system that is fit for purpose.

However, major challenges lie ahead. For example, those posed by the physical re-structuring of the Scottish Courts estate due to court closures are matched by the intellectual re-structuring required by the anticipated abolition of the corroboration rule. Both of these challenges are occurring at a time when access to justice due to legal aid constraints is a constant concern.

This book cannot supply answers to these pressing issues, but it aims to provide a modest contribution to the understanding of the law of evidence, the policy behind the law and some of the practical consequences that result. It is hoped it will be of use to those approaching the subject for the first time, as well as those more familiar with the subject who wish a concise commentary on the law. The Victims and Witnesses (Scotland) Bill and the Criminal Justice (Scotland) Bill are both likely to be in force during 2014 and the book takes account of this with discussion of key provisions in the relevant chapters. In particular, the forthcoming abolition of corroboration is acknowledged, but much of the discussion in the previous edition concerning the application of the rule is retained. It is speculated that in determining sufficiency of evidence in a post-corroboration world, recourse to previous jurisprudence to construct arguments will be useful. Time will reveal the merits of this speculation!

I was very fortunate to have the assistance of Eamon Keane in the researching and drafting of this edition. Any omissions and errors are of course my sole responsibility.

The team at W. Green have exhibited extraordinary patience while the book was completed. I am indebted to them and most appreciative of their support and professionalism throughout the process. In particular, my thanks to Janet Campbell, Frances Reid Rowland, Kirsty Price and Alan Bett.

Fiona Raitt
September 2013

CONTENTS

TABLE OF CASES

TABLE OF STATUTES

TABLE OF STATUTORY INSTRUMENTS

Chapter 1

THE ADVERSARIAL PROCESS

Scotland, in keeping with the other two jurisdictions of the United King- **1–01**
dom, namely England and Wales, and Northern Ireland, adopts an adversarial process of proof. Scots law is principally a common law legal system,
though tempered by its roots in civil law. The adversarial tradition, sometimes described as an accusatorial process, is in contrast to the continent
where virtually all countries have codified systems of law and operate within
an inquisitorial system.[1] In the adversarial system there are at least two sides
pitted against each other. In a criminal trial, there is the prosecution against
the defence, and in civil proceedings there is a pursuer against the defender.
These two sides argue out the dispute before a judge who operates as an
umpire or arbitrator but is supposed to intervene only when essential.
Excessive intervention can form a ground of appeal for interfering with the
parties' conduct of the case. According to Lord Justice Clerk Thomson[2]:

> "A litigation is in essence a trial of skill between opposing parties,
> conducted under recognised rules and the prize is the judge's decision.
> We have rejected inquisitorial methods and prefer to regard our judges
> as entirely independent. Like referees at a boxing contest, they see the
> rules are kept and count the points."

The reference by Lord Thomson to judges as "entirely independent" is not a
reference in this context to independence from political interference of any
sort, but to independence from the issues in dispute. In the adversarial
process, the parties, not the court, decide which issues will be litigated, while
the judge oversees fair play. In that adjudicative role, judges hold considerable discretion in interpreting the rules and advising the jury, as the
trier of fact, on the evidence. In most civil proceedings, and in summary
criminal trials, the judge, rather than the jury, will be the fact-finder.[3]

In contrast, in the inquisitorial system, at all times the judge effectively **1–02**
acts as the investigator and is instrumental in deciding which issues are
relevant. Judges in the inquisitorial system are much more in charge of the
conduct of the case, its pace and direction, and of the witnesses who are to
be called to give evidence, than their counterparts in the adversarial system.

---

[1] For comparative accounts of these two systems, see M. Damaska, "Structures of Authority
and Comparative Criminal Procedure" (1975) 84 Yale LJ 480.
[2] *Thomson v Glasgow Corporation*, 1962 S.C. (HL) 36 at 52; 1961 S.L.T. 237 at 246.
[3] In Scotland civil jury proofs are still competent. See A. Hajducki, *Civil Jury Trials*, 2nd edn
(Edinburgh, Avizandum, 2006).

1–03   In the inquisitorial system, a great deal of reliance is placed upon evidence contained in written witness statements compiled into a *dossier*, whereas the principle of oral testimony lies at the heart of the adversarial process. The emphasis is on evidence obtained by live, direct testimony from witnesses in the courtroom in the presence of the trier of fact—the judge or the jury depending on the nature of the case. These witnesses are then subject to cross-examination, a process that many ardently believe to be a crucial element in the search for the "truth" and for justice.

1–04   It would, however, be a mistake to think that criminal trials and civil proofs can necessarily uncover the "truth". Peter Murphy[4] has provided a more accurate and pragmatic description of what the trial can achieve:

> "A judicial trial is not a search to ascertain the ultimate truth of the past events inquired into, but to establish that a version of what occurred has an acceptable possibility of being correct."

One arrives at the acceptable "version of what occurred" through investigation, enquiry, fact-finding, examination and cross-examination. Each party, faced with the same set of facts, will seek to offer a different interpretation of these facts in order to persuade the trier of fact that their interpretation, their version of events, is the more probable one. In this way, the art of advocacy, of the ability to marshal arguments and to interpret and persuade becomes critically important. You may believe your case in law is sounder than that of your opponent, but you still have to present that case to the court persuasively if you are to have a chance of success.

1–05   In recent years there has been a series of shifts in Scots criminal procedure to embrace features of the inquisitorial approach, encouraged by the impact of the jurisprudence of the European Court of Human Rights in Strasbourg. These shifts are apparent, for example, in changes to the rules for disclosure of evidence by prosecutors to the defence, and in the use of prior statements in court in lieu of oral testimony. These are discussed in more detail in the relevant chapters. Suffice to note meantime, that assimilation of inquisitorial practices in Scotland's adversarial system is likely to increase, not least due to the advantages of harmonised legal procedures in countering global crime, especially cybercrime which has no physical boundaries.

The law of evidence

1–06 According to William Twining, one of the foremost evidence scholars, "[m]any teachers of evidence continue to cling to the absurd fallacy that the subject of evidence is co-extensive with the rules of evidence".[5] Twining's criticism is that the teaching of the law of evidence has been reduced to a rather unreflective exposition of a disparate collection of rules that regulate the way that facts are admitted into court. The focus is then heavily orientated towards the trial process, when actually it may be the pre-trial process, when evidence is being gathered, that is determinative of disputed issues. Pre-trial, the police will be faced with an array of choices at the

---

[4] P. Murphy, *Murphy on Evidence*, 8th edn (Oxford: Oxford University Press, 2003), p.3.
[5] W. Twining, *Theories of Evidence: Bentham and Wigmore* (London: Weidenfeld and Nicolson, 1985) p.174.

investigation stage that influence the kind of evidence obtained. For example, if police officers are convinced of the guilt of a suspect, alternative lines of enquiry that might implicate another person may not be followed up. It may be months or years later, if the case constructed against suspect A collapses at trial, that the police may explore other avenues, by which time the trail is cold.[6] The pre-trial stage can be pivotal for the outcome of the trial in other ways. Sadly, the annals of miscarriages of justice are replete with the situations where evidence was available but not disclosed to the defence,[7] not analysed[8] or simply not sought.[9]

Twining therefore urges evidence teachers to pay much more attention to **1–07** the role of fact-finding in legal disputes and to take account of the potential insights offered to fact-finding by, for example, logic, reasoning, probability theories and psychology. Other scholars have also urged an escape from the treadmill of teaching the rules of evidence absent of factual context, moral underpinning or socio-political backdrop.[10] This is a demanding challenge and deserves to be taken seriously, not least because of the significance for practitioners who handle facts. As Nicolson observes, "[i]t is indisputable that most lawyers spend far more time dealing with facts than with law".[11] Undoubtedly, this book has not entirely escaped "the treadmill of teaching the rules", but it tries to contextualise these rules, to keep a focus on the influence of facts and to offer criticism where appropriate.

Scottish universities have been liberated to teach beyond the rules since **1–08** the Law Society of Scotland decided, in 2011, to drop the study of evidence as a compulsory independent component of the curriculum for students embarked on a law degree that qualified graduates for entry to the Diploma in Professional Legal Practice and thereafter the legal profession. As an intellectual study, the law of evidence has more in common with jurisprudence and theories of knowledge, dimensions which may be by-passed in the rush to deliver an understanding of "how it all works in practice".[12] In the new regime, evidence lecturers are free to explore some of the more complex and challenging aspects of evidence rules, such as the definition of "fair" in the context of a fair trial, or what constitutes "due process" or "reliable" evidence in legal proceedings. The description of the rules of evidence as merely a series of exclusionary rules does little to excite interest in the subject. The task here is therefore to try to give meaning and purpose to the study of evidence by teasing out the important underlying values, such as due process, fairness, informed consent, public interest and absence of deception.

---

[6] G. Chambers and A. Millar, *Investigating Sexual Assault* (Edinburgh: Scottish Office, 1983).
[7] *R. v Clark* (Sally) [2003] EWCA Crim 1020.
[8] *R v Maguire (anna Rita)* [1992] 94 Cr. App. R. 133.
[9] *Preece v HM Advocate*, Note and Commentary, A. Brownlie [1981] Crim.L.R. 783.
[10] See D. Nicolson, "Facing facts: the teaching of fact construction in university law schools" (1996–1997) 1 *International Journal of Evidence and Proof*, 132; and P. Roberts, "Rethinking the Law of Evidence: A Twenty-first Century Agenda for Teaching and Research," (2002) *Current Legal Problems*, 297.
[11] D. Nicolson, "Facing Facts" (1996–1997) 1 E. & P. at 132.
[12] P. Roberts, "Rethinking the Law of Evidence" (2002) C.L.P. 297.

Fact construction and interpretation

1–09 When parties are contemplating litigation, they start to gather facts in order
to establish what kind of a case can be proved in court. The rules of evidence
constrain the type and nature of information that is admissible in court and
thus regulate the process of proof of fact in both civil and criminal cases.
Twining has urged that we "take facts seriously" as they are easily taken for
granted and the critical attention they deserve is more often focused on the
rules of evidence that regulate their admissibility in court.

1–10 Facts are only admissible in court if they comply with these rules of
evidence. It is sometimes fondly thought that facts are self-evident and once
proved must be true. Students of evidence should be quickly disabused of
that notion. Indeed, most come to realise that facts are constructed, that is,
they are often woven together into a particular story to support a case that is
being built by one party to litigation, whether the prosecutor in a criminal
trial for theft, or the pursuer in a civil action for breach of contract. In
Thomson v Glasgow Corporation, discussed above, Lord Justice-Clerk
Thomson observed:

> "Our system of administering justice in civil affairs proceeds on the
> footing that each side, working at arm's length, selects its own evidence.
> Each side's selection of its own evidence may, for various reasons, be
> partial in every sense of the term."

Presentation of evidence is therefore aimed at being purposeful, rather than
necessarily truthful. As Nicolson and Webb explain[13]:

> "The argument for the adversary system's superiority is that it is best
> suited to ascertaining the facts ... Unfortunately, however, this claim is
> impossible to verify empirically ... No-one can ever know what the
> 'true' facts of particular disputes are."

What is meant by claiming that facts are constructed is that "facts have to
be selected, interpreted and communicated. The process is neither
mechanical nor neutral, but is aimed at persuading the reader of the logical
and emotional force of the decision."[14] In their account of how prosecutors
reached decisions, Moody and Toombs illustrated how the personal and
professional beliefs and attitudes of the prosecutor can influence decision-
making, both in the decision whether to prosecute and in trial tactics.[15]

1–11 In addition, the adversarial system accords a great deal of discretion to
judges who have considerable interpretive power. When acting in civil
proceedings, or in summary proceedings without a jury, the judge is the trier
of fact.[16] They are required to select and prioritise facts and to allocate

---

[13] D. Nicolson and J. Webb, *Professional Legal Ethics: Critical Interrogations* (Oxford: Oxford
University Press,1999) at 185.

[14] D. Nicholson, "Facing Facts" (1996–1997) 1 E. & P. at 134.

[15] S. Moody and J. Tombs, *Constructing Prosecution Decisions: The case of the procurator fiscal*
(Edinburgh: Scottish Academic Press, 1982).

[16] Even in solemn proceedings when the jury is the trier of fact the judge stills performs a vital
role in deciding which items of evidence are admissible and thus available for the jury to
consider.

weight to these facts. How are such judicial decisions made? It has been suggested that "a judge with discretion should reach the best decision on the basis of relevant non-legal standards, such as those of sound political morality or social justice".[17] In the 1986 Reith Lectures, Lord McCluskey, then a senior Scottish judge, acknowledged that judges are indeed influenced by factors other than "law"[18]:

> "It is difficult to escape the conclusion that the choices which the system leaves the judge free to make are influenced by the judge's personality, his instincts and preferences, his accumulated social and philosophical make-up and his sense of the public mood."

The common law has often been described as "a living system of law"[19] so it is quite proper that judges, who shape the common law through interpretation and re-interpretation will have regard to their "sense of the public mood" when exercising discretion. One can think of major reforms that interpretation of case law has brought about, where judges have acknowledged that shifts in social attitudes have been instrumental to the decision. For example, in *HM Advocate v Stallard*[20] the court accepted for the first time that a husband could be guilty of raping his wife. In a subsequent case, the *Lord Advocate's Reference No.1 of 2001*,[21] the definition of rape was re-framed when a seven bench court held, by a majority (two judges dissenting) that the crime is committed if there is sexual intercourse without a woman's consent, thus altering the actus reus of rape. Prior to the *Reference*, the crime of rape consisted of sexual intercourse in circumstances where a woman's will had been overcome. Of course, how the Crown now proves lack of consent remains a matter for the law of evidence and is problematic.[22]

Judges have to be just as conscious of shifting attitudes in civil matters. **1–12** We have recently seen the abandonment of "maternal preference" in disputes over the residence of children. There is no longer a doctrine that only mothers can parent children, or that they are necessarily the better parent. Instead, a mother's claim to residence of the child must be founded upon evidence that it is in the child's best interests to be with his or her mother. In determining best interests, judges acknowledge they need to have regard to some general principle as a "point of reference" that "represents the consensus of society".[23] Similarly, there is no assumption that it is necessarily in a child's best interests to have contact with a biological father—*Sanderson v McManus*.[24] The father's claim must be supported by evidence.

There is obviously also a political dimension to the "public mood". We **1–13** can see this very clearly in relation to the perceived threat from global

---

[17] S. Burton, *Judging in Good Faith* (Cambridge, Mass.: Cambridge University Press, 2002), p.47.

[18] Lord McCluskey, *Law, Justice and Democracy*, (London: Sweet and Maxwell, 1987), p.8.

[19] *Kleinwort Benson Ltd v Lincoln City Council* [1999] 2 A.C. 349 per Lord Goff of Chieveley at 377.

[20] *HM Advocate v Stallard*, 1989 S.C.C.R. 248.

[21] *Lord Advocate's Reference (No.1 of 2001)*, 2002 S.L.T. 466.

[22] See *McKearney v HM Advocate*, 2004 J.C. 87 and discussion in Chs 5 and 12.

[23] *White v White*, 2001 S.L.T. 689 per Lord President Rodger at 696.

[24] *Sanderson v McManus*, 1997 S.C. (HL) 55.

terrorism that has undoubtedly influenced the passage of much anti-terrorist legislation since 9/11 and the attack on the Twin Towers in New York.

1–14   Through a series of measures, we have legislation that encroaches quite deeply on previously held freedoms. Under the Anti-Terrorism, Crime and Security Act 2001, when deciding whether to deport persons suspected of terrorist offences, Special Immigration and Advisory Courts were empowered to operate on the basis they could admit incriminating evidence against a suspect. They did so even if that evidence might have been obtained by torture, so long as the torture did not take place on British soil. Although the House of Lords has ruled this practice unlawful[25]—in doing so upholding the principle of freedom from torture, one of the most hallowed constitutional rights—repeated surveys of the British public indicate a high level of sympathy with restricting the civil liberties of individuals in the greater interest of protecting the rest of society.[26] Their sympathy extends to accepting that evidence obtained by torture may be necessary in the interests of national security.

1–15   The point here is that, but for 9/11, and the intense political reaction to that event, the notion that the courts in the United Kingdom might start to admit evidence obtained by torture would have been unthinkable, let alone an actuality. We also now know from prosecutions in England in 2012 that British personnel have been implicated in rendition and torture of prisoners, a finding which is both shameful and deeply undermining of the reputation of a jurisdiction which maintains its adherence to the rule of law.[27] This issue is discussed at greater length in Ch.10.

1–16   A final example of a factor influencing how facts are selected and interpreted is economics. The rule of relevancy prevents a great deal of factual information from being heard in court because, unless it is directly relevant to the case, it will unduly lengthen litigation which is already very costly. Economics drive the legal process of proof in other ways that are less readily justified. A party's ability to fund litigation or to instruct experts to challenge evidence may be unduly influential on outcomes. For example, if a party cannot afford an expert witness, important facts in a proof or trial may go uncontested, and thus be regarded as proven, but that does not necessarily mean these facts are accurate.

1–17   The adversarial process requires the trier of fact to make choices about the credibility and reliability of witnesses. Ultimately it requires that one version of events is chosen over another. There is no magic formula for this—the truth is not something tangible hanging in the ether and waiting to be captured. Facts are rarely pure, neatly defined or objective. They are often incomplete, messy and capable of multiple interpretations. In the case of *R. v Cannings*[28] a mother was wrongfully convicted of the murder of two of her children who died suddenly in unexplained circumstances. The trial

---

[25] *A and others v The Secretary of State for the Home Department* [2001] 24 UKHL 56.

[26] e.g. the Anti-Terrorism Crime and Security Act 2001, the Prevention of Terrorism Act 2005; and the Terrorism Act 2006. For discussion of the international law obligations binding the UK see R. Pattenden, "Admissibility in criminal proceedings of third party and real evidence obtained by methods prohibited by UNCAT", (2006) 10(1) E.& P. 1.

[27] A.T. Williams, *A Very British Killing—The Death of Baha Mousa* (London: Johnathan Cape, 2012).

[28] *R v Cannings (Angela)* [2004] EWCA Crim. 1; [2004] 1All E.R. 725.

judge, Mrs Justice Hallet, said when sentencing Cannings to imprisonment[29]:

> "I have no doubt that for a woman like you to have committed the terrible acts of suffocating your own babies there must have been something seriously wrong with you. All the evidence indicates you wanted the children, apart from these terrible incidents you cherished them, so in my layman's view, it is no coincidence that these events took place within weeks of your giving birth. It can, in my view, be *the only explanation* for why someone like you could have committed these acts when you have such a loving and supportive family."

In seeking an explanation for the "murder" Mrs Justice Hallet overlooked the possibility that the evidence was incomplete. The Court of Appeal, on the second occasion the case was referred to it, found there was another plausible reason for the children's deaths—natural causes—plus serious disagreement amongst the experts about the cause of death, sufficient to render the conviction unsafe.

It is rare that there will be only one explanation for events. Allegations **1–18** arise because at least two parties cannot agree on the interpretation of the facts. Both may be entirely sincere as to their position, but one or both may be mistaken as to a person's identity, or as to the events that have occurred, or as to the interpretation of behaviour. These may be genuine and well-intentioned mistakes, but they would also prevent a fact becoming objectively true. Therefore, one must approach every set of "facts" with an open mind and remain alive to the possibility that there may be alternative plausible interpretations. The task of the law of evidence is to help identify the most accurate interpretation available. The next chapter takes up this theme and considers some of the main rules that govern what kind of evidence is admissible in court.

---

[29] *R v Cannings* [2004] EWCA Crim 1 at [5] (emphasis added).

Chapter 2

THE CONCEPTUAL FRAMEWORK OF EVIDENCE

INTRODUCTION

2–01 Although it is possible to characterise the law of evidence as merely a set of rules that determine the admissibility of facts into the court process, it is also possible to view these rules as constituent parts of a broad conceptual framework. It is a framework that serves both a pragmatic purpose, in making the administration of justice more efficient, as well as a principled one, in articulating the key values and ideals for conducting litigation. This chapter is concerned with some of the more important principles and features of that framework.

Categories of facts

2–02 There are various ways of characterising facts. In every criminal trial or civil proof there are facts in dispute (also known as facts in issue) between the parties that will have to be considered by the court and proven or disproven in order to determine the case. These facts must themselves be relevant to the eventual outcome of the case. The facts in issue are traditionally referred to as the *facta probanda*, or "those matters in dispute between the parties".[1] While in each case there is only one ultimate issue to be determined (whether or not the accused is convicted, or whether the pursuer succeeds in a civil action), the process of arriving at that determination involves decisions about various facts in issue which, taken together, make up the case. The facts in issue are also known as the "crucial facts or essential facts".

2–03 It is possible for a party to lose on one or more of the crucial facts, i.e. fail to establish them in his or her favour by means of admissible evidence, and yet still succeed on the ultimate issue. Equally, but unusually, a party could prove every one of the points raised as facts in issue and still lose the case. This might occur, for example, when an accused offers no evidence in contradiction of the prosecution case, but is acquitted following a successful defence submission of "no case to answer".[2] The court in such a situation has found the totality of the prosecution case insufficient to prove the accused's guilt beyond reasonable doubt.

2–04 The role of the trier of fact—the jury in a solemn criminal trial or the judge in summary criminal proceedings and in civil cases—is to disentangle the facts and assess the weight to be attached to each of them before ruling

---

[1] Walker and Walker, *The Law of Evidence in Scotland*, 3rd edn, M. Ross (Edinburgh: T & T Clark, 2000) para.1.3.1.

[2] See s.97 (solemn proceedings) and s.160 (summary proceedings) of the Criminal Procedure (Scotland) Act 1995.

on the ultimate issue: the innocence or guilt of the accused. Exactly the same process operates in a civil action, where the ultimate issue is whether the pursuer succeeds in their claim.

A court may be asked to consider facts that are not themselves facts in issue, but which have some bearing on the probability or improbability of the facts in issue.[3] Such facts comprise circumstantial evidence and are known as *facta probationis*. For example, it would be important for a court hearing testimony from an eye-witness to a robbery to know that the witness was short sighted since that could affect the reliability of the witness and may result in the testimony being disregarded. The fact that a witness has such an impairment is circumstantial evidence, in that it has no immediate bearing on the ultimate issue, but it may be highly relevant to a fact in issue, i.e. the accurate identification of the accused. **2–05**

Another illustration of the distinction between the facts in issue and circumstantial evidence can be drawn from a civil reparation action. In a case of alleged medical negligence of a surgeon, the facts in issue—crucial facts— include the fact of the injury, the existence of a duty of care, the fact of a breach of that duty and the existence of a causal link between the injury and the breach of the duty. The fact that the surgeon has previously been found negligent in two similar cases is not in itself an essential fact, but it certainly has a bearing on the probability or improbability of the facts in issue, and is thus circumstantial evidence. **2–06**

Relevance

Evidence that a party wishes to bring to the attention of a court must be relevant. What do we mean by "relevant"? We can begin with the deceptively simple statement that in a court of law, "all admissible evidence must first of all be relevant, but not all relevant items of evidence will be admissible". It is dangerous to generalise about relevance: it is highly contingent on context and depends very much on the individual facts and circumstances in any given case. However, in broad terms, facts which a party wishes to adduce as evidence must have a logical link with an issue raised by the case in hand. **2–07**

The concept of relevance is complex. It can be expressed in general terms as a relationship that exists between two facts. Fact A is relevant to fact B when it appears that the two tend to exist together. When one of those two facts requires to be proven, then the existence of the other fact, when it appears to be "logically connected with those matters in dispute"[4] is potentially an item of evidence. Or, to put in another way, "the ultimate test [of relevance] is whether the material in question has a reasonably direct bearing on the subject under investigation".[5] **2–08**

For example, where an accused person is found to be in possession of recently stolen property, in incriminating circumstances, that fact is an **2–09**

---

[3] Walker and Walker, 3rd edn, para.1.3.1. When the fact sought to be proved is insufficiently relevant to a primary issue to justify its tendency to confuse matters, it will be rejected as an inadmissible collateral issue. See *Swan v Bowie*, 1948 S.C. 46 at 51.

[4] *Inland Revenue Commissioners v Stenhouse's Trustees*, 1993 S.L.T. 248.

[5] per Lord Osborne in *Strathmore Group Ltd v Credit Lyonnais*, 1994 S.L.T. 1023 at 1031H.

admissible item of evidence in that person's subsequent trial for almost any crime of dishonesty relating to that property.[6] Why? Because it is part of human experience that persons who are found to be in possession of property shortly after its theft, and who cannot give an innocent explanation of such possession, tend to have been involved in some way in its dishonest appropriation, usually as thieves or as resetters. Fact A (the possession of recently stolen property in criminative circumstances) is so logically related to fact B (the guilt of the person in possession) that it cannot be ignored and is therefore relevant to the case. In this example, the logical link between the two facts is so strong that it creates a presumption of guilt against the person in possession, which must then be rebutted by some innocent explanation.[7]

2–10   The facts offered by the prosecution as evidence must be relevant (i.e. logically related to) the central issue in the case, namely the guilt or innocence of the accused. Of equal relevance to the same central issue will be items of defence evidence, which might stem from an alibi, e.g. the fact that the accused was 100 miles away from the locus at the time a crime was committed, or character evidence that the accused has never been in trouble before,[8] and that the accused gives evidence on oath denying any knowledge of the crime. The extent to which all or any of these items of evidence are admissible in court is a separate consideration.

2–11   Although these examples are from criminal proceedings, the basic requirement of all items of evidence—that they be relevant—is equally applicable in civil proceedings. For example, in an action for damages arising from the negligent driving of a motor vehicle, it is relevant to know how the vehicle was being driven shortly before, and shortly after, the collision that gave rise to the action.[9] Or, when it is alleged that a local highway authority ignored the known state of a road, in breach of its statutory duty, it is relevant to cite examples of other accidents on the same stretch of road in the weeks prior to the accident in question.[10] In each of these examples, the item of evidence is relevant because of its logical link with a fact in issue, i.e. respectively, the care the driver took at the time of the accident and the state of knowledge of the local authority concerning the condition of the road. The resulting inference is that one fact is probably accompanied by the other. As with criminal cases, the logical connection between the two facts is sometimes so strong in civil actions that it gives rise to a presumption, albeit a rebuttable one. Thus, a child born to a married couple will be presumed to be the biological child of that couple—a presumption that could be rebutted with DNA evidence of paternity.

Admissibility of facts and the Exclusionary Rules

2–12 Once an item of evidence is regarded as relevant it then has to pass the test of admissibility, i.e. not be excluded on one of the many grounds upon

---

[6] For an example of this principle in action, see *Cassidy v McLeod*, 1981 S.C.C.R. 270: see also Gordon, "The Burden of Proof on the Accused", 1968 S.L.T. (News) 29 and 37 at 40.

[7] This presumption is dealt with more fully in Ch.7. It pre-dates Alison, *Principles of the Criminal Law of Scotland*, p.320.

[8] Character evidence is generally admissible in favour of the accused; see *Slater v HM Advocate*, 1928 J.C. 94 at 105, and Ch.12.

[9] Lord President Cooper in *Bark v Scott*, 1954 S.C. 72 at 76.

[10] *W. Alexander & Sons v Dundee Corporation*, 1950 S.C. 123.

which even relevant evidence can be withheld from the court. The fact that an item of evidence is relevant does not guarantee that the court will admit it as evidence, let alone that it will attach any great weight to it. The Anglo-American adversarial system does not permit "free proof" whereby all potentially relevant evidence is placed before the court. Instead, most of the rules of evidence function as exclusionary rules in that they prevent evidence being considered by the court on the ground that it is not admissible. To give an example, a confession obtained through duress will not be admissible because it is not freely given and it is not reliable. Equally, the "planting" of incriminatory evidence is deception and therefore unlawful.[11] Thus, the fingerprints of an accused person found at the scene of a murder may be highly relevant and apparently incriminating, but the evidence in relation to these fingerprints will not be admissible if it turns out they have been "planted" by the police. The decision as to the admissibility of any item of evidence lies with the judge—it lies within his or her judicial discretion.

Exclusionary rules have a common objective, namely the desire to ensure **2–13** that every issue before a court is considered fairly and accurately. Later chapters examine the main exclusionary rules in depth, but five specific rules are mentioned here as illustrations of the type of evidence that will be excluded and the rationale for exclusion.

(1) Hearsay evidence is regarded as "second-hand" evidence as it is only **2–14** B's account of what A told him. It is not "best evidence" because it does not come from the original source, much might have been lost or confused in transition and so it is generally prudent to exclude hearsay evidence on the grounds of unreliability.

(2) Opinion evidence is not generally admissible unless the witness is an **2–15** expert on the matter in issue. Thus, a witness is expected to give an accurate statement of what they saw, heard or smelt, etc., but the court does not want a lay witness's opinion of how these facts should be interpreted, since interpretation of facts is for experts or the court.

(3) Character evidence, such as the previous misdeeds of the accused, is **2–16** usually excluded because of its tendency to mislead the trier of fact and potential to be unduly prejudicial. As a general rule, a criminal court is only concerned to establish whether the accused committed the offence libelled on the occasion libelled. It is not concerned with what may or may not have been done by the accused on a previous occasion. However, there are some statutory exceptions to this general rule which are discussed in detail in Ch.12.

(4) The public interest may demand that certain information, whilst **2–17** relevant, is not disclosed to a court. If a government department or agency claims that disclosure in court of specific information is contrary to the public interest, a government minister can issue a public interest immunity certificate preventing disclosure. When successful, this can result in evidence that is highly relevant, or even conclusive to a dispute, being denied to the court. In 1992 this issue became the focus of much public concern following the collapse of the highly publicised *Matrix Churchill* trial in England. In those proceedings, various businessmen narrowly escaped conviction, and

---

[11] Note that not all countries regard evidence that is unlawfully obtained as inadmissible. For example, English law adopts a different approach. See Ch.10 for discussion.

likely imprisonment, when certain government documents essential to their defence were initially withheld on the ground of public interest.[12] More recently, in England, policies have been developed to enable prosecutions of alleged terrorists to take place in circumstances where intelligence-derived material relied upon by the prosecution is not disclosed to the defence in the usual way, but is instead disclosed solely to a "special advocate" appointed to represent the accused persons but not permitted to discuss with them the contents of protected intelligence material.[13] These arrangements are highly controversial as withholding from the defence information that is critical to the proof of the crime charged offends against the basic tenets of a fair trial. On the other hand, the state has a duty to protect its citizens from potential acts of terrorism and it is argued that the provision of special advocates satisfies both the need for equality of arms within the trial whilst preserving details of intelligence activities and identity of agents.[14]

2–18   (5) Evidence that has been obtained improperly or illegally is often excluded from the court on grounds of public policy. For example, if the police conduct a non-urgent search of premises without a warrant and exceed their common law powers of search, any evidence recovered, no matter how relevant will be excluded. In a democracy which seeks to uphold the rule of law and the rights of individuals against the state such illegal activity is not acceptable. Under certain political conditions this causes considerable tension. The admissibility of evidence obtained by torture may appear an extreme example to cite here, but, as mentioned earlier, it is a real issue today.

Weight of evidence

2–19 The "weight" of an item of evidence is simply the degree of reliance that the court places upon it. While admissibility of evidence is a matter of law for the judge, its weight is a question of fact for the trier of fact. There is no pre-assessment of weight and no legal rules governing it. The trier of fact has to assess the evidence for themselves, using what has been described as "rules of common sense".[15] In so doing, there is a wide discretion, though in a jury trial, where the evidence is complex, the judge has a responsibility to provide guidance in directions to the jury before they retire to consider their verdict.[16] As weight is a question of fact, it is rarely the subject of an appeal. However, the significance that the issue of weight can command is apparent in *Thomson v Kvaerner Govan Ltd*,[17] a claim for damages by an injured worker. The House of Lords upheld the decision of the Lord Ordinary at first instance to reject the claim for damages. The Lords concluded, overturning the decision of the Inner House, that although the precise details of the accident could not be determined, and the pursuer had given an honest

---

[12] For background to this unreported case see I. Leigh, "Matrix Churchill, Supergun and the Scott Inquiry", *Public Law* (1993) 630.
[13] See e.g. the provisions in the Anti-terrorism Crime & Security Act 2001.
[14] See, Counter-Terrorism Policy and Human Rights: Prosecution and Pre-Charge Detention, *http://www.official-documents.gov.uk/document/cm69/6920/6920.pdf* [accessed July 15, 2013].
[15] Lord Blackburn in *Lord Advocate v Lord Blantyre* (1879) 6 R. (H.L.) 72 at 85.
[16] *Shepherd v HM Advocate*, 1997 S.L.T. 525 per Lord McCluskey at p.528.
[17] *Thomson v Kvaerner Govan Ltd*, 2004 S.C. (H.L.) 1.

account of the accident, the weight of the evidence did not support the pursuer's explanation of events.

Sufficiency of evidence

Separate from the question of the weight to be attached to any individual **2–20** item of evidence, there is always a question as to whether a party has adduced sufficient evidence for the case to succeed. Sufficiency is a question of law. As a matter of law, a party's evidence must reach a certain minimum standard of persuasion before it can succeed.[18] It is linked to weight and is often a matter of inference.[19] You have to know the law to establish what amounts to sufficiency. For example, in a civil action based on negligence you need to know what it is you have to prove (duty of care, breach of duty, resultant loss, etc) before you can establish the amount of evidence you need to prove your case.

In a criminal prosecution, as in Scotland, at present there is a rule that **2–21** essential facts must be corroborated. This means that a sufficiency of evidence normally requires at least two items of evidence emanating from separate sources.[20] Sometimes the construction of what is a separate source is strained, as in *Langan v HM Advocate*[21] where the two sources were, first, the accused's fingerprint in the house where the murder victim was found and, second, the accused's bare denial that he had ever been in the house. Lord Justice-Clerk Ross declared that:

> "...[M]uch would in this connection turn upon whether any explanation was put forward by the appellant for the presence of his fingerprint. In this case not only was there an absence of any explanation from the appellant as to how his fingerprint got onto the tap, but he really put forward the position that there was no explanation because he maintained that he had never been in the house."

It is possible for one party to produce sufficient evidence in law to prove the case, but the other party still succeeds because their evidence is more convincing. It is also possible for one party to produce the only evidence in a case, but find that this evidence is insufficient in law to justify a decision in their favour. This is what happens in criminal cases when a judge rules that there is "no case to answer",[22] or where a trial judge refuses to allow a particular point to go to the jury because insufficient evidence has been led to justify it. For example, on an indictment libelling "assault to severe injury and to the danger of life", the prosecution must adduce sufficient evidence to establish that the victim's life was actually in danger. Otherwise, the prosecution, possibly at the invitation of the judge, will delete reference in the indictment to "danger of life" before the judge's charge to the jury.

---

[18] See, for example, *White v Mackinnon,* 1987 G.W.D. 4-110. For a discussion and application of sufficiency, see *F. v Kennedy,* 1988 S.L.T. 404.
[19] See, for example, *Donaghy v Normand,* 1992 S.L.T. 666.
[20] Note that the Criminal Justice (Scotland) Bill, s.57, published by the Scottish Government on June 21, 2013 proposes to abolish the corroboration rule. See Ch.8.
[21] *Langan v HM Advocate,* 1989 S.C.C.R. 379 at 381.
[22] See *Lockhart v Crockett,* 1987 S.L.T. 551 and *Wallace v McLeod,* 1986 S.C.C.R. 678.

2–22   In determining the legal question of sufficiency, more than one principle may be involved. It may be that there is no conviction in a criminal case because there is a lack of corroboration.[23] Or it may be that a vital ingredient of a party's case in a reparation action, such as failure to take reasonable care, has not been established. These issues are concerned with the concept of the burden of proof which is dealt with in Chs 5 and 6.

Best evidence

2–23   The best evidence rule is both an aspiration and a statement of common sense. The law of evidence aspires to have admitted into the proof process the best, i.e. original, or best quality, evidence that is available to the court as this will be the most reliable and persuasive evidence. According to Dickson,[24] it is a primary rule of evidence:

> "...[T]he rule, namely, that a party must adduce the best attainable evidence of the facts he means to prove. ... The rule is chiefly directed against the admission of copies or parole of the contents of documents and of hearsay evidence; these all inferring the existence of more original proof of the facts which they set forth."

The Scottish Law Commission in their *Report on Hearsay Evidence in Criminal Proceedings* stated that rules of evidence should aim to achieve reasonable expedition and a reasonable degree of certainty, while avoiding needless expense.[25] They also noted that the best evidence rule was rarely applied today,[26] though examples can be found in the law reports.[27] In any event, the rule continues to influence many other rules of evidence, such as the hearsay rule, which in its pure form rejects "second-hand evidence", but whose common law and statutory exceptions are permitted precisely because they are the best *available* evidence.

Best evidence in civil cases

2–24   The best evidence rule in civil cases requires that if a document is fundamental to a claim made by one of the parties, then the original of that document, not a copy, must be produced. In the absence of an original document, there are alternative procedural options, including the parties' acceptance of a copy.[28] However, the essential principle remains that best evidence is preferred. Acceptance of a copy can be set out in a joint minute, or by an admission in the closed record to the effect that the document

---

[23] Corroboration is dealt with in Ch.8.
[24] William G. Dickson, *Evidence, A Treatise on the Law of Evidence in Scotland*, with P. J. Hamilton Grierson, 3rd edn (Edinburgh: T & T Clark, 1887) para.195.
[25] See 2.26–2.31, Scottish Law Commission, *Evidence: Report on Hearsay Evidence in Criminal Proceedings*, HMSO, 1995. Scot. Law Com. No.149.
[26] See para.3.5. *Report on Hearsay Evidence in Criminal Proceedings*. HMSO, 1995. Scot. Law Com. No.149.
[27] See *Scottish & Universal Newspapers Ltd v Gherson's Trs*, 1987 S.C. 27; *Crichton v Wood*, 1981 S.L.T. (Notes) 66; and *Inverclyde D.C. v Carswell* (Sh. Ct) 1987 S.C.L.R. 145.
[28] Also, s.6(1) of the Civil Evidence (Scotland) Act 1988 provides that a copy document properly authenticated by the person making the copy shall be deemed a true copy. Another option is a separate court action to "prove the tenor" of the document.

quoted at length in the pleadings is genuine. When the missing document does not constitute the foundation of a party's claim (but is, for example, simply an adminicle of evidence of it), then it is the normal practice for a party to seek to adduce secondary evidence of its terms to be admitted in proof. Whether or not a party will succeed in this will depend upon the circumstances of the case.[29]

Ideally, other real evidence, beyond documents, should also be produced **2–25** in their original state. In *McGowan v Belling & Co*[30] a claim for injuries sustained in a house fire hinged upon the allegedly defective state of an electric fire. The electric fire was not inspected at any time after the house fire and was not lodged as a production. During the proof the pursuers attempted to adduce expert evidence from two witnesses based on their examination of a similar appliance that was allegedly identical to the one involved in the accident. The court rejected this approach on the ground that the best evidence rule required the production of the actual appliance that had been examined. It was considered unreasonable for that appliance not to have been produced, as it was still in existence. In its absence, the court held that "an oral description of its condition . . . was inadmissible and any expert evidence based on its alleged condition was also inadmissible".[31] In all such cases, clearly it is for the court to assess how much the failure to adduce potential evidence detracts from the overall case of the party who should have adduced it.

Best evidence in criminal cases

In criminal cases the effect of the best evidence rule is that any production **2–26** relied on by the Crown must be lodged in court if its absence would be prejudicial to the accused. However, where no such prejudice would arise, and where production would be totally impracticable, as in the case of very large or fixed items, then the court may dispense with it.[32] The High Court has stated that:

> "[I]n a criminal trial the best evidence rule applies to the extent that where it is both convenient and practicable, productions which are referred to, or to be referred to, must be produced or an adequate explanation furnished for their non production."[33]

One of the most common reasons for not lodging potential productions is the fact that they are perishable. In *Anderson v Laverock*[34] salmon seized from the accused were destroyed prior to the trial. Although the court

---

[29] e.g. *Eliott v Galpern*, 1927 S.C. 29; *Young v Thompson*, 1909 S.C. 529; and *Ritchie v Ritchie* (1857) 19 D. 505.
[30] *McGowan v Belling & Co*, 1983 S.L.T. 77.
[31] *McGowan v Belling & Co*, 1983 S.L.T. 77.at 78.
[32] *Morrison v Mackenzie*, 1990 G.W.D. 4-174, where tyres alleged to be defective in a prosecution under the Road Vehicles (Construction and Use) Regulations 1986 were not produced in court. The appeal court upheld the sheriff's view that it was unnecessary to produce the tyres given the inconvenience for the Crown and that there was no resulting prejudice to the accused. For a commentary on this and best Evidence in criminal cases, see D. Nicol, "Best Evidence in Criminal Cases", 1990 S.L.T. (News) 149.
[33] *Hughes v Skeen*, 1980 S.L.T. (Notes) 13.
[34] *Anderson v Laverock*, 1976 J.C. 9.

accepted that it was not practicable or convenient to retain the fish, it was held that the accused should have been informed of the intention to destroy the fish. As the failure to do so had materially prejudiced him, the conviction was quashed. In circumstances where the condition of the items is crucial to the case the accused should therefore be given the opportunity to examine the items and take photographs.

2–27   If an accused is going to claim "material prejudice" due to the failure to produce an item central to the case, then intimation of the need for production may have to be given to the Crown. For instance it is normal practice not to produce motor cars that are allegedly stolen. In *Kelly v Allan*[35] the issue concerned reset of a motorcycle. The owner had identified the motorcycle to the police despite missing registration plates, frame and engine numbers. Kelly did not deny being in possession of the cycle, and did not challenge police witnesses' descriptions of its condition when found in his possession. He did not deny that it belonged to the true owner. The Crown did not produce the motorcycle at the trial, nor did they produce photographs. An appeal against conviction was rejected as the failure caused no "such material prejudice as to lead to the conclusion that his conviction represented a miscarriage of justice".[36] Although the best evidence rule is still promoted in regard to criminal cases, it is clear from recent case law that unless there is significant prejudice to the accused resulting from a failure to produce best evidence, the admissibility of "less than best" evidence will often be acceptable.[37]

Oral, real and documentary evidence

2–28   There are various approaches to classifying evidence, most of which are descriptive rather than necessarily purposive. This section looks briefly at one set of commonly used categories—oral, real and documentary evidence. There are other categories, some of which also appear in this text, e.g. the terms direct or circumstantial evidence (discussed again in Ch.8), and primary or secondary evidence (discussed in the context of hearsay evidence in Ch.11).

Oral evidence

2–29   Oral evidence is simply the verbal testimony of a witness in court. As already explained, the adversarial system of proof lays great store on the oral testimony of a witness. Allied to this is the opportunity for an accused or, more commonly, their representative, to cross-examine a witness in the courtroom. It remains an important feature of oral testimony that an accused person has a right to "confront" their accuser, but even that right is not absolute, in terms of entitling the accused to a face-to-face meeting. The

---

[35] *Kelly v Allan*, 1984 S.C.C.R. 186. See also, *Tudhope v Stewart*, 1986 J.C. 88, another case in which lack of material prejudice to the accused seems to have been regarded as the main test of whether or not failure to lodge a production was fatal.

[36] *Kelly v Allan*, 1984 S.C.C.R. 186. at 189.

[37] e.g. *Hamilton v HM Advocate*, 1980 J.C. 66 (written confession); *HM Advocate v Dennison*, 1978 S.L.T. (Notes) 79 (fingerprint "lifts"); *Hamilton v Grant*, 1984 S.C.C.R. 263 (photographs of fingerprints); *HM Advocate v Swift*, 1983 S.C.C.R. 204 (tape-recording of confession); and *McLeod v Fraser*, 1987 S.C.C.R. 294 (computer printout of blood/alcohol reading).

European Court of Human Rights (hereafter ECtHR) has declined to interpret the reference in art.6(3)(d) of an accused's right "to examine or have examined witnesses against him and to obtain the attendance and examination of witnesses on his behalf under the same conditions as witnesses against him" to amount to an entitlement to insist a witness is entirely visible, or even physically present, in the courtroom.[38] The question is whether "adequate counterbalancing procedures have been utilised" rendering the trial as a whole fair to the accused.[39]

Thus, statutory provisions which permit a witness to give their evidence **2–30** from behind screens or by live television link do not breach art.6. Debates over the rights of an accused, those of witnesses and the wider public interest, together with increasing recognition that vulnerable and intimidated witnesses are unlikely to give their best evidence in the witness box in open court, are all examined in the next chapter.

Real evidence

Real evidence is something tangible and physical. According to Walker and **2–31** Walker it is "a thing, which may be a human being, any features of the thing which are significant, and the inferences to be drawn from the existence of the thing or from its significant features".[40] Real evidence includes all types of evidence lodged as productions in a criminal trial or civil proof, for example a weapon, forensic samples or tape[41] and audio-visual recordings.[42] Real evidence serves various purposes. It may be needed to prove an essential fact and not because anything particularly significant may be deduced from its appearance. Thus, in a routine shoplifting case, the Crown will normally produce the items stolen, but they are unlikely to yield any evidence themselves. In contrast, in a rape case the items of clothing of an alleged rape victim could be important items of evidence if they yield body fluids which aid the identification of the accused person. Real evidence may also be produced because of inferences that the court can draw from it. Thus, in *Sandells v HM Advocate*[43] the production in the courtroom of a cigarette vending machine enabled the jury to assess the likelihood of whether it was wrenched and stolen from the wall of premises by one man or two. In *Patterson v Nixon*[44] the behaviour of a police tracker dog proved sufficiently reliable and systematic to corroborate a partial confession by the accused.

Real evidence still requires to be spoken to by a witness. Such evidence **2–32** must be formally lodged as a production by whichever party is relying upon it. It must be spoken to by at least one witness (or be covered by joint minute of the parties) in order to make it available as evidence, unless by statute

---

[38] e.g. *Doorson v Netherlands* (1996) 22 E.H.R.R. 330.
[39] *Van Mechlen and Others v Netherlands* (1988) 25 E.H.R.R.647; *Birutis and Others v Lithuania*, nos 4768.99 and 48115/99 28.03.2002.
[40] Walker and Walker, *Evidence*, 3rd edn, para.18.1.1.
[41] *Hopes and Lavery v HMA*, 1960 J.C. 104.
[42] *Lord Advocate's Reference No.1 of 1983*, 1984 S.L.T. 337. See too *Bowie v* Tudhope, 1986 S.C.C.R. 205.
[43] *Sandells v HM Advocate*, 1980 S.L.T. (Notes) 45.
[44] *Patterson v Nixon*, 1960 J.C. 42.

there is no requirement to call such a witness.[45] For example, scenes of crime officers may require to interpret fingerprint evidence,[46] while police doctors may need to speak to the forensic certificate that accompanies the samples taken for blood/alcohol readings in drunk-driving cases.[47] In civil cases, expert witnesses may be required to speak to blood samples taken to determine disputed paternity claims.[48] Refusal to provide such samples to aid the resolution of paternity claims can attract adverse inferences.[49] In a consumer dispute, a party who claims goods purchased are defective will have to identify the goods in question and produce proof of purchase.[50]

Documentary evidence

2–33 When a document is adduced in evidence for its content, it is classified as documentary evidence. Documentary evidence is a form of real evidence, not least when its relevance to the case stems from its very existence, e.g. an allegedly forged document in an indictment for forgery. Many statutes provide their own definition of a document. Section 9 of the Civil Evidence (Scotland) Act 1988 defines a document as a written matter including any map, plan, graph, drawing, photograph, disc, tape, film, sound track or other device in which sounds or visual images are recorded so as to be capable of being reproduced.[51] The essence of a document is not its form, but the information recorded on it. Given the pace of technological developments of electronic material, the courts tend to a flexible interpretation, an approach that is consistent with the general principle of admitting all relevant evidence not otherwise excluded.

2–34 Writings do not come within the definition of documentary evidence unless they contain some fact that their contents tend to prove. When such writings are relied upon in court they must either be incorporated into the pleadings in civil cases or "noted" by the court during a criminal trial. This is so that in the event of any appeal, the appeal court has available to it all the evidence upon which the first instance judgment was based.[52] When a witness is shown a document in court for the purpose identifying it, it is a production, whereas if it is shown to the witness to speak to for its content then it is documentary evidence.[53]

---

[45] For example, s.16(1) of the Road Traffic Offenders Act 1988, in the case of a certificate relating to a blood or urine sample taken in the course of a drink-driving investigation. On the requirement for a witness to speak to a production before it becomes evidence, see *Hamilton v HM Advocate*, 1980 J.C. 66. The jury may not necessarily insist on taking a production into the jury room with them, see *Hamilton v HM Advocate*; *Sandells v HM Advocate*, 1980 S.L.T. (Notes) 45, and *McMurdo v HM Advocate*, 1987 J.C. 61.

[46] *HM Advocate v Dennison*, 1978 S.L.T. (Notes) 79

[47] The samples themselves may no longer be available because of the destructive nature of the test itself.

[48] *Docherty v McGlynn*, 1985 S.L.T. 237. The case pre-dated the Law Reform (Parent and Child) (Scotland) Act 1986 which reduced the standard of proof from beyond reasonable doubt to that of a balance of probabilities.

[49] See s. 70(1)(a) of the Law Reform (Miscellaneous Provisions) (Scotland) Act 1990.

[50] *Docherty v McGlynn*, 1985 S.L.T. 237. The case pre-dated the Law Reform (Parent and Child) (Scotland) Act 1986 which reduced the standard of proof from beyond reasonable doubt to that of a balance of probabilities.

[51] See too Sch.8 of the Criminal Procedure (Scotland) Act 1995.

[52] Lord MacLaren in *Ogilvy v Mitchell* (1903) 4 Adam 237 at 245.

[53] *Jacobs v Hart* (1900) 3 Adam 131 per Lord McLaren at 140.

Disclosure of evidence in criminal cases

It is a fundamental principle of the adversarial process in criminal trials that **2–35** there is appropriate disclosure by the Crown, as prosecuting authority, to the defence, of all material witness statements, videos or transcripts and lists of productions available to the Crown even if they do not intend to rely upon them in court.[54] The Crown clearly has substantially greater resources at its behest to investigate crime and prepare for trial. The Crown prosecutes in the public interest, one dimension of which is to strive to ensure proceedings are conducted fairly and in keeping with the aspiration of the European Convention of Human Rights (hereafter ECHR) to equality of arms. This means that prosecutors must give fair notice to the accused and to defence lawyers, not only of the case against the accused, but also of material which could have an exculpatory or mitigatory effect.[55] The precise statutory test is that the prosecutor must disclose information if[56]:

(a) the information would materially weaken or undermine the evidence that is likely to be led by the prosecutor in the proceedings against the accused;
(b) the information would materially strengthen the accused's case; or
(c) the information is likely to form part of the evidence to be led by the prosecutor in the proceedings against the accused.

Although the principle of disclosure is long-standing in Scots common law, the two Privy Council decisions in *Sinclair v HM Advocate*[57] and *Holland v HM Advocate*,[58] together with jurisprudence from the ECtHR,[59] compelled significant changes in the way that the principle operates.

First of all, it is now on a statutory footing. In 2006 the Scottish Gov- **2–36** ernment appointed Lord Coulsfield, to conduct a review of disclosure practices in the criminal courts.[60] Based upon the Coulsfield recommendations, a statutory framework for disclosure was enacted as Pt 6 of the Criminal Justice & Licensing (Scotland) Act 2010.

In both *Holland* and *Sinclair* the Scottish judges, Lord Hope and Lord **2–37** Rodger considered that the Crown's (then) approach to disclosure was not wholly compliant with the Convention rights of the accused.[61] The Privy Council confirmed that the duty was a pro-active one—it did not have to be triggered by a defence request for release of information, or even an assertion of its relevance, not least because the defence might not be aware of the existence of any specific relevant information. The statutory provisions implicitly accept this analysis and therefore require disclosure of much more information than had previously been assumed was necessary, and to locate the duty to disclose entirely upon the Crown. The onerous obligations

---

[54] *McLeod v HM Advocate (No.2)*, 1998 J.C. 67.
[55] *Johnston v HM Advocate*; *Allison v HM Advocate*, 2006 S.C.C.R. 236.
[56] Criminal Justice & Licensing (Scotland) Act 2010 s.121(3).
[57] *Sinclair v HM Advocate*, 2005 1 S.C. (P.C.) 28; 2005 S.L.T. 553.
[58] *Holland v HM Advocate*, 2005 1 S.C. (P.C.) 3; 2000 S.L.T. 563.
[59] *Edwards v United Kingdom* (1992) 15 EHRR 417; *Rowe and Davis v United Kingdom* (2000) E.H.R.R. 1; and *Edwards and Another v United Kingdom* (2003) 15 BHRC 189.
[60] The Rt Hon. Lord Coulsfield, *Review of the law and practice of disclosure in criminal proceedings in Scotland*, Scottish Government, 2007.
[61] e.g. *Sinclair v HM Advocate*, 2005 1 S.C. (P.C.) 28.

upon the Crown include a statutory responsibility to produce a code of practice on the disclosure process,[62] and there is admirable electronic web access to Crown policy documents in this regard.[63] Access apart, it should be remembered that disclosure is primarily a principle intended to satisfy equality of arms and ensure a fair trial for the accused person. However, the impact of disclosure extends beyond those accused of crimes. The information disclosed often relates to the private lives of Crown witnesses, including the complainer, and has been critiqued in Scotland and in other common law countries for its effect on privacy rights and as material for cross-examination.[64]

Disclosure of evidence in civil cases

2–38   Disclosure procedures in civil litigation operate very differently from those in criminal cases. Although there may well be disparity between the parties in terms of resources and power, such disparity is not regarded as equivalent to the scale of inequality in the criminal trial. Neither are parties in civil disputes at risk of losing their liberty. There is therefore no duty on parties to disclose to each other the evidence that they are gathering. However, there are procedures for seeking recovery of documents, etc. under the supervision of the court using commission and diligence.[65] Fundamentally, though, the evidence gathered in preparation for civil litigation is privileged, that is, it remains confidential to the parties who have acquired it unless and until they are ordered to disclose it by the court.

The Human Rights Act 1998

2–39   Undoubtedly, the enactment of the Human Rights Act in 1998 has changed the environment within which litigation is conducted. By virtue of the devolved powers contained in the Scotland Act 1998, Scots law became the first legal system within the United Kingdom to experience the full impact of Convention rights and the law of evidence has been shaped and developed significantly since 1998. The most influential article of the ECHR is art.6, the right to a fair trial. When interpreting the relevance and application of the various rights described in that article, it is important to bear in mind that the Convention case law repeatedly stresses that these individual rights are not absolute, but have to be seen in the round. Article 6 guarantees the overall fairness of the trial. That does not mean that each of the sub-sections of the article must be satisfied on every occasion. The larger question is always: taking into account all aspects of the proceedings, did the accused have a fair trial?[66]

---

[62] s.164 of the Act.

[63] See *COPFS Disclosure Manual*, 9th edn (2011) paras 9.7.4, 29.12.1.

[64] See P. Duff, "Disclosure, PII and the confidentiality of personal records" (2010) S.L.T. 181; F. Raitt, "Disclosure of Records and Privacy Rights in Rape Cases" (2011) 15 Edin. L.R. 33.

[65] For details of this procedure consult the major texts on civil procedure, such as D. Maxwell, *Practice of the Court of Session*, (Edinburgh, Scottish courts Administration, 1980); I. D. Macphail, *Sheriff Court Practice*, 3rd edn, T. Walsh (ed) (Edinburgh: W. Green, 2006).

[66] *HM Advocate v McLean* [2009] HCJAC 97.

The fair trial

The necessity for a trial to be fair and for the accused to be treated fairly is a **2–40** long standing principle of the Scottish common law.[67] The elements and importance of a fair trial, particularly in regard to compliance with the ECHR, are a recurrent feature in this book so a brief comment is provided here to set the context for subsequent chapters. The Scottish law of evidence cannot be studied in isolation. Much of the impact of the rules of evidence relate to their relationship with other aspects of the law, including procedural rules, the behaviour of the police, the quality of expert witnesses, as well as the substantive criminal and civil law. There are multiple components that contribute to a fair trial in terms of the ECHR jurisprudence and there is a margin of appreciation afforded to the ambit of a fair trial as there are currently 27 signatories to the Convention, all with distinctive national laws and procedural rules. Article 6 is as follows:

Right to a fair trial

1. In the determination of his civil rights and obligations or of any criminal charge against him, everyone is entitled to a fair and public hearing within a reasonable time by an independent and impartial tribunal established by law. Judgment shall be pronounced publicly but the press and public may be excluded from all or part of the trial in the interests of morals, public order or national security in a democratic society, where the interests of juveniles or the protection of the private life of the parties so require, or to the extent strictly necessary in the opinion of the court in special circumstances where publicity would prejudice the interests of justice.

2. Everyone charged with a criminal offence shall be presumed innocent until proved guilty according to law.

3. Everyone charged with a criminal offence has the following minimum rights:

    (a) to be informed promptly, in a language which he understands and in detail, of the nature and cause of the accusation against him;

    (b) to have adequate time and facilities for the preparation of his defence;

    (c) to defend himself in person or through legal assistance of his own choosing or, if he has not sufficient means to pay for legal assistance, to be given it free when the interests of justice so require;

    (d) to examine or have examined witnesses against him and to obtain the attendance and examination of witnesses on his behalf under the same conditions as witnesses against him;

    (e) to have the free assistance of an interpreter if he cannot understand or speak the language used in court.

The ECtHR frequently affirms that the concept of a fair trial is to be interpreted to mean the trial *as a whole* must be fair and not that each of the

---

[67] *McLeod v HM Advocate (No.2)*, 1998 J.C. 67.

individual subsections of art.6 must be all be fully complied with to the same degree (emphasis added). For example, the Court has recognised that although art.6(3)(d) refers to the right of an accused person "to examine or have examined witnesses ..." that did not necessarily mean *that witnesses have to be examined in full sight of the court, if, for example, as in* Doorson, *the investigating judge had heard the evidence of the witness.*[68] There may be good reason for some witnesses to remain anonymous and to give their evidence from behind a screen, such as witness intimidation, or to preserve the identity of undercover agents.

---

[68] *Doorson v Netherlands* (1996) 22 E.H.R.R. 330.

Chapter 3

WITNESSES: COMPETENCE, COMPELLABILITY AND VULNERABILITY

INTRODUCTION

In the last two decades the dominant concern of policy-makers has been to **3–01** improve the experiences of the victims and witnesses who encounter the criminal justice system.[1] It is a truism to say that the judicial process is dependent upon members of the public being willing to appear as witnesses, but the central role for witnesses in jurisdictions such as Scotland, which have adversarial systems, can hardly be over-stated.[2] The principle of orality, i.e. sworn testimony by witnesses present in the courtroom before the trier of fact, is at the heart of the process of proof and creates particular challenges. Whereas the inquisitorial systems of continental Europe place much more reliance upon written witness statements, in Scotland the best evidence is evidence which is delivered "live" under oath or affirmation from the witness in the witness box. It is generally presumed that the witness will be present in court and their identity revealed to the court.

There are some exceptions, however. Vulnerable and intimidated wit- **3–02** nesses may be shielded from sight of the accused by a screen placed between them and the dock. The accused however, will be able to see them by virtue of a small camera fitted to the screen. In rare circumstances witnesses such as undercover police or members of the security services may be permitted to retain anonymity with a screen as shield and their voice disguised, in the interests of protecting themselves and other serving officers.[3] The European Court of Human Rights has held that anonymity can be justified if strictly necessary for operational effectiveness. The determining issue is whether, taken as a whole, the proceedings are fair to the accused and that the accused can exercise their rights of defence if witnesses remain anonymous.[4]

---

[1] See, for example, Scottish Law Commission, *The Evidence of Children and Other Vulnerable Witnesses,* Report 125 (1990); *Vital Voices: Helping Vulnerable Witnesses Give Evidence*, Scottish Executive, 2002. All common law countries have acknowledged this concern, e.g. New Zealand Law Commission, Preliminary Paper 26, *The Evidence of Children and Other Vulnerable Witnesses* (1996); Home Office, *Speaking Up for Justice—Report of the Inter-departmental Working Group on the Treatment of Vulnerable or Intimidated Witnesses in the Criminal Justice System* (1998).

[2] Unnecessary distress and inconvenience to witnesses created by the practices of the justice system was acknowledged in the report by the Hon Lord Bonomy, Improving Practice: 2002 *Review of the Practices and Procedure of the High Court of Justiciary*, The Stationery Office, 2002.

[3] *HM Advocate v Smith*, 2000 S.C.C.R. 910.

[4] *Kostovski v Netherlands* (1996) 12 E.H.R.R. 434; *Ludi v Switzerland* (1993) 15 E.H.R.R. 173; *Doorson v Netherlands* (1996) R.H.R.R. 330; *Van Mechelen v Netherlands*, 1988 25 E.H.R.R 647.

There are some situations where statements can be used in court in lieu of oral testimony, but by their very nature, such statements may not carry as much weight or have as much value as evidence elicited direct from the witness.

3–03   Increasing concerns about the reluctance of victims to report sexual crimes in particular, and the hesitation to expose young child victims, especially those involved in sexual offences, to the harsh realities of the criminal process, has generated a raft of legislation to support and protect witnesses. This ranges from the provision of online information about the court process for the benefit of anyone cited to appear as a witness,[5] to an entire statutory regime to support those classed as vulnerable and/or intimidated witnesses. Such witnesses are treated as exceptions to the general rule and entitled to certain protective measures to enable them to give the best evidence of which they are capable. Developments in Scotland are influenced by EU legislation, the most recent of which is the EU Directive 2012/29.[6] The Scottish Government's Victims and Witnesses (Scotland) Bill published in 2013 reflects the provisions of the Directive and its implications are discussed later in this chapter.

3–04   The chapter focuses upon three distinct issues. First, who is competent to be a witness; and second, who can be compelled to be a witness. These two questions are considered together as they tend to be closely connected. Third is the question of who is considered a vulnerable or intimidated witness. Such witnesses are at particular risk of being unable to provide good quality evidence and thus deemed in need of special measures to enable them to produce their best evidence.

Competent and Compellable Witnesses

3–05 Witnesses are said to be competent to give evidence when they are permitted by law to testify. Witnesses can only give evidence in court if they are competent to do so, and in most circumstances competent witnesses can also be compelled to give evidence. They are said to be compellable when they can be forced to testify under threat of a charge of contempt of court.[7] Historically, many categories of people were considered incompetent, including the accused, children, women and the mentally ill. As with other rights and entitlements of citizenship in earlier periods, assumptions of competency were linked to gender, wealth and the trappings of class or economic power. There is a much stronger assumption today that every person who is capable of giving intelligible evidence is both a competent and a compellable witness.[8] However, there are a few exceptions to that general rule.

---

[5] *http://www.copfs.gov.uk/* [accessed July 11, 2013].

[6] Directive 2012/29/EU of the European Parliament and of the Council of October 25, 2012 establishing minimum standards on the rights, support and protection of victims of crime. This Directive replaces the 2001 Council Framework Decision on the standing of victims in criminal proceedings.

[7] See *HM Advocate v Airs*, 1975 J.C. 64.

[8] Walker and Walker, *Evidence*, 3rd edn, para.13.1.1.

Witnesses are either required to take an oath before testifying, or elect **3–06** to "affirm" their testimony,[9] a practice which continues to place faith in the symbolic power of a higher moral authority to encourage witnesses to be truthful.[10] It is established that children over the age of 14 will normally be expected to take the oath, while children aged between 12 and 14 should be sworn by the judge only if he or she is satisfied that the child understands the nature of the oath. The oath is not usually administered to a child under the age of 12. Instead, such children will be admonished by the judge to tell the truth.[11]

The next section discusses the exceptions to the general rule that everyone **3–07** is both a competent and a compellable witness. Unless indicated to the contrary, the principles discussed apply equally to civil and criminal cases.

THE ACCUSED

The accused, even when competent, is not a compellable witness because the **3–08** accused has, in effect, a right to silence arising from the presumption of innocence. This presumption is not an absolute right. There are circumstances, discussed below, where a failure to offer a comment may attract negative inferences. However, the presumption is both a fundamental principle of the common law and integral to the right to a fair trial in terms of art.6.

There are three contexts in which the accused person in a criminal trial **3–09** might enter the witness box, namely:

(1) as a witness for himself or herself;
(2) as a witness for a co-accused; and
(3) as a witness for the prosecution.

In each context, subject to certain safeguards, the accused may be a competent witness, but there are separate issues concerning the compellability of the accused in each case.

(1) The accused as a witness on their own behalf

At common law, the accused had no status as a witness in his own trial, and **3–10** had to be content with making an unsworn judicial declaration from the dock. In 1898 the accused was made a competent witness in their own defence. The current law is contained in s.266(1) of the Criminal Procedure (Scotland) Act 1995 which states that the accused is a competent witness for the defence at every stage of the trial, whether he is tried alone or with a co-accused. Section 266(11) provides that where the accused is to be called as a witness by the defence, he must be the first witness called unless the court directs otherwise.

---

[9] See ss.1(1), (3) and 5(1) of the Oaths Act 1978.
[10] For guidance on the provision courts should make for the different faiths of witnesses see *Equal Treatment Benchbook*, 2nd edn (2008), available at *http://www.scotland-judiciary.org.uk/Upload/Documents/Equal-TreatmentBenchBook_1.pdf* [accessed July 11, 2013].
[11] See Dickson, n.5, paras 1548–9, *Rees v Lowe*; *Kelly v Docherty*, 1991 S.L.T. 419 and *M v Kennedy*, 1993 S.C. 115. See too the *Equal Treatment Benchbook of the Scottish Judiciary*, 2nd edn, 2008, at para.4.4: *http://www.scotland-judiciary.org.uk/Upload/Documents/Equal-TreatmentBenchBook_1.pdf* [accessed July 11, 2013].

3–11   When giving evidence, the accused is sworn, or affirms, in the normal way, testifies from the witness box and is liable to a perjury charge if he gives false evidence.[12] In solemn cases, although the defence must give advance notice to the Crown of their intention to call all other witnesses, they need not do so in the case of an accused who may testify at the trial without prior intimation.[13] Although the right to make an unsworn judicial declaration was lost in 1898, the Criminal Justice (Scotland) Act 1980 introduced another form of unsworn declaration—the concept of judicial examination. This permits an accused person who appears on petition before a sheriff to advance a defence or make any other comment in response to questions put by the prosecutor.[14] The current provisions are contained in s.35 of the Criminal Procedure (Scotland) Act 1995.

3–12   The accused is not on oath during judicial examination and has the right to refuse to answer any questions put by the Crown, as they try to establish a preliminary response to the charge(s) against the accused. However, a record of the proceedings (subject to deletions called for in advance by either party and agreed by the court after hearing both sides) must be lodged as a production by the Crown at the trial.[15] This creates the potential for introducing to the jury a statement by the accused on which he or she cannot be cross-examined if they decline to go into the witness box. This can arise in so-called mixed statements where an accused person has made a statement which is both incriminatory and exculpatory. Section 266 states that the accused may only be called as a witness for himself upon his own application and it follows that an accused can never be compelled to give evidence on his own behalf. There may, however, be dangers in such a course of action as the Crown is entitled to comment on the accused's failure to give evidence and to suggest adverse implications might be drawn from his or her silence.[16]

3–13   In a solemn trial the judge is entitled to comment adversely on an accused's failure to give sworn testimony, though if such comment is excessive it can give rise to grounds for appeal, and a reasonable balance should be struck.[17] In some cases adverse comment may be unavoidable if justice is to be done to both sides. There are circumstances in which an accused is expected to give an innocent explanation of circumstances that otherwise imply guilt.[18] Silence from the accused in such cases is an invitation to the jury to draw the adverse inferences from the unchallenged prosecution evidence. The guidelines to be followed in cases in which evidence ought reasonably to be expected from the accused are those laid down by Lord Justice-General Normand in *Scott v HM Advocate*,[19] who advised trial judges that:

---

[12] *HM Advocate v Cairns*, 1967 J.C. 37.

[13] *Kennedy v HM Advocate* (1898) 2 Adam 588.

[14] For further details of this procedure, see Renton and Brown, n.46, paras 12.10–12.31. Note that s.63 of the Criminal Justice (Scotland) Bill abolishes judicial examination.

[15] Criminal Procedure (Scotland) Act 1995, s.68(1).

[16] *Beggs v HM Advocate* [2010] HCJAC 27.

[17] *Stewart v HM Advocate*, 1980 J.C. 103.

[18] See *McHugh v HM Advocate*, 1978 J.C. 12 and *HM Advocate v Hardy*, 1938 J.C. 144; see also Lord Justice-Clerk Grant in *McIlhargey v Herron*, 1972 J.C. 38, who pointed out that "the silent defender does take a risk". See also *Dorrens v HM Advocate*, 1983 S.C.C.R. 407 at 411.

[19] 1946 J.C. 90 at 98. See also *Knowles v HM Advocate*, 1975 J.C. 6.

"Although a comment of the kind is, in my view competent, it should be made with restraint and only when there are special circumstances which require it; and, if it is made with reference to particular evidence which the panel might have explained or contradicted, care should be taken that the evidence is not distorted and that its true bearing on the defence is properly represented to the jury."

It is now settled that a co-accused can comment on the failure of an accused to give sworn testimony.[20] If an accused fails to testify, there cannot then be any cross-examination by a co-accused, and it only fair to allow the frustrated co-accused the right to comment on this.

In the course of giving evidence on his or her own behalf, if an accused **3–14** (A1) gives evidence which is adverse to, or even incriminatory of a co-accused (A2), then A1 can be cross-examined by A2, separate of course from any cross-examination by the Crown.[21] An accused may also call a co-accused as a witness, with his or her consent.[22]

When more than one accused appears on the same charge(s), and any one **3–15** of them gives evidence, then, as regards the remainder, the evidence of each becomes the evidence of a *socius criminis*. However, it is incompetent and improper to issue the *cum nota* warning to the jury in respect of that evidence because of the prejudicial effect which it may have on a person whose guilt has yet to be established.[23] This is true even though there is evidence to incriminate a co-accused.[24] If before the end of the trial an accused pleads guilty to, or is convicted of, the charges in which he or she is *socius criminis* and thereafter gives evidence for the Crown, then the warning may be administered, if appropriate.[25] It is competent to proceed to trial against an accused who is charged with an offence while acting along with another, even though that other person has been previously acquitted of the charge.[26]

Further issues which arise from the position of the accused as a witness **3–16** for him or herself include issues of privilege, and cross examination as to character and previous convictions. These are dealt with in later chapters.

(2) The accused as a witness for a co-accused

An accused may, with the consent of a co-accused, call that other accused as **3–17** a witness on the accused's behalf.[27] While one accused may be competent as a witness for another accused, he or she cannot be compellable while the two remain co-accused, i.e. still facing a verdict on charges on a complaint or indictment in which they are both named. However, if one of the accused has the charges withdrawn, or pleads guilty, after the start of the trial then s.266(10) of the 1995 Act states that:

---

[20] *Shevlin v HM Advocate*, 2002 S.L.T. 729 citing the analogous English authority of *R. v Wickham* (1971) 55 Cr.App.R. 199 as "consistent with Scots law".

[21] S.266(8) (b) Criminal Procedure (Scotland) Act 1995.

[22] S.266(8) (a) of the 1995 Act.

[23] *Martin v HM Advocate*, 1960 S.L.T. 213.

[24] *Slowey v HM Advocate*, 1965 S.L.T. 309.

[25] *Docherty v HM Advocate*, 1987 J.C. 81, a nine bench decision which discusses when it may be required.

[26] *Howitt v HM Advocate*, 2000 J.C. 284.

[27] It will be recalled that by subs.(9)(b) in each case, he may also cross-examine him if he gives evidence, but he may not do both.

"The prosecutor or the accused may call as a witness a co-accused who has pleaded guilty to or been acquitted of all charges against him which remain before the court (whether or not in a case where the co-accused has pleaded guilty to any charges, he has been sentenced) or in respect of whom the diet has been deserted; and the party calling such co-accused as a witness shall not require to give notice thereof, but the court may grant any other party such adjournment or postponement of the trial as may seem just."

In such circumstances, the accused is a compellable witness.[28] Before the subsection can operate, it is necessary for all the charges which the former accused faced at the start of the trial diet to have been disposed of by either a guilty plea or an acquittal or a desertion of the diet by the Crown.[29] It is not necessary for the accused to have been convicted or sentenced.[30]

3–18   Before a person can be classed as the "co-accused" of another for the purposes of s.266(9) it is necessary for them both to appear at a trial diet on the same complaint or indictment. They will no longer be co-accused if their trials have been separated as the result of some earlier diet prior to trial. In such cases, each will be a competent and compellable witness for the other in their separate trials, whether or not their respective cases have been disposed of.[31] Where the trial proceeds by solemn procedure the potential witness must appear on the witness list of the accused for whom he or she will be testifying.

3–19   It was held in *Monaghan v HM Advocate*[32] that when an accused is originally charged along with a co-accused on an indictment, but pleads guilty by the accelerated procedure available under s.76 of the 1995 Act, that accused remains a co-accused and qualifies to be called as a witness for a co-accused by virtue of s.266(10).

3–20   If the Crown drop charges against one, of two, original co-accused prior to the commencement of the trial, then at common law the person in respect of whom the charges have been dropped is a competent and compellable witness for the remaining accused. In solemn cases that person must appear on the defence witness list and, unless the Crown have deserted simpliciter, may refuse to answer any questions which could be incriminating in regard to those charges.

3–21   No co-accused giving evidence on behalf of another co-accused can be classed as *socius criminis*, a term which is confined to witnesses giving

---

[28] s.266(10). In accordance with the normal rule that competence implies compellability, and by contrast with the wording of s.266(9)(a).

[29] Unless the Crown desert these charges *simpliciter,* the accused giving evidence for a co-accused enjoys a privilege against answering questions which are incriminating, even in respect of charges which have been withdrawn. The accused will, however, come within the purview of the subsection because he or she will have pled guilty to all the charges "remaining before the court", a phrase clearly intended to make allowance for withdrawals by the Crown.

[30] *HM v Ferrie*, 1983 S.C.C.R. 1. This was a case in which the former accused was called by the Crown, but the point at issue is the same for both types of case.

[31] *Morrison v Adair,* 1943 J.C. 25. In such a case, of course, the accused called as a witness will enjoy a privilege against self-incrimination in respect of the charges still outstanding against him.

[32] 1983 S.C.C.R. 524, another case in which the co-accused was in fact called for the Crown.

evidence against another accused, and probably to those who do so as Crown witnesses.[33]

(3) The accused as a witness for the prosecution

While a person remains on trial on charges which have yet to be proved or admitted, they cannot be a competent witness for the prosecution, either against themselves or against a co-accused. However, since *Young v HM Advocate*[34] an accused giving evidence on their own behalf may well assist the prosecution by giving evidence adverse to a co-accused upon which the prosecution may rely. **3–22**

The process of judicial examination, discussed above, provides for an accused person arrested for a serious crime to be brought before a sheriff on petition and given an opportunity to make a judicial declaration regarding the charges. The accused is invited to make any comments in respect of: **3–23**

- (i)   any of the charges in the petition;
- (ii) any defence he or she wishes to put forward; or
- (iii) any confession which he or she is alleged to have made to the police.[35] Although there is a theoretical right to remain silent on this occasion, this is qualified by s.36(8) of the 1995 Act which provides that an accused's silence may be made the subject of adverse comment by the Crown, the judge or any co-accused if, at the subsequent trial any matter is raised (such as a defence of alibi or incrimination) which might appropriately have been raised at the judicial examination.[36]

As already noted an accused may become a witness for the Crown in a number of circumstances:

- (i)   If a person ceases to be an accused, by virtue of having pled guilty or had the charges deserted, they can be called as a prosecution witness against a former co-accused.
- (ii) If the trials of an accused and a co-accused are separated, each becomes a competent and compellable witness for the Crown at the trial of the other.[37]
- (iii) If during the course of a trial an accused pleads guilty to all remaining charges, or where such charges are dropped by the Crown, or where the Crown accepts a partial plea of guilt, the former co-accused may be called as a witness by either a continuing accused or the prosecution and is then both competent and compellable for the Crown.

---

[33] *Slowey v HM Advocate*, 1969 S.L.T. 309.
[34] 1932 J.C. 32, and in practice since before then.
[35] ss.35–36 of the 1995 Act. For details of this process see Renton and Brown's *Criminal Procedure*, 6th edn, Pt VIII, Evidence.
[36] e.g. *Alexander v HM Advocate*, 1989 S.L.T. 193 where nothing was said at the judicial examination on the instructions of the accused's solicitor. When a defence of alibi was put forward at the trial, it was held competent for the trial judge to comment on this in his charge to the jury, leaving them to assess what weight to attach to the accused's evidence.
[37] See *Morrison v Adair*, 1943 J.C. 25.

All that was written previously concerning the statutory provisions in regard to a former accused testifying for a former co-accused applies equally to evidence given by such a person for the Crown.[38] When an accused is a witness for a co-accused in circumstances in which the Crown have not deserted the charges simpliciter against the accused, a privilege may be claimed against answering any incriminating question in relation to the offences charged. This cannot arise when the accused appears for the Crown in those cases in which the Crown has given up the right to prosecute in respect of these charges. This occurs whenever an accused is called specifically as a *socius criminis* in respect of those charges that the remaining accused still faces. The *socius* in such cases is said to have immunity against further prosecution, and this operates to all intents and purposes like a desertion simpliciter. The same rule applies when the Crown have secured an accused as a *socius criminis* witness by a separation of trials. If, however, an accused is not specifically called as a *socius criminis* the immunity does not apply and that accused will require to fall back on the privilege against self-incrimination.

3–24   The immunity was expressed by Hume thus, "By the very act of calling him as a witness, the prosecutor discharges all title to molest him for the future with relation to the matter libelled".[39] The modern interpretation of this is more restricted. In *O'Neill v Wilson*[40] the accused, a police officer, was charged with assaulting M, but claimed immunity on the ground that on an earlier occasion, as a witness for the Crown, he had given evidence against M on a charge of an assault on himself. It was held on appeal (a) that the immunity from prosecution applies only to a person expressly called as a *socius criminis* in the crime with which the then accused is charged, and (b) that such immunity covers only the charges contained in the libel in support of which he has given evidence.

SPOUSES AND CIVIL PARTNERS

3–25   In the last decade the general rule in relation to spouses and civil partners is that they are competent and compellable witnesses for each other. Previously, spouses and, briefly, civil partners had a privileged status whereby they were competent witnesses for their spouse or civil partner, but they could not be compelled to be a witness. That privileged status did not extend to cohabitants, whether heterosexual or same-sex, which is arguably an anachronistic and discriminatory distinction that produces unintended consequences. It is simplest to consider the various categories separately.

Spouses of a party in civil cases

3–26   Section 3 of the Evidence (Scotland) Act 1853 abolished the historical rule whereby a party to a civil action was not a competent witness. That section also declared that parties' spouses were competent witnesses but gave

---

[38] *Docherty v HM Advocate*, 1987 J.C. 81.
[39] David Hume, *Commentaries on the law respecting crimes*, II366–367.
[40] *O'Neill v Wilson*, 1983 J.C. 42.

spouses a privilege against testifying to matters characterised as "marital communications", i.e. "any matter communicated (to each other) during the marriage". The wording of the section has given rise to some doubts as to the compellability of the spouse in circumstances other than those comprising marital communications.[41]

Civil partners of a party in civil cases

Civil partners are competent and compellable witnesses in civil cases. The **3–27** Civil Partnership Act 2004 which extended virtually all of the rights and responsibilities of married persons to same sex couples, makes no specific reference to the competence or compellability of civil partners in civil proceedings. This is because there is no pre-existing legal obstacle to their competence or compellability, unlike the historical prohibition on spouses explained above.

Spouses and civil partners of accused in criminal cases

The spouse or civil partner of an accused is a competent and compellable **3–28** witness for the prosecution, the accused, or any co-accused in the proceedings against the accused.[42] This reflects the principle that, "subject to appropriate safeguards, all relevant evidence should be available to the court at a criminal trial in the interests of justice".[43] This provision was introduced by the Criminal Justice and Licensing (Scotland) Act 2010,[44] sweeping away previous common law rules which gave spouses and civil partners a status whereby they were competent but *not* compellable witnesses.[45] One of the problems with that status was that it impeded child protection investigations in circumstances where a child of a married or civilly partnered couple was assaulted, injured or neglected, but in the absence of evidence as to whether either or both parent was culpable, neither parent was obligated to give evidence against the other. The legitimate interests of children were therefore not served and the current provisions are an important improvement in this regard.

Where a spouse or civil partner is compellable they are entitled to the **3–29** usual privilege that they need not answer any question which might be self-incriminating in any future charge. They must of course answer questions which might incriminate the accused.[46] There is a separate category of privilege known as "matrimonial communications" which is discussed in Ch.13.

---

[41] Macphail, *Evidence*, Ch.4, paras 4.03–4.06.
[42] Criminal Procedure (Scotland) Act 1995, s.264(1).
[43] *Hunter v HM Advocate*, 1984 S.L.T.434 at 437.
[44] Criminal Justice and Licensing (Scotland) Act 2010, s.86(1).
[45] Other than in cases where the spouse/civil partner was the victim. *Harper v Adair*, 1945 J.C.21.
[46] *Bates v HM Advocate*, 1989 S.L.T. 701.

Cohabiting partners of either sex

3–30 Cohabiting partners of either sex are competent and compellable witnesses for the Crown, the defence, and any co-accused.[47] The Court of Appeal in England has criticised any type of familial exceptions to the general rule that all witnesses are compellable as that denies the court having access to otherwise admissible evidence.[48]

PERSONS WITH MENTAL ILLNESS

3–31 The fact that a person is mentally ill, or is suffering from cognitive incapacity does not, by itself, render that person incompetent as a witness. The test in all cases is whether the witness understands the difference between truth and falsehood, appreciates the duty of telling the truth and can give coherent testimony.[49]

3–32 Witnesses with physical disabilities which inhibit their speech, but who are otherwise competent, can give evidence with communication aids, or through an interpreter or an expert in sign language.[50] Interpreters can also be used for witnesses who do not understand the English language provided their qualifications and competence satisfy standards of fairness.[51] There is no legal bar to the admissibility of their testimony and indeed every effort ought to be made to facilitate them. A learning disability will not prevent a person being a competent witness, provided their disability is not of such severity as to preclude their understanding of questions, or their ability to give comprehensible answers. A witness will only be deemed incompetent if all reasonable attempts at communication fail.

3–33 The decision on the competency of a witness is that of the presiding judge, if necessary, after hearing evidence on that point.[52] Once competency is determined, the witness is either sworn in the normal way or admonished to tell the truth. The nature and extent of any disability may, however, affect the weight given to that witness's evidence. Thus, in *HM Advocate v Stott*[53] a patient in an asylum gave evidence at the trial of a night attendant charged with the murder of another patient. The court heard conflicting medical evidence. One view was that the witness had a reliable memory, while another view was that he suffered from gross delusions. In his charge to the jury the judge commented that the witness had given a perfectly distinct account of what he had seen but that he was "obviously insane". He advised them that since it was impossible to tell how much of the witness's evidence was a reliable product of his memory and how much emanated from a diseased mind, they should not rely on that evidence except in so far as it was corroborated by other witnesses.

---

[47] *Casey v HM Advocate (No.1)*, 1993 S.L.T. 33 per LJ-C Ross at 35, where the court said as matter of statutory interpretation the rule did not extend to unmarried partners.

[48] *R. v Pearce* [2002] 1 Cr App Rep 39.

[49] Dickson, *Evidence*, paras 1550–1554.

[50] *HM Advocate v Wilson*, 1942 J.C. 75. A witness may also be permitted to give replies to questions in writing.

[51] *HM Advocate v Regufe*, 2003 S.C.C.R. 579.

[52] *Black* (1887) 1 White 365.

[53] (1894) 1 Adam 386.

Competency is a matter of physical and mental capability rather than **3–34** moral background. Thus, the fact that a person is of bad character, has previous convictions or has an interest in the outcome of the case does not prevent them from testifying, since "moral turpitude or interest is a ground of criticism not of the admissibility of the witness but of the reliability of his evidence".[54]

JUDGES AND JURORS

When judges are acting in their private capacity, as members of the public, **3–35** they are competent witnesses to anything they see or hear. For example, a judge involved in a road traffic incident would be competent to give evidence as to the facts of that incident. When judges are acting in their official capacity their competency as witnesses varies depending on their status as a judge. In *Muckarsie v Wilson*[55] it was held that a judge of the Supreme Court could not be called as a witness to evidence given before him.[56] However, judges of the lower courts are competent witnesses to cases heard by them,[57] notably when the testimony of a witness heard by the judge results in a subsequent perjury charge.[58] The distinction would seem to be based on the twin considerations of the dignity of the office and the fact that senior judges are often sitting with a jury.[59]

Jurors may not testify to matters which arise in the jury room,[60] whether **3–36** in civil[61] or in criminal[62] cases, although in all other matters they remain competent witnesses, e.g. to an incident occurring during the trial.

PROSECUTORS, SOLICITORS AND COUNSEL

Procurators fiscal and advocates-depute, as prosecutors, are competent **3–37** witnesses to any matter on which they can assist the court, provided they are not also conducting the case and, preferably, have had no direct involvement in its preparation.[63] Any suggestion of a conflict of interest should be avoided otherwise the fairness of proceedings may be jeopardised.[64] In *Ferguson v Webster*[65] Lord Deas noted that:

---

[54] *Dow v McKnight,* 1949 J.C. 38 at 56. This case contains a comprehensive summary of the development of Scots law in this area. For the possibility of attacking a witness's *credibility* on the grounds of bad character, etc. see Criminal Procedure (Scotland) Act 1995, s.265(1)(a).

[55] 1834 Bell's Notes 99.

[56] But he could be called as a witness to a physical incident such as a disturbance in court.

[57] *Monaghan* (1844) 2 Broun 131.

[58] e.g. *Davidson v McFadyean,* 1942 J.C. 95.

[59] See Macphail, *Evidence,* Ch.3, paras 3.08–3.13.

[60] At least, not so far as concerns their deliberations; see *McGuire v Brown,* 1963 S.C. 107 at 109 and 112.

[61] *Pirie v Caledonian Ry* (1890) 17 R. 1157 at 1161.

[62] Hume, II, 429.

[63] *Mackintosh v Wooster,* 1919 J.C. 15

[64] See generally, *Code of Conduct for Scottish Solicitors,* 2002, Law Society of Scotland; and A. Paterson and B. Ritchie, Law, *Practice & Conduct for Solicitors* (Edinburgh: W. Green, 2006) Ch.7.

[65] *Ferguson v Webster* (1869) 1 Coup. 370 at 375. The effect of *Mackintosh* is that the only strict bar arises when the prosecutor is actually presenting the case.

"It would be the duty of anyone so situated to decline from the outset all interference, either official or judicial, in a case in which he knew he had important testimony to give from his own personal knowledge."

In contrast, it is possible for a defence solicitor, defence counsel or solicitor-advocate to testify to matters within their knowledge even while conducting a client's case.[66] Parties, their counsel and agents may testify even though they have been present during the whole of the prior evidence, and this applies equally to the accused.[67] If an accused calls their legal agent as a witness then they cannot also claim confidentiality for any information given in evidence.[68]

HEADS OF STATE

3–38 There is no direct authority on the competence of the monarch as a witness, but it is generally considered that the monarch is a competent, but not compellable, witness.[69] The remaining members of the Royal Family are both competent and compellable.[70] In terms of s.20 of the State Immunity Act 1978, foreign heads of state, their families and domestic retinue, have the same basic privilege as foreign diplomats, in that they are competent but not compellable as witnesses.[71]

3–39 Civil law suits or prosecutions against present or former heads of state of a foreign country used to be extremely rare. However, the traditional state immunity afforded to heads of state has been called into question in recent cases where there are allegations of serious crimes under international law having been committed with the endorsement of the head of state. For example, in 1999, Spain asked the British government to extradite Senator Pinochet, the former President of Chile, to Spain to stand trial for state-sanctioned crimes, including torture, hostage-taking and murder. A majority in the House of Lords held that a head of state could not claim state immunity from prosecution, at least in regard to the internationally recognised crime of torture. The speeches reveal the diplomatic, political and legal complexities of the arguments and the limited circumstances in which immunity will be waived.[72]

DIPLOMATS AND CONSULAR STAFF

3–40 There are a number of categories of witness who, although competent in law to give evidence, cannot be forced to do so, largely for reasons of public

---

[66] *Campbell v Cochrane*, 1928 J.C. 25.
[67] *HM Advocate v Ferrie*, 1983 S.C.C.R. 1.
[68] See Legal Professional Privilege in Ch.13.
[69] See Macphail, *Evidence*, paras 3.04–3.06; Stewart, *Stair Memorial Encyclopaedia*, para.26; and F. Davidson, *Evidence*, para.8.11.
[70] Wilkinson, *Scottish Law of Evidence*, p.154.
[71] s.21 of the Act.
[72] *R. v Bartle & Ors, Ex p. Pinochet* [1999] 2 W.L.R. 827 (HL) Jan 36. Ultimately, the British government relied upon expert medical evidence that Pinochet was unfit to stand trial and declined to extradite him.

policy. Under the Diplomatic Privileges Act 1964, the head of a diplomatic mission based in the United Kingdom and members of the diplomatic staff, while competent to give evidence if they wish, cannot be compelled to do so. This privilege extends to the families and staff of diplomats and to the families of members of staff, as long as these persons are not also citizens of the United Kingdom and colonies. A witness who seeks diplomatic immunity needs to obtain a certificate of their status from the Foreign Office.[73]

BANKERS

Financial information frequently forms part of the evidence in criminal and **3–41** civil proceedings and, as a matter of public policy, to insist on personal appearances by banking staff would generally be unreasonable and unnecessary to achieve justice. In criminal proceedings, s.6 of the Bankers Books Evidence Act 1879 makes a bank official competent but not compellable as a witness in matters relating to entries in the bank's books. This extends to appearances or to production of any bank book or record, unless ordered by the court to do so for "special cause" as shown by the party wishing to call him.

Where it is necessary to call a bank witness to testify that a copy of an **3–42** entry in the bank's records is an authentic copy of the original, ss.4–5 make that witness compellable for that purpose. The position is broadly the same in civil proceedings.[74]

VULNERABLE AND INTIMIDATED WITNESSES

Given the importance of witnesses to the functioning of a criminal trial, or **3–43** indeed to civil proceedings, those cited to appear in court ought to be treated with respect and dignity, the fundamental values of human rights instruments.[75] From a pragmatic perspective, the justice system is best served if witnesses are enabled and supported to give their best evidence.[76] Unfortunately, there is a wealth of empirical research to show that many witnesses find respect and dignity in rather short supply, especially in criminal proceedings.[77] In the last decade sustained lobbying from organisations such as Victim Support, as well as from bodies representing particular constituencies, e.g. children and those with learning disabilities, have

---

[73] The Consular Relations Act 1968 and the Diplomatic and Other Privileges Act 1971, applies similar rules to full-time consular officials. All part-time consular officials and their staff, however, are both competent and compellable, except in relation to matters covered by their diplomatic work.

[74] s.7(2) of the Civil Evidence (Scotland) Act 1988 extends the effect of s.6 of the Bankers' Books Evidence Act 1879 to civil matters. See too, *Lord Advocate's Reference No.1 of 1996*, 1996 S.L.T. 740.

[75] See, for example the terms of s.275(2)(b) of the Criminal Procedure (Scotland) Act 1995 which requires the judge in sexual offence trials the ensure the "appropriate protection of a complainer's dignity and privacy",

[76] See *Achieving Best Evidence in Criminal Proceedings: Guidance for Vulnerable or Intimidated Witnesses, including Children*, Home Office, London, 2006.

[77] *Speaking Up for Justice—Report of the Interdepartmental Working Group on the Treatment of Vulnerable or Intimidated Witnesses in the Criminal*, Home Office 1998.

campaigned to make the issue of the treatment of witnesses and victims a central plank of criminal justice policy for the Scottish Government. As a result, there has been a determined improvement to the levels of support given to witnesses, especially complainers.[78] In Scotland the office of Victim Information and Advice ("VIA") was established in 2004 and is now part of the Crown Office and Procurator Fiscal Service ("COPFS"), offering an advice and support service to victims, witnesses and also, in cases of sudden, unexpected or crime-related deaths, to the next of kin. The work of VIA is complemented by the Witness Support Service and there is a whole raft of new publications and information guides for lay and practitioner consumption available online.[79] More recent policy developments have been advanced under the banner "Making Justice Work".[80] Following a public consultation the Government published the Victim and Witnesses (Scotland) Bill in February 2013. The policy memorandum accompanying the Bill provides a history of the developments in this area and a justification for the proposed legislation.[81] The Bill reflects some of the provisions of the EU Directive 2012/29/EU which entitles European Union citizens who become victims of crime to certain minimum standards of treatment from the member country in whose jurisdiction the crime occurs.[82]

3–44   The Bill as introduced proposes extending existing provisions, such as wider availability of special measures, improving compliance with service standards; and new provisions concerning compensation for complainers in certain circumstances, giving victims the right to a choice about the gender of those who interview them at the investigative stage and a right to information about an offender's release from prison.[83]

The Impact of the ECHR

3–45 The incorporation of the ECHR into domestic law offers potential for improved treatment of witnesses. Although the interests of witnesses, whether as victims or complainers, are not specifically constituted as a "right" in the ECHR, their interests are recognised in various articles and there is a well developed jurisprudence within the case law of the European Court of Human Rights that recognises the interests of witnesses. Articles 3 and 8 of the ECHR often feature in arguments about the appropriate weight to give witnesses' interests. Article 3 states, "No one shall be subjected to torture or to inhuman or degrading treatment". Article 8 states, "Everyone has the right to respect for his private and family life, his home and his correspondence". Both these articles are capable of an interpretation that

---

[78] See, for example, *Vital Voices: Helping Vulnerable Witnesses Give Evidence*, Scottish Executive, 2002.

[79] The list is available at *http://www.crownoffice.gov .uk/Publications* [accessed July 11, 2013].

[80] Scottish Government, *Making justice work for victims and witnesses—Victims and Witnesses Bill—a consultation pape*r, 2012.

[81] *http://www.scottish.parliament.uk/S4_Bills/Victims%20and%20Witnesses%20(Scotland)%20Bill/b23s4-introd-pm.pdf* [accessed July 11, 2013].

[82] Directive 2012/29/EU of the European Parliament and of the Council of October 25, 2012 establishing minimum standards on the rights, support and protection of victims of crime.

[83] See *http://www.scottish.parliament.uk/parliamentarybusiness/Bills/59133.aspx* [accessed August 26, 2013].

protects witnesses, notably vulnerable complainers in rape and sexual assault cases, from techniques of cross-examination that witnesses, at least, often characterise as "degrading".[84]

Although the overarching principle is that the accused must receive a fair **3–46** trial, that does not exclude the interests of complainers or other witnesses. As the European Court has acknowledged[85]:

> "[The] principles of fair trial also require that in appropriate cases the interests of the defence are balanced against those of witnesses or victims called upon to testify."

Child witnesses receive explicit recognition in art.6(1) of the ECHR in that "the press and public may be excluded from all or part of the trial ... where the interests of juveniles ... so require". The explanatory memorandum to the Council of Europe's Recommendation on the Intimidation of Witnesses and the Rights of the Defence states that "the welfare of the child witness must, in general, be the paramount concern over other interests, even the interests of justice".[86]

DOMESTIC LEGISLATION

A range of statutory reforms has been introduced in Scotland since 1990 to **3–47** enable certain categories of witness to give their best quality evidence. Initially, these reforms were focused on those deemed most in need of support, namely children, but recently these measures have been extended to other categories of persons described as "vulnerable" and/or intimidated. A witness who has experienced intimidation may very well also be vulnerable. The current statutory framework still takes the child as the paradigmatic vulnerable witness and the special measures set out in the legislation to support testimony are designed with children in mind. It is therefore appropriate to consider the position of the vulnerable child witness first before turning to other groups.

Children

Children comprise by far the single largest group of witnesses to have **3–48** statutory protection. There are various reasons for this, including the increasing number of prosecutions of cases involving children who are the complainers in cases of child sexual abuse.[87] Numbers have increased in parallel with our better understanding of the phenomenon of child sexual abuse and with the behaviour of those who perpetrate it. In addition to

---

[84] For comment see, P. Duff, "The Scottish 'rape shield': as good as it gets", Edin. LR (2011) 218; L. Ellison, *The Adversarial Process and the Vulnerable Witness* (Oxford: Oxford University Press, 2001); M. Burman, L. Jamieson, J. Nicholson, and O. Brooks, *Impact of Aspects of the Law of Evidence in Sexual Offence Trials: An Evaluation Study* (Scottish Government, 2007).

[85] *Doorson v Netherlands* (1996) E.H.R.R. 330 at para.70.

[86] (R. (97) 13) at para.100.

[87] L. Hoyano and C. Keenan, *Child Abuse: Law and Policy across Boundaries*, (Oxford: Oxford University Press, 2010).

more cases being reported as a result of growing public awareness of the issue, child protection strategies and agencies have become better co-ordinated, resulting in improved methods of interviewing and fact-finding,[88] and prosecutors being more willing to pursue reports by adults of historic abuse.[89]

3–49 Growing numbers of children thus face the possibility that they will require to give evidence in criminal proceedings. At the same time it is widely acknowledged that children generally do not have the resources to cope with the rigours of cross-examination, especially when the nature of the evidence being given is of a difficult or embarrassing nature or, as is often the case, the alleged perpetrator is a previously trusted family member.[90]

3–50 As noted earlier, art.6 of the ECHR describes the welfare of the child as "the paramount concern" even over other interests and permits clearing the court so that "the press and public may be excluded from all or part of the trial ... where the interests of juveniles ... so require".[91]

3–51 The Scottish reform process began in earnest in 1990 with the Scottish Law Commission report, *Evidence of Children and Other Potentially Vulnerable Witnesses*, which made a number of recommendations, many of which were subsequently enacted.[92] Following the publication of the Report, the Lord Justice General issued a *Memorandum on Child Witnesses*[93] suggesting a variety of practical measures that could be taken to alleviate the formality of the court setting. The objective was to ensure that "so far as is reasonably practicable ... the experience of giving evidence by all children under sixteen causes as little anxiety and distress to the child as possible in the circumstances".[94]

3–52 The key recommendation from the SLC report, namely permitting child witnesses the option of giving evidence by live television link, was introduced in 1990[95] and re-enacted in s.271 of the Criminal Procedure (Scotland) Act 1995. Subsequent legislation extended the statutory protection offered to child witnesses to all witnesses who were considered vulnerable.[96] The current terms of s.271 incorporate the reforms contained in the Vulnerable Witnesses (Scotland) Act 2004 and the Criminal Justice and Licensing (Scotland) Act 2010 and represent two and a half decades of reform. Although the emphasis is on supporting children in criminal proceedings, the 2004 Act extended the support measures offered in the legislation to children in civil proceedings and to adults who are vulnerable due to mental disorder, or fear and distress associated with giving evidence.[97]

---

[88] e.g. *Guidance on Joint Investigative Interviewing of Child Witnesses in Scotland*, Scottish Government, 2011.

[89] P. Lewis, *Delayed Prosecution for Childhood Sexual Abuse* (Oxford: Oxford University Press, 2006).

[90] J. Spencer and M. Lamb (eds), *Children and Cross-Examination: Time to Change the Rules?* (Oxford: Oxford University Press, 2012).

[91] The explanatory memorandum to the Council of Europe's Recommendation on the Intimidation of Witnesses and the Rights of the Defence, discussed earlier in this chapter.

[92] Scottish Law Commission, *The Evidence of Children and Other Vulnerable Witnesses*, Report 125, 1990.

[93] *http://www.scotland.gov.uk/Resource/Doc/47049/0025079.pdf* [accessed July 11, 2013].

[94] Dent and Flin (eds), *Children as Witnesses*, (Chichester: Wiley, 1992).

[95] Law Reform (Miscellaneous Provisions) (Scotland) Act 1990.

[96] s.29 of the Crime and Punishment (Scotland) Act 1997.

[97] s.271(1) Criminal Procedure (Scotland) Act 1995.

Part X11 of the Criminal Procedure (Scotland) Act 1995 sets out the **3–53** statutory framework for the special measures and the arrangements for application to the court to be granted their use. Under the heading "Special measures for child witnesses and other vulnerable witnesses", ss.271A–M detail the provisions which define who is a vulnerable witness, the circumstances in which such witnesses are entitled to special measures to enable them to give evidence and the nature of these special measures. The following discussion of these provisions highlights the key terms and draws attention to potential difficulties in implementation. Section 271(1) states that a person is a vulnerable witness if:

    (a) the person is under the age of 16 on the date of commencement of the proceedings in which the trial is being or to be held (such a vulnerable witness being referred to in this Act as a "child witness"), or

    (b) where the person is not a child witness, there is a significant risk that the quality of the evidence to be given by the person will be diminished by reason of—

        (i) mental disorder (within the meaning of s.328 of the Mental Health (Care and Treatment) (Scotland) Act 2003), or

        (ii) fear or distress in connection with giving evidence at the trial.

The accused who is a child is also eligible to be classed as a vulnerable witness.[98] The trial refers to proceedings in either the sheriff court or the High Court under either summary or solemn procedure.

Section 271A provides that a child witness has an entitlement to certain **3–54** special measures.

Section 271B provides that children under 12 years of age should be able **3–55** to give evidence remotely, i.e. not in the court building.[99]

Section 271C deals with vulnerable witnesses other than children.   **3–56**

Section 271(2) explains that in determining whether a person who is an **3–57** adult is a vulnerable witness the court shall take into account:

    (a) the nature and circumstances of the alleged offence to which the proceedings relate;

    (b) the nature of the evidence which the person is likely to give;

    (c) the relationship (if any) between the person and the accused;

    (d) the person's age and maturity;

    (e) any behaviour towards the person on the part of—

        (i) the accused;

        (ii) members of the family or associates of the accused;

        (iii) any other person who is likely to be an accused or a witness in the proceedings; and

    (f) such other matters, including—

        (i) the social and cultural background and ethnic origins of the person;

---

[98] s.271F.

[99] Note that the Victims & Witnesses (Scotland) Bill 2013 proposes removing this requirement.

    (ii)   the person's sexual orientation;

   (iii)   the domestic and employment circumstances of the person;

   (iv)   any religious beliefs or political opinions of the person; and

   (v)   any physical disability or other physical impairment which the person has, as appear to the court to be relevant.

The matters which the court is directed to take into account in (a)–(f) above represent a much broader set of circumstances than the legislation which the 2004 Act replaced. This reflects the growing appreciation that prosecutions simply could not be mounted, or if mounted would collapse, unless adequate measures were in place. Such measures aim to support witnesses already traumatised by the initial offence and further distressed by the prospect of having to give their evidence in a witness box placed a short distance from the alleged perpetrator. Child complainers in cases of physical or sexual abuse are at particular risk of feeling intimidated.[100] An area which could make a significant difference to the quality of the evidence that children give in court is the investigative interview. The arrangements for the conduct of these interviews currently have only advisory status and research demonstrates that police practice varies, with some interviews conducted so poorly that potential high quality evidence is lost or contaminated.[101] This is disappointing as, if conducted in compliance with the guidance, the interview can carry substantial weight. Ironically, the Victims and Witnesses (Scotland) Bill, which is an opportunity to remedy this problem, proposes only that interviewers "must have regard to any guidance issued by the Scottish Ministers about the carrying out of interviews with a child in relation to those matters".[102] If the guidance were to be made mandatory, and embodied in legislation, interview practice would have to improve.

Vulnerable adult witnesses

3–58   An adult can be considered a vulnerable witness either on grounds of mental disorder (i.e. mental illness, personality disorder or learning disability),[103] or if there is a significant risk that the quality of their evidence will be diminished by reason of fear or distress in connection with giving evidence.[104] In order to satisfy these provisions a court is likely to require production of a medical, psychiatric or psychological report, although this is not made explicit in the Act.[105] At common law, rape complainers have been recognised as entitled to a screen to shield them from sight of the accused.[106]

3–59   In relation to adults, the intimidation is just as likely to be experienced prior to, as during, the trial, whether from the accused, his or her family or

---

[100] K. Murray, *Preparing Child Witnesses for Court*, Scottish Office, 1997.

[101] D. La Rooy, "The Quality of Joint Investigative Interviews in Scotland", S.L.T. 2010, Issue 24, p.133.

[102] s.4(2) of the Victims and Witnesses (Scotland) Bill 2013.

[103] It is mental disorder with the meaning of s.328 of the Mental Health (Care and Treatment) (Scotland) Act 2003.

[104] s.271(1)(b)(i) and (ii).

[105] The application form is contained in an Act of Adjournal and requires the applicant to specify the reasons why the witness is likely to be vulnerable. If granted the order must be served on the other party. See: *http://www.legislation.gov.uk/ssi/2006/76/made* [accessed July 11, 2013].

[106] *Hampson v HM Advocate*, 2003 S.L.T. 94.

associates. There are already concerns about delays in the time it takes to bring prosecutions to trial and these are compounded if adjournments are necessary because intimidated witnesses have failed to respond to a citation.

Protective measures for vulnerable child witnesses in criminal proceedings

Child witnesses are entitled to one or more special measures to reduce their **3–60** exposure to the normal processes of the adversarial trial, unless they do not wish to have the benefit of these (and the court thinks that appropriate)[107] or the court decides that one of the two following situations applies[108]:

(i)   the use of any special measure for the purpose of taking the evidence of the child witness would give rise to a significant risk of prejudice to the fairness of the trial or otherwise to the interests of justice; and

(ii) that risk significantly outweighs any risk of prejudice to the interests of the child witness if the order is made.

The special measures available for a child witness are listed as follows:

- s.271H—taking of evidence by a commissioner;
- s.271I—use of a live television link;
- s.271K—271J use of a screen;
- s.271L—use of a supporter;
- s.271M—giving evidence in chief in the form of a prior statement.

There is now, in effect, a statutory presumption that a child witness is vulnerable and will require special measures. This will overcome the difficulties presented under the previous legislation which required a child to "show cause" for the grant of special measures as they were not automatic and, for example, the mere witnessing of a "traumatic event" was not sufficient cause.[109] The special measures of a screen, live television link and a supporter are regarded as "standard" special measures and the court has to grant them.[110] Any other measure will only be granted if the judge considers it appropriate to do so.[111]

In addition to the above, judges retain discretion to follow the recom- **3–61** mendations of the Lord Justice General's *Memorandum on Child Witnesses*, including the removal of wigs and gowns; clearing the court of unnecessary persons, such as members of the public; and relocating the child, judge and lawyers to a table in the well of the court.[112]

---

[107] s.271A(a).
[108] s.271A(b).
[109] *HM Advocate v Birkett*, 1992 S.C.C.R. 850. See Gordon in his Commentary to the case report at 854.
[110] s.271A(5)(a)(i).
[111] s.271A(5)(a)(ii).
[112] Discussed earlier in this chapter.

Using the special measures

3–62 The provisions of the Vulnerable Witnesses (Scotland) Act were introduced over a lengthy period, starting with solemn proceedings, rolled out to include summary proceedings and finally extending to civil proceedings by April 2007. However, there is variable availability of certain facilities, such as the remote television link, as not every sheriff court district has a suitable remote location.

Evidence on Commission

3–63 This is a procedure whereby the court appoints a commissioner (either an advocate or solicitor of five years' standing) to take evidence from the vulnerable person.[113] The witness's responses to questions asked by the commissioner are recorded on videotape and seen by the accused in a separate room. The taking of evidence on commission has been available since 1990, but has been used very rarely.[114] There appears to be some concern that the loss of immediacy of the examination and cross-examination of the witness impacts negatively on juries. This was an argument that used to be made in regard to the live television link, with some justification in the early days of less sophisticated technology and poorly-equipped courtroom facilities.[115] It is less valid today and empirical research confirms that the live link is now a well-accepted procedure in both the High Court and sheriff courts.[116]

Live television link

3–64 The live link includes an option of a remote link, i.e. the witness gives evidence from another building not just another room in the courthouse. As noted above, remote links are not yet available in all parts of the country. With both live links and screens (which are wheeled between the witness box and dock) arrangements are made to meet the expectation that an accused should be allowed to see the accuser. The witness's image appears on the monitor placed above the screen so the accused can see the witness but the witness cannot see the accused. The European Court of Human Rights has ruled that there is no absolute right to face-to-face confrontation. For example, in cases involving policing or national security, or where there is a fear of reprisal, witnesses may remain hidden from the accused and have their voices disguised.[117] The Appeal Court in *I v Dunn*[118] ruled that s.271C has to be read down to ensure it is compliant with art.6. The appellant had argued that the legislation was contrary to a fair trial in that the accused

---

[113] For details of the procedures involved generally in taking evidence on commission see The Hon Lord Macphail, Sheriff T. Welsh QC (ed), *Sheriff Court Practice*, 3rd edn (Edinburgh, W. Green, 2006) para.15.18.

[114] M. Mackarel, F. Raitt and S. Moody, *Legal Issues and Witness Protection in Criminal Cases*, 2001.

[115] See for example, *Brotherston v HM Advocate*, 1996 S.L.T. 1154 at 1156.

[116] For discussion of this research, see F. Raitt, "Robust and Raring to go?—judges' perceptions of child witnesses", (2007) 34(4) *Journal of Law and Society* 465.

[117] *Doorson v Netherlands* (1996) E.H.R.R. 330; *Van Mechelen v Netherlands* (1998) 25 E.H.R.R. 647. See too, the rather limited discussion in *Brotherston v HM Advocate*, 1996 S.L.T. 1154, a case from a period when references to the ECHR were rare.

[118] *I v Dunn* [2012] HCJAC 108.

person had no opportunity to oppose the application for special measures at the stage when the sheriff considered it in chambers in the absence of the parties. The defence objection that this might prevent a fair trial was rejected by the appeal court on the grounds that even if there was no specific provision for opposing an application, there were alternative procedural options to address the court on the question of any unfairness to the accused. The court noted there was statutory protection for a review of the fairness of the special measures at any stage on the trial.[119]

If it is demonstrated that the special measure(s) would "give rise to a **3–65** significant risk of prejudice to the fairness of the trial or otherwise to the interests of justice", and that the risk "significantly outweighs any risk of prejudice to the interests of the witness if the order is made", the judge may revoke the order and (depending on the circumstances and the submissions) may, or may not, substitute a different special measure (s.271D(4)(b)).

It has been proposed that the legislation should be amended to permit **3–66** objections to applications for special measures at the point of application.[120]

Clearing the court

At common law the presiding judge can order the courtroom to be cleared **3–67** of all persons except the parties and their legal advisers, other persons directly concerned with the case, officers of the court and the press.[121] An application to clear the court would only be necessary if the witness was actually giving evidence in open court. If the witness is giving evidence by live television link they are only able to see the solicitor, counsel or judge who is at any stage asking them a question.[122]

Prior statement

Giving evidence in chief in the form of a prior statement, i.e. instead of the **3–68** child appearing as a witness, is a significant innovation. At common law, the admissibility of such prior statements constituted hearsay evidence and the circumstances where a child could have prior statements considered by the court were very limited. A statutory exception introduced through s.259 of the Criminal Procedure (Scotland) Act 1995 permits a prosecutor to lodge a prior statement and seek its acceptance as evidence in circumstances where the child has started to give evidence, but then, not untypically, is unable to continue. If a child or other vulnerable witness satisfies s.259(2)(5)(a), namely that they are unable to give evidence "by reason of his bodily or mental condition", or is "unfit or unable to give evidence in any competent manner" then a prior statement is permitted. That section had been interpreted as meaning that a child's hearsay statement could only be used as evidence if certain pre-conditions applied. The child had to be present in court and then refused or been unable to give evidence, *having been ordered* by the judge to do so. A "refusal" was not therefore just an inability or

---

[119] *1 v Dunn* [2012] HCJAC at para.39.
[120] s.9 of the Victims and Witnesses (Scotland) Bill 2013.
[121] It is specifically mentioned in the Lord Justice General's *Memorandum on Child Witnesses* referred to earlier.
[122] The Victims and Witnesses (Scotland) Bill, s.16, proposes making this a statutory provision.

difficulty in giving evidence—it was a refusal in response to an order.[123] The expectation that a fearful or distressed child might be encouraged to testify by being ordered to do so is unconvincing to say the least. Fortunately, s.260 was amended by s.27M(2)[124] so that a child's prior statement can be used as evidence in chief *in place of* the child's entire or partial live testimony in chief, without the child having to confirm the statement was theirs, or having to adopt the statement as their evidence.

Use of a supporter

3–69 The supporter permitted to accompany the child would usually be an adult the child knows and trusts, but obviously not someone who will be a witness. When this provision was introduced, it was widely assumed that the supporter would be known to the child, but it appears this is not always the case.[125] Research from England, where commonly the child is allocated an unknown court official as a supporter, suggests, unsurprisingly, that children give evidence better if they have with someone of their choosing as a supporter.[126]

Applications for special measures

3–70 The party wishing to cite the witness—often, but not always the Crown—has the responsibility to apply timeously for a grant of the special measure or measures thought most appropriate for the individual child's circumstances and in their best interests. However, since the child should not suffer on account of error or negligence on the part of the lawyers involved, the procedures for late application, including during the trial, are flexible. The court and the party citing the witness must take into account the child's wishes if expressed, their best interests and the wishes of the child's parent (unless they are the accused).[127] Children ought to be consulted about their preferences for special measures and if they are aged 12 or over they are presumed to be of sufficient age and maturity to form a view.[128] If the child's view conflicts with any views expressed by their parent, the child's views have greater weight.[129]

Protective measures for adult vulnerable witnesses

3–71 Adult witnesses deemed vulnerable currently have no automatic entitlement to special measures. However, the Victim and Witnesses (Scotland) Bill 2013 proposes raising the age of a vulnerable child witness from 16 years to 18 years, and extending, but still as discretionary, the availability of special measures offences to categories of witnesses in certain cases, e.g. domestic abuse, stalking and people trafficking,[130] and to named crimes. The party

---

[123] *MacDonald v HM Advocate*, 1999 S.L.T. 533.
[124] Criminal Procedure (Scotland) Act 1995
[125] J. Plotnikoff and R. Woolfson, *Measuring up Report* (London: NSPCC, 2009).
[126] J. Plotnikoff and R. Woolfson, *In Their Own Words* (London: NSPCC, 2004).
[127] s.271E.
[128] s.271E(3)(a).
[129] s.272E(3)(b).
[130] Victims and Witnesses (Scotland) Bill 2013, s.6. The Bill also proposes a right of victims to specify the gender of the police interviewer in specific crimes; and circumstances for "deeming" a witness vulnerable and thus eligible for special measures.

citing a witness who is eligible for special measures must apply for one or more measures and set out the justification in the application, providing evidence, such as a medical report where appropriate.[131] Solicitors are responsible for assessing whether a witness they propose to cite would be more able to give their evidence with the benefit of one or more special measures. The court considering applications for special measures will assess whether the witness would be likely to give more complete, coherent or accurate testimony if a special measure was in place. Detailed guidance on the legislation, criteria for eligibility and for making applications is available online.[132]

Protective measures for vulnerable child witnesses in civil proceedings

The provision of special measures, and the criteria for eligibility, applies **3–72** equally to child witnesses in civil proceedings and in criminal proceedings.

Future directions

Despite the considerable progress made with arrangements for vulnerable **3–73** witnesses to give evidence, there are a number of further reforms which have been proposed but not yet implemented. Two of these are worthy of comment, given the likelihood that the pressure to foreground the interests of witnesses in the justice system will not abate. First, for many years now there has been a proposition that children should not be required to appear in court or on a CCTV link to give live testimony. Instead, both their evidence-in-chief and cross-examination should be video-recorded.[133] It is argued this would have the advantage of capturing children's evidence at a much earlier stage in proceedings when their recall would be sharper. In addition, earlier examination would save them from lengthy periods of stress and anxiety while anticipating the trial. Arguments against this proposal include the difficulty for the defence in conducting a cross-examination before full preparations for trial have been concluded.

Second, examination and cross-examination of children requires parti- **3–74** cular skills and the art of examining children or other vulnerable persons is not necessarily a skill every litigator has at their fingertips In England and Wales the use of an intermediary appointed by the court is permitted in terms of s.29 of the Youth Justice and Criminal Evidence Act 1999. Following a successful pilot study, the intermediary programme has been introduced throughout England.[134] Intermediaries are trained professionals, typically speech therapists and linguists, who have the skills to convert complex or poorly constructed questions into a form that is more readily comprehensible to the witness. In 2007 the Scottish Government issued a Consultation Paper on the possible introduction of such a scheme in Scotland, but to date no progress has been made with this.[135]

---

[131] s.271C.
[132] At *http://www.scotland.gov.uk/Publications/2008/04/21142140/0* [access August 26, 2013].
[133] See, e.g. Responses to Scottish Government Consultation Paper.
[134] See research evaluation by J. Plotnikoff and R. Woolfson, "The Go-Between: evaluation of intermediary pathfinder projects", *Lexicon Limited*, 2007.
[135] Consultation on the use of intermediaries for vulnerable witnesses in Scotland, Scottish Government, 2007.

Chapter 4

EXPERT WITNESSES AND OPINION EVIDENCE

INTRODUCTION

4–01 The emphasis in the adversarial process is on fact-finding. Thus, the court is interested in the testimony of a witness as to the *facts* of which they have personal knowledge or experience and which are relevant to the case. Generally, the court is not interested in the witness's *opinion* of what might have happened, or how the court should interpret the facts offered during their testimony. The one exception to this rule is that witnesses who are able to lay claim to specialist knowledge may be permitted to give expert opinion evidence to assist the trier of fact to reach an informed conclusion on the facts as a whole.

4–02 Critics have pointed out that the distinction between fact and opinion is artificial and without substance. The accounts of non-expert witnesses who testify to the circumstances of something they have personally experienced necessarily involves recounting some element of personal opinion. According to the American jurist, J.B. Thayer, writing in the nineteenth century, "in a sense all testimony to matter of fact is opinion evidence, i.e. it is a conclusion formed from phenomena and mental impressions".[1] For example, the witness who identifies the accused as the person who assaulted her is, in effect, telling the court that in her opinion the person who assaulted her is the person now sitting in the dock.

4–03 Whether evidence is derived from fact or opinion, the legal duty of adjudicating on the facts and drawing any conclusions from those facts— known as deciding the ultimate issue—is the responsibility of the trier of fact. Expert witnesses may give their opinion of the facts proven in court, but they should not pre-empt the responsibility of the trier of fact by giving their opinion on *how* the court should assess what it has heard:

> "The general rule is that it would be quite wrong, and inadmissible, to put a witness into the witness box to tell the jury what the evidence they have been listening to ought to convey to them."[2]

Expert opinion evidence is admissible where the issues in dispute involve matters so specialist or technical that they are considered to be beyond the everyday experience of the judge or jury as the fact-finder. The range of potential opinion evidence from an expert is infinite, but commonly it arises in criminal trials when scientific evidence is led to incriminate or exculpate

[1] *A Preliminary Treatise on Evidence at the Common Law*, 1898, at 524.
[2] Lord Sorn, *Hopes and Lavery v HM Advocate*, 1960 J.C. 104 at 113.

46

an accused, and in reparation actions where causation must be proven, e.g. mechanical failure in road traffic accidents or medical negligence in wrongful birth suits.[3]

The use of expert opinion evidence in the courtroom tends to attract **4–04** media attention and is often central to alleged miscarriages of justice. High profile cases frequently involve some element of expert scientific evidence, subsequently proven to have been withheld from the defence, either by the police or the prosecution, or never even relayed to any party by the expert.[4] Furthermore, there is a steady stream of historic cases being reviewed by the police and defence teams as new techniques in forensic technology and medical science raise the possibility of analysing evidence previously too tiny or too contaminated to be capable of analysis.[5]

Unsurprisingly therefore the role of the expert in the courtroom has come **4–05** under increasing public and critical scrutiny.[6] This chapter examines the role of expert witnesses and the shifting climate within which they now have to operate.

The Role of the Expert Witness

The role of the expert witness in civil and criminal cases, and the limitations **4–06** placed by law on that role, were summarised by Lord President Cooper in *Davie v Magistrates of Edinburgh*.[7] He said:

"Their duty is to furnish the Judge or jury with the necessary scientific criteria for testing the accuracy of their conclusions, so as to enable the Judge or jury to form their own independent judgment by the application of these criteria to the facts proved in evidence."

The expert witness is only required in order that certain facts may be assessed and understood in their specialist, and often scientific, context. The standard of proof to which an expert gives evidence on an essential fact is on a balance of probability.[8] The facts themselves must still be established by evidence, usually from the expert, and may be challenged, and even discarded, as indeed may the opinion itself if the court is not satisfied with it for some reason.[9] Unlike non-expert witnesses, in the absence of any objection, an expert witness is permitted to remain in court during the hearing of other testimony, other than for the opinion element of other experts' testimony.

---

[3] For a detailed examination of this topic see C. Jones, *Expert Evidence: science, medicine and the practice of law* (Oxford: Clarendon Press, 1994); Kenny, "The Expert in Court", 99 L.Q.R. 197; and M. Redmayne, *Expert Evidence and Criminal Justice* (Oxford: Oxford University Press, 2001).

[4] See, for example, the cases of *Preece v HM Advocate*, Note and Commentary, A. Brownlie, [1981] Crim. L.R. 783; and Sally Clark discussed later in this chapter.

[5] e.g. *R. v Hanratty* [2002] E.W.C.A. Crim 1141.

[6] See the report by the House of Commons Science and Technology Committee, *Forensic Evidence on Trial* (7th Report of Session 2004–05). HC 96-I (2005). See too House of Commons Science and Technology Committee, Forensic Science Second Report of Session 2013–14 (HC London, 2013).

[7] *Davie v Magistrates of Edinburgh*, 1953 S.C. 34 at 40.

[8] *Hendry v HM Advocate*, 1988 S.L.T. 25.

[9] See e.g. *HM Advocate v Grimmond*, 2001 S.C.C.R. 708.

Their presence in court better equips them to comment upon the evidence being led.[10]

4–07 An appeal may be successfully taken on the ground that expert evidence should have been led but was not.[11] Alternatively, a court may refuse to make a finding on a particular point where expert evidence was required but was not led. In *Columbia Steam Navigation Co Ltd v Burns*[12] a collision occurred between two vessels during a thick fog on the River Clyde. The trial court refused to draw inferences concerning the speed of one of the vessels at the time of the collision from the nature and extent of the damage to the other, because no expert evidence was led on the point. Although the court was sitting with a nautical assessor, it was held to be incompetent simply to invite his opinion as he was not in a position to give evidence as an independent expert.

4–08 In a recent action against a large cigarette manufacturer, Lord Nimmo-Smith held that the court required guidance from experts on the specialist area of epidemiology as that was a central plank in the basis of a claim of a causal connection between smoking and lung cancer. In the absence of such evidence the court was unable to form a judgment.[13]

4–09 With rapid medical, scientific and technological advances, there is increasing emphasis on trying to prove or disprove the accuracy of contested issues through the application of expert testimony. This has given rise to concerns that, as the parties turn to expert testimony to vindicate their cause, the courtroom will become the arena for a "battle of the experts" consuming ever larger proportions of the courts' time and adding considerably to the legal costs of the parties. Major reforms to the role of experts have been proposed and at least partially undertaken in other jurisdictions.[14] These have tried to anticipate the appropriate response of law to the admissibility of new scientific discoveries amidst fears that unreliable science will creep into the courtroom.

ESTABLISHING THE EXPERTISE OF THE EXPERT WITNESS

4–10 The credentials of an expert should be established before any opinion is admissible in evidence. This is to safeguard against false claims of expertise which might invalidate the reliability of the opinion. In the normal course of things, the expert witness will belong to a profession or a branch of the sciences. In such cases, it is normally only necessary for the party calling the expert to establish the witness's identity and then enumerate their academic and professional qualifications, their reputation in their field and other

---

[10] *HM Advocate v Laurie* (1889) 2 White 326.

[11] See, e.g. *U.S. Shipping Board v The St Albans* [1931] A.C. 632.

[12] (1895) 22 R. 237. See also *Muir v Stewart*, 1938 S.C. 590, where a reparation action against a pharmacist failed for lack of evidence of the relevant professional standards of care.

[13] *McTear v Imperial Tobacco Ltd*, 2005 2 S.C. 1.

[14] e.g. Lord Woolf report on the civil courts of England and Wales, *Access to Justice*, 1996, available at: *http://www.dca.gov.uk/civil/final/index.htm* [accessed July 11, 2013]; Lord Justice Auld's *Review of the Criminal Courts of England and Wales*, 2001, available at *http://www.criminal-courts-review.org.uk/auldconts.htm* [accessed July 11, 2013]; and the Law Commission Report, *Expert Evidence in Criminal Proceedings in England and Wales* (Law Com No.325) 2011.

relevant information such as any honours bestowed upon them or details of publications. Leading an expert witness through this personal biography provides a context from which judges and juries can better assess the weight to be attached to expert testimony. While expertise is frequently underpinned by academic and professional qualifications, those are not essential qualities. The law also recognises the expertise of the "skilled witness"[15] who may have acquired specialist knowledge from years of relevant experience. Their claim to specialist, expert knowledge still has to be proven to the court.[16]

Sometimes it is necessary to prove that an expert has the specialist **4–11** knowledge they claim.[17] Thus, in *Hewat v Edinburgh Corporation*[18] the Court of Session held that it would be competent to ask a police officer and three council employees whether they believed a particular hole in the road to be dangerous because it was their duty to report such dangers. Thus, one can infer that those with such responsibilities must be presumed to have some specialist knowledge of the subject. In *Hopes and Lavery v HM Advocate*[19] Lord Sorn held that a typist might have become an expert on the authenticity of a transcript from a tape recording on which she had worked. This was on the basis that there was "no rigid rule that only witnesses possessing some technical qualification can be allowed to expound their understanding of any particular item of evidence".

What matters is not so much the academic qualification or the formal **4–12** recognition as proof of the expertise. The source of that proof does not determine admissibility provided that the court is satisfied that it exists, and that the person called as an expert witness is fit to guide the court in an area beyond its experience. For example, in an early English case[20] a solicitor was allowed to give expert evidence on handwriting, a matter in which he had acquired expertise as a skilled amateur. It also follows from this general principle that an expert should not tread beyond the boundaries of their field of expertise, even if those matters appear to be closely related to the matter on which the expert is testifying.[21] Containing experts to their area of expertise is an increasingly difficult task as burgeoning advances in science and technology present opportunities for emerging or novel science—science that is in its infancy—to be available in the investigation and detection of crime. Litigators in turn require expert witnesses to explain the relevance and value of new knowledge and there may be temptations on some witnesses to step beyond the parameters of their expertise, whether in accepting instructions to appear as a witness, or under pressure to make claims or concessions in cross-examination. It is therefore vital that legal representatives select their witnesses with care and with due regard to their qualifications, experience and reputation. Various high profile miscarriages

---

[15] Dickson defined "skilled witness" as "a person who through practice, or study, or both, is specially qualified in a recognised branch of knowledge, whether it be art, science or craft". *Evidence*, 3rd edn, para.398.

[16] *Davie v Magistrates of Edinburgh*, 1953 S.C. 34.

[17] *Davie v Magistrates of Edinburgh*, 1953 S.C. 34.

[18] 1944 S.C. 30.

[19] 1960 J.C. 104 at 114. See also *Haq v HM Advocate*, 1987 S.C.C.R. 433.

[20] *R. v Silverlock* [1894] 2 Q.B. 766.

[21] As for example in *U.S. Shipping Board v The St Albans* [1931] A.C. 632 in which it was held that land surveyors could not testify to a diagram constructed from a photograph.

of justice have demonstrated the need for greater diligence and training on the part of both expert witnesses and those who instruct them. We return to the complexities posed by the admissibility of emerging science later in this chapter.

4–13   Notwithstanding the warnings against experts straying from the boundaries of their expertise, it is permissible for an expert to refer to literature in a related field provided the literature has a bearing upon the subject in which the witness has expertise.[22] It is not regarded as hearsay for an expert to discuss literature other than that which they have authored. Thus, while giving evidence an expert witness may well draw upon the published research of the discipline, whether empirical studies or peer-reviewed journal articles, in support of their own testimony. In doing so, the passages are in effect adopted as the expert's evidence and become part of the general body of evidence available to the court. The reason this is permissible is because "expert witnesses are regarded as the living embodiment of a corpus of learning, so are not constrained by the hearsay rule from adopting the views of other experts in the field".[23] But it is only the extracted sections of books and journals which become evidence in the case. The remainder of any literature is not evidence and may not be relied upon, even to challenge that expert witness's opinion.[24] Published academic literature may be put to an expert in chief or cross-examination without such literature being previously lodged as a production.[25]

LIMITATIONS ON EXPERT TESTIMONY

4–14 In addition to an expert only testifying to matters within their area of expertise, an expert witness may *not* testify as to matters that are well within the knowledge and experience of the trier of fact. This rule was established in 1975 in the English case of *R. v Turner*,[26] and it remains the guiding principle today in English and Scots law.[27] Turner was charged with the murder of his girlfriend, apparently carried out while he was in a blind rage induced by her sexual taunts and admissions of infidelity. His defence was that of provocation[28] and his counsel sought to lead psychiatric evidence to the effect that, although the accused was not suffering from a mental illness, the sort of experience to which he had been subjected might provide intense provocation even to a normal person. The trial judge excluded the opinion evidence, a ruling upheld by the Court of Appeal, which declared that although the opinion evidence was admissible it was irrelevant. L.J. Lawton reminded the parties of the purpose and parameters of opinion evidence[29]:

---

[22] *Main v McAndrew Wormald Ltd*, 1988 S.L.T. 141.
[23] P. Alldridge, "Scientific Expertise and Comparative Criminal Procedure" (1999) E. & P. 141 at p.149.
[24] *Davie v Magistrates of Edinburgh*, 1953 S.C. 34.
[25] *Roberts v British Railways Board*, 1998 S.L.C.R. 577.
[26] *R v Turner* [1975] Q.B. 834.
[27] *HM Advocate v Grimmond*, 2002 S.L.T. 508.
[28] Provocation has the same function under English law as under Scots law, in that it reduces a murder charge to the lesser charge of manslaughter, the equivalent of culpable homicide.
[29] *R v Turner* [1975] Q.B. 834 at 841.

"An expert's opinion is admissible to furnish the court with scientific information which is likely to be outside the experience and knowledge of a judge or jury. If on the proven facts a judge or jury can form their own conclusions without help, then the opinion of an expert is unnecessary. In such a case if it is given dressed up in scientific jargon it may make judgment more difficult. The fact that an expert witness has impressive scientific qualifications does not by that fact alone make his opinion on matters of human nature and behaviour within the limits of normality any more helpful than that of the jurors themselves; but there is a danger that they may think it does."

The appeal court stated that once the psychiatrist had determined that the accused was mentally normal, there was no further role for expert evidence, because:

"Jurors do not need psychiatrists to tell them how ordinary folk who are not suffering from any mental illness are likely to react to the stresses and strains of life."[30]

The *Turner* rule, as it has become known, has been criticised for revealing a narrow and uninformed view of the behavioural sciences. It presupposes human behaviour is common sense and transparent, a belief that is much contested by researchers who claim that "'ordinary, reasonable men and women' have a systematically biased understanding of normal human behaviour".[31]

Although *Turner* was concerned with the behaviour of a defendant who **4–15** was claiming the defence of provocation, the broader principle encapsulated in the *Turner* rule is that of excluding opinion evidence from areas which are the clear preserve of the jury (or other trier of fact). One such area is that of the credibility of witnesses, an area that creates considerable difficulties in practice.

EXPERT EVIDENCE AND CREDIBILITY

The assessment of a witness's credibility and reliability are the province of **4–16** the trier of fact. Jurors who have observed the demeanour of the witness giving evidence are best placed to decide how much eight to attach to the testimony of a particular witness and expert opinion evidence should not usurp this important function of the jury.[32] Members of the jury are assumed to have the capability to make decisions about a witness's credibility and reliability without the assistance of expert evidence. It is argued that to permit opinion evidence on credibility would unduly prolong the proof

---

[30] *R v Turner* [1975] Q.B. 834 at 841.
[31] A. Colman and R. Mackay, "Legal Issues surrounding the admissibility of expert psychiatric and psychological testimony", (1993) 20 *Issues in Criminological and Legal Psychology*, 46 at 48–49. See too D. Sheldon, "The admissibility of psychiatric and psychological evidence" (1992) S.L.T. (News) 301.
[32] There is a long line of English authority stemming from *Folkes v Chadd* [1782] 3 Doug KB 157 through to *R v Turner* [1975] Q.B. 834 which expresses this rule and which has been followed in Scotland: *HM Advocate v Grimmond*, 2002 S.L.T. 508.

process and would constitute "oath-helping" and add nothing to the quality of the witness's testimony.[33]

4–17   However, where there is a suggestion that external psychiatric or psychological factors (short of a recognised mental illness) may be influencing a witness's behaviour and thus credibility, it may be legitimate to admit expert evidence to explain to the jury how these external factors might typically affect a person in such a position.[34] For example, in *Green v HM Advocate*[35] psychiatric evidence that a rape complainer had previously made false complaints was admitted as an item of fresh evidence in an appeal against conviction. However, a key distinguishing factor in *Green* was that no objection was taken to the admissibility of this expert evidence. Moreover, because it constituted "facts relevant to the question at issue",[36] i.e. consent to sexual intercourse, one can see why there would be less objection to admitting expert evidence.

4–18   Where expert evidence is permitted, it is directed only at explaining to juries the general trends, patterns or aetiology of the phenomenon, and not how they have affected the witness in question. To attempt to give evidence on the latter is to decide the ultimate issue and that is not the role of the expert. This point is well-illustrated in *HM Advocate v Grimmond*[37] where Lord Osborne approved *R. v Turner* remarking that he considered it "properly reflects the approach taken by Scots law".[38]

4–19   *Grimmond* concerned allegations of sexual assault of two boys aged seven and eight from different families. Initially the boys had independently told their mothers of an incident which led to Grimmond being convicted of shameless and indecent behaviour. Some weeks later one boy described the incident in terms that suggested the much more serious assault of anal rape had occurred. The other boy corroborated this account. The Crown pursued a further prosecution. They anticipated that these secondary allegations, described by the trial judge as a "two-stage disclosure" process, would likely lead to an attack on the credibility of the complainers. The Crown therefore sought to call a clinical psychologist, an expert in sexual abuse cases, to give opinion evidence as to the commonality of the pattern of partial, then full, disclosure of revelations in child sexual abuse cases and thus to counter any negative inferences that the jury might otherwise draw.

4–20   Opinion evidence perceived as merely reinforcing a witness's credibility is not generally permitted, as it falls into the category of "oath-helping", but the Crown argued that their expert would go further by giving evidence of matters beyond the knowledge of the jury. The defence objected to the Crown's proposed line of evidence, founding upon the *Turner* rule, an approach the trial judge, Lord Osborne, preferred[39]:

---

[33] Walker and Walker, *Evidence*, 3rd edn, para.1.6.2.
[34] For a recent English case which illustrates the fine lines that are often drawn in this area, see *R. v H (Childhood Amnesia)* [2005] EWCA Crim 1828.
[35] 1983 S.C.C.R. 42.
[36] The view expressed in Walker and Walker, *Evidence*, 3rd edn, para.1.6.2.
[37] *HM Advocate v Grimmond*, 2002 S.L.T. 508.
[38] *HM Advocate v Grimmond*, 2002 S.L.T. 508 at para.11.
[39] *HM Advocate v Grimmond*, 2002 S.L.T. 508 at para.11.

"...[T]here is no suggestion that either of the children who are the complainers in this case is other than an ordinary and normal child. That being so, it appears to me that the assessment of their credibility is exclusively a matter for the jury, taking into account their experience and knowledge of human nature and affairs."

In his judgment Lord Osborne therefore comes down squarely on the side of the argument that holds understandings of how children react to sexual abuse is within the knowledge of the jury. That is highly debatable.[40] As Sheriff Gordon remarked, in an editorial commentary to the case[41]:

"This area is probably ripe for detailed consideration ... Does this decision mean that it is irrelevant to lead evidence of the way children usually behave in relation to telling or not telling about sexual abuse ... just how much does a jury's experience of life help in assessing the behaviour of abused children?"

The decision in *Grimmond* caused disquiet because it may have presumed too much about a juror's state of comprehension and thus their ability to assess credibility. Research in other disciplines informs us that the ways victims react to sexual offences are neither universal nor predictable.[42] If law is closed to admitting expert evidence to inform the trier of fact about such research and knowledge then it may be erecting artificial barriers. It is not the principle of the *Turner* rule that is problematic, so much as where the line is drawn in deciding whether jurors have an appropriate level of knowledge in order to make an informed assessment of credibility. Jurors cannot be tested on their individual knowledge and understanding. Instead, courts make assumptions about what constitutes "common sense" or "common knowledge" in areas of human behaviour where research repeatedly points the accurate answer is often counter-intuitive to what people actually think and believe.[43]

It is possible to admit opinion evidence without substituting the trier of **4–21** fact's judgment for that of the expert. Indeed, some argue judicious use of opinion evidence will improve the quality of fact-finding.[44] In the wake of *Grimmond* the Scottish Parliament enacted a significant, if limited, relaxation of rules on the admissibility of expert evidence. Section 5 of the Vulnerable Witnesses (Scotland) Act 2004[45] provides:

---

[40] See F. Raitt, "Credibility and the Limits of Scots Criminal Law" (2003) *Juridical Review*, 29; A. Lothian, "Time for Fundamental Review of Children's Evidence" (2001) JLSS, December, 40. See too Lord Macphail's analysis of this point in *HM Advocate v A*, 2005 S.L.T. 975 below.

[41] *HM Advocate v Grimmond*, 2001 S.C.C.R. 708 at 713–714.

[42] e.g. A. Burgess and L. Holmstrom, "Rape Trauma Syndrome and post-traumatic stress response" in. A. Burgess (ed) *Research Handbook on Rape and Sexual Assault*, (New York: Garland, 1985).

[43] R. Mackay and A. Colman, "Equivocal rulings on expert psychological and psychiatric evidence: Turning a muddle into a nonsense" [1996] Crim. L.R. 88.

[44] P. Roberts, "Towards the principled reception of expert evidence of witness credibility in criminal trials' (2004) 8(4) International Journal of Evidence and Proof, 215.

[45] Inserting s.275C into the Criminal Procedure (Scotland) Act 1995.

"Expert psychological or psychiatric evidence relating to any subsequent behaviour or statement of the complainer is admissible for the purpose of rebutting any inference adverse to the complainer's credibility or reliability as a witness which might otherwise be drawn from the behaviour or statement."

The reference to "any subsequent behaviour or statement of the complainer" means separate from the acts constituting the offence and not otherwise relevant to any fact in issue at the trial.[46] This provision applies to the more serious sexual offences, including rape, sodomy, induction with intent to rape and indecent assault.[47]

4–22   Where expert testimony offered by psychiatrists or psychologists has a firm psychiatric association, i.e. is a form of mental disorder that is recognised by the psychiatric community, then it is usually admissible in court. Thus, expert evidence has been admitted in relation to a person's suggestibility in making a confession, but only because their suggestibility derives from a subsisting psychological deficiency.[48] The courts will not entertain expert evidence on the general impact of the pressures of a police interview. However, where, for example, there is evidence of a witness's suggestibility due to a learning disability that enhances an individual's vulnerability, there is a case for expert evidence.[49]

4–23   In *HM Advocate v A*[50] Lord Macphail had to determine an application from the defence to lead expert testimony from a psychiatrist to suggest that one of two complainers of allegations of sexual assault was suffering from false memory syndrome, thus making false allegations. To contend that a person suffers from false memory syndrome is to suggest that they have, after a prolonged period of time, recalled or "recovered" a memory previously unknown to them. Researchers and practitioners are deeply divided over the issue.[51] Some claim that one can never suppress traumatic memories and thus when adults (as it is typically occurs later in life) supposedly "recover "early childhood trauma, these are not reliable memories. Other experts claim that suppression and temporary erasure of traumatic memories are a natural protective process. They explain that these memories may unfold later in life, sometimes, but not always, as a result of therapeutic intervention.

4–24   . . .In *A*, the expert had provided the defence with a report that indicated she considered the complainer, D, had a subsisting mental illness and that this subsisting illness led her to make the allegations. In response, the Crown sought to introduce their own expert, a clinical psychologist, who disputed the existence of false memory syndrome and argued that D's allegations were consistent with a history of childhood sexual abuse and was a pattern commonly encountered in clinical practice.

---

[46] Now s.275C(3) of the 1995 Act.
[47] Now specified in s.288C of the 1995 Act. Note that many of these offences have been re-classified in the Sexual Offences (Scotland) Act 2009.
[48] See *Blagojevic v HM Advocate*, 1995 S.L.T. 1189.
[49] *Blagojevic v HM Advocate*, 1995 S.L.T. 1189.
[50] *HM Advocate v A*, 2005 S.L.T. 975.
[51] For a discussion of the debates see F. Raitt and S. Zeedyk, "False Memory Syndrome: Undermining the Credibility of Complainants in Sexual Offences", International Journal of Law & Psychiatry 26(5) 453.

If one sets to one side the validity or otherwise of the syndrome, one can **4–25** nevertheless see how presenting one expert's evidence as to its existence and then another expert's contrary evidence as to the association between abuse and subsequent behaviour, could directly affect the jury's view of D's credibility.

Lord Macphail resolved that this was a case that came within the **4–26** exception to the general rule prohibiting opinion evidence as it amounted to "expert evidence relevant to a witness's veracity ... where *some special feature is present* which, in Dickson's phrase, 'involves scientific knowledge ... with which men of ordinary intelligence are not likely to be familiar'". It was not merely a collateral issue as the reliability of D's evidence was central to the proof of the charges—without it there would be insufficient evidence against the accused. Evidence of D's history suggested she was "in a complex mental state that was likely to be outside the experience of the members of a jury, and that they would need skilled assistance in order to understand her state of mind and reach a conclusion as to her credibility and reliability".[52] Lord Macphail therefore ruled the evidence of both experts admissible, rejecting the defence objection that the Crown's expert would merely be oath-helping. As he explained, this objection[53]:

"[W]as decisively trumped by the fundamental duty of the court to ensure that the trial was conducted with fairness, and it was essential for the Crown, prosecuting in the public interest, to be entitled to anticipate expert evidence and to demonstrate to the jury that there was another expert explanation and assessment of the complainer's state of mind which tended to indicate a different conclusion as to her veracity."

Under the shadow of the *Turner* rule, the Scottish courts have been willing to admit expert evidence of battered women's syndrome, a form of post-traumatic stress disorder ("PTSD"). Battered women's syndrome seeks to explain the context of why some battered women kill their abusive partners.[54] The syndrome is listed as a sub-category of PTSD in the Diagnostic and Statistical Manual ("DSM"), one of the most authoritative diagnostic manuals relied upon by health professionals.[55]

In *Galbraith v HM Advocate (No.2)*[56] the appellant had killed her hus- **4–27** band and pleaded diminished responsibility. Both psychiatric and psychological evidence was led at trial on her behalf. The psychiatrist testified that the appellant had a form of clinical depression, while the two psychologists

---

[52] *HM Advocate v A*, 2005 S.L.T. 975 at para.12 and para.15 (emphasis added).
[53] *HM Advocate v A*, 2005 S.L.T. 975 at para.21.
[54] There is a large literature on this subject. See, for example, R. Dobash (ed.), *Women, Violence and Social Change* (London: Routledge, 1992); Walker, *The Battered Woman Syndrome* (New York: Springer, 1994); and R. Dobash and R. Schuller, Regina and P. Hastings, "Trials of battered women who kill: the impact of alternative forms of expert evidence" (1996) 20 Law and Human Behavior 20: 167.
[55] The DSM (*Diagnostic and Statistical Manual of Mental Disorders*) (Arlington, USA: American Psychiatric Association, although it is frequently used in the UK. It is updated regularly. The current edition is the DSM 5, 2013. An alternative Manual is the 1CD-10, endorsed by the WHO (World Health Organisation).
[56] 2002 J.C. 1.

argued that she suffered from a type of post-traumatic stress disorder caused by years of physical and sexual abuse. A five bench court clarified the nature of the evidence that was required to sustain a plea of diminished responsibility in such circumstances[57]:

> "If the law has accepted that external causes, such as 'strokes of the sun' and head injuries, may give rise to a relevant mental abnormality for the purpose of diminished responsibility, we can see no reason in principle why a recognised abnormality caused by sexual or other abuse inflicted on the accused might not also be relevant for the same purpose. We stress, of course, that the abuse must result in some recognised mental abnormality. Subject to that important qualification, we again see no reason in principle why evidence of such a condition could not be given by those, such as psychologists, having the appropriate professional expertise, even though they were not medically qualified."

The courts have also recognised other types of syndrome evidence that are sub-categories of PTSD, especially in civil reparation actions involving damages for psychiatric injury or "nervous shock".[58]

CHALLENGING THE EXPERT WITNESS

4–28 In common with all witnesses an expert witness is open to challenge, both as to the validity of their opinion and the accuracy of the facts or assumptions on which it is based. The testimony of experts may be persuasive, but it must still pass the usual tests of relevancy and reliability. There will often be several experts in a case and it is very possible that they will disagree with each other, sometimes even when instructed by the same party, as occurred in *Davie v Magistrates of Edinburgh*.[59] This is to be expected, given that experts are frequently providing specialist knowledge which is itself derived from judgment and interpretation—it is rarely a precise science. Moreover, if all the expert witnesses in a case agreed, it is unlikely there would be a need for a trial or proof on these issues. They could be the subject of a minute of agreement lodged with the court and no evidence on those points would require to be led.

4–29 The function of the expert witness is to assist the court in coming to a conclusion, and not to proclaim some set of universal truths.[60] There is often a fine line between drawing appropriate inferences and speculation based on assumed facts.[61] Even if the expert gives evidence that is not contradicted, and it appears credible and reliable, the court is not bound to accept it.[62] The two most likely grounds upon which expert opinion will be challenged are

---

[57] At para.53, per Lord Justice-General Rodger.
[58] *Walker v Northumberland County Council* [1995] 1 All E.R. 737. For discussion see B. Baratt, "Psychiatric stress—an inacceptable cost to employers" (2008) Journal of Business Law, 64.
[59] n.7 above.
[60] *Dempster v Motherwell Bridge and Engineering Co*, 1964 S.L.T. 353.
[61] For examples of the rejection of evidence on this latter ground, see *S.S. Rowan v S.S. Malcolm*, 1923 S.C. 316 and *Gardiner v Motherwell Machinery and Scrap Co*, 1961 S.C. (H.L.) 1.
[62] *Beaton v HM Advocate*, 1994 S.L.T. 309.

first, a failure to lay a suitable basis of fact for the opinion; and second, the reliability of the scientific technique or conclusions being put forward. These are addressed in turn.

LAYING A BASIS OF FACT

The opinion of an expert must be based upon facts proved to the satisfaction **4–30** of the trier of fact and to the appropriate standard of proof. Generally speaking, expert testimony is a mixture of fact and professional opinion. The expert is called in to make an examination, or conduct a series of tests, and the court is receiving the expert evidence not just as a pure opinion, but also as evidence of the physical condition of something or someone. Illustrations of this include the evidence of pathologists describing post-mortem examinations on the deceased, police surgeons describing the results of examinations of rape victims and psychiatrists giving evidence of the mental state of persons they have examined. In both criminal and civil cases, experts are frequently instructed by solicitors to describe the condition of vehicles and roads in connection with road accidents, or machinery and plant in connection with injuries at work. In such circumstances, there may be the potential for civil reparation actions and/or criminal prosecutions under the health and safety legislation.

The onus of laying a relevant basis of fact, from which to invite sub- **4–31** sequent opinion evidence from an expert, lies on the party that wishes to lead the expert. Otherwise, the expert evidence may not be admissible. *Blagojevic v HM Advocate*[63] was an appeal against conviction for murder. The appellant, Blagojevic, had not given evidence at his trial. Counsel for the appellant had unsuccessfully sought to lead evidence at the trial from a clinical psychologist to show that Blagojevic was suggestible under the pressure of a police interview and thus susceptible to agreeing with suggestions put to him. The trial judge ruled the expert's testimony was inadmissible as no foundation in fact for the alleged suggestibility had first been laid. The appeal court upheld the ruling and conviction, noting that[64]:

> "In the absence of evidence from the appellant himself that his statement was influenced by these factors, or from the police that he was seen to be suffering from emotional stress or was under any pressure while they were talking to him, the jury could only speculate as to whether his vulnerability affected him on this occasion."

A similar finding of inadmissibility due to failure to lay a foundation of fact arose in *Forrester v HM Advocate*.[65] Forrester was convicted of charges of safe-blowing. It was central to the Crown's case to prove a connection between fibres from a bedspread used in the crime and fibres from material in Forrester's pocket. Although microscopic fibres had produced potentially incriminating results, the Crown had not led any evidence of the source of

---

[63] 1995 S.L.T. 1189.
[64] *Blagojevic v HM Advocate*, 1995 S.L.T. 1189 at 1192.
[65] 1952 J.C. 28. See also *Ritchie v Pirie*, 1972 J.C. 7; and *Russell v HM Advocate*, 1946 J.C. 37.

these fibres. As it could not be established that material found in Forrester's pocket corresponded with the bedspread, the conviction was quashed.

4-32   In criminal cases, each essential fact to which an expert speaks must be corroborated. That is not to say the expert's opinion must itself be corroborated,[66] but the facts upon which the opinion is based must be if these facts are essential to the proof of the charges beyond reasonable doubt.[67] Moreover, the absence of corroboration invites challenge and may increase the scope for querying reliability.

4-33   Since 1988 there has been no need to corroborate essential facts in civil cases, but the pre-1988 position prevailed in *Stewart v Glasgow Corporation*,[68] which illustrated the significance of corroboration of the facts that give rise to the opinion evidence. It is suggested the principle of corroboration set out in *Stewart* holds good in criminal cases. In *Stewart*, evidence was led from an expert concerning the condition of a clothes pole which had allegedly caused the death of a child. The accident had occurred in October 1953. The expert examined the pole in January 1954. He gave his opinion in court that, based upon his examination of the pole, it must have been in a manifestly dangerous state for at least the previous six months. He was not cross-examined on this point. The pursuer had sought to have the pole examined by a second expert witness, but the defenders had failed to produce the pole for this purpose. The second expert therefore simply gave his opinion, which agreed with that of the first expert, on the assumption that the pole was in the state described by the first expert at the date of his examination of it. It was held that there was insufficient evidence in law upon this factual point to form a basis for any expert opinion. There was no corroboration of the evidence of the first expert, either from the second expert or from the lack of cross-examination of the first expert. The corroboration required was the actual state of the pole in January 1954.

PRESERVING THE ULTIMATE ISSUE FOR THE COURT

4-34 The function of the expert witness is to assist the trier of fact to come to a decision on the ultimate issue in the case, but not to offer the court a view on the ultimate issue. The ultimate issue is the guilt of an accused in a criminal trial or the liability of a defender in a civil proof. For example, an expert may give an opinion on whether the skid marks on the road indicate the car was swerving violently, but may not say whether the driver was at fault. However closely the evidence of the expert is associated with the ultimate outcome of the case, a clear distinction ought to be maintained between the expert's role as a guide through a specialist area, and the role of the judge or jury as the ultimate arbiter of fact.

4-35   Expert testimony that illuminates matters for the trier of fact is admissible, provided it does not encroach upon their territory and does not stray

---

[66] See, for example *M v Kennedy*, 1992 S.C.C.R. 69.
[67] See Davidson, *Evidence*, para.11.25.
[68] 1958 S.C. 28.

in to expressions of view about the standard of proof. According to Lord Justice-General Emslie in *Hendry v HM Advocate*[69]:

> "[T]hough a skilled witness may be asked to express an opinion, he should not be asked to express an opinion as to whether he is satisfied of some essential fact beyond reasonable doubt. Determining whether an essential fact has been established beyond reasonable doubt is within the province of the jury, and a witness should not be invited to usurp the function of the jury."

Similarly, in *Meehan v HM Advocate*[70] the High Court refused to arrange for an accused to be examined under the influence of sodium pentothal and methedrine, commonly known as "the truth drug", because in respect of any resulting statement, the court considered "the medical man would take the place of the jury as a judge of credibility".

If the substantive law reserves discretion entirely to the court, expert **4–36** evidence may not be appropriate at all. In *Gellatly v Laird*[71] a magistrate was held to have correctly refused to hear expert evidence on whether or not books were indecent or obscene, since that was "the very matter remitted to the opinion of the magistrate". It was therefore the magistrate's sole responsibility to decide if the material was obscene or indecent, without resort to opinion evidence.

The rules governing the use of expert testimony are largely the same in **4–37** criminal and civil cases. In *Morrison v Maclean's Trs*[72] it was alleged that a testator was mentally unfit at the time when he signed his will. The medical witnesses in the case had been asked to comment on his mental state and no objection had been taken to this line of questioning by counsel for the executors. Nevertheless, the jury were directed that the issue of capacity to sign was a matter for them, and not the medical witnesses.

In a similar vein, if there is an issue over the interpretation of the terms of **4–38** a contract, the usual rule of contract law prevails, namely, that the court must interpret the contract using the normal everyday meaning given to each word used by the parties, and without the aid of experts.[73] It becomes competent to refer to experts if a contract uses technical words which require specialist interpretation.

DISCLOSURE OF EXPERTS' REPORTS

The party who instructs the expert report has ownership of it, but may in **4–39** some circumstances be obliged to disclose its contents to other parties prior to the proof or trial. There are both ethical and pragmatic reasons for this. The position largely depends on the nature of the proceedings.

---

[69] at 69–70. The court in *Hendry* corrected an erroneous dictum in *HM Advocate v McGinlay*, 1983 S.L.T. 562, suggesting that medical experts would be expected to express their opinion in terms that put it "beyond reasonable doubt". See *Hendry v HM Advocate*, 1988 S.L.T. 25.
[70] 1970 J.C. 11 at 14.
[71] 1953 J.C. 16 at 27. This case was followed in *Ingram v Macari*, 1983 S.L.T. 61.
[72] (1862) 24 D. 625 at 631.
[73] See *Tancred, Arrol & Co. v Steel Co. of Scotland* (1887) 15 R. 215; affd. (1890) 17 R. (H.L.) 31.

Criminal cases

4–40 In criminal cases it has long been accepted that expert reports, in keeping with much other evidence in the hands of the Crown, must be disclosed to the defence. The statutory test requiring disclosure applies where[74]:

(a) the information would materially weaken or undermine the evidence that is likely to be led by the prosecutor in the proceedings against the accused;

(b) the information would materially strengthen the accused's case; or

(c) the information is likely to form part of the evidence to be led by the prosecutor in the proceedings against the accused.

There is no equivalent reciprocal obligation of disclosure on the defence in relation to their experts reports.[75] As an organ of the State, the Crown has far greater access than the defence lawyers to forensic and other resources to enable them to obtain expert reports. The defence will often be dependent upon legal aid and have to obtain special permission from the Scottish Legal Aid Board for sanction before they incur the costs of instructing independent experts. Cause needs to be shown. Where the Crown reports implicate the accused then the defence lawyers need access to the reports in order to establish whether there are grounds for challenge and/or in order to advise their client of the extent of the options available in the light of any incriminating evidence.

4–41 There are statutory provisions that facilitate agreement between the parties of undisputed expert evidence to limit the number of witnesses who need to appear in court and to speed up the proof process.[76] In the wake of the decisions in *Holland v HM Advocate*[77] and *Sinclair v HM Advocate*[78] and the subsequent review by Lord Coulsfield of the Crown's duty of disclosure,[79] a statutory regime was introduced to clarify the extent of the duty.[80]

Civil cases

4–42 In civil cases in Scotland there is no general rule of disclosure between parties of expert reports.[81] The instructing party retains a right of confidentiality and privilege over the report. They may of course choose to waive that right, perhaps as part of a negotiating strategy in anticipation of a settlement of the action.

---

[74] s.121 Criminal Justice and Licensing (Scotland) Act 2010.

[75] Although the accused has an obligation to notify the Crown of the nature of his defence in certain circumstances. See s.78(1) to (3) of the Criminal Procedure (Scotland) Act 1995. See Ch.5—there is no obligation pre-trial to disclose the evidence in support of that defence.

[76] Criminal Procedure (Scotland) Act 1995, ss.256–258.

[77] 2005 S.L.T. 563.

[78] 2005 S.L.T. 553.

[79] Lord Coulsfield's Report, *Review of the Law and Practice of Disclosure*, (Scottish Government), August, 2007).

[80] Criminal Justice and Licensing (Scotland) Act 2010, Pt 6, in particular ss.121–126.

[81] *W's Parent and Guardian v Douglas* (2007) 93 B.M.L.R. 42.

THE RELIABILITY OF EXPERT TESTIMONY

Expert evidence has no value unless it is reliable. Confidence in the reliability **4-43** of expert evidence is vital to the integrity of the justice process. Unreliable science can lead to miscarriages of justice in the criminal courts, or to mistaken outcomes in the civil courts. The pace of advances in areas of medical and scientific evidence make it imperative that the rules regulating the admissibility of expert opinion evidence in these areas are rigorous and robust. In criminal cases a great deal of expert forensic evidence is obtained by established techniques, such as blood tests,[82] breathalyser results,[83] identification by video,[84] fingerprints,[85] palm prints,[86] dental impressions,[87] handwriting[88] and DNA profiling.[89] In these everyday situations, courts routinely admit expert evidence without challenge or complication. The process of proof may involve more than one set of experts. For example, the use of DNA profiling may require specialist forensic experts to give evidence in this field, as well as experts on statistical probabilities.

Typically, proof is reduced to a straightforward set of procedures. Often **4-44** evidence relating to real evidence is uncontested, not least because it is accepted as verging on the conclusive, or at least highly persuasive, to the trier of fact. Numerous statutory provisions ease the passage of evidence of these routine procedures into the courtroom and greatly expedite the proof process. In the great majority of cases, these procedures are executed without incident. However, occasionally, the identification, analysis and production of real evidence samples for litigation purposes give rise to procedural irregularities that are challengeable. Such challenges may question the reliability of the scientific method or technique, the competence or even good faith of the expert, or all.

The reliability of the scientific method or technique

Quite apart from the issue of procedural correctness, there is an increasing **4-45** tendency to challenge the very legitimacy of the methods or techniques associated with even established science. The miscarriage of justice that occurred in the case of *Shirley McKie* illustrates the importance of remaining vigilant about the quality of evidence routinely admitted in court and the risks of misplaced confidence in science that is generally regarded as well-established and therefore "safe". No science or scientific technique is inherently infallible and human intervention of any sort increases the risk of error. This willingness to challenge the science derives from the appreciation that much expert testimony goes to the core of scientific developments, which, as discussed earlier, are contingent and always subject to further discovery and refinement. What we know today is sometimes very different

---

[82] *Docherty v McGlynn*, 1985 S.L.T. 237. In relation to establishing paternity, now regulated by s.70 of the Law Reform (Miscellaneous Provisions) (Scotland) Act 1990.
[83] *Valentine v Macphail*, 1986 J.C. 131.
[84] *Bowie v Tudhope*, 1986 S.C.C.R. 205.
[85] *Hamilton v HM Advocate*, 1934 J.C. 1.
[86] *HM Advocate v Rolley*, 1945 J.C. 155.
[87] *Hay v HM Advocate*, 1968 J.C. 40.
[88] *Richardson v Clarke*, 1957 J.C. 7; *Campbell v Mackenzie*, 1974 S.L.T. (Notes) 46.
[89] *Welsh v HM Advocate*, 1992 S.L.T. 193.

from what we knew yesterday, opening up a new vista for review of historical cases due to the scope for scientific advances and technological developments to unearth new understandings and potential previous injustices.[90]

CCTV and similar technology

4–46 Accepting video evidence as competent[91] is distinct from any endorsement of the merits of such a form of evidence in providing reliable identification. Advances in technology and the growth of CCTV to monitor crime in public places have given rise to concerns that the increase in the use of such technology will compound the inherently unreliable nature of eyewitness testimony. The risk of mistaken identity whenever eye witness testimony is involved is widely acknowledged. Vicki Bruce,[92] a leading researcher in this field, noted that:

> "CCTV images are very variable in quality, and camera and lighting angles may conspire to produce no more than a poorly lit messy image of the top or back of a person's head. Recent research findings suggest, however, that the process of matching identities across different images may be remarkably error-prone even when image quality is reasonably high."

Juries in England and Wales are given a specific warning about the dangers of over-reliance on such evidence and there are detailed Codes of Guidance in relation to police powers and the obtaining of evidence, including provisions on both eye witness testimony and identification using CCTV images.[93] Scotland has no equivalent codes or guidance but at common law, judges frequently warn juries to be aware of the dangers of accepting identification evidence. The existence of the corroboration rule has served as a safeguard until 2013 at least, but its likely abolition will make this type of human identification evidence a greater risk than hitherto and alternative safeguards might be required to bolster the reliability of CCTV evidence. Separate procedural risks arise from the circumstances in which CCTV images may be used by the police officers to identify suspects. Although Scotland has no equivalent published guidance to that available, in English law the appeal court has acknowledged that "their content may provide some useful guidance to best practice".[94]

4–47   Identification of accused persons using CCTV images cannot simply be lodged as productions—they must be brought to the attention of the jury if they are to contribute to the sufficiency of the evidence in the case.[95]

---

[90] See the website of the Scottish Criminal Cases Review Commission for details of case reviews. *http://www.sccrc.org.uk/home.aspx* [accessed July 11, 2013].

[91] *Bowie v Tudhope*, 1986 S.C.C.R. 205.

[92] "Fleeting images of shade: Identifying people caught on video" (1998) 11(7) The Psychologist, 331 at 332. See too, Bruce and Hall, *In the Eye of the Beholder: The Science of Face Perception* (Oxford: Oxford University Press, 1998).

[93] The statutory framework is the Police and Criminal Evidence Act 1984 together with the related Codes of Practice A–D.

[94] *Strachan v HM Advocate*, 2011] HCJAC 66, para.6 which sheds some light on inappropriate police practices.

[95] *Robertson v HM Advocate*, [2007] HCJAC 12, Appeal No.XC486/06.

DNA profiling

In the last decade DNA (deoxyribronucleic acid) profiling or genetic fin- **4–48**
gerprinting has featured regularly in criminal cases, though few contested
cases are reported in the Scottish law reports. The technique seems attractive
for the degree of certainty that it appears to produce though the reliability of
DNA continues to generate much debate. Undoubtedly, DNA evidence has
huge potential to provide reliable incriminating—and exonerating—evidence. But critics have questioned the methodology of the testing procedures and the risk of human error.[96]

DNA evidence is presented to court as a "match probability", i.e. sta- **4–49**
tistical scientific evidence of the probability of finding the DNA profile of an
accused (or party in a civil case) in a person randomly selected from the
population. However, the presentation of this evidence can easily give the
impression of a much greater match than is appropriate, resulting in a
situation that has become known as "the prosecutor's fallacy". This fallacy
was explained in the English case of *R v Deen*[97] thus:

> "The prosecution case had confused the DNA match probability with
> the likelihood ratio. It was necessary to ask what the probability was
> that a defendant's sample could match the crime sample given that he
> was innocent (match probability), and what the probability was of a
> defendant being innocent although his sample matched the crime
> sample (likelihood ratio). Giving the answer to the first question as the
> answer to the second is 'the prosecutor's fallacy'. In the instant case, the
> fallacy in the expert evidence led the judge to sum up on the basis that
> probability was near to certainty, when on a proper assessment of the
> evidence the unexplained discrepancy was fatal to the prosecution's
> case."

The Scottish courts have been far less willing to grapple with the contested
dimensions of DNA than their English counterparts. In *Welsh v HM
Advocate*[98] it was suggested by experts in relation to the match probability of
blood samples, that the DNA profile of a sample of fresh blood found on
the deceased's clothing was identical to that of Welsh. Moreover, the experts
contended that Welsh's profile was common to only one person in every 88–
99 million. There is an obvious risk that a contention of this sort could be
assigned disproportionate weight by the trier of fact unless it was presented
in its full scientific context, and it was clear that it represented an expert's
opinion as opposed to a fact.[99] The appeal court refused to lay down any
particular standard of statistical probability that had to be reached before a
jury would be entitled to rely on DNA profiling. The court preferred instead

---

[96] The extensive literature on DNA includes: P. Alldridge, "Recognising Novel Scientific
Techniques: DNA as a test case", 1992 Crim. L.R. 687; M. Redmayne, "Doubts and
Burdens: DNA Evidence, Probability and the Courts," 1995 Crim. L.R. 464; M. Redmayne,
"Presenting Probabilities in Court: The DNA Experience", 1997 1 E & P 187; I. Evett, A.
Foreman, G. Jackson and J. Lambert, "DNA Profiling: A discussion of issues relating to the
reporting of very small match probabilities", 2000 Crim. L.R. 341.
[97] *The Times*, January, 10, 1994.
[98] 1992 S.L.T. 193.
[99] An inherent risk with the evidence of experts, discussed in relation to fingerprint evidence
later in this chapter.

to rest on the usual principle that if there was sufficient evidence a jury could convict.

4–50   A related controversial aspect of the debate on DNA profiling is the admissibility of expert evidence based on Bayes theorem, a statistical method of analysis which compares probabilities to those obtained by more traditional DNA profiling based upon the random occurrence ratio. The use of expert evidence on Bayes theorem has been decisively rejected in England on the ground that it is apt to confuse and mislead a jury.[100] The potential for misunderstanding and misinterpretation of such fundamental concepts related to statistical evidence and probabilities prompted the Royal Statistical Society to publish a series of a reports aimed at legal practitioners who wish to use but are not expert in statistical evidence.[101]

Fingerprint evidence

4–51   Ineptitude, procedural irregularities and bad faith were also alleged in the case of *HM Advocate v McKie*,[102] which concerned mistaken identification from fingerprint evidence. Until *McKie,* the reliability of fingerprint evidence was virtually unchallenged in Scotland. Shirley McKie was a detective police constable with Strathclyde police. She was involved in the murder investigation of Marion Ross in Kilmarnock in January 1997. Fingerprint officers, backed up by expert witnesses from the Scottish Criminal Records Office ("SCRO") Fingerprint Bureau, alleged that McKie's fingerprints were on a door frame in the murder victim's house in a sealed-off scene of crime area. McKie denied she had ever been to that area of the house. She gave evidence to that effect at the trial of David Asbury who was accused of the murder of Marion Ross.[103] McKie was subsequently prosecuted for perjury. At her trial in May 1999 two expert fingerprint witnesses from the United States appeared on her behalf and successfully discredited the evidence from the SCRO Fingerprint Bureau. She was acquitted. It was apparently the first time in the history of the SCRO that there had ever been a challenge to the expertise of its staff and McKie's acquittal had far-reaching ramifications.

4–52   The interim findings of a report by the Chief Inspector of Constabulary, Sir William Taylor, exonerated Shirley McKie and concluded that the Fingerprint Bureau was "not fully effective and efficient", resulting in tightened procedures in all cases involving fingerprint evidence.[104]

4–53   One key outcome of the *Taylor Report* was that the reliance (until then) on a 16-point match in similarity between sets of fingerprints be discontinued. In its place there is now a non-numeric scale which as to be

---

[100] *R. v Adams* (No.2) [1997] 1 Cr.App.R. 369. See too, *R. v Doheny*, [1997]1 Cr. App. Rep.

[101] The first two of four planned Guides in the series, *Communicating and Interpreting Statistical Evidence in the Administration of Criminal Justice* are: *Fundamentals of Probability and Statistical Evidence in Criminal Proceedings* (2011); and *Assessing the Probative Value of DNA Evidence* (2012). See *http://www.rss.org.uk* [accessed July 11, 2013].

[102] Unreported, For background see *McKie v Scottish Ministers*, 2006 S.C. 528.

[103] Asbury was convicted and sentenced to life imprisonment. Part of the Evidence against him was the victim's fingerprint supposedly found on a biscuit tin in his house. His conviction was subsequently quashed as unsafe.

[104] See Report by HM Inspectorate of Constabulary for Scotland, "The Lessons to be Learned for Future Inspection Procedures" (2007) available at *http://www.scotland.gov.uk/Resource/Doc/179539/0051043.pdf* [accessed July 11, 2013].

approved by three fingerprint staff instead of the previous two. Although fingerprint evidence still requires to be corroborated, where there is an assumption of the reliability of a long-established scientific method, it is extremely difficult to challenge such expert evidence. For example, the defence team may find it difficult to obtain legal aid in order to fund an independent fingerprint analysis. While the proposed abolition of the corroboration rule may encourage more challenges, legal practice will still be influenced by the availability of legal aid. The aftermath of *HM Advocate v McKie* is an important reminder of the dangers in over-dependence on scientific testimony, not least because it is always subject to interpretation by individuals and that invariably carries risks of human error.[105]

The most positive legacy of the *McKie* case was the publication of the **4–54** *Fingerprint Inquiry*, chaired by the former Northern Ireland Appeal Court judge, Sir Athony Campbell.[106] In a comprehensive and highly informative analysis, the Report concluded that there was no evidence that McKie had entered the crime scene and found that the identification of some marks as her finger prints were misidentifications due to human error by SCRO fingerprint examiners.[107] The Report produced 86 recommendations, of which 10 were nominated as key. Seven of these are listed here,[108] because the underlying principles are succinct and could be readily applied as recommended best practice for many forms of forensic evidence:

1. Fingerprint evidence should be recognised as opinion evidence, not fact, and those involved in the criminal justice system need to assess it as such on its merits.

2. Examiners should discontinue reporting conclusions on identification or exclusion with a claim to 100 per cent certainty or on any other basis suggesting that fingerprint evidence is infallible.

3. Examiners should receive training which emphasises that their findings are based on personal opinion; and that this opinion is influenced by the quality of the materials that are examined, their ability to observe detail in mark and print reliably, the subjective interpretation of observed characteristics, the cogency of explanations for any differences and the subjective view of "sufficiency".

4. Features on which examiners rely should be demonstrable to a lay person with normal eyesight as observable in the mark.

5. Explanations for any differences between a mark and a print require to be cogent if a finding of identification is to be made.

6. A finding of identification should not be made if there is an unexplained difference between a mark and a print.

7. An emphasis needs to be placed on the importance not only of learning and practising the methodology of fingerprint work, but also of engaging with members of the academic community working in the field.

---

[105] Responsibility for fingerprint examination is now part of the wider remit for forensic services investigations vested in the Scottish Police Authority in terms of the Police and Fire Reform (Scotland) Act 2012.

[106] *http://www.thefingerprintinquiryscotland.org.uk/inquiry/21.html* [accessed July 11, 2013].

[107] Fingerprint Inquiry, Pt 8, Ch.42.

[108] Fingerprint Inquiry, Pt 8, Ch.42.

The competence and integrity of the expert

4–55 First and foremost, the expert witness has a duty to the court, whether or not they are called to give oral evidence, if any report by them has been lodged as a production. Thus, although some experts may perceive tensions in their duties to the instructing party (who may be paying them) and to the court, in law the latter prevails. The principal duties owed by a witness have been expressed as follows[109]:

- to give objective, unbiased opinion in relation to matters within his or her expertise;
- to produce an independent opinion, uninfluenced by the litigation context;
- not to omit from the opinion material facts which could detract from it;
- to stay within their area of expertise;
- if insufficient data is available to reach a conclusion, to state the opinion is provisional; and
- to state within the report any qualifications to the accuracy of it.

Perhaps the most fundamental challenge an expert who gives opinion evidence faces is a question over their competence or integrity. Disputes over opinion evidence may arise from a genuine disagreement amongst experts about the state of the science but they may also involve alleged procedural irregularities, and/or questions of professional incompetence or misconduct. Experts may be inseparable from the method of enquiry, the analysis and the exercise of judgement and can expect, as part of the normal process of cross-examination, to have their views challenged, for example through suggestions that they lack the requisite knowledge and experience, or that their opinion runs counter to the dominant views in the field.

4–56 In some areas of expertise it may be difficult to identify the parameters of the discipline, and therefore to know who is a genuine expert. It is increasingly likely emerging science will produce pockets of expertise of far greater complexity than the more traditional discipline in which they may have their roots or with which they continue to have some affiliation. Failure to understand the processes by which science acquires status, credibility and validity in their field, can lead to error and misrepresentation. For example, in the case of *Hainey v HM Advocate*[110] the appeal court failed to grasp the distinctive nature of the discipline of forensic anthropology, in particular, its fundamental difference from medical science.

4–57 Challenges to an expert's competence based upon allegations of bias or ineptitude are more serious. A few examples are given here to illustrate the range of problems that have arisen.

---

[109] *The Ikarian Reefer (No.1)*, also known as *National Justice Compania Naviera SA v Prudential Assurance Co Ltd* [1993] 2 Lloyd's Rep. 68.
[110] [2013] HCJAC 47.

Forensic body fluid samples

In *Preece v HM Advocate*[111] the appellant had served seven years of a life **4–58** sentence for murder before his conviction was quashed on the ground that the Crown forensic evidence had been deeply flawed. Evidence of blood samples and seminal stains had played a significant part in his conviction. However, it was subsequently claimed that the tests had been conducted and the results had been interpreted in such a way that the Crown's chief forensic expert, Dr Clift, a leading biologist with the Home Office, had omitted significant information from his written expert report. In their re-assessment of the scientific evidence, the appeal court found that at the trial Clift had made unsustainable claims based upon the evidence and had presented unwarrantable conclusions. These flaws in the expert evidence were fatal to the conviction since the testimony fell short of the standards of accuracy and objectivity required of an expert witness. The court held that Clift's evidence did not display the level of objectivity required of a person in his position and it was wholly unreliable.

Simple errors of calculation by an expert can lead to devastating con- **4–59** sequences. In *McCreight v HM Advocate*[112] one of the experts was presented with data in the morning at court shortly before giving his evidence relating to the quantity of chloroform in the liver of the deceased. He failed to interpret the data correctly and subsequently gave evidence concerning a quantity which much later after conviction transpired to be a "1000 fold magnification of the true result".[113] The conviction was quashed but only 20 years later, after a referral by the Scottish Criminal Cases Review Commission.

Medical science

In the last few years, evolving engagement with medical science, especially in **4–60** the area of child protection, has yielded a raft of highly contentious cases. Between 2003 and 2005 there was a series of wrongful convictions of mothers for the murder of their newly born children, all of which arose out of the withholding or misapplication of medical evidence at trial.[114] In *R. v Clark* the practices of two experts drew criticism from the Court of Appeal. Clark was convicted of the murder of her two sons, Christopher and Harry, by smothering them. She denied murder and claimed they both died of natural causes. Fresh evidence was produced to the appeal court that demonstrated that one of the prosecution experts, the Home Office pathologist, Dr Alan Williams, failed to disclose to any other expert, or to the Crown or defence lawyers, the results of microbiological tests which he had conducted on blood samples from Harry. His explanation that he had discounted them as they were not consistent with his belief that the child did not die from natural causes was sharply criticised by the Court of Appeal as being "completely out of line with the practice accepted by other

---

[111] Note and Commentary, A. Brownlie [1981] Crim. L.R. 783.
[112] [2009] HCJAC 69.
[113] *McCreight v HM Advocate* [2009] HCJAC 69 at para.49.
[114] *R. v Clark* [2003] EWCA Crim 1020, *R. v Cannings* [2004] EWCA Crim 1, *R. v Anthony* [2005] EWCA 952.

pathologists to be the standard".[115] The pathologist's role in recording the results from all tests is crucial as all subsequent interpretations of these results depend upon there being a full and accurate account. If such experts produce only partial results then, as the court went on to note[116]:

> "It is likely to mislead others, who may work on the same case and who will be denied the opportunity of considering the material in the way that Dr Williams explained that he found necessary, in reaching their own properly informed conclusions. It runs a significant risk of a miscarriage of justice."

The Court of Appeal also rejected the statistical evidence given by another Crown expert witness, Professor Sir Roy Meadow. His assertion that there was a one in 73 million chance of two sudden deaths of children within the same family from unexplained, but natural causes, was considered a gross over-statement of the correct statistical position and provided without a full context. The court said the statistical evidence should have been withdrawn from the jury, especially as its validity was challenged by the defence.[117]

4–61   The General Medical Council subsequently took disciplinary proceedings against Dr Williams and Professor Meadow. Both were found guilty of serious professional misconduct and struck off. Meadow's subsequent appeal against the GMC ruling was successful. The Court of Appeal[118] confirmed that at common law, all witnesses, including experts, had immunity in civil proceedings from any party who may be disaffected by the evidence given in court.[119] Given the absolute nature of the immunity the Court were unwilling to agree that the immunity in civil proceedings extended to disciplinary proceedings before the GMC. The latter has the protection of the public uppermost in its mind, which is a different priority from that which pertains in civil proceedings more generally.

4–62   The court also held, by a majority, that the GMC were wrong to conclude that the errors which Professor Meadow made, in good faith, amounted to serious professional misconduct. In a powerful dissenting judgment Sir Stephen Clark adopted the principles upon which experts should give evidence set out in *The Ikarian Reefer (No.1)*,[120] ruling:

> "It is, in my opinion, of the utmost importance that an expert should only give evidence of opinion which is within his particular expertise and that, where a statement, whether made in writing or orally, is outside his expertise, he should expressly say so. If, for example, it depends upon work done or opinions expressed by others, that work or those opinions should be identified in the statement, so that their validity can be ascertained by the parties to the proceedings or by the court. All reasonable attempts should be made to check the validity of

---

[115] *R. v Clark* [2003] EWCA Crim 1020 at para.167.
[116] *R. v Clark* [2003] EWCA Crim 1020 at para.267.
[117] *R. v Clark* [2003] EWCA Crim 1020 at paras 177–178.
[118] *Meadow v General Medical Council* [2006] EWCA Civ 1390.
[119] Note that such immunity no longer exists in English law: see *Jones v Kaney* [2011] UKSC 13.
[120] See *The Ikarian Reefer (No.1)*, also known as *National Justice Compania Naviera SA v Prudential Assurance Co Ltd* [1993] 2 Lloyd's Rep. 68 at 81–82.

an opinion which is not within the expert's expertise. These are simple precautions which should be taken by experts because of the risk that the opinion might be wrong, with what may be very serious consequences. This seems to me to be of particular importance in a serious criminal matter such as the trial of a defendant for murder."[121]

In short, according to Sir Stephen Clark, Meadow's failure to adopt these fundamental precautions amounted to serious professional misconduct.

The need to protect children from abuse, amidst concerns of unchallenged **4–63** allegations of parental harm by paediatricians, places continuing pressure on medical experts to produce reliable opinion evidence in an atmosphere of considerable tension and suspicion of experts, such that there is concern many will withdraw from undertaking expert witness work. As a step towards resolving this tension, the circumstances of the convictions of these Clark, Cannings and Antony, as well as the role of expert witnesses, were the subject of a inquiry convened by the Royal College of Pathologists and Royal College of Paediatrics and Child Health, and chaired by Baroness Helena Kennedy. The Inquiry's report, *Sudden Unexpected Death in Infancy*, produced a set of recommendations and proposed protocols for the investigation and management of unexplained sudden deaths of infants, including the gathering and storage of evidence.[122]

EMERGING SCIENCE

The limitations of expert opinion evidence are more readily apparent where **4–64** the science is emerging. The possibilities offered by novel science and new discoveries in disciplines, such as biotechnology and the forensic sciences, are constantly stretching the parameters of knowledge and with varying degrees of reliability. As noted earlier in this chapter, confidence in the reliability of scientific evidence is critical to the criminal trial and the rules of admissibility ought to ensure appropriate levels of reliability if public confidence is to be maintained and miscarriages of justice are to be avoided. Expert evidence will not assist the trier of fact if the courts are confronted with conflicting and contradictory expert opinions unless there is a rigorous framework for evaluating the reliability of such evidence. This is usually less of a problem in regard to the "hard" or physical sciences, e.g. quantum physics, chemistry, or mechanical engineering because such expert evidence tends to be long established.

However, testimony that seeks to introduce evidence that is on the per- **4–65** iphery of the discipline, perhaps because it is cutting edge and at the forefront of discovery, is unlikely to have had the opportunity to become sufficiently established or have been satisfactorily validated to merit the wider support of the community. In other words, it will not have become "generally accepted" within that community and thus may be attacked in court for its novelty. Recent decisions in the English courts on admissibility

---

[121] *Meadow v General Medical Council* [2006] EWCA Civ 1390 at para.71.
[122] The Report was published jointly by the Royal College of Pathologists and the Royal College of Paediatrics and Child Health, London, 2004.

of novel science have ruled that expert evidence concerning psychological autopsies[123] and gait analysis[124] to be inadmissible evidence; and ear print evidence to be admissible in some limited circumstances.[125] The term "junk science" is sometimes used pejoratively to refer to scientific evidence that fails to persuade the court it has a scientific foundation recognised by experienced and respected members of the relevant scientific community. By its very nature, the scientific method of validating novel or innovative techniques or research findings tends to take a while before such new "knowledge" can be said to be generally accepted.[126] Regulation of junk science is a major pre-occupation in the US where courts are generally more willing to admit expert opinion evidence on all manner of issues despite concerns over reliability.[127] This has resulted in a huge corpus of case law and academic literature on the framework for admissibility.[128]

4–66   In response to the challenges of ensuring that only reliable science, especially from new disciplines, is admitted in court, most common law countries—though not Scotland—have reviewed their framework for the use and management of expert scientific evidence in court. The Law Commission (England & Wales) Report in 2011 identified similar issues to those facing Scotland, including concerns over the quality of the evidence given by some experts; the adequacy of the knowledge and skill of some lawyers in examining and cross-examining scientific experts; how well-equipped judges were to exercise their discretion in admitting or refusing to admit expert evidence, and whether juries might too readily be swayed by apparently persuasive but potentially unreliable expert evidence. The Law Commission report included a draft Bill that proposes an enhanced gate-keeping role for judges in decision-making over the reliability of any evidence admitted. This is an approach which most common law jurisdictions now regard as unavoidable.[129] In light of developments elsewhere, an appraisal of the Scottish approach is therefore arguably overdue.[130]

4–67   In common law jurisdictions the orthodoxy of the courts is to limit the contribution of expert witnesses to those areas of knowledge irrefutably beyond the informed understanding of the average juror, e.g. to medical and forensic science. There is an anxiety that the traditional judicial process should not simply be replaced by a system of trial by experts, given that

---

[123] *R v Gilfoyle* [2001] Crim. L.R. 312
[124] *Elroy Otis Otway v Regina* [2011] EWCA Crim 3, where there is a useful discussion of what constitutes a "proper scientific foundation" for novel science or a developing technology.
[125] *R. v Dallagher*, [2002] EWCA Crim 1903, but see *R v Kempster* (No.2). [2008] EWCA 975.
[126] The concept of general acceptance was established in the Frye test: *Frye v United States*, 1923 F. 1013 (D.C. Cor 1923).
[127] S. Jasanoff, *Science at the Bar* (Cambridge, Mass: Harvard University Press, 1995).
[128] The leading case authority is the Supreme Court decision in *Daubert v Merrell Dow Pharmaceuticals Inc.*113 S. Ct. 2786 (1993). For a review and introduction to the post-Daubert guidelines see D. Bernstein, "Junk Science in the United States and the Commonwealth," (1996) 21 Yale J. Int'l L. 123.
[129] See, e.g. National Academy Sciences, *Strengthening Forensic Science in the United States: A Path Forward*, (2009) available at *http://www.nasonline.org/* [accessed July 11, 2013].
[130] *Scots law of Evidence in the digital age—Fit for Purpose?* Final Report, (Glasgow, Scottish Universities Insight Institute, 2011), at *http://www.scottishinsight.ac.uk/Portals/50/ScotsLawEvidence.pdf* [accessed July 17, 2013].

"[t]he parties have invoked the decision of a judicial tribunal, and not an oracular pronouncement by an expert".[131] However, as science and technology have developed, producing new insights and complexities, there is a constant tension between the desire of parties to have expert testimony favourable to their cause admitted and the pressure on the courts to control its admittance quite strictly.

A decision in 2005, where the English Court of Appeal ruled on conjoined **4–68** appeals in four cases involving the deaths of infants, illustrates this tension.[132] The Court acknowledged the contingent state of science in regard to the uncertainties associated with the phenomenon of so-called shaken baby syndrome, the precise cause of which is thought to be extremely hard to determine and remains a divisive issue within the medical community.[133] Rather than shrinking from admitting such evidence altogether until it was deemed safe science and thus reliable, the Court of Appeal was alive to, if wary of, the contribution expert evidence could make in such situations. Lord Justice Gage noted, *obiter*[134]:

"...[I]n our judgment, developments in scientific thinking should not be kept from the Court, simply because they remain at the stage of a hypothesis. Obviously, it is of the first importance that the true status of the expert's evidence is frankly indicated to the court."

The final sentence is of paramount importance to the integrity of the testimony—it is a reminder that the expert has a duty to the court, over and above any duty owed to the party for whom they are giving evidence, or to the solicitor who has cited them to appear.[135]

In *Leihne (Walker) v HM Advocate*[136] the appeal court held that the judge **4–69** had a duty to provide the jury with a structured set of directions to enable them to perform a systematic analysis of the evidence in arriving at their decisions. Although there is no prescribed set of judicial directions for dealing with expert evidence, the Appeal Court in *Leihne* noted that a fair trial in terms of art.6 of the ECHR required the trial judge to provide the tools to enable the fact-finder to evaluate the evidence in a transparent and fair manner, a task made all the more vital in a case such as *Leihne* where a total of 15 expert witnesses gave complex and conflicting evidence.

---

[131] per Lord President Cooper in *Davie v Magistrates of Edinburgh*, 1953 S.C. 54. See also *Hendry v HM Advocate*, 1987 J. C. 63.

[132] *Shaken Baby Appeals* [2005] EWCA Crim 1980.

[133] See, for example, "The evidence base for shaken baby syndrome: response to Reece et al from 41 physicians and scientists" (BMJ. 2004) (available *http://www.ncbi.nlm.nih.gov/pubmed/15388625* [accessed July 11, 2013]; "Retinal hemorrhages and shaken baby syndrome: an evidence-based review" (J Emerg Med. 2009) (available *http://www.ncbi.nlm.nih.gov/pubmed/19081701* [accessed July 11, 2013]).

[134] *Shaken Baby Appeals* [2005] EWCA Crim 1980, at para.70.

[135] *The Ikarian Reefer (No.1)*, also known as *National Justice Compania Naviera SA v Prudential Assurance Co Ltd*, [1993] 2 Lloyd's Rep. 68.

[136] *Liehne (Walker) v HM Advocate*, 2011 S.L.T. 1114.

Chapter 5

BURDENS AND STANDARDS OF PROOF IN CRIMINAL PROCEEDINGS

INTRODUCTION

5–01 This chapter is concerned with two issues in criminal proceedings: the burden of proof and the standard of proof. It considers upon whom the burden rests to prove a fact or to challenge the prima facie proof of a fact; and then to what standard a fact must be proven. Incidentally, it is concerned with the question of sufficiency, which arises in every case, for, in order to prove a fact in a court of law, a party has to produce sufficient admissible evidence to the standard required in the particular case. Thus, sufficiency, burden and standard are inextricably linked in the legal process of proof. Standard of proof is dealt with later in this chapter. It is simply noted here that in criminal cases the prosecution generally has to prove the case to a standard beyond reasonable doubt.

BURDEN OF PROOF

5–02 The burden of proof is the obligation that rests upon the party who seeks to have a particular issue decided in their favour to adduce sufficient evidence to support their argument. In Scots law there are two distinct burdens of proof,[1] namely:

(1) the *persuasive burden*: the burden of satisfying a court to the appropriate standard of proof on a particular issue; and
(2) the *evidential burden*: the burden of adducing enough evidence on a particular issue to warrant the court at least considering that issue.

Each of these burdens is fixed by law and applies in respect of every issue in a case. Because the burden of proof is fixed by law, it never shifts from whichever party it is allocated to the commencement of the trial. The next section considers the different purpose and function of each burden.

---

[1] See Macphail, *Evidence*, para.22.01. The terminology employed is that used there. See too *Hendry v Clan Line Steamers Ltd*, 1949 S.C. 320 where there were various attempts by the Inner House to explain the difference between the standard of proof in criminal and civil cases, e.g. Lord Justice-Clerk Thomson at 323–324 and Lord Jamieson at 328–329.

THE PERSUASIVE BURDEN

In a criminal case the onus is on the prosecution to prove the guilt of an **5–03** accused person. The burden of proof resting with the Crown is known as the persuasive burden. The law rarely places any obligation upon the accused to produce exculpatory evidence. The two principal common law exceptions which place an onus on the accused are the defences of mental disorder and diminished responsibility. There are also numerous statutory provisions that impose an onus of proof on the accused. When a party bears the persuasive burden on an issue, the court must be satisfied on that issue to the required degree or standard of proof, or the party will lose on that issue. Whether or not the entire case is then lost depends upon how crucial that issue is to the overall case. As Walker and Walker put it,[2] "if on any issue of fact no evidence is led, or the evidence leaves the matter in doubt, the party upon whom the burden of proof rests has not discharged it, and accordingly fails on that issue".

At the conclusion of a trial the Crown may fail to discharge the persuasive **5–04** burden because the trier of fact considers a sufficient doubt has been raised by the defence, whether through cross-examination or through witnesses led on behalf of the accused. Alternatively, it is possible for the Crown to fail to discharge the persuasive burden without the defence leading any evidence at all. If the evidence that has been led is insufficient in law the defence can submit a motion that there is "no case to answer"—in other words, even if all the evidence led by the Crown was proven, it would not amount to a sufficient case in law for a conviction. If the judge upholds the motion of no case to answer the accused is acquitted. Unless the standard in criminal cases of proof beyond reasonable doubt is reached, the persuasive burden has not been discharged, and the prosecution will fail.

The persuasive burden does not transfer from the Crown at any stage. It is **5–05** fixed by law and at the outset of the trial. All that the accused has to do to prevent a conviction is to raise a reasonable doubt.

THE EVIDENTIAL BURDEN

The evidential burden may be defined as the burden of adducing sufficient **5–06** evidence on a particular issue to allow the court to begin considering it as a live issue. The party wishing to rely upon the evidence has the duty to lay down a basis for its proof. For example, if a person accused of murder wishes to claim she could not have committed the crime because she was out of the country at the time, it will strengthen her case if she provides some evidence of where she was at the time of the murder. Although she does not have a persuasive burden to prove her alibi (for the persuasive burden remains with the Crown throughout) she does carry the burden of adducing sufficient evidence on the issue to warrant its consideration by a court and thus, she will hope, raise a reasonable doubt. This type of burden is known

---

[2] Walker and Walker, *Evidence*, para.2.1.1; see also *Brown v Rolls Royce*, 1960 S.C. (H.L.) 22.

as the evidential burden.[3] Evidence adduced to satisfy the evidential burden does not have to be corroborated.[4]

5–07   Like the persuasive burden, the evidential burden is fixed by law and allocated to a particular party. As a general rule the party bearing the persuasive burden on any given issue also bears the evidential burden. Thus, in criminal cases, because the Crown almost always carries the persuasive burden, it also almost always carries most of the evidential burden. The logic of that position derives from the presumption of innocence that prevails in our adversarial system. Allegations of criminal offending levelled at an accused person are automatically accompanied by a common law presumption of innocence and it is for the Crown, with all the resources of the state behind it, to dislodge that presumption.

THE PRESUMPTION OF INNOCENCE

5–08 In *Mackenzie v HM Advocate*[5] Lord Justice-Clerk Thomson stated, "[t]he presumption of innocence is a fundamental tenet of our criminal procedure. It follows that the burden of proof rests on the Crown to displace this presumption." This is essentially another way of saying that the Crown bears both the persuasive and evidential burdens on every issue in a case which tends to prove the guilt of the accused of the crime(s) libelled in the complaint or indictment. With one exception, at common law, these burdens remain with the Crown throughout the trial and never shift to the accused.[6] At the conclusion of the trial any reasonable doubt which remains in the minds of the jury or sheriff must be exercised in favour of the accused. This general rule is not absolute, however—there are various exceptions to the rule that are considered below—but the paramount nature of the presumption of innocence shapes much of the body of rules of evidence and procedure concerning a fair trial. The common law presumption of innocence has more recently been reinforced by the terms of art.6(2) of the ECHR which states, "[e]veryone charged with a criminal offence shall be presumed innocent until proved guilty according to law".

5–09   This is the guiding principle to keep in mind when faced with the temptation to think that an accused person who has an alibi to state or who claims to be acting in self-defence therefore carries the burden to prove their defence. Other than in very limited circumstances, they do not have any such burden. This is so whether they give a general denial of guilt, offer a specific

---

[3] A description in general use in England: see Cross and Tapper (ed), *Cross and Tapper on Evidence*, 11th edn (Oxford: Oxford University Press. 1990). Although the existence of this second burden has been recognised in Scotland, and is implicit in several recent criminal appeal judgments (see *Earnshaw v HM Advocate*, 1982 J.C. 11, 1982 S.L.T. 179, the use of the term evidential burden seems still to be confined to academic works. See Gordon, "The Burden of Proof on the Accused", 1968 S.L.T. (News) 29, and Macphail, *Evidence*, at para.22.01, Walker and Walker, *Evidence*, 3rd edn, para.2.1.2, and Davidson, *Evidence*, paras 4.05.4.08

[4] *Lambie v HM Advocate*, 1973 J.C. 53.

[5] 1959 J.C. 32 at 36–37.

[6] See, e.g. Lord Justice-General Normand's judgment in *Lennie v HM Advocate*, 1946 J.C. 79 at 80. See also *Owens v HM Advocate*, 1946 J.C. 119, and Renton and Brown, *Criminal Procedure*, 6th edn, para.24–01. NB also *Tallis v HM Advocate*, 1982 S.C.C.R. 91.

explanation or raise a special defence. These three situations are now considered in turn.

An accused person is entitled to make a general denial of guilt and say no **5–10** more. They are also entitled to say nothing at all. They are entitled to put the Crown to the test, i.e. to insist that the Crown prove the case alleged beyond reasonable doubt. One consequence of the presumption of innocence is that an accused cannot be compelled to go into the witness box to give evidence.

If an accused offers some specific explanation in response to questioning **5–11** at the police station or in court, such as suggesting his alleged reckless driving was due to a cardiac arrest whilst driving, then the accused has an evidential burden to lead sufficient evidence to allow the trier of fact to consider the issue.[7] The onus of an evidential burden is relatively easily discharged. If the accused raises a special defence in response to a charge then they also carry an evidential burden in relation to that defence to lead sufficient evidence to have the issues considered.

CRIMINAL DEFENCES

There are numerous specific defences to criminal charges and often the **5–12** defence relied upon will reflect the nature of the charge against the accused, e.g. a defence of consent in a prosecution for rape and certain other sexual offences.[8] Ferguson and McDiarmid[9] list the following defences: alibi; impeachment/incrimination; non-age; error; mental disorder; intoxication; automatism; coercion/necessity; self-defence; and provocation. Of these, four are known as special defences, so called because at least seven days' notice must be lodged with the court prior to the preliminary hearing to ensure the prosecution has adequate warning of the line of evidence the defence will take at trial. The special defences are: alibi, self-defence, incrimination or impeachment and automatism/coercion.[10] In regard to all of these defences the onus remains with the Crown to discharge the persuasive burden on the issue raised by the defence.

They are termed special because where an accused puts forward a defence **5–13** of, for example, alibi, the evidential and persuasive burdens are divided between the defence and the prosecution. The accused must produce *some* credible evidence to suggest the existence of an alibi (the evidential burden), but it remains for the Crown to prove their version of the facts beyond reasonable doubt (the persuasive burden).[11] That, in effect, may mean proving that the alibi is false.

In order to discharge the evidential burden an accused need only put **5–14** forward the explanation. There is no requirement to produce corroboration, though if corroboration exists it will obviously strengthen the defence case. However, the Crown retain the onus to adduce sufficient credible evidence

---

[7] *HM Advocate v Hardy*, 1938 J.C. 144.
[8] i.e. those detailed in s.288C of the Criminal Procedure (Scotland) Act 1995.
[9] P. Ferguson and C. McDiarmid, *Scots Criminal Law: A Critical Analysis* (Dundee: DUP 2009).
[10] s.149B, Criminal Procedure (Scotland) Act 1995.
[11] See *Lambie v HM Advocate*, 1973 J.C. 53.

to counter the accused's explanation and to discharge the persuasive burden beyond reasonable doubt. For example, in *Campbell v Mackenzie*,[12] the accused in a drink-driving case sought to explain why the analyst's certificate showed his blood/alcohol level to be higher than that permitted by law at the time the sample was taken. He claimed that he had consumed enough alcohol between the time of his driving and the taking of the sample to account for the excess reading. The sheriff ruled that since the accused raised the explanation of post-accident drinking, it was for him to prove it on a *balance of probabilities*.[13] This is the appropriate standard of proof for an accused who bears the persuasive burden on an issue. On appeal, therefore, it was pointed out that in such cases, once the accused has raised the issue (i.e. discharged the evidential burden) it is for the Crown to discharge the persuasive burden and to do so beyond reasonable doubt.

5–15   In *Ritchie v Pirie*[14] Lord Justice-Clerk Wheatley noted that the sort of evidence required to raise such a defence, which the Crown then have to disprove beyond reasonable doubt, can come from any source, and not necessarily the accused:

> "The onus of proving the case beyond reasonable doubt rests with the prosecution, and remains on the prosecution throughout, and whether that has been done depends upon all the evidence before the court, whether adduced by the prosecution or by the defence, and on the view which the court takes of it."[15]

The Crown is not expected to anticipate every possible explanation that an accused might put forward in cases that do not involve special defences. However, very often the police statements of what the accused said during questioning and/or in response to caution and charge will reveal the outline of an explanation and thus forewarn the prosecutor. Occasionally, the statements from other witnesses, including the Crown witnesses will suggest the basis for a defence.[16] This is an important element of preparing a case for trial.

BURDEN OF PROOF AND THE SPECIAL DEFENCES

5–16   The special defences of alibi, self-defence, incrimination (otherwise known as impeachment) automatism and coercion conform to the general rule, namely none of these defences impose a persuasive burden on the accused—it rests with the Crown alone.[17] They only place an evidential burden on the

---

[12] 1982 S.L.T. 250; see also *Earnshaw v HM Advocate*, 1982 J.C. 11, 1982 S.L.T. 179; and *McGregor v Jessop*, 1988 J.C. 98.

[13] The so-called "hip flask defence".

[14] 1972 J.C. 7.

[15] *Ritchie v Pirie*, 1972 J.C. 7 at 17.

[16] Although, if it did, it would have precisely the same effect: *Ritchie v Pirie*, 1972 J.C. 7.

[17] See Renton and Brown, *Criminal Procedure*, 6th edn, para.14–26. Since *HM Advocate v Cunningham*, 1963 J.C. 80 it is assumed that somnambulism is no longer (if it ever was) a special defence, and as such belongs in the category of specific defences referred to below. Similarly, automatism: *Ross v HM Advocate*, 1991 S.L.T. 564, and coercion: *Trotter v HM Advocate*, 2001 S.L.T. 1996, are specific defences.

accused. Early case law created some confusion about the nature of the burden carried by the accused, but the position was settled in *Lambie v HM Advocate*[18] where Lord Justice-General Emslie stated:

"The only purpose of the special defence is to give fair notice to the Crown and once such notice has been given the only issue for a jury is to decide upon the whole evidence before them whether the Crown has established the accused's guilt beyond reasonable doubt."

Lambie involved a special defence of incrimination. Although the trial judge advised the jury that the Crown was required to prove the accused's guilt, he withdrew the special defence from them on the ground that it was not supported by corroborated evidence.[19] This was an error. There is no requirement for the accused to produce corroboration of his defence as the burden he carried was evidential only.

The misunderstanding regarding the burden carried by an accused who **5–17** relies on a special defence stemmed from dicta in various earlier cases involving special defences, in particular *Lennie v HM Advocate*,[20] *Owens v HM Advocate*[21] and *HM Advocate v Cunningham*.[22] These cases treated the special defence (a) as a defence in itself, which it was for the accused to prove; and (b) as a possible source of reasonable doubt which might lead to an acquittal.[23] Reviewing earlier cases, Lord Justice-General Emslie concluded in *Lambie* that "references in *Lennie* and *Owens* to there being an onus upon the defence were unsound". The correct position was instead:

"When a special defence is pleaded, whether it be of alibi, self-defence or incrimination, the jury should be so charged in the appropriate language, and all that requires to be said of the special defence, where any evidence in support of it has been given, either in course [sic] of the Crown case or by the accused himself or by any witnesses led by the defence, is that if that evidence, whether from one or more witnesses, is believed, or creates in the minds of the jury reasonable doubt as to the guilt of the accused ... the Crown case must fail and that they must acquit."[24]

Although the appeal court in *Lambie* did not refer to the evidential and persuasive burdens as such, it is clear from subsequent opinions that the special defence has no special evidential implications.[25] It is therefore misleading to direct a jury, as in *Lambie*, in terms which suggest that the

---

[18] 1973 J.C. 53 at 58–59.
[19] In the event in *Lambie* the appeal court held that taken as a whole the charge to the jury narrowly avoided amounting to a misdirection. The appeal was sustained on a different ground.
[20] 1946 J.C. 79.
[21] 1946 J.C. 119.
[22] 1963 J.C. 80.
[23] The historical position is examined by Gordon in "The Burden of Proof on the Accused", 1968 S.L.T. (News) 29.
[24] *Lambie v HM Advocate*, 1973 J.C. 53 at p.59.
[25] See for example, *Dunn v HM Advocate*, 1987 S.L.T. 295 and *Harrison v HM Advocate*, 1993 S.C.C.R. 1087.

accused bears the persuasive burden of proof of a special defence. The position today is that the accused requires *only* to raise a reasonable doubt to secure an acquittal. Once an accused has produced some credible evidence to support a defence raised, it is for the prosecution to disprove that defence as part of their duty to discharge the persuasive burden. As Renton and Brown observe:

> "There is no duty on the prosecution to refute any specific defence until it is raised in evidence by the accused or arises out of the evidence led for the Crown, but once a specific defence, whether or not technically 'special', has been raised, it is for the prosecution to exclude it beyond reasonable doubt. The only burden laid on the defence is what is sometimes called the 'evidential burden', the onus of raising the issue. The 'persuasive burden' remains on the Crown."[26]

Macphail states that as a result of *Lambie*, in the case of the special defences other than insanity and diminished responsibility, "the persuasive burden of proof remains on the Crown and the only duty on the defence is to discharge the evidential burden of raising the issue in such a way that it has to be left to the jury".[27] The correct way for a trial judge to approach any specific defence raised by an accused is that laid down by Lord Justice-General Cooper in *Crawford v HM Advocate*[28] who ruled, in the context of a plea of self-defence, that:

> "[It] is the duty of the presiding Judge to consider the whole evidence bearing on self-defence and to make up his own mind whether any of it is relevant to infer self-defence as known to the law of Scotland. If he considers that there is no evidence from which the requisite conclusion could reasonably be drawn, it is the duty of the presiding Judge to direct the jury that it is not open to them to consider the special defence. If, on the other hand, there is some evidence, although it may be slight, or even evidence about which two reasonable views might be held, then he must leave the special defence to the jury subject to such directions as he may think proper."

The need for a clear direction to the jury on burdens is illustrated in *Gilmour v HM Advocate*.[29] The accused had raised special defences of alibi and incrimination. The sheriff directed the jury that "there is no special burden on the accused to prove his special defence—corroboration is not necessary...". The appeal court described this charge to the jury as "quite unsatisfactory" and "defective" because of the failure to explain to the jury

---

[26] At para.24–01. Another effect of *Lambie* became apparent in *McAvoy v HM Advocate*, 1982 J.C. 117 and *Fraser v HM Advocate,* 1982 S.C.C.R. 458 in which it was held that, with the exception of the defence of insanity, there is no need for any direction to be given to a jury on any requirement for a corroborated case to support such a defence. *Lambie* was also followed in *Mullen v HM Advocate*, 1978 S.L.T. (Notes) 33 and *Donnelly v HM Advocate*, 1977 S.L.T. 147.

[27] Macphail, *Evidence*, para.22.08.

[28] 1950 J.C. 67 at 69. See also the direction given to trial judges in *Dunn v HM Advocate*, 1987 S.L.T. 295.

[29] 1989 S.L.T. 881.

the key information that, "if what is raised by the special defence leaves them *with any reasonable doubt*, the accused must be given the benefit of that doubt".[30]

In addition to the common law exceptions to the general rule on the **5–18** persuasive burden, there are numerous statutory provisions that seek to impose an onus of proof on an accused person. Such provisions often appear in road traffic offences, as well as those relating to organised crime and terrorism. In recent years a number of these have been challenged as contrary to the Human Rights Act 1998 and Strasbourg jurisprudence as they appear to undermine the presumption of innocence by imposing a persuasive burden on the accused. Such provisions have become known in England as the reverse onus of proof. Before we turn to consider these, there is one further category of defence to discuss which was previously a common law defence but was made a statutory defence in 2010.

DEFENCES CONCERNING MENTAL DISORDER

Defences relating to the state of the mental health of the accused have been **5–19** acknowledged for centuries. Hume recognised that when an accused person sought to plead insanity at the time of the commission of the offence, both the persuasive burden and the evidential burden shifted from the prosecution and instead rested on the accused.[31] This represented a major departure from the general rule that the persuasive and evidential burdens lay with the prosecution. Historically, insanity and the lesser, but associated, plea of diminished responsibility represented the sole common law exceptions to the general rule whereby the persuasive burden of proof lies with the prosecutor.[32] Contemporary understandings of the appropriate responses to offenders with mental health disorders inspired the Scottish Law Commission's *Report on Insanity and Diminished Responsibility*.[33] The Report recommended the replacement of the common law defence of insanity with a new statutory defence of mental disorder in circumstances where an accused lacked criminal responsibility. It also recommended the codification of the law relating to pleas of diminished responsibility.[34]

Part 7 of the Criminal Justice and Licensing (Scotland) Act 2010 largely **5–20** implemented the Law Commission proposals. It abolished the common law defences of insanity, diminished responsibility and insanity as a plea in bar of trial, and replaced them with new statutory versions of the defences. These new statutory defences are set out in ss.51A and 51B of the Criminal Procedure Scotland Act 1995.[35] Section 51A(1) provides that person is not

---

[30] At 882F, emphasis added.
[31] Hume, *Crimes*, I, 43.
[32] Diminished Responsibility has historically always been regarded as a form of partial insanity in Scots law; see *HM Advocate v Braithwaite*, 1945 J.C 55.
[33] Scot Law Com No.195, 2004.
[34] Scot Law Com No.195, 2004 at Pt 3.
[35] Acquittal involving mental disorder (previously insanity in bar of trial) is also dealt with by the Criminal Justice and Licensing (Scotland) Act 2010 by the insertion of s.53E into the Criminal Procedure (Scotland) Act 1995. The consideration of this procedural matter is beyond the scope of this book; see Renton and Brown, *Criminal Procedure*, 6th edn, para.26–05.

criminally responsible for conduct constituting an offence, and is to be acquitted of the offence, if the person was, at the time of the conduct, unable by reason of mental disorder to appreciate the nature or wrongfulness of the conduct. Section 51B(1) provides that a person who would otherwise be convicted of murder is instead to be convicted of culpable homicide on grounds of diminished responsibility if the person's ability to determine or control conduct for which the person would otherwise be convicted of murder was, at the time of the conduct, substantially impaired by reason of abnormality of mind.

5–21   Section 171 of Criminal Justice and Licensing (Scotland) Act 2010 Act abolished "any existing common law rules regarding the special defence of insanity, the plea of diminished responsibility and the plea of insanity in bar of trial".[36]

5–22   Despite this provision, the statutory provisions in the 2010 Act do not represent a significant departure from the previous common law evidential rules governing this area. In particular, the burden of proof of mental disorder remains with the accused person who wishes to rely upon such a defence.[37] The new statutory defence of "non-criminal responsibility of persons with a mental disorder". We refer to this hereafter as the "mental disorder" defence[38] and it is a special defence (requiring notice to be lodged by the defence seven days prior to the commencement of the preliminary hearing in a trial).[39] As with its common law predecessor—the defence of insanity—the defence of mental disorder must still be established by an accused on the balance of probabilities.[40] However, in contrast to the previous position under the common law in relation to insanity, the accused is now the *only* party in a trial who may seek to raise the defence.[41] The Act applies to proceedings commenced on or after the June 25, 2012 in relation to the s.51A defence (which replaced insanity) regardless of when the alleged conduct occurred.[42] The statutory plea of diminished responsibility implemented by the Act largely reinstates the evidential position under the common law as set down in the full bench decision in *HM Advocate v Braithwaite*.[43] Only the accused may raise the plea and, if raised, the accused has to prove diminished responsibility on the balance of probabilities.[44] The common law rules relating to diminished responsibility continue to apply in

---

[36] s.171 of the Criminal Justice and Licensing (Scotland) Act 2010.

[37] s.51A(a) of the Criminal Procedure (Scotland) Act 1995.

[38] The name suggested by Gerry Maher who was the Law Commissioner with responsibility for the 2004 report. For discussion of the new provisions, see G. Maher, "The new mental disorder defences: some comments", S.L.T. (News) 2013, 1, 1–4. An alternative name of "the irresponsibility defence" has been adopted by the editors of Renton and Brown.

[39] s.78(3), Criminal Procedure (Scotland) Act 1995. In a positive shift, against discrimination linked to mental illness, the archaic language of "insanity" was dispensed with, a full thirty years after its use was first criticised by the Thomson Committee (see *Criminal Procedure in Scotland (Second Report)* (Cmnd 6218, 1975) paras 52.13 and 53.10.

[40] s.51A(4), Criminal Procedure (Scotland) Act 1995.

[41] s.51A(4), Criminal Procedure (Scotland) Act 1995. The Crown has at least on one reported occasion in the past sought to counter the suggestion that the accused is of diminished responsibility and assert instead that the accused is insane, albeit unsuccessfully. See *HM Advocate v Harrison* (1968) SC 32 JCL 119.

[42] SSI 2012/160.

[43] 1945 J.C. 55.

[44] s.51B(4) of the Criminal Procedure (Scotland) Act 1995.

respect of proceedings where the conduct alleged took place prior to June 25, 2012.[45] The effect of a successful plea of diminished responsibility remains the same as it was under the common law. Thus, in regard to a murder charge, if a plea of mental disorder is upheld, a verdict of culpable homicide will be returned. If a plea of mental disorder at the time the offence was committed is upheld, then the accused will be acquitted. If the accused is unfit to plead due to mental disorder then he may be subject to compulsory measures under the mental health legislation.[46]

When an accused person seeks to assert that he was insane at the time of the offence, the persuasive burden of proof rests upon that accused.[47] So too does the evidential burden, though there may be sufficient evidence of the accused's state of mind from other sources to discharge this burden. The previous statement of the common law on this point was that of Lord Justice-Clerk Thomson in *HM Advocate v Mitchell*,[48] who directed a jury that the burden of proof is on the defence, "because in our law there is a presumption that a man is sane". **5–23**

In some circumstances the Crown may seek to counter the suggestion that the accused is mentally disordered and argue instead that the accused should become the subject of an order under the Mental Health (Care and Treatment) (Scotland) Act 2003.[49] **5–24**

There is no clear and authoritative ruling on this point, but dicta and commentary suggest that the persuasive burden of proving insanity (now mental disorder) in such a case will rest with the Crown.[50] Despite the historical and procedural differences between insanity and diminished responsibility,[51] the latter has always been regarded as a form of "partial insanity"[52] and it is logical to continue to treat the evidential implications of a plea of diminished responsibility in the same way as those for mental disorder, even if the outcomes of a successful plea are different.[53] Thus in *Carraher v HM Advocate*[54] Lord Russell directed the jury that: **5–25**

> "If the Crown have established here that the accused did this thing, it is not for the Crown to go further and show that the accused was fully responsible for what he did; it is for the accused to make good his defence of partial irresponsibility. . ."

---

[45] SSI 2012/160

[46] Criminal Procedure (Scotland) Act 1995, s.53F.

[47] Hume, Crimes, I, 43, representing the common law, now swept away. The new statutory rules concerning unfitness in bar of trial are procedural matters outwith the scope of this book. See Renton and Brown, *Criminal Procedure*, 6th edn, Ch.26. Evidence from two medical practitioners is required to support a plea of unfitness for trial. See s.54(1)(c)(i).

[48] 1951 J.C. 53 at 53–54; see also *Lambie v HM Advocate*, 1973 J.C. 53 at 58.

[49] See For which procedure see Renton and Brown, *Criminal Procedure*, 6th edn, Ch.26.

[50] See Macphail, Ch.22.06, citing *HM Advocate v Harrison* (1968) 32 J.C.L. 119. For a discussion of the standard and onus of proof in a plea of insanity in bar of trial see *Jessop v Robertson*, 1989 S.C.C.R. 600.

[51] For which see Gordon, *Criminal Law*, 3rd edn, Chs 10 and 11.

[52] Described as such in *HM Advocate v Braithwaite*, 1945 J.C. 55. Alison, *Practice of the Criminal Law in Scotland*, described a person suffering from diminished responsibility as being "partially deranged" (II, 652).

[53] i.e. in terms of any treatment required under the mental health legislation.

[54] 1946 J.C. 108 at 113. This passage was adopted in *Braithwaite*, above. The categories of special defences are probably now closed: *Sorley v HM Advocate*, 1992 S.L.T. 867.

In other words, both the persuasive and evidential burdens on the issue of diminished responsibility are upon the accused. In practice, it will normally be sufficient for the accused to raise enough evidence to suggest that he was not fully responsible for his actions to warrant the judge leaving that possibility open for the jury's consideration.

STATUTORY PROVISIONS AND REVERSE ONUS OF PROOF

5–26 Statutory exceptions that endeavour to reverse the onus of proof typically require the accused to show that they had some lawful justification or excuse for what they did,[55] or which require them to prove that they had no knowledge of some vital fact essential to the commission of the offence.[56] For example, in terms of ss.4(3) and 5(2) of the Road Traffic Act 1988, it is an offence to be in charge of, or driving, a motor vehicle under the influence of drink or drugs. It is a defence to such a charge for an accused to "prove that at the material time there was no likelihood of his driving" the vehicle while he remained in such a condition.

5–27   Does this onus on an accused impose a persuasive or an evidential burden? It is often difficult to determine from the language of the statute precisely what kind of burden the accused bears. The case law leans strongly towards a view that when statutory provisions impose an onus on an accused to prove matters that are, or ought to be, within their knowledge, the effect is to impose a persuasive burden on that accused.[57] Thus, requiring an accused to prove that, although "over the limit" for driving, they had no intention of driving anyway, is arguably a particular kind of knowledge that only an accused can provide.[58] To favour that standpoint may be to assume that the subjective knowledge of the accused of their intention is of greater weight than the objective knowledge derived from other sources from which it can be inferred that the accused did intend to drive.[59] Davidson has pointed out that it is illogical to impose a persuasive burden on the accused while at the same time find that there is no duty upon the accused to corroborate their account.[60] Macphail, too, is critical of the imposition of a persuasive burden, proposing that all burdens falling upon an accused should be evidential only.[61]

---

[55] Such as the Prevention of Crime Act 1953, s.1(1), which makes it an offence to carry an offensive weapon in a public place without lawful authority or reasonable excuse, the proof whereof shall lie on him (i.e. the accused).

[56] e.g. Misuse of Drugs Act 1971, s.28(2). See also Licensing (Scotland) Act 1976, s.126.

[57] See, e.g. *Neish v Stevenson*, 1969 S.L.T. 229 for the imposition of such a burden on the accused in a drink/driving case involving a defence of "no likelihood of driving".

[58] Sometimes referred to as "special knowledge", discussed below.

[59] *King v Lees*, 1993 S.L.T. 1184, which held there was a persuasive burden on the accused to prove his statutory defence, though the court said the evidence led need not be corroborated. See also *Grieve v Macleod*, 1967 J.C. 32, in which the accused in a complaint under s.1 of the Prevention of Crime Act 1953 lost his appeal because the court was not satisfied that it was "reasonable" for an Edinburgh taxi driver to protect himself from customers with a length of rubber hose. The persuasive burden was clearly regarded as being his. For a discussion critical of these issues, see Sheldon, "Hip Flasks and Burdens", 1993 S.L.T. (News) 33.

[60] *Evidence*, para.4.26, alluding to *King v Lees*, 1993 J.C. 19.

[61] See Macphail, *Evidence*, paras 22.19 and 22.23.

Since the enactment of the Human Rights Act 1998, the issue of the **5–28** nature of the burden imposed upon the accused in statutory offences has sparked considerable controversy in English law. A series of Court of Appeal level and House of Lords' decisions revealed deep divisions within the judiciary. These decisions are of persuasive authority in the Scottish courts, in part because the burden and standard of proof across the jurisdictions of the United Kingdom is so similar and in part because many of these appellate decisions concern legislation with UK-wide application, including legislation dealing with road traffic offences, anti-terrorism, serious and organised crime and misuse of drugs. A distinction is drawn here between two classes of offences. The first class comprises those cases where statute imposes a persuasive burden in summary proceedings, or offences with a mainly regulatory function, such as possession of a licence. These provisions create less difficulty for the courts in finding the existence of a persuasive burden because the penalties and sentencing powers in summary cases are comparatively low. It is the second class—offences on indictment—that are especially problematic as the consequence of a conviction potentially carries a long prison sentence. These are discussed later after consideration of the first class of offences.

SUMMARY AND REGULATORY OFFENCES

Although the statutory provisions that purport to impose a persuasive **5–29** burden on the accused may appear uncomplicated, precisely what the prosecution or accused has to prove is not always immediately clear. One particular provision that has created confusion and contradiction is para.16 of Sch.3 to the Criminal Procedure (Scotland) Act 1995.[62] This is intended to have over-arching effect on the interpretation of clauses that seek to impose an onus on the accused. Paragraph 16 provides:

> "Where, in relation to an offence created by or under an enactment any exception, exemption, proviso, excuse or qualification, is expressed to have effect whether by the same or any other enactment, the exception, exemption, proviso, excuse or qualification need not be specified or negatived in the indictment or complaint, and the prosecution is not required to prove it but the accused may do so."

In *Earnshaw v HM Advocate*[63] the accused relied upon "reasonable excuse" for failure to provide a blood or urine sample in a drink/driving case. In his charge to the jury, the trial judge interpreted para.16 as imposing a persuasive burden upon the accused to prove that he had a reasonable excuse for failing to provide a specimen. The appeal court disagreed. Earnshaw's conviction was quashed on appeal. The court explained that the Crown carried the persuasive burden throughout of proving that no specimen was provided *and* that there was no reasonable excuse for that failure. The burden resting on the accused was simply an evidential one of presenting

---

[62] See Renton and Brown, *Criminal Procedure*, 6th edn, para.8–57.
[63] 1982 J.C. 11.

sufficient evidence to raise the issue of reasonable excuse. It was then for the Crown to exclude that possibility.[64]

5–30 The courts are understandably reluctant to find a persuasive burden exists unless statutory provisions are clearly drafted to reveal such parliamentary intent. This is discussed in more detail below.

FACTS PECULIARLY WITHIN THE KNOWLEDGE OF THE ACCUSED

5–31 As we have seen, it is generally contrary to the presumption of innocence to require an accused to prove his or her own innocence in the face of merely prima facie evidence from the Crown. However, it may be unwise for the accused to remain silent in the face of events that demand an explanation, as otherwise negative inferences may be drawn. As Lord Justice-Clerk Grant explained in *McIlhargey v Herron*[65]:

> "...[T]he silent defender does take a risk, and, if he fails to challenge evidence given by witnesses for the Crown by cross-examination or, in addition, by leading substantive evidence in support of his challenge, he cannot complain if the Court not merely accepts that unchallenged evidence but also, in the light of all the circumstances, draws from it the most unfavourable and adverse inferences to the defence that it is capable of supporting."[66]

In such circumstances there is no "burden of proof" as such upon the accused. However, by opting for silence an accused is unable to put any evidence before the court to raise a reasonable doubt. The choice is that of the accused. Where the courts consider that the silence relates to facts "that are peculiarly within the knowledge of the accused" then there may be no protection for the accused who does not offer an explanation:

> "We have not had from the accused one single word of explanation ... Now there are certain cases in which the proved facts may raise a presumption of guilt, and in which, in the absence of some explanation by the accused—where the person accused is the one person who can know the real truth—a jury may be entitled to draw an inference of guilt."[67]

In many cases, all that the defence require to do once the Crown appears to have discharged the evidential burden on an issue, is to cross-examine to try to challenge, contradict or weaken that evidence, i.e. to take action to prevent the Crown from discharging the persuasive burden on that issue. Where the Crown has already produced sufficient evidence to discharge the persuasive burden, the defence would have to introduce another issue

---

[64] But the court did not consider the application of s.66 in depth as the Crown conceded they had the persuasive burden of proof. See also *Kennedy v Clark*, 1970 J.C. 55.

[65] 1972 S.C. 38.

[66] At 42.

[67] *HM Advocate v Hardy*, 1938 J.C. 144 at 146 per Lord Justice-Clerk Aitchison. See too *Mochan v Herron*, 1972 S.L.T. 218

altogether in order to raise a reasonable doubt against the case which the Crown has constructed. This is often just a question of tactics in the adversarial process, not a formal burden of proof, but the somewhat imprecise language used within some of judgments, often without specific reference to the evidential and persuasive burdens, may suggest the existence of a burden.

In *Cruikshank v Smith*[68] the accused was charged with a statutory offence **5–32** involving illegal fishing. It was held that the persuasive burden of on the issue rested with the Crown, but that they only produce prima facie evidence of illegal fishing, which the accused had then to rebut. Sheriff Kermack described the onus in *McNeill v Ritchie*, thus[69]:

> "I interpret the effect in Scots law of a fact being peculiarly within the knowledge of the accused as requiring him to produce evidence of that fact and not as requiring him to substantiate it by full legal proof."

In the recent of case *Cunningham v HM Advocate* the Appeal Court referred to "the wisdom of the rule that it be for the accused pleading a particular exemption or excuse peculiarly within his knowledge to establish that excuse or exemption".[70] The rational is if the activities with which the accused is charged are plainly a matter within his knowledge, it is unreasonable to require the Crown to embark on potentially fruitless searches for evidence.

Many expressions are used to convey the general rule that the Crown carries the persuasive burden of proof but in certain circumstances, not much evidence, perhaps just prima facie evidence,[71] will suffice to place the accused in a position where a failure to produce some evidence (i.e. discharge an evidential burden) will lead to a conviction.

The next section considers those cases which are giving rise to greater **5–33** interpretive challenges. These are the more serious cases when there is more at stake for both the state and the individual, the legislator seeks to impose a persuasive burden on the accused, and the presumption of innocence comes under greater pressure.

SOLEMN CASES ON INDICTMENT

The reverse onus of proof in serious cases on indictment before a jury has **5–34** created considerable disquiet in the English appellate courts. Senior judges have acknowledged that if the persuasive burden is imposed on an accused it means that a jury may have to convict even if they think there is much more than a reasonable doubt that the accused did not commit the offence. As Lord Nicholls has warned[72]:

---

[68] 1949 J.C. 134 at 154 per Lord Justice-Clerk Thomson.
[69] 1967 S.L.T. (Sh. Ct) 68. See now *Irving v Jessop*, 1988 S.L.T. 53, which supports the view that the Crown need only produce a prima facie case. For a recent case outlining the difficulties facing the Crown in such circumstances, see *R. v Gibson* [2000] Crim. L.R. 479.
[70] [2012] HCJAC 90.
[71] *Cruickshank v Smith*, 1949 J.C. 134.
[72] *R. v Johnstone* [2003] 1 W.L.R. 1736 at 1750.

"...[R]emember that if an accused is required to prove a fact on the balance of probability to avoid conviction, this permits a conviction in spite of the fact-finding tribunal having a reasonable doubt as to the guilt of the accused."

How is this possible? It occurs because the imposition of a persuasive burden on the accused requires the accused to prove some fact or other on a balance of probability. If an accused fell just short of that standard, they would not have produced sufficient evidence on a balance of probability to secure their acquittal, but they will at least have produced evidence sufficient to raise a reasonable doubt—the usual criminal standard for an acquittal— and possibly considerably more than that. Clearly, such a position cuts across the presumption of innocence. It is why so many appeals have been made on grounds that statutory provisions which reverse the onus of proof are in conflict with art.6(2) of the European Convention on Human Rights. A brief history of the treatment in the courts of these reverse onus clauses illustrates the complexities.

5–35   In *R. v DPP, Ex p. Kebilene*[73] the House of Lords had to determine what kind of onus s.16A(3) of the Prevention of Terrorism (Temporary Provisions) Act 1989 placed upon an accused. The section related to possession of articles for commission of terrorist offences. It provided that "[i]t is a defence for a person charged with an offence under this section to prove that at the time of the alleged offence [the articles in question] were not in his possession...". Relying on the European Court of Human Rights decision in *Salabiaku v France* (A/141–A)[74] the Lords held that it was not necessarily a reversal of the presumption of innocence to place an onus of proof, whether evidential or persuasive, on an accused. The issue was whether there was a reasonable balance between the public interest and an individual's rights. *Salabiaku* is the leading ECHR authority on this issue. There, the court declared:

"Presumptions of fact or of law operate in every legal system. Clearly, the Convention does not prohibit such presumptions in principle. It does, however, require the Contracting States to remain within certain limits in this respect as regards criminal law. ... Article 6(2) does not therefore regard presumptions of fact or of law provided for in the criminal law with indifference. It requires States to confine them within reasonable limits which take into account the importance of what is at stake and maintain the rights of the defence."

Despite this ruling in *Salabiaku*, the decision in *Kebilene* drew a great deal of criticism from commentators who felt the balance had not been struck correctly, to the detriment of the accused. They called for urgent legislation to amend the effects of those statutes that impose a persuasive burden on an accused.[75] The 1989 Act was repealed, but the relevant sections discussed

---

[73] [1999] 4 All E.R. 801.
[74] (1991) 13 E.H.R.R. 379 at 388.
[75] See, for example, J.C. Smith, Commentary in [2000] Crim. L.R. 480–481 and the discussion in P. Lewis, "The Human Rights Act 1998: Shifting the Burden" [2000] Crim. L.R. 667.

here were re-enacted in the Terrorism Act 2000, albeit with the addition of a defence in s.118(2) which provides that:

"If the person adduces evidence which is sufficient to raise an issue with respect to the matter the court or jury shall assume that the defence is satisfied unless the prosecution proves beyond reasonable doubt that it is not."

The effect of s.118(2) is that the persuasive burden in the previous legislation, the 1989 Act, was now to be regarded as an evidential burden only.

The House of Lords had to consider reverse onus clauses in *R v Lambert*[76] **5–36** where Lambert appealed against his conviction under s.28 of the Misuse of Drugs Act 1971 for being in possession of drugs in circumstances where he claimed he did not know the bag he carried contained drugs. Section 28(2) provides that:

". . .[I]t shall be a defence for the accused to prove that he neither knew of nor suspected nor had reason to suspect the existence of some fact alleged by the prosecution which it is necessary for the prosecution to prove if he is to be convicted of the offence charged."

In a five bench decision, Lord Hutton dissenting, the majority, obiter dicta,[77] noted that s.28 did not require the Crown to prove that the accused *knew* he was carrying a controlled drug. They had to establish only that the accused was in possession of such a drug. It was then for the accused to prove one of the available defences set out in the Act. The particular difficulty with this position is that one is asking the accused to prove a negative, e.g. he did not know that what he was carrying was other than he thought it was, and that may be manifestly unfair and unreasonable. Accordingly, the majority read down the persuasive burden in the statute as an evidential burden.[78] The "reading down" of statutory provisions refers to situations where the courts interpret the provision in such a way that it is rendered compatible with the Human Rights Act.

There have been numerous decisions in regard to reverse onus clauses **5–37** where the courts have identified that, in the interpretation of Convention rights, there has to be balanced compromise between the right of governments to secure a public policy objective in the national interest and the right of the accused to a fair trial. Signatories to the ECHR do have a margin of appreciation in the implementation of Convention rights. The test is "whether the modification or limitation of that right [to a fair trial] pursues a legitimate aim and whether it satisfies the principle of proportionality".[79]

---

[76] [2002] A.C. 545. The case was a series of three conjoined appeals—the two others, *Jordan* and *Ali* concerned the burden imposed by s.2(2) of the Homicide Act 1957.

[77] It was obiter dicta, as *Lambert* was decided on the procedural issue of whether the Human Rights Act had retrospective effect.

[78] *R v Lambert* [2002] A.C. 545 at para.41 per Lord Steyn.

[79] *R v Lambert* [2002] A.C. 545, per Lord Hope at para.88. See too, *Brown v Stott*, 2001 S.C. (P.C.) 43 per Lord Bingham at 60.

5–38   In regard to road traffic offences, in *Sheldrake v DPP*[80] the Lords held that the imposition of an onus on the accused to prove that at the material time there was no likelihood of him driving while "under the influence" was an acceptable persuasive burden. Delivering the leading judgment, Lord Bingham explained[81]:

> "Plainly the provision is directed to a legitimate object: the prevention of death, injury and damage caused by unfit drivers. Does the provision meet the tests of acceptability identified in the Strasbourg jurisprudence? In my view, it plainly does. I do not regard the burden placed on the defendant as beyond reasonable limits or in any way arbitrary... The defendant has a full opportunity to show that there was no likelihood of his driving, a matter so closely conditioned by his own knowledge and state of mind at the material time as to make it much more appropriate for him to prove on the balance of probabilities that he would not have been likely to drive than for the prosecutor to prove, beyond reasonable doubt, that he would."

A number of English cases have endeavoured to clarify the conflicting dicta from the House of Lords. The Court of Appeal in *Attorney-General's Reference (No.1 of 2004)*[82] produced its own guidance for the lower courts, in a judgment which also acknowledged that reverse onus of proof clauses were too complex to be readily reduced to a simple set of guidelines. We will not repeat here all 10 points of guidance (listed at para.52) of the judgment. However, the first was an instruction to the lower courts to follow the guidance given in the *Reference* and, "strongly discourage the citation of authority to them other than the decision of the House of Lords in *R. v Johnstone*"[83] as it (then) represented the most recent authority on the matter. Two other points are worth emphasising as being of wider interest for the evaluation of all reverse onus clauses. Paragraph 52(g) states:

> "The easier it is for the accused to discharge the burden the more likely it is that the reverse burden is justified. This will be the case where the facts are within the defendant's own knowledge. How difficult it would be for the prosecution to establish the facts is also indicative of whether a reverse legal burden is justified."

Paragraph 52(i) states:

> (i)   Caution must be exercised when considering the seriousness of the offence and the power of punishment. The need for a reverse burden is not necessarily reflected by the gravity of the offence, though, from a defendant's point of view, the more serious the offence, the more important it is that there is no interference with the presumption of innocence.

[80] [2005] 1 A.C. 264 at 313, para.51.
[81] *Sheldrake v DPP* [2005] 1 A.C. 264 at 313, at para.41.
[82] *Attorney-General's Reference (No.1 of 2004)*, 2004 EWCA Crim 1025.
[83] [2003] UKHL 28.

As Lord Woolf explained in *Attorney General of Hong Kong v Lee Kwong-kut*[84]:

> "In order to maintain the balance between the individual and the society as a whole, rigid and inflexible standards should not be imposed on the legislature's attempts to resolve the difficult and intransigent problems with which society is faced when seeking to deal with serious crime. It must be remembered that questions of policy remain primarily the responsibility of the legislature."

Three significant cases in the Scottish courts illustrate the approach taken in
this jurisdiction to reverse onus clauses. First, *Agar v HM Advocate* held that the term "balance of probabilities" when referring to the standard of proof of the burden placed upon the accused should be interpreted at face value: **5–39**

> "[T]hese are simple English words and it is difficult to see how their meaning could be improved upon, particularly as it was emphasised [by the trial judge] that the standard of proof was lower than that applicable to the Crown."[85]

Agar was cited in *Glancy v HM Advocate*[86] which reviewed a number of the key English authorities and where the appellant argued unsuccessfully that the statutory defence provided by s.49(4) of the Criminal Law (Consolidation) (Scotland) Act 1995—having a reasonable excuse or lawful authority to carry a knife in a public place—ought to impose an evidential burden of proof only and not the more onerous standard of balance of probabilities. The arguments put forward to the effect that a balance of probabilities standard "offended against the presumption of innocence and the Convention rights under art.8(1)" were rejected by the court. In so doing, Lord Clarke noted that in determining the appropriate onus the legislature intended in any given case:

> "[T]he authorities taken as a whole ... require a careful examination of (a) the relevant statutory provisions in each case, (b) the measures that are taken in those provisions directed at the activity in question, which is made an offence, and (c) what justification can be made out for a departure from the presumption of innocence, balancing the interests of the public and the individual's fundamental rights."

Despite the many detailed expositions of the law in this area, it has clearly been difficult for the courts to avoid an individualistic case-by-case approach to interpretation. Although this has been criticised as a failure of the courts to call the legislature to account,[87] given the repeated emphasis on

---

[84] [1993] A.C. 951 at 975.
[85] *Agar v HM Advocate*, Unreported, High Court of Justiciary, March 17, 2000 (2000 G.W.D. 12-421) at para.8.
[86] [2011] HCJAC 104.
[87] V. Tadros and S. Tierney, "The Presumption of Innocence and the Human Rights Act" (2004) 67(3) M.L.R. 402.

the need for careful scrutiny and balancing of interests, it appears that such an approach is the only viable one.

THE STANDARDS OF PROOF AND THE PERSUASIVE BURDEN

5–40 The standard of proof is the term used to describe the amount and quality of evidence that is sufficient to discharge a burden of proof. In criminal proceedings, the standard for discharging the persuasive burden of proof is proof beyond reasonable doubt. This is in contrast to the standard in civil proceedings, which is proof on a balance of probabilities.

Beyond reasonable doubt

5–41 The trial judge will explain in the directions to the jury that the prosecution must establish the guilt of the accused beyond reasonable doubt, since this is the standard of proof required whenever the Crown bears the persuasive burden. The concept of beyond reasonable doubt cannot be rigidly defined. But it is understood as meaning the sort of doubt which a reasonable person would entertain. It cannot be reduced to a quantitative amount, but has been described as something more than "a strained or fanciful acceptance of remote possibilities"[88] and "more than a merely speculative or academic doubt".[89] Jurors are sometimes told in the judge's charge to the jury that before they convict they need to be *sure* of the accused's guilt. This may be compounded when loose language is used in criminal cases that infer an injustice to the accused in regard to the presumption of innocence. Thus, in *Guest v Annan*[90] a conviction for excessive chastisement of a child was quashed because the sheriff used the words, "on balance ... I convict", language in a criminal case that was inappropriately reminiscent of the civil standard of proof.[91]

5–42 As already discussed, there are a few situations in which an accused person bears a persuasive burden on a particular issue. The question then arises as to the standard of proof required to discharge that. Dealing first with the criminal defences, there is only one special defence which places a burden on the accused—it is the statutory defence in s.51A of the Criminal Procedure (Scotland) 1995 which provides "[a] person is not criminally responsible for conduct constituting an offence, and is to be acquitted of the offence, if the person was at the time of the conduct unable by reason of mental disorder to appreciate the nature or wrongfulness of the conduct". If the accused raises this defence s.51A(4) of the Act provides, "[t]he special defence may be stated only by the person charged with the offence and it is for that person to establish it on the balance of probabilities".

---

[88] Lord Justice-Clerk Cooper in *Irving v Minister of Pensions*, 1945 S.C. 21 at 29. See also *HM Advocate v McGinlay*, 1983 S.L.T. 562 and *Tudhope v Craig*, 1985 S.C.C.R. 214.
[89] Lord Justice-Clerk Thomson in *McKenzie v HM Advocate*, 1959 J.C. 32 at 37.
[90] 1988 S.C.C.R. 275.
[91] See also *Ward v Chief Constable of Strathclyde*, 1991 S.L.T. 292, an action of damages for injuries allegedly sustained when mounted police cantered into a crowd. The appropriate standard was held to be on a balance of probabilities, but it was observed that it would be difficult for a pursuer to overcome evidential hurdles and demonstrate want of probable cause and malice on the part of the police.

There is a second statutory defence of diminished responsibility available **5–43** only in murder cases. Section 51B(1) provides:

"A person who would otherwise be convicted of murder is instead to be convicted of culpable homicide on grounds of diminished responsibility if the person's ability to determine or control conduct for which the person would otherwise be convicted of murder was, at the time of the conduct, substantially impaired by reason of abnormality of mind."

Again, it is for the person charged with murder to establish, "on the balance of probabilities, that the condition set out in subsection (1) is satisfied".

In terms of both s.51A and 51B "conduct" includes acts and omissions.[92] **5–44**

The "balance of probabilities standard" is the standard applied in civil **5–45** cases and is discussed in more detail in Ch.6. It imposes a significant burden on the accused, which, as we have already discussed, is unusual as it is contrary to the presumption of innocence. The reason it is permitted in cases involving mental disorder is because there is a presumption of sanity[93] and if an accused person wishes to rely upon that defence they will have to submit to a psychiatric examination by two medically qualified doctors to obtain reports to substantiate their claim. As such examinations require the consent of the patient, they can only be instigated by the accused and the burden of producing evidence on a balance of probabilities therefore lies with them.

At common law, in respect of all other issues in a criminal trial, the **5–46** persuasive burdens rest and remain with the Crown. If, at the end of the day, the trier of fact has any reasonable doubt, that doubt must work in favour of the accused and lead to an acquittal (or possibly a not proven verdict) because the Crown has failed to discharge the persuasive burden.

In those situations where a statute places a persuasive burden upon an **5–47** accused, the appropriate standard of proof is also on a balance of probabilities. For example, in *Robertson v Watson*,[94] a prosecution under Sale of Milk Regulations, milk found to have been adulterated was presumed to have been adulterated by the accused unless and until he proved otherwise. Lord Justice-General Cooper considered the appropriate standard of proof required for the accused to discharge the persuasive burden thus placed upon him[95]:

"I adopt, as an accurate statement of Scots law of general validity the rule laid down in *R. v Carr-Briant*[96] that, when (as in this instance) some matter is presumed against an accused person unless and until the contrary is proved, the burden of proof on the accused is less than that required at the hands of the prosecutor in proving the case beyond

---

[92] ss.51A(5) and 51B(5).

[93] *HM Advocate v Mitchell*, 1951 J.C. 53 at 54 (emphasis added). The same standard was established for the defence of diminished responsibility in *Carraher v HM Advocate*, 1946 J.C. 108 at 113, and *HM Advocate v Braithwaite*, 1945 J.C. 55, in which Lord Justice-Clerk Cooper at 58 directed the jury that "[i]f you think the balance of probability to be in favour of that defence, you must sustain it".

[94] 1949 J.C. 73.

[95] *Robertson v Watson*, 1949 J.C. 73, p.88.

[96] [1943] K.B. 607, which is still the leading authority on the same point in England.

reasonable doubt, and that this burden may be discharged by evidence satisfying the jury or the Court of the probability of that which the accused is called upon to establish."

For the reasons discussed above, any suggestions of a standard of proof higher than on a balance of probabilities would run counter to the presumption of innocence contained in art.6.

5–48   It is arguable that the principle expounded in *Robertson v Watson* is of general applicability to any situation in which some fact is presumed against an accused unless the contrary is proved. This is how *R. v Carr-Briant* has been interpreted in the English courts. In *Farrell v Moir*[97] it was held that an accused who bore the persuasive burden of showing "special reason" why he should not be disqualified for drunken driving need only discharge it on a balance of probabilities.[98]

5–49   In those cases where an accused bears an evidential burden on an issue, either because he or she is peculiarly in possession of the necessary facts or because they have been found in possession of recently stolen property in criminative circumstances, they need only raise a reasonable doubt on the evidence. In other words they do not have to reach any particular standard and, as discussed later, the evidence in question does not have to be corroborated. Any suggestion that the accused must in some way prove their innocence is deeply flawed. In *Tallis v HM Advocate* the sheriff wrongly directed the jury in the following terms[99]:

> "[T]he situation may arise, ladies and gentlemen, that the Crown puts forward such a strong case that it is only if you are satisfied with the explanation given by the accused, that you would be entitled to acquit him."

On appeal, this charge was described as a "serious misdirection in law" in that it was a "plain indication to the jury that in certain circumstances the onus of proof shifts to the accused and unless he can discharge it by an explanation which satisfies the jury, i.e. of his innocence, then conviction must follow".[100]

---

[97] 1974 S.L.T. (Sh. Ct) 89.
[98] For an analysis of the confusion created in this area see David Sheldon, "Hip Flasks and Burdens", 1993 S.L.T. (News) 33.
[99] 1982 S.C.C.R. 91 at 99.
[100] *Tallis v HM Advocate*, 1982 S.C.C.R. 91.

Chapter 6

BURDENS AND STANDARDS OF PROOF IN CIVIL PROCEEDINGS

INTRODUCTION

The general rule with respect to both the persuasive and evidential burdens **6–01** of proof in civil cases is that the burdens rest with the party who will lose on that issue if no other evidence is led.[1] This is another way of saying that the party who raises an issue must prove it.

To illustrate: if A seeks a court order that B owes her money then she **6–02** must produce some evidence of the debt or she will fail in her action. To this extent, therefore, A carries a burden of proof of the debt. At the same time, if it is B's contention that he did indeed at one time owe A money, but has since repaid it, then B bears a burden of proof on the separate issue of repayment. However, B is under no obligation to begin discharging this burden, i.e. to begin leading evidence to show that the debt has been repaid, until A has satisfied the court that the money is still due.

On each issue in a case, there is a persuasive burden of proof which **6–03** attaches to one or other of the parties. If no evidence at all is led on that issue, or if the evidence leaves the matter finely balanced, then the party relying on that issue as part of their case will lose, at least on that issue. A defended civil action is a series of related issues and often in the course of the proof the persuasive burden of proof is distributed among the parties in accordance with the issues raised.

The actual allocation of these burdens between the parties is always a **6–04** matter of law, since it is the substantive law that determines what each party must prove in order to succeed in any given case. Thus in the debt example above, if A wishes to secure decree for the repayment of money due to her, it is incumbent upon her to produce evidence of the existence of the debt. However, even if she does so, she will not obtain decree if the court is satisfied that the money has been repaid, hence the obligation placed upon B to prove repayment once the existence of the debt has been established.

The evidential burden may be defined as the burden of adducing sufficient **6–05** evidence on a particular issue to allow the court to begin considering it as a live issue. In the debt example above, A cannot expect the court to consider the possibility that B owes her money unless and until she produces *some* credible evidence of the existence of the debt. Without at least this, her case has no foundation. Once she *has* produced some such evidence, and the court is prepared to consider the possibility that a debt exists, she will hope to go on to reinforce the point with further evidence. The same item of

---

[1] Dickson, *Evidence*, para.25.

evidence may of course achieve both objectives at once, but often a stage can exist in connection with any issue at which the court has accepted that some evidence exists, but is looking for more before it will regard the persuasive burden as having been discharged.

THE PERSUASIVE BURDEN OF PROOF

6–06 In *Brown v Rolls Royce*,[2] an action in delict, Lord Denning articulated the role of burdens in civil cases. Brown had contracted industrial dermatitis whilst employed as a machine-oiler by the defenders. He claimed damages for negligence, alleging that his employers, the defenders, had not provided him with the same barrier cream that other employers supplied in similar circumstances. The defenders admitted this fact, but argued medical advice suggested the barrier cream was not effective. They further claimed that the provision of good washing facilities, which they had made available, was an effective precaution against dermatitis.

6–07   On appeal from the Court of Session to the House of Lords, Lord Denning made various comments about the disparity in the Inner House over the nature of the persuasive burden[3] (referring to it in the following extract as the legal burden, the term used to describe it in English law):

> "This difference of opinion shows how important it is to distinguish between a *legal* burden properly so called, which is imposed by the law itself, and a *provisional* burden which is raised by the state of the evidence. The legal burden in this case was imposed by law on the Pursuer. In order to succeed, he had to prove that the Defenders were negligent, and that their negligence caused the disease ... In order to discharge the burden of proving negligence, the pursuer proved that 'barrier cream was commonly supplied by employers to men doing such work as the pursuer was doing.' This was a cogent piece of evidence and raised no doubt a 'presumption' or a 'prima facie' case, in this sense, that if nothing more appeared, the Court might well infer that the defenders were negligent, and in that sense it put a burden on the defender to answer it. But this was only a provisional burden which was raised by the state of the evidence as it then stood. The defender might answer it by argument, as indeed they did ... In this way, a provisional burden may shift from one party to the other as the case proceeds or may remain suspended between them. But it has no compelling force. At the end of the day the Court has to ask itself—not whether the provisional burden is discharged—but whether the legal burden has been discharged, that is to say: Has the pursuer proved that the defenders were negligent?"[4]

In essence, Lord Denning was suggesting the issue is more easily conceptualised as a question of whether there has been sufficient evidence on a

---

[2] 1960 S.C. (H.L.) 22.
[3] See *Brown v Rolls Royce*, 1958 S.C. 600, though the Inner House did not discuss it in detail, save for Lord Carmont at 607 who referred simply to the "onus of proof".
[4] *Brown v Rolls Royce*, 1960 S.C. (H.L.) 22 at 27.

balance of probabilities to discharge the requirements of the substantive law of negligence.

Civil cases may well consist of more than one issue and the evidential **6–08** burdens on these issues are likely to arise between the parties in a sequential pattern. Take the example of an action for payment by B (builder) against H (householder) in respect of a conservatory which B has erected for H in compliance with a building contract. In scenario 1, assume that following completion of the contract H fails to pay B, who then raises an action for payment of the invoice. In order to be assured of payment the persuasive burden is on B to show (i) the existence and extent of the contract; and (ii) the fact of non-payment by H without good cause. If B is able to do that he will have discharged the persuasive burden. Assume that H acknowledges the invoice is due but explains she has just been made redundant and cannot afford to pay the sum sought. That explanation from H is not an answer which the law recognises as justification for non-payment. The court will therefore grant a decree for payment in favour of the pursuer B as he has discharged the persuasive burden to prove the debt is due.

In scenario 2, assume H admits the existence and extent of the contract **6–09** but claims that she is withholding payment from B because the conservatory leaks and the under-floor heating system which he installed is not functioning properly. In order for H to persuade the court that she is justified in withholding payment she will obviously have to produce evidence of the defects, i.e. she carries an evidential burden in this respect. She would usually do this by calling witnesses, e.g. a surveyor or another builder in respect of the leak, and a heating engineer in respect of the under-floor system. As B is asserting that H owes him money, B must produce the necessary evidence of this, but he carries the further responsibility of countering H's arguments about defects. B therefore still carries the persuasive and evidential burdens on the issue of payment, even though it is a slightly more complex set of issues than scenario 1.

Finally, in scenario 3, assume H has paid B's invoice before she realises **6–10** that the conservatory leaks and the heating system is mal-functioning. Assume too that B has failed to respond to requests from H to return to remedy these defects. In these circumstances H will have to raise an action for specific implement or have the work carried out by an alternative contractor and sue B for the costs incurred. Either way, in this type of court action it is H who will carry the persuasive and evidential burden of proving B is due her money or performance.

It ought to be possible in a civil action to examine the closed record (the **6–11** written pleadings lodged prior to the proof), identify the remaining live issues and allocate the burdens of proof according to which party is making which assertion. However, it is not always as simple as this. Sometimes a party appears to be asserting a negative (e.g. that the defender has failed to honour a contract, or that the pursuer failed to take reasonable care for her own safety) and it can seem that a party is being asked to prove a negative. However, if it is "the substance and not the grammar"[5] which is considered, such averments[6] are positive ones and not negative. Thus, in order to show

---

[5] Dickson, *Evidence*, para.35.
[6] An averment is the term for a claim or assertion in the written pleadings of the parties which they will be expected to prove.

that the pursuer in a negligence action failed to take reasonable care for her own safety (the essence of a defence of contributory negligence) the defender will require to lead evidence of the pursuer's behaviour. This might be a failure to follow safety procedures, or a failure to look both ways at a road crossing. For this reason, an averment, whether phrased in the positive or the negative, will normally impose the burdens of proof on the party making it.

6–12   The general rule is that it is for the pursuer to lead at the outset of the proof. This reflects the fact that in most cases the pursuer must discharge the burdens of proof on at least some of his averments before the defender is required to prove anything. Thus, in scenario 2 of the original example, B had to prove the existence of the debt before H was required to prove why it had not been repaid.

6–13   However, there may be some occasions when the court rules that the defender should lead. This could occur, for example, if the defender has raised an issue on the record, which, if proved, would end the case without the need to hear evidence from the pursuer. In such a case the burdens of proof remain where the averments have placed them—it is simply that the court has altered the order in which the parties set about discharging them.

STANDARDS OF PROOF IN CIVIL CASES

6–14 In civil cases the appropriate standard of proof to discharge the persuasive burden is proof on a balance of probabilities.[7] The balance of probabilities means "more sure than not" that the evidence supports a particular contention. While it might be better to avoid attempting to convert this into a quantitative figure, it could be expressed as more than 50 percent sure.

6–15   The standard of proof applicable to persuasive burdens in civil cases generally creates less confusion than in criminal cases as judges only rarely have to explain the concept of balance of probabilities to a jury. In civil cases, in order to succeed on a particular issue, the party bearing the persuasive burden must persuade the court that their version of the facts is more probable than that of their opponent. As the late Lord Macphail explained, "[w]hat is being weighed in the 'balance' is not quantities of evidence but the probabilities arising from the acceptable evidence and all the circumstances of the case".[8]

6–16   There is often no material distinction between the persuasive and evidential burdens in civil cases because of the broader general rule that the party who needs to succeed in respect of a particular argument bears the burden on proving it on a balance of probabilities. This is apparent in the case of *Inglis v L.M.S.*[9] an action for damages raised by the parents of a young boy killed when he fell from the doorway of a moving train. Once the pursuers had shown that no one, including the boy, had interfered with the door handle, they had established prima facie evidence of negligence on the part of the defenders. The defenders, the train company, offered no evidence

---

[7] *Hendry v Clan Line Steamers*, 1949 S.C. 320 per Lord Justice Clerk Thomson at 323.
[8] Macphail, *Evidence*, at Ch.22.30. See also Lord Jamieson in *Hendry v Clan Line Steamers*, n.9 above at 328.
[9] 1941 S.C. 551, referred to above.

to counter that prima facie case. Their silence on this crucial issue permitted the pursuers to discharge their persuasive burden and obtain a decree of damages. One can see that as a matter of tactics the defenders in such situations are required to counter with some evidence of their own, or accept the pursuer's case. The decision in *Inglis* is authority for the proposition that if a pursuer establishes a prima facie case that is unchallenged by evidence to the contrary, they have reached the standard of proof to satisfy the evidential burden.[10] There is no obligation on the pursuer to have to exclude all other possible explanations for the events that have led to the court action.[11]

Notwithstanding the general rule that the party bearing the persuasive **6–17** burden on an issue also bears the evidential burden on that same issue, a distinction can be drawn in cases in which a fact which requires proof one way or the other lies exclusively (or, to use the accepted legal term, "peculiarly") within the knowledge of one of the parties. Thus, in *McClure, Naismith, Brodie and Macfarlane v Stewart*[12] a client instructed his solicitor to secure a loan on a patent he was taking out. The solicitor persuaded another client to lend £5,000 on the patent. The patent was subsequently found to be invalid because it had been anticipated. The creditor client sued the solicitor, alleging that the solicitor had known of the invalidity of the patent, but had failed to communicate that fact to him in time. The court determined that where one party (in this case the creditor) is obliged to make a negative averment (i.e. the failure to communicate with him), the proof or otherwise of which lies peculiarly within the knowledge of the other party (i.e. the solicitor), then that other party, who is asserting the affirmative, must prove it. But, he is not obliged to do this unless and until the party asserting the negative has at least produced some evidence (in this case that he had received no communication from the solicitor). In other words, the persuasive burden on the issue (in this case the issue of communication) rests with the person with the knowledge of the facts, but he is not obliged to begin discharging it until the party without the knowledge has discharged the evidential burden.[13]

EFFECT OF PRESUMPTIONS ON THE PROCESS OF PROOF

As will be discussed in Ch.7, a presumption is no more than a device—a **6–18** construction—to speed up the process of proof. It operates in civil law in much the same way as in criminal law, i.e. when a particular collection of facts pertain, a presumption flows from it such that there may be no need for a party to lead all or any direct evidence in order to discharge the burden which they would otherwise bear on the issue. Once the facts upon which a presumption is based have been established, the burden is deemed to be

---

[10] See too *Brown v Rolls Royce*, 1960 S.C. (H.L.) 22 per Lord Denning at 28 to the effect that once the pursuer has established what amounts to a prima facie case, then "if nothing more appeared, the Court might well infer that the defenders were negligent".

[11] *Scottish Water v Dunne Building & Civil Engineering Ltd*, 2012 G.W.D. 28-569.

[12] (1887) 15 R. (H.L.) 1.

[13] See also *Cruickshank v Smith*, 1949 J.C. 134 at 151–152. The significance of these cases is not, of course, that the pursuer is asserting a negative, but that the facts are almost exclusively within the knowledge of the defender. See also *Burns v Royal Hotel (St Andrews) Ltd*, 1958 S.C. 354.

discharged and the party who benefits from it need not prove anything further. From a common law perspective, compared to the criminal law, there are many more examples of presumptions still operating in civil law. There are none that carry the same significance as the presumption of innocence, but they are important for practitioners when preparing for a proof in that the existence of a presumption will dictate whose duty it is to lead evidence on a particular point and the consequences of failing to do so.

6–19   The closed record of the pleadings should reveal, ideally explicitly, but at worst implicitly, any presumptions arising from the averments. It is then for the party against whom that presumption operates to lead evidence so as to counter its effect. For example, there is a common law presumption against donation which reflects the belief that people as a rule do not give away their money or their possessions to strangers. Thus, if I lend my lawnmower to my neighbour because hers is not working, and she subsequently refuses to return it, arguing that she thought it was a gift, I would have the benefit of a presumption against donation if I were to go to court seeking its return. In terms of the burden of proof in such a court action, as soon as I had shown that the lawnmower was in my neighbour's possession, and that I had not gifted it to her, I have discharged the persuasive burden. It would then be for her to rebut the presumption against donation—perhaps by producing a receipt for her payment to me![14]

CONCEPTUALISING THE STANDARD OF PROOF

6–20 Over the years, problems have arisen in determining the appropriate standard of proof in civil actions that either have dimensions of criminal activity or have consequences that have criminal sanctions. In all civil actions the standard of proof required is always proof on the balance of probabilities. However, some cases have created ambiguity by suggesting that where there is an element of criminal activity in a civil action, e.g. fraud in an insurance claim or in tax returns, or allegations of sexual abuse against a child in the context of divorce or separation, this requires a higher quality of evidence on order to tip the balance of probabilities.[15] Despite authority that firmly rejects the notion of a third or intermediate standard,[16] there is a significant body of case law that implies where criminal behaviour is averred the standard of proof is of a different quality if it is to succeed on a balance of probabilities. Such cases include alleged malpractice, potentially fraudulent tax returns to the Inland Revenue,[17] reduction of a deed for forgery[18] and allegations of professional misconduct in civil disciplinary proceedings but where there was a potential outcome of considerable severity.[19]

6–21   The language used in some cases often suggests the level of proof is of a standard somewhere between balance of probability and beyond reasonable

---

[14] *Penman v White*, 1957 S.C. 338 provides an illustration of the presumption against donation.
[15] For discussion see *L v L*, 1996 S.L.T. 767.
[16] *Brown v Brown*, 1972 S.C. 123; *Lamb v Lord Advocate*, 1976 S.C. 110.
[17] *Inland Revenue v Ruffle*, 1979 S.C. 371, and *Irving v Minister of Pensions*, 1945 S.C. 21.
[18] *Sereshky v Sereshky*, 1988 S.L.T. 426 at 427E, where Lord Weir observed that the standard of proof was less than that required in a criminal case but, "must be proved to a very high degree of probability having regard to the criminal implications involved".
[19] *Bhandari v Advocates Committee* [1956] 3 All ER 742.

doubt. Judicial dicta contribute to this ambiguity, on occasion creating the perception of an intermediate standard. For example, in *Lennon v Co-op Insurance Society Ltd*, Lord Kincraig, rather unhelpfully, opined[20]:

> "There is, in my judgment a higher onus on the defenders where such an allegation of wilful fire-raising is made. I am not able to state in words the extent of that onus, but it is enough that I consider that it is higher than on a balance of probabilities, somewhere half way between that and beyond reasonable doubt."

Similarly, in *Anderson v Lambie*,[21] a civil action for reduction of a probative deed, Lord Reid claimed that "a heavy onus" was placed upon the pursuer. In that case, the House of Lords held that the pursuer "has proved his case beyond reasonable doubt".[22]

Such terminology compounds the linguistic ambiguity over standards of **6–22** proof and is confusing in the context of civil cases, especially where no criminal conduct is alleged. However, these terms are better interpreted as emphasising the quality of evidence and degree of persuasion required of a pursuer in such an action. This point was made by Lord Allanbridge in *Sloan v Triplett*[23]:

> "Where a crime is alleged in a civil case in Scotland, the standard of proof required is based on probability, but the more serious the allegation, the higher the degree of probability that is required: but it need not, in a civil case, reach the very high standard required by the criminal law."

This last dictum is a more helpful interpretive approach in that it underlines that is not the *standard* of proof that alters when allegations of criminal behaviour are integral to a civil suit as much as the *quality* of the evidence required to satisfy that standard.

In his recommendations to the Scottish Law Commission,[24] the late Lord **6–23** (then Sheriff) Macphail confirmed the frequency with which, as a matter of practice, allegations of statutory crimes are accepted on a balance of probabilities in actions for damages for personal injuries. He cited the authority of *King v Patterson*,[25] in which it was held that it was for the defender to show "on a balance of probabilities, that the conviction was wrong and that the presumption of negligence has been rebutted".[26] Macphail recommended that in all cases in which a crime is alleged in the course of a civil action, the standard of proof should be on a balance of probabilities. He addressed the issue of the gravity of certain behaviour sometimes justifying a higher standard of proof by explaining that,"[t]he nature of the offence with which the court was concerned would cause variations in

---

[20] 1986 S.L.T. 98.
[21] 1954 S.C. (H.L.) 43.
[22] *Anderson v Lambie*, 1954 S.C. (H.L.) 43 at 63. See too *Rehman v Ahmad*, 1993 S.L.T. 741 per Lord Penrose at 745J.
[23] 1985 S.L.T. 294 at 296.
[24] Macphail, *Evidence*, para.22.33.
[25] 1971 S.L.T. (Notes) 40.
[26] *King v Patterson*, 1971 S.L.T. (Notes) at 40.

the *amount* of evidence required to tilt the balance of probability, but would not alter the standard of proof".[27]

6–24   Any ambiguity over an intermediate standard has now been authoritatively settled in the five bench decision in *Mullan v Anderson*.[28] In this case a widow whose husband had been murdered raised an action for damages against the man who had been acquitted of the murder. In her pleadings she alleged that the defender had indeed murdered her husband. The question arose as to what was the appropriate standard of proof. The appeal court had no difficulty in affirming that there was a "well established principle that in civil cases the standard of proof required of a pursuer is that he prove his case on a balance of probabilities".[29] Referring to some of the case law that proposed an intermediate standard, Lord Morrison declared:[30]

> "In my view these authorities are plainly insufficient to displace the well-established principle that in civil cases the standard of proof required of a pursuer is that he prove his case on a balance of probabilities, and the suggestion that there exists in Scotland some standard intermediate between balance of probabilities and beyond reasonable doubt must be rejected."

Lord Morrison went on to observe:[31]

> "My view that any civil case, including this one, must be determined on a balance of probabilities does not ignore the obvious fact that it is more difficult to prove, according to the required standard, an allegation of murder or serious crime, because it is inherently unlikely that a normal person will commit such a crime."

The point that "it is more difficult to prove" alluded to by Lord Morrison lies at the heart of any perceived confusion regarding the sufficiency of evidence required to persuade a court over the balance of probabilities.

CIVIL ACTIONS WITH CRIMINAL PENALTIES

6–25   When considering allegations of criminal activity in the context of a civil case, a distinction can be drawn between those cases where the pleadings contain averments that infer criminal activity, e.g. a forged document, and those cases which, if proven, lead to a criminal sanction or penalty. This section is concerned with the latter.

---

[27] Macphail, *Evidence*, Ch.22.34 (emphasis added). See the opinion of Lord Cowie in *Ashcroft's C.B. v Stewart (O.H.)*, 1988 S.L.T 163. The Scottish Law Commission (Memo 46, para.V 16) accepted his basic proposal, but see *Lennon v Co-operative Insurance Society*, n.38.

[28] 1993 S.L.T. 835.

[29] *Mullan v Anderson*, 1993 S.L.T. 835 at 842D.

[30] *Mullan v Anderson*, 1993 S.L.T. 835 at 842D.

[31] *Mullan v Anderson*, 1993 S.L.T. 835 at 842D.

Breach of interdict

An action for interdict is purely a civil action and, in itself, creates no **6–26**
criminal consequences. However, if a defender breaches an interdict then the
party who obtained it in the first place may raise an action for breach of
interdict.[32] In these circumstances, the possible sanctions upon proof of such
a breach include criminal penalties.[33] The concurrence of the Lord Advocate
is required before such an action may be raised. This is because the Crown
may proceed with a prosecution arising out of the alleged breach of interdict
and that would pre-empt any civil action. Despite the possibility of criminal
penalties, proceedings for breach of interdict are civil proceedings within the
meaning of s.1(1) of the Civil Evidence (Scotland) Act 1988 and corroboration is unnecessary.[34] However, since the proceedings have criminal
implications the question arises as to the appropriate standard of proof. In
Gribben v Gribben[35] it was held that where a wife raised an action alleging a
breach by her husband of an interim interdict to prevent him from molesting
her, she was required to prove the breach beyond reasonable doubt.

Breach of interdict is a breach of a court order and as such is a contempt **6–27**
of court. It is logical for proof beyond reasonable doubt to be the appropriate standard of proof for all cases of alleged contempt of court, of which
breach of interdict is only one example. Persons who are accused of contempt of court, an offence which is punishable with criminal penalties, such
as admonition, censure, fine or imprisonment, are entitled to all the protections and safeguards implicit in art.6 of the ECHR and the right to a fair
trial.[36]

Action of lawburrows

In *Morrow v Neil*[37] the pursuer brought an action under the ancient remedy **6–28**
of lawburrows[38] against her neighbours as she feared further assaults by
them. Noting that the standard of proof had never been determined, but
that since the case of *Brown v Brown*[39] he had only two standards of proof to
choose from, after assessing the merits and implications of each standard,

---

[32] Though if a party holds a matrimonial interdict with a power of arrest attached then the
police can invoke it immediately if a breach is suspected: Matrimonial Homes (Family
Protection) (Scotland) Act 1981 as amended by ss.10 and 32 of the Family Law (Scotland)
Act 2006. These provisions also amended s.1 of the Protection from Abuse (Scotland) Act
2001.
[33] See Scott Robinson, *The Law of Interdict*, 2nd edn (Edinburgh: Butterworths, 1994) Ch.16.
[34] *Byrne v Ross*, 1993 S.L.T. 307.
[35] 1976 S.L.T. 266, following *Eutectic Welding Alloys Ltd v Whitting*, 1969 S.L.T. (Notes) 79.
[36] See Macphail, *Evidence*, para.22.37, and *HM Advocate v Airs*, 1975 J.C. 64, in which all
contempts of court were judged to be essentially the same in nature. The Scottish Law
Commission opted also for proof beyond reasonable doubt in such cases (Memo. 46,
para.V.18). *Gribben* was followed in *Inland Revenue v Ruffle*, 1979 S.C. 371, in regard to a tax
penalty.
[37] 1975 S.L.T. (Sh. Ct) 65.
[38] Essentially a civil action brought by someone fearing harm to either themselves or their
family. The defender is required to find caution for good behaviour, with the threat of
imprisonment unless he or she does so. The circumstances of any breach may also be made
the subject of criminal charges: see Stair Memorial Encyclopaedia, *The Laws of Scotland*,
Vol.13, paras 901–926.
[39] 1972 S.C. 123, dealt with more fully below.

Sheriff Macphail held that that an the appropriate standard was proof on a balance of probabilities.

6–29   Situations where the criminal standard of proof beyond reasonable doubt has been held to apply include contempt of court.[40]

CHILDREN'S HEARINGS

6–30 In the Scottish Children's Hearings system, if the grounds of referral of a child to the Children's Panel are contested, they require to be proved in the sheriff court. The Children's Hearings (Scotland) Act 2011 came into force in June 2013 and overhauled the previous legislation in regard to children's hearings contained in the Children (Scotland) Act 1995. There are 17 grounds of referral under the new Act. If, following a referral to the Panel, the ground or grounds of referral are not accepted by the child or their parent or carer, then the case is sent to the sheriff court for a proof of the ground(s). The only ground that must be proven beyond reasonable doubt is that in terms of s.37(2)(j), i.e. that the child has committed an offence.[41]

---

[40] *Scottish Daily Record and Sunday Mail Ltd v Thomson* [2009] HCJAC 24;

[41] s.102(3) of the Children's Hearing (Scotland) Act 2011 applies where s.67(2)(j) is engaged. It provides "[t]he standard of proof in relation to the ground is that which applies in criminal proceedings".

Chapter 7

PRESUMPTIONS

INTRODUCTION

Normally, a party seeking to establish the existence of a fact must prove that **7–01** fact with evidence. However, in some circumstances even though a party may bear a burden of proof on a particular issue, there may be no need to lead all or any direct evidence to discharge that burden. There are four main situations when this arises:

   (i)   when a presumption operates in favour of a party;
  (ii)   when the matter is "judicially noted";
 (iii)   when a matter between the parties is said to be "*res judicata*"; and
 (iv)   when the point is formally admitted by the other party at the outset.

Later chapters discuss judicial notice, facts which are *res judicata* and formal admissions. This chapter concentrates on presumptions.

PRESUMPTIONS DEFINED

The law sometimes presumes a fact to exist without requiring proof. A **7–02** presumption has been defined as "an inference as to the existence of one fact, drawn from the existence of another fact".[1] Thus, a party may offer to the court certain facts from which the court is invited to conclude that other facts must also exist. For example, the fact that an accused person charged with a crime of dishonesty is found in "criminative" circumstances, and in possession of recently stolen property, is sufficient evidence to bring into operation a presumption that they are guilty of a crime of dishonesty in respect of that property. Fact A (the possession, etc.) gives rise to a suggestion that Fact B (the guilt of the accused) is established. A presumption is intended to expedite the process of proof. It obviates the need for evidence to be led in order to discharge the burden which a party would otherwise bear on the issue. The rationale for the rules relating to presumptions is that if a certain set of facts prevails, then ordinary human experience permits us to make certain inferences from those facts without the need for formal proof.

Presumptions are found in a wide variety of contexts, and may arise either **7–03** under statute or as the result of common law. In many cases their rationale

---

[1] Dickson, *Evidence*, para.109.

is founded upon practical convenience, public policy or long usage, and in some cases they fail to reflect modern attitudes and practices. There are too many presumptions to discuss all of them here—instead some of the more common ones are examined, along with others that may create particular difficulties.[2] Presumptions fall into three general categories, according to their effect on the evidence, if any, which has to be led once the particular presumption has been invoked: irrebuttable presumptions of law; rebuttable presumptions of law; rebuttable presumptions of fact. These are considered in turn.

IRREBUTTABLE PRESUMPTIONS OF LAW

7–04 An irrebuttable presumption of law is a presumption which has been established by either statute or common law and, once the basic facts which give rise to the presumption are proved, no evidence can be led which would be sufficient to counter it. In some contexts these presumptions can seem like legal fictions, but they will, at least historically, have a rationale and a purpose. An irrebuttable presumption is really a point of substantive law, but it impacts upon the evidence that needs to be led and possibly even whether proceedings can be raised at all. This can be illustrated with some examples relating to child protection and children's autonomy, where policy considerations have shaped irrebuttable presumptions.

(1) Presumptions relating to the age of a child

(a) Age of criminal responsibility

7–05 The age of criminal responsibility in Scotland is eight years. However, that does not mean that children of eight years can be prosecuted. Section 41A of the Criminal Procedure (Scotland) Act 1995 states "[a] person aged 12 years or more may not be prosecuted for an offence which was committed at a time when the person was under the age of 12 years". This is an irrebuttable presumption. There are no exceptions. Age is proven by the production of a valid birth certificate.

7–06 If a child under the age of 12 committed a crime he or she would likely be referred to the Children's Hearing system as in need of care and protection. These statutory provisions reflect the recommendations of the Scottish Law Commission *Report on Age of Criminal Responsibility*, published in 2002.[3]

7–07 A prosecutor cannot take any criminal proceedings against a child who has not reached the age of 12 years.[4]

7–08 Davidson reasonably points out that this provision is more accurately described as a rule of law rather than an irrebuttable presumption.[5] However, the presumptive element that underlies the rule is the proposition that,

---

[2] Textbooks dealing with the substantive law of a topic will generally include reference to relevant presumptions in their respective areas.

[3] Scot Law Com No.185.

[4] s.41A.

[5] *Evidence*, at para 4.46.

irrespective of a particular child's maturity and understanding, the law deems it impossible for any child under 12 to be capable of forming the necessary mens rea for the commission of a crime. This statutory presumption is a matter of public policy and the logic of a given age of criminal responsibility is of course challengeable. It is not self-evident, but a policy choice. Scotland's age of criminal responsibility is the lowest in Europe and it is frequently criticised for being contrary to human rights jurisprudence[6] and international conventions, such as the United Nations Convention on the Rights of the Child, 1989. The Scottish Law Commission recommended that the term "age of responsibility" should be abandoned in favour of the principle that children below a certain age should be immune from prosecution and that the earliest age at which a child could be prosecuted be raised from 8 to 12.[7] Instead the Scottish Parliament retained the age of eight as the age of criminal responsibility and raised the age at which a child could be prosecuted to 12 years (it was previously eight). In practice, as indicated above, most children between 8 and 12 years are likely to be referred to the Children's Hearing system and dealt with in its more child-focussed. welfare-orientated regime. At present, no child under 16 can be prosecuted without the consent of the Lord Advocate.

(b) Lack of sexual consent by a girl under 12

According to Hume,[8] a girl under the age of 12 was to be regarded as **7–09** incapable of giving the necessary consent to intercourse which would reduce a charge of rape to one of a less serious sexual offence. The origin of this rule has been said to be a legal presumption that a girl so young cannot give effective consent in a matter so serious.[9] Gordon describes the offence with which an accused is charged in such a case as one of "constructive rape".[10]

At common law, the age of 12 appears to have been chosen as it was **7–10** commensurate with the onset of puberty in a girl.[11] Puberty itself is of course not a fixed state—over the years it has been occurring at an earlier biological age. However, in the contemporary context of child protection and public policy there is little support for the age of consent to be lowered. Instead, statutory provisions ought to reflect the reality of sexually active teenagers. Both the draft Criminal Code for Scotland[12] and the Scottish Law Commission's *Report on Rape and Other Sexual Offences*[13] criticised the unsatisfactory state of the criminal law in regard to sexual offences and supported modernising the law. The Sexual Offences (Scotland) Act 2009 reflected these criticisms and radically changed the statutory rules. The new

---

[6] *T v UK and U v UK*, 2000 30 E.H.R.R.121.
[7] *Report on Age of Criminal Responsibility*, Scot Law Com No 185 at paras 3.19–3.20.
[8] Hume, I, 303.
[9] See, e.g. *Chas Sweenie* (1858) 3 Irv 109 at 138 and 147.
[10] *Criminal Law*, para.33–14.
[11] Stair, I, iv, 35.
[12] Available from the Scottish Law Commission at *www.scotlawcom.gov.uk*.
[13] Scot Law Com No.209. See too the preceding Discussion Paper on the topic, DP 131, 2006. The Report was made the subject of a Scottish Government Consultation in 2008 which informed the 2009 legislation.

provisions contain a number of presumptions which aim to satisfy the twin objectives of protecting children from sexual exploitation whilst recognising the sexual autonomy of older children and avoiding criminalising sexual behaviour unnecessarily. The following examples are selected to illustrate the way that statutory provisions are used to create presumptions[14] concerning sexual intercourse with a young person under 16 years of age. For example there is a new offence of having intercourse with an older child, older child being defined as aged 13 to 16 years at the time of the offence. The presumption is that a child within this age frame cannot give consent, although there is a defence of reasonable belief that the child was aged between 13 and 16, if in fact they were not.[15] In addition to vaginal penetration or intercourse, there is a whole range of new criminal offences based on penetrative sexual activities.[16]

(c) Capacity in the law of contract

7–11 The Age of Legal Capacity (Scotland) Act 1991, s.1, deems a child aged 16 years and over to have legal capacity to enter into any transaction. The Act took effect from September 25, 1991 and is not retrospective. Prior to it, a boy under 14 and a girl under 12[17] were deemed incapable of giving the consent necessary for the formation of a legally binding contract, and any contracts by a pupil had to be entered into through the medium of his or her tutor. The presumption of the pre-1991 position was reflected in the fact that any purported contract by a pupil would be regarded as a nullity.[18]

(2) Prescription

7–12 Prescription can both create and extinguish legal rights through the mechanism of the passage of time. The modern law is contained in the Prescription and Limitation (Scotland) Act 1973, which deals with both positive and negative prescriptions.[19] The effect of the positive prescription is to establish conclusively a party's right to an interest in land. This can arise where such a right is either founded upon a recorded title accompanied by 10 years' continuous possession; or upon 20 years of such possession, either in certain special cases, or where there is no foundation writ which the party claiming title would ordinarily be required to register. Once the party has established these facts, and there is no evidence of any "judicial interruption" of the qualifying period of possession (e.g. by court action), then the effect of s.1 of the 1973 Act is to exclude "all inquiry into the previous titles

---

[14] Readers who require a more detailed account of the changes to sexual offences should consult a criminal law book.

[15] s.39.

[16] For a detailed discussion of these see P. Ferguson and McDiamard, *Scots Criminal Law: A Critical Analysis* (Dundee: DUP, 2009).

[17] The ages again reflecting the legal view of the age of puberty: see Stair I, iv, 35.

[18] *McGibbon v McGibbon* (1852) 14 D. 605.

[19] For a detailed discussion see Gloag and Henderson, *Introduction to the Law of Scotland*, 13th edn (Edinburgh: W. Green, 2012) Ch.4.

and rights to the lands".[20] A 10-year prescriptive title is valid against the whole world.[21]

Negative prescription extinguishes certain obligations after they have been enforceable for 5, 10 or 20 years,[22] and have been neither claimed by the creditor nor acknowledged by the debtor. On proof of these facts, the court has to declare the obligation extinguished, since it is conclusively deemed to be so by statute. **7–13**

Every irrebuttable presumption of law, once invoked, has the effect of excluding further argument on the subject. Only a limited number of examples have been discussed here and numerous additional examples may be encountered under statute.[23] However, as with all presumptions, the basic facts must first be proven, so that in many cases a party must appear before a court in order to establish the facts necessary for the operation of the presumption in their favour. If the other party is then unable to refute the facts, the point will be settled in favour of the first party. **7–14**

REBUTTABLE PRESUMPTIONS OF LAW

Like the first category, rebuttable presumptions of law are the creation of law. This category of presumption is also known as a presumption *juris tantum*.[24] Unlike the first category, a rebuttable presumption may be countered by evidence to show that in the particular case it is unsafe to arrive at Conclusion B purely on the basis of Fact A. However, unless some rebutting evidence is produced, the conclusion almost certainly will be drawn. The effect of a presumption *juris tantum* is therefore to place a burden of proof on the party against whom it operates to lead evidence to prevent the operation of the presumption. **7–15**

In common with their irrebuttable counterparts, presumptions *juris tantum* may be created by statute[25] or common law, though in practice many of the best-known presumptions *juris tantum* are judge-made, e.g. the presumption against donation. Certain presumptions, including those relating to commercial life or medical science, are prone to become quickly **7–16**

---

[20] See Gloag and Henderson, *Introduction to the Law of Scotland*, 13th edn, paras 34.30–34.37. So final is the effect of this presumption that it forms the basis of the modern conveyancing practice of seeking only a 10 year prescriptive process of titles when confirming that the seller has title to the subjects of the disposition.

[21] The presumption being that the title is valid. It would seem to proceed upon what Lord Chancellor Halsbury, in *Clippens Oil Co Ltd v Edinburgh and District Water Trs*, 1903 6 F. (H.L.) 7, referred to at p.8 as "that principle of presumption in favour of long-continued use or possession, from which the presumption arises that such use or possession was lawful in its origin".

[22] ss.6, 22A and 7 respectively of the 1973 Act as amended—the appropriate period depends upon the nature of the obligation.

[23] e.g. Companies Act 1985, s.13(7) of which makes a certificate of incorporation "conclusive" evidence of (i) the existence of the company from the date thereof, and (ii) compliance with all the statutory formalities of incorporation: see Gloag and Henderson, *Introduction to the Law of Scotland*, Ch.51.7.

[24] Walker and Walker, *Law of Evidence in Scotland*, para.3.1.1.

[25] See, for example that created by s.13 of the Bills of Exchange Act 1882, under which a bill of exchange, and any acceptances and endorsements thereon, are presumed, until the contrary is proved, to have been executed on the dates which they bear.

overtaken by technological advances. For example, *G's Trs v G*[26] laid down the rebuttable presumption that, in any case where no interests are affected, other than a possible unborn child, a woman of 53 years or older is incapable of child-bearing.[27] This is a presumption that would be more easily rebutted today given recent advances in reproductive technology as the facilities now exist to permit women to bear children at a much later age than was once assumed possible.

7–17   Some of the better-known presumptions are discussed below as illustrations of the concept. First though, we should acknowledge an important general presumption that impacts on all areas of law, that of *omnia praesumuntur rite et solemniter acta esse*, a phrase usually referred to by its shortened name, *omnia praesumuntur*. It means that there is a general presumption that where an act is performed in accordance with normal procedure, it is an act lawfully and properly done. In the words of Lord Chancellor Halsbury in *Bain v Assets Co*,[28] "every intendment should be made in favour of what has been done as being lawfully and properly done".

7–18   In all cases involving the presumption *omnia praesumuntur*, the use of a valid process is taken to be evidence of the validity of the action taken under that process. Thus, where a person purports without challenge to act in an official capacity, the law presumes they were duly appointed.[29] Similarly, a decree duly recorded in old judicial records will be presumed to have been validly and properly pronounced.[30] The doctrine of *omnia praesumuntur* extends to a mixed range of business or administrative practices, which may be used to set up a presumption that they were followed on a particular occasion simply because they are normally followed.[31] They include the validity of a marriage based upon the performance of the formalities of a wedding ceremony and the issue of an authorised certificate.[32] The rationale of the principle *omnia praesumuntur* was provided by Lord Simons in *Morris v Kanssen*,[33] who observed, "[t]he wheels of business will not go smoothly round unless it is assumed that that is in order which appears to be in order".

7–19   Three areas of law are used to illustrate where rebuttable presumptions operate on a regular basis to permit the "wheels of business" to go round smoothly.

(a) Criminal law

7–20   The common law presumption of innocence of an accused person is intimately connected to the persuasive burden of proof of guilt that rests on the prosecution. The presumption also has statutory form by virtue of the incorporation of the ECHR into domestic law. As discussed in Ch.5, art.6(2) of the ECHR states that "[e]veryone charged with a criminal offence shall be

---

[26] 1936 S.C. 837.
[27] For an example of a similar presumption of a man's ability to father a child see *Munro's Trustees v Monson*, 1965 S.C. 85.
[28] (1905) 7 F. (H.L.) 104 at 106.
[29] As in *Marr v Procurator Fiscal of Midlothian* (1881) 8 R.(J.) 21, in which the presence on the bench of an interim sheriff substitute was taken to be evidence of his appointment.
[30] *Duke of Athole v Lord Advocate* (1880) 7 R. 583 at 589.
[31] *Edinburgh District Council v MacDonald*, 1979 S.L.T. (Sh. Ct) 58.
[32] *Burke v Burke*, 1983 S.L.T. 331.
[33] [1946] A.C. 459 at 475.

presumed innocent until proved guilty according to law". This presumption is operative from the point of charge—there are no facts that require to be proved before an accused person has the benefit of the presumption. The responsibility of displacing the presumption lies with the prosecution.

Equally, every accused person is presumed to be sane. Thus, if an accused **7–21** person claims that due to mental disorder they were not criminally responsible for their actions at the time of the commission of the offence, they carry the persuasive burden of proof to demonstrate this.[34] An accused person who pleads mental disorder or diminished responsibility in order to argue that they were not responsible for their actions will therefore need to adduce psychiatric and/or psychological evidence to discharge the persuasive burden and rebut the presumption of sanity.[35]

(b) Family law including succession

Ownership of moveables

The Family Law (Scotland) Act 1985 contains two presumptions designed **7–22** to settle arguments over the division of moveable property during or after a marriage or civil partnership.[36] First, it is presumed that household goods are owned equally by the spouses or civil partners.[37] Second, it is presumed that any savings made from a household allowance paid by one spouse or civil partner to another is owned equally.[38]

Presumption of continuance—domicile of origin

There is a general presumption of continuance that arises quite often in **7–23** family law cases (though not exclusively so) concerning status and domicile. Dickson noted the existence of a common law presumption to the effect that conditions which are proved to have existed at one time may be presumed to have continued in existence.[39] There is a well-established common law rule[40] that a person's domicile of origin (i.e. the domicile acquired at birth) is presumed to continue as their domicile for legal purposes until they are shown to have acquired another domicile not only by residence (*facto*) but also by intentionally abandoning that domicile of origin (*animo*). The persuasive burden of proof rests with the party seeking to rebut the presumption and rely upon the new domicile.[41]

---

[34] Criminal Procedure (Scotland) Act ss.51A and 51B.
[35] The standard of proof being a balance of probabilities: see Ch.6.
[36] For ownership of moveable property generally there is a common law rebuttable presumption that the person in possession of it is the rightful owner: Lord President Cooper in *George Hopkinson Ltd v Napier & Sons*, 1963 S.C. 139. For detailed discussion see Gloag and Henderson, *Introduction to the Law of Scotland*, 13th edn, Ch.31.
[37] s.25(1) as amended by para.28 of Sch.28 to the Civil Partnership Act 2004.
[38] s.26 as amended by para.29 of Sch.28 to the Civil Partnership Act 2004.
[39] Dickson, *Evidence*, para.114(5) and Walker and Walker, *Law of Evidence in Scotland*, para.3.5.1.
[40] Dickson, *Evidence*, para.27.
[41] *Liverpool Royal Infirmary v Ramsay*, 1930 S.C. (H.L.) 83.

Presumption of continuance—presumption of death

7–24 At common law, there is a general presumption that human life extends for a period of between 80 and 100 years. In the absence of specific indications to the contrary, a person cannot be presumed dead until he or she has reached at least 80 years. There are two statutory exceptions to this general rule: first in terms of the Succession (Scotland) Act 1964, where a person dies in a "common calamity"; and second, in terms of the Presumption of Death (Scotland) Act 1977 where a person is not known to be alive for at least seven years. The statutory presumption of death is discussed below. First, the common law rule is examined in circumstances in which neither statutory provision applies, e.g. if a person has not been missing for seven years, and the case is not one involving succession.

7–25 The common law rule is illustrated in *Secretary of State v Sutherland*.[42] The defender, Mrs Sutherland, found that her right to a pension depended upon the validity of her marriage to Mr Sutherland, a point which was in turn dependent upon whether or not her previous husband was still alive. If he was still alive, he would have been 72 at the date of the hearing, but evidence was given that he had deserted Mrs Sutherland some 44 years previously and had not been heard of for the past 40 years. Mrs Sutherland had heard a rumour to the effect that he had died many years before, but she had not bothered to investigate. The underlying legal principle was neatly summarised by Lord Moncrieff,[43] who ruled that:

> "[While] in a case in which there are no special features our common law assumes life will continue up to the age of eighty years[44] or even longer, it is always a jury question in each particular case whether or not the presumption of continuance of life has been displaced. The considerations which influence a finding for or against that presumption have long been well established; either there must be direct proof of something amounting to a proper *casus amissiones*, or there must at least be facts and circumstances indicating such a break in the continuing relations of the absentee as would have been wholly out of character with his conduct had he been in life."

The court held there was no reason why Mrs Sutherland would have seen her first husband, and indeed, in the words of Lord Normand, they "had every motive for avoiding one another". The wife therefore failed to discharge the onus of proof placed upon her of proving that he was dead, and therefore failed in her claim for pension rights as the widow of the second "husband". It was also held that the presumption of death after seven years' absence, which could be invoked under the Divorce (Scotland) Act 1938[45] did not diminish her burden of proof, since it was relevant only on a direct application for declarator of death and dissolution of marriage.[46]

---

[42] 1944 S.C. 79.
[43] At 85–86.
[44] The period suggested by the Institutional writers; Lord President Normand at 84 referred to "a period of between eighty and a hundred years".
[45] Now subsumed under the 1977 Act.
[46] For an illustration of the sort of circumstances in which the common law presumption can be rebutted, see *Greig v Merchant Company of Edinburgh*, 1921 S.C (H.L.) 83.

As a counterweight to the common law presumption of life (at least until **7–26** a person has reached the age of 80), which can produce inequitable outcomes, there are statutory provisions which can be used in two principal sets of circumstances. The first set of circumstances applies when two persons die in what is referred to as a "common calamity".[47] At common law there would be no presumption as to which of them died first. If, for example, father and son died in a house fire or an air crash, there would be no presumption that the son had survived the father, so as to regulate the problems of succession which might thereby arise. Some of the older authorities reveal that such a rule could clearly defeat the testamentary intentions of the parties. For example, in *Drummond's Judicial Factor v HM Advocate*[48] the court held that there was no presumption under Scots common law as to survivorship among those killed in a common calamity. In order to prove survivorship, some factual evidence was required.[49] In the absence of that, the wife's savings fell to the Crown as *ultimus haeres*.

This potentially harsh outcome of the common law led to the enactment **7–27** of s.31 of the Succession (Scotland) Act 1964 in order to regulate succession. Under the section, where two persons have died in circumstances indicating that they died simultaneously, or rendering it uncertain which of them (if either) survived the other, then there is a presumption that they died in order of seniority, that is, that the younger survived the elder. There are two exceptions to this rule. If either apply the old common law rule will prevail and no survivorship will be presumed.

The first exception is where the two persons in question are married or **7–28** civilly partnered. There is then a statutory presumption that neither survived the other.[50] The second exception is where the older person (i.e. the one presumed to have died first) has left a testamentary provision in favour of the younger (i.e. the presumed survivor), whom failing to some third party, and that younger person has died intestate. In such a case, to enable the third party beneficiary to inherit that testamentary provision, there is a presumption that the older person survived the younger, thus enabling the legacy to pass to the third party. The presumption only applies where two people die in circumstances that render it uncertain which of them survived the other. If there is evidence that one of them survived the other, then s.31 does not apply at all.[51]

The second set of circumstances is when a person is missing, presumed **7–29** dead. By virtue of s.1 of the Presumption of Death Act 1977 any person "having an interest"[52] may apply to the court for a declarator that a person who is missing is in fact dead. This may be for any legal purpose, such as divorce or inheritance. The pursuer must produce either evidence that points to the conclusion that the missing person has died, or evidence to the effect that he or she "has not been known to be alive for a period of at least seven years". The standard of proof is on a balance of probabilities.[53]

---

[47] i.e. circumstances, not necessarily the same incident, in which two people are found to be dead such that it is impossible to tell which, if either, died first.

[48] 1944 S.C. (H.L.) 298.

[49] *Ross v Martin*, 1955 S.C. (H.L.) 56.

[50] s.1(1).

[51] *Lamb v Lord Advocate*, 1976 S.L.T. 151 per Lord Wheatley at 153.

[52] Which can include the Lord Advocate, for the public interest, per s.17.

[53] s.2.

Presumption of fatherhood

7–30 The status of illegitimacy was abolished by s.21 of the Family Law (Scotland) Act 2006 which came into force on May 4, 2006. Previous presumptions of legitimacy have now much less significance in the law of evidence. However, one remaining aspect is contained in s.5 of the Law Reform (Parent and Child) (Scotland) Act 1986 which provides that:

> "(1) A man shall be presumed to be the father of a child—
>
> > (a) if he was married to the mother of the child at any time in the period beginning with the conception and ending with the birth of the child;
> >
> > (b) where paragraph (a) does not apply, if both he and the mother of the child have acknowledged that he is the father and he has been registered as such in any register kept under section 13 ... or section 44 ... of the Registration of Births, Deaths and Marriages (Scotland) Act 1965 or in any corresponding register kept under statutory authority in any part of the United Kingdom other than Scotland."

Subsection (4) provides that "[a]ny presumption under this section may be rebutted on a balance of probabilities". Thus, once the facts come within s.5(1)(a), even if a husband denies that he is the father of the child, it will be presumed that he is, until he is able to prove otherwise on a balance of probabilities.[54]

7–31 The only situation in which there is now no presumption of legitimacy, either at common law or under the 1986 Act, is that in which the husband marries the mother of the child after its birth and fails to comply with the provisions of s.5(1)(b). There is no presumption that, if a man marries a woman who has an illegitimate child, that child is his child.[55] The burden of proof to produce positive evidence of legitimacy is on the party seeking to prove that a child born outside the marriage is in fact the child of the subsequent husband.

Rebuttable Presumptions of Fact

7–32 The final category discussed here is that of rebuttable presumptions of fact. These do not arise from the operation of an established legal principle, but from the facts specific to a particular case. When these facts are taken together and read in the context of knowledge derived from common human experience they may amount to a rebuttable presumption of fact. Because rebuttable presumptions of fact arise from a set of facts and not from legal principle, they are difficult to classify and do not make particularly reliable precedents. In one sense this set of facts constitutes nothing more than circumstantial evidence. Nonetheless, because human experience in certain

---

[54] Such evidence may take the form of blood tests which can be used to provide a genetic fingerprint through DNA techniques. See s.6.

[55] *Brooks' Executrix v James*, 1971 S.C. (H.L.) 77 per Lord Reid at 81.

circumstances suggests proof of set of Facts A and B usually means Fact C is proven too, the set of facts in question are considered to raise a presumption that imposes a burden of proof on the party against whom they operate. This party then needs to produce some evidence in rebuttal of Facts A and B if Fact C is not to be deemed proven as well.

The main distinction between a rebuttable presumpsion of law and an **7–33** equivalent one of fact is that the former is usually invoked by the production of relatively few facts which are required by law, and which are well identified in advance. In contrast, the latter may require a whole battery of facts of an imprecise nature before the court is persuaded that a presumption operates. For example, as was seen earlier, the legitimacy of a person can be presumed by adducing evidence he or she was born during the continuance of their parents' marriage. Once these facts are established the presumption must be invoked, although it may of course be rebutted.

Unlike circumstantial items taken singly, the facts that together invoke **7–34** the presumption of fact also impose a burden of proof on the party against whom they operate. If that party is unable to discharge their burden they will almost certainly lose on that issue.[56] Two of the more common presumptions of fact are now considered.

Presumption of guilt from possession of recently stolen property

There are rare occasions when there is sufficient proof of a particular set of **7–35** facts to create, in effect, a presumption of guilt, such that it becomes especially pressing for the accused to provide an explanation to prevent being convicted. For example, if an accused person is found in possession of recently stolen property in "criminative" circumstances, there is a sense in which it is argued the persuasive burden shifts to the accused to offer evidence to rebut a presumption of guilt. In the principal authority on this point, *Fox v Patterson*,[57] Lord Justice General Cooper explained that, provided three conditions were met—possession of stolen goods; a short interval between theft and discovery[58]; and other criminative circumstances beyond the bare fact of possession—the full effect of the rule was "in shifting the onus from the prosecution to the accused, and raising a presumption of guilt which the accused must re-argue or fail".[59]

This dictum has been criticised by Gordon who declared Lord Cooper's **7–36** attempt to define the conditions when the onus shifts as "misleading and tautologous".[60] Gordon argues that the fact of possession of recently stolen goods in criminative circumstances is merely a cogent item of circumstantial evidence and claims there is no historical basis for any persuasive burden to

---

[56] For examples of the process in action, see *Pickup v Thames Insurance Co.* (1878) 3 Q.B.D. 594, especially at 599, and *Klein v Lindsay*, 1911 S.C. (H.L.) 9.

[57] 1948 J.C. 104, followed in many subsequent cases, including *Simpson v HM Advocate*, 1952 J.C. 1; *Brannan v HM Advocate*, 1954 J.C. 87; and *Cassidy v McLeod*, 1981 S.C.C.R. 270.

[58] It was noted obiter in *L v Wilson*, 1995 J.C. 29, that possession seven days after the theft was too long a period to be recent.

[59] *Fox v Patterson*, 1948 J.C. 104 at 108. The same assertion was made in *Cameron v HM Advocate*, 1959 J.C. 59 at 63, and *Cryans v Nixon*, 1955 J.C. 1 at 6.

[60] G. Gordon, "The Burden of Proof on the Accused", 1968 S.L.T. (News) 29 at 42.

be placed on an accused found in such circumstances.[61] The so-called presumption is therefore arguably no more than any illustration of the inferences that a trier of fact could be expected to draw from a given set of facts presented by the Crown. The accused found in possession of property shortly after it was stolen, in circumstances suggestive of guilt, has "a lot of explaining to do", in the face of a formidable body of circumstantial evidence. But the onus falling upon an accused is not a persuasive burden, but an evidential one to lead some evidence to raise a reasonable doubt and counter the presumption established by the Crown.

7–37   Mere recent possession of stolen goods is not enough to raise the presumption. There must be *some* other criminative circumstances. In *Fox*, the appeal court held there was not even sufficient evidence of possession on the part of the accused shortly after the theft, let alone any evidence that he had attempted to conceal his actions. There therefore could not have been any "criminative circumstances" such as to invoke the presumption and the conviction was set aside.

7–38   It seems from the authorities that the three constituent factors of the presumption—possession, brevity of time since the theft, and criminative circumstances—may be used to complement each other. Thus, strong evidence of recent possession may compensate for relatively weak additional evidence of criminative circumstances, and vice versa. As Lord Justice-Clerk Thomson put it in *Cryans v Nixon*[62]:

> "The necessity for the presence of other criminative circumstances arises because the degree and character of possession may vary greatly, and the fact of possession may be so bare as not by itself to be incriminating. Of course, the fact of possession may be in the circumstances so suspicious that very little in the way of incriminating circumstance may be enough ... Very different circumstances may rule according to whether a stolen article is found in an accused's pocket or in his back garden."[63]

The necessary criminative circumstances may come from all manner of sources. For example, in *Cameron v HM Advocate*[64] the criminative circumstance which secured the accused's conviction was the fact that he ordered his wife to throw the stolen property out of the window only seconds before the police knocked on his door. In *Cassidy v McLeod*,[65] on the other hand, it came from a persuasive series of circumstantial items of evidence. The presumption may be invoked in respect of any offence

---

[61] G. Gordon, "The Burden of Proof on the Accused", 1968 S.L.T. (News) 29 at 40–43, in which he describes this doctrine as "[t]he clearest example of the tendency to discuss a tactical burden of proof in terms which suggest that it is a persuasive burden".

[62] *Cryans v Nixon*, 1955 J.C. 1 at 5. The necessary possession must occur in a personal capacity, and not, e.g. as an employee: *Simpson v HM Advocate*, 1952 J.C. 1. In *MacLennan v Mackenzie*, 1988 S.L.T. 16, where possession more than two months after the theft was not recent.

[63] Nor may the accused's silence when cautioned and charged, or thereafter, be said to constitute criminative circumstances: see *Wightman and Collins v HM Advocate*, 1959 J.C. 44. A failure to answer preliminary police questions, or a false explanation, may however be sufficient—see *Cryans v Nixon*, 1959 J.C. 1.

[64] 1959 J.C. 59.

[65] S.C.C.R. 270.

involving theft, including aggravated theft,[66] and whether the accused is charged as actor or art and part.[67] It will also support a conviction for reset.[68]

To conclude, where the facts suggest an accused person has custody of **7–39** recently stolen goods, those facts give rise to an inference of guilt that may be sufficiently strong to permit the Crown to discharge their persuasive burden of proving guilt beyond reasonable doubt. To prevent this occurring, the accused has to put forward some explanation such as to persuade a trier of fact that a reasonable doubt exists.[69] Since the enactment of the Human Rights Act it would not be appropriate to interpret any presumption in the common law as placing anything other than an evidential burden on the accused.

Presumption of negligence, known as res ipsa loquitor

In an action arising from the alleged negligence of the defender, in some **7–40** circumstances the courts can infer negligence on the part of the defender from the facts adduced in proof by the pursuer. In order to succeed a defender then needs to produce evidence to rebut that inference of negligence.[70] In *Gunn v McAdam & Son*[71] a railway company was held liable for the negligence of its employees when an unmanned and loaded bogey (trolley) careered down the rail track and collided with another trolley whose operator was killed. The loaded bogey had been on an incline and supposedly held by a brake and a scotch (block) against a wheel. The pursuer, the widow of the deceased trolley operator, was unable to explain precisely how the accident had happened. It occurred in darkness and the runaway trolley was unlit. However, the appeal court overturned the decision of the Lord Ordinary and held that the pursuer had demonstrated "a relevant case of prima facie fault against the contractors, giving them the amplest notice of the case against them, and, I think, clamorously calling for some explanation from them".[72] Later, Lord President Cooper said:

> "In that situation it seems to me that the onus has completely shifted on to the first-named defenders to account for what happened consistently with the observation of the most elementary precautions for the safety of those whom they knew were going up that line on a single track a few miles away."[73]

The pursuer's pleadings in the court action and the evidence led thus raised a presumption of negligence that was never rebutted by defence evidence. This

---

[66] *Christie v HM Advocate*, 1939 J.C. 72; *Cameron v HM* Advocate, 1959 J.C. 59 at 63.
[67] *Christie v HM Advocate*, 1939 J.C. 72.
[68] *Christie v HM Advocate*, 1939 J.C. 72 and *Cameron v HM* Advocate, 1959 J.C. 59 at 63.
[69] G. Gordon, "The Burden of Proof on the Accused", 1968 S.L.T. (News) 29 at 43, who recommends a rule to the effect that "guilt can be proved by circumstantial evidence".
[70] e.g. *Inglis v L.M.S.*, 941 S.C. 551, discussed in Ch.6.
[71] 1949 S.C. 31.
[72] *Gunn v McAdam & Son*, 1949 S.C. 31, at p.40.
[73] *Gunn v McAdam & Son*, 1949 S.C. 31, at p.40.

presumption is known as the doctrine of res ipsa loquitur,[74] the development of which has attracted much criticism.[75]

7–41   The doctrine of res ipsa loquitor emerged in *Scott v London and St Katherine Docks Co*,[76] a case in which a barrel had fallen from the window of a warehouse owned and operated by the defenders and injured the plaintiff. In his judgment Erle C.J. observed:

> "There must be reasonable evidence of negligence. But where the thing is shown to be under the management of the defender and his servants, and the accident is such as in the ordinary course of things does not happen if those who have the management use proper care, it affords reasonable evidence, in the absence of explanation by the defendants, that the accident arose from want of care."

Res ipsa loquitor has been applied in many Scottish cases.[77] In the five bench House of Lords decision in *Ballard v North British Railway Company*[78] Lord Shaw was at pains to point out that res ipsa loquitor was a maxim and not a legal principle, pithily observing, "[i]f that phrase had not been in Latin, nobody would have called it a principle".[79] As a maxim, it is therefore merely a presumption of fact and its force depends on the facts in each case. The authorities show that it is limited to cases in which the facts are so suggestive of liability on the part of the defenders that the court will look to them for an explanation of what happened, which is at least consistent with a lack of negligence on their part. According to Lord Moncrieff in *O'Hara v Central S.M.T. Co.*[80]:

> "The characteristic of such cases is, or in my opinion ought to be, that the action or conduct which is charged as negligent has not been open to observation by witnesses, and so must be spoken to by according a voice to the subsequent event itself."

The leading modern authority on res ipsa loquitur is *Devine v Colvilles Ltd*[81] where a steelworks employee was injured after jumping 15 feet from a platform on which he had been working. He jumped because of a violent explosion nearby which had alarmed him. The cause of the explosion was unexplained, but was known to have resulted from a fire in a hose conveying oxygen to a converter. It was established that the defenders were responsible for filtering impurities from the oxygen stream, but they could not prove that their filters were working properly. Even after accepting the opinion of the court below (the Inner House of the Court of Session) that "the maxim

---

[74] i.e. things speak for themselves.
[75] See, for example, P. S. Atiyah, "Res Ipsa Loquitor in England and Australia" (1972) *Modern Law Review*, 344. For recent misapplications of the principle, see *Fryer v Pearson and Another* [2000] T.L.R. 260 and *Dewar v Winton*, 1999 S.C.L.R. 1014.
[76] (1865) 3 H. & C. 596 at 601.
[77] For example, *Milliken v Glasgow Corporation*, 1918 S.C. 857; *Craig v Glasgow Corporation*, 1919 S.C. (H.L.) 1; *Moffat v Park* (1877) 5 R. 13.
[78] 1923 S.L.T. 219.
[79] *Ballard v North British Railway Company*, 1923 S.L.T. 219 at 227.
[80] 1941 S.C. 363 at 388.
[81] 1969 S.L.T. 154.

[of res ipsa loquitur] is of limited ambit",[82] the House of Lords nevertheless had no doubt that it applied in this situation. In the words of Lord Guest[83]:

> "The res which is said to speak for itself was the explosion. I must say that, without evidence to the contrary, I should have thought it self evident that an explosion of such violence that causes fear of imminent danger to the workers does not occur in the ordinary course of things in a steel works if those who have the management use proper care ... [The appellants] are absolved if they can give a reasonable explanation of the accident and show this explanation was consistent with no lack of care on their part."

The court held that the defenders had failed to show that the filters for which they were responsible had been working properly. They could not therefore rebut the presumption of negligence raised against them.

It would seem, therefore, that res ipsa loquitur will only normally operate **7–42** where (a) there is no direct evidence of how an accident happened; and (b) the fact that the cause of the accident was something within the exclusive management and control of the defender. The presumption will not apply when there is some direct evidence of what happened,[84] or where the offending item was not in the exclusive management or control of the defender.[85]

---

[82] *Devine v Colvilles Ltd*, 1969 S.L.T. 154, Lord Guest at 154.
[83] *Devine v Colvilles Ltd*, 1969 S.L.T. 154, 154–155.
[84] See e.g. *O'Hara v Central S.M.T.*, 1941 S.C. 363 at 388.
[85] *McLeod v Glasgow Corp*, 1971 S.L.T. (Notes) 64; *Murray v Edinburgh D.C.*, 1981 S.L.T. 253; *Carrigan v Mavisbank Rigging Co*, 1983 S.L.T. 316.

Chapter 8

PROOF AND SUFFICIENCY OF EVIDENCE

INTRODUCTION

8–01 A fact is not proven unless there is sufficient evidence to support that conclusion. At the time of publication of this book, Scotland was unique in retaining a general principle that crucial facts in criminal cases cannot be proved by the testimony of one witness alone, but must be corroborated by evidence derived from a second independent source. According to Sir Gerald Gordon, writing in 1993, the corroboration requirement "is generally regarded by Scots lawyers as one of the most notable and precious features of Scots criminal law".[1] However, all that seems poised to change. In June 2013 the Scottish Government introduced legislation to abolish the centuries old rule of corroboration.[2] If enacted this will align Scots law with the position elsewhere in the common law world, where all other jurisdictions have long since abandoned a general rule of corroboration in favour of a regime which evaluates the weight to be accorded to a single item of evidence based on its reliability. The debates over the proposal to abolish corroboration occupy opposite ends of a spectrum. There are those who see abolition as a progressive move towards a more modern "free proof" approach to establishing facts. There are others who see the removal of the corroboration rule as significantly increasing the risk of miscarriages of justice. In 2010, following the decision of the UK Supreme Court in the case of *Cadder*,[3] the Rt Hon Lord Carloway was appointed by the Scottish Government to conduct a review of the law and practice of detaining and questioning suspects in a criminal investigation and to make recommendations for legislative change and new guidance. The Review process led to the Carloway Report,[4] as well as two public consultations by Scottish Government. The first of these was on the merits of the recommendations in the Carloway Review, central to which was the recommendation that corroboration be abolished.[5] The second consultation was on the type of changes that might be required to the criminal justice system if corroboration were to be removed.[6] Extensive responses were made to the

---

[1] G. Gordon, "At the mouth of Two witnesses: some comments on corroboration", in *Justice and Crime—essays in honour of the Rt Hon the Lord Emslie* (Edinburgh: T & T Clark, 1993) at 33.

[2] Criminal Justice (Scotland) Bill 2013.

[3] *Cadder v HM Advocate* [2010] UKSC 43 (SC).

[4] The *Carloway Review: Report and Recommendations* (Scottish Government, 2011).

[5] The *Carloway Review*: Scottish Government Consultation Paper, 2012.

[6] *Reforming Scots Criminal Law and Practice: Additional Safeguards Following the Removal of the Requirement for Corroboration.*

first consultation.[7] Many of the detailed arguments in the debate were also analysed in various academic and practitioner publications.[8] Proponents of abolition include many of the organisations which support victims of crime, e.g. Victim Support, Rape Crisis Scotland and Scottish Women's Aid, as well as ACPOS (the Chief Police Officers for Scotland), though their support is not without some reservations. Opponents of abolition included the judiciary (Lord Carloway excepted), the Faculty of Advocates and the Law Society of Scotland whose concern focussed on the loss of a rule that served a valuable purpose in preventing miscarriages of justice.

Abolition is proposed in s.57 of the Criminal Justice (Scotland) Bill 2013 **8–02** which provides:

"(1) This section—

(a) relates to any criminal proceedings,
(b) is subject to sections 58 and 59.

(2) If satisfied that a fact has been established by evidence in the proceedings, the judge or (as the case may be) the jury is entitled to find the fact proved by the evidence although the evidence is not corroborated."

Legislation that declares corroboration is no longer required is quite distinct from a law that seeks to prevent corroboration being admitted in court.

The above provision concerns the common law. Section 78 excludes **8–03** statutory requirements for corroboration from the ambit of the proposed legislation. It provides:

"Section 57 does not affect the operation of any enactment which provides in relation to the proceedings for an offence that a fact can be proved only by corroborated evidence."

Section 59 provides that s.57 does not take effect until a date appointed for that purpose, and importantly, in circumstances where corroboration might be applied to prove part of a course of continuing conduct, the start date of such conduct is permitted to pre-date the date of the section coming into force. This is enabled through a "deeming clause"[9] and is clearly intended to capture cases prosecuted using the *Moorov* doctrine, discussed later in this chapter.

The terms of s.57 may reassure some opponents to abolition as it does not **8–04** seek to abolish corroboration, merely to state that it is no longer a requirement. This is an important distinction. While the abolition of a corroboration requirement dispenses with the *need* for a second independent source of evidence to prove a fact, that does not mean that those who

---

[7] "*Reforming Scots Criminal Law and practice: The Carloway Report—analysis of consultation responses*". Scottish Government, 2012 at *http://www.scotland.gov.uk/Resource/0041/00410913.pdf* [accessed July 29, 2013].

[8] See, for example, P. R. Ferguson and F. E. Raitt, "A Clear and Coherent Package of Reforms: The Scottish Government consultation paper on the Carloway Report?" in 2012 Crim.L.R. 909, and D.Nicolson and J.Blackie, "Corroboration in Scots Law: 'archaic rule' or 'invaluable safeguard'?" 2013 Edin. L.R. 152.

[9] s.60, Criminal Justice (Scotland) Bill 2013.

investigate and prosecute crime will stop searching for as much evidence as they can reasonably obtain to justify an arrest or to achieve a conviction. The terms of s.57 envisage the use of corroborating evidence, if required, in order to establish a fact and ensure sufficiency to the criminal standard of *beyond reasonable doubt*. This continues the current arrangements which accord the fact-finder a high degree of discretion in assessing the weight to be attached to individual items of evidence. No case in the civil or criminal courts can ever succeed unless there is sufficient evidence at a proof or a trial respectively. The *sufficiency* of evidence required for a case to succeed is a well-established principle in the Scottish legal system and that principle will continue to operate within the framework of a fair trial, and to the required standard of proof, regardless of whether or not a formal rule of corroboration is in place.

8–05   An analogy can be drawn with civil law. When the need for corroboration in Scottish civil cases was removed in 1988, it affected the way that pleadings were drafted and cases argued to the extent that solicitors and counsel were able to pursue cases where the pursuer was the only witness to their accident or other event underpinning the litigation. That did not deter the diligent lawyer from seeking any available evidence possible to support the pursuer's case and courts were not persuaded on the proof of a claim unless it was credible and supported by sufficient evidence. While quality of evidence is the principal factor, where there are plausible competing accounts of the facts there may be a need to have quantity as well to succeed. The experience of other adversarial jurisdictions which have abolished corroboration demonstrate that even if the formal rule is removed, in practice, in criminal cases in particular, the prosecutor has a duty to ensure there is enough evidence to justify prosecuting in the public interest. The experience in England and Wales, where any lingering corroboration rules were fully abolished in 1994 by the Criminal Justice and Public Order Act, s.32(1). Roberts and Zuckerman have observed "[a]bolishing the law of corroboration no more dispenses with epistemic standards for assessing evidential support than abolishing the law of hearsay would cure the inherent infirmities of second-hand evidence".

The Effect of Corroborating Evidence

8–06   As noted above, the terms of s.57 envisage the use of corroborating evidence, if required to establish a fact and ensure sufficiency. It would therefore be premature to ignore the existing body of case law concerning corroboration especially in those difficult areas of law, where obtaining sufficient proof is often problematic. These include sexual offences and offences against children and other vulnerable persons, as such offences tend to occur in private with no independent eye-witnesses. As a mechanism to ameliorate injustice to victims, the common law developed various responses to the effect of the strict rule of corroboration, an approach which Peter Duff has memorably described as "fiddles".[10] There is another reason to retain knowledge of the previous case law. It is a vital resource if we are to

---

[10] P. Duff, "The requirement for corroboration in Scottish criminal cases: one argument against retention", 2012 Crim. L.R. 513.

make meaningful evaluations of the effectiveness of the reforms to corroboration.

Corroboration is evidence that "strengthens, or confirms, or supports a **8–07** statement or the testimony of a witness".[11] Scots law was unusual in retaining a general principle of corroboration well into the 21st century. The rule applied to crucial facts in common law criminal cases (though not civil cases). Crucial facts could not be proved by the testimony of one witness alone but had to be corroborated by evidence deriving from a second independent source. That second source could take numerous forms. Occasionally there might have been two eye witnesses to an incident, but it might also have derived for example, from a document, blood sample or finger print. As the Scottish Law Commission Report No.100[12] noted, "in practice it [corroboration] is commonly found in a combination of direct testimony and circumstantial evidence".[13] The rationale for a rule of corroboration is that evidence from a second, separate source provides an independent check on the reliability of the fact in question.[14]

It was only the "crucial facts or facts in issue" that required corrobora- **8–08** tion.[15] Other facts tend to be evidential facts that comprise circumstantial evidence and did not require to be corroborated. In civil cases the general requirement for corroboration was abolished by s.1(1) of the Civil Evidence (Scotland) Act 1988.

DISTINGUISHING CRUCIAL FACT FROM EVIDENTIAL FACTS

The crucial facts of any case are what were referred to in Ch.1 as the facta **8–09** probanda, or "those matters in dispute between the parties".[16] In a criminal case they are "the facts which ... establish the accused's guilt of the crime charged and must be libelled in an indictment or complaint, expressly or by statutory implication".[17] In a civil case they are "the facts which a party must, or ought to, aver in order to make a case relevant to be sent to proof".[18] The essential facts in a case will emerge in a criminal case from the nature of the charge, and in a civil case in the course of the pleadings. In contrast, evidential facts are facts which are circumstantial, in that inferences can be drawn from them to support proof of crucial facts.

Crucial facts will obviously vary with the substantive law. In *Lockwood v* **8–10** *Walker*[19] the accused was charged with lewd and libidinous practices with a girl below the age of puberty. He was acquitted because of insufficient evidence of the age of the child. The only evidence of her age came from the child herself. Holding that "unimpeachable evidence of the age of the child

---

[11] *Fox v HM Advocate*, 1998 S.L.T. 335 at 339.
[12] *Report on Corroboration, Hearsay and Related Matters* (1986).
[13] Quoting Dickson, *Evidence*, paras 1808 and 1811.
[14] Sometimes also referred to as the essential facts.
[15] The term "crucial" is used here.
[16] Walker and Walker, *Law of Evidence in Scotland*, para.1.3.1.
[17] Walker and Walker, *Evidence*, 3rd edn, para.5.3.1.
[18] Walker and Walker , *Evidence*, 3rd edn, at para.5.3.1.
[19] 1910 S.C. (J.) 3. Note that in that case the facts in issue were described as crucial facts.

was necessary where it was central to the offence charged that the complainer was under the age of puberty", the Lord Justice-Clerk affirmed[20]:

> "No doubt our law does not require that every fact in a case shall be proved by two witnesses, but it most certainly does require that every crucial fact shall be so proved, or proved where there is only one witness by corroborative facts and circumstances proved, or by corroborative documentary evidence."

In *Stewart v Glasgow Corporation*,[21] a civil case from an era before the need for corroboration in civil cases was abolished, a mother sought compensation for the death of her son in an accident involving a clothes pole on a Glasgow drying green. She required to prove that the pole was badly corroded at the time of the accident and that the local authority must have known this. She lost her case, inter alia, because there was no corroborated evidence of the state of the pole at the time. Lord Russell[22] ruled that "[i]t is true that not every part of the evidence of a witness requires to be corroborated but, in the present case, the existence and extent of the corrosion which is claimed to have rendered the pole dangerous is vital to the establishment of the pursuer's case and requires to be affirmatively proved".

8–11   If there had been no legal requirement for corroboration at the time of this case we cannot know if the pursuer would have succeeded, but the importance of persuading the court about the state of the clothes pole would not change and there is no doubt that if there is an option of leading evidence from the pursuer alone or from the pursuer *and* another independent source of evidence, the prudent litigator would choose the latter. Therefore, we could reasonably anticipate, regardless of whether or not corroboration is abolished, if independent corroborating evidence is available to a party it will be the norm to lead it rather than leave the outcome of the case resting on the testimony of one witness alone and risk there being insufficient evidence.

8–12   As explained in Lockwood, corroboration of crucial facts to produce sufficient evidence to prove the offence charged in the indictment or complaint may take several forms. In a criminal case, in the simplest situation, it could be the eye-witness accounts of two independent witnesses, both of whom, for example, saw X hit Y. Or, again in a criminal case, it may take the form of a confession by the accused coupled with a forensic report that links the accused to the crime. Eyewitness accounts, confessions and forensic reports provide direct evidence of the proof of a fact in issue. Such evidence is not always available and a party seeking to prove a particular fact may have to rely on indirect evidence, i.e. evidence that does not point directly to what actually occurred, but nevertheless tends to support another item of direct evidence.

---

[20] *Lockwood v Walker*, 1910 S.C. (J.) 3 at 5. Section 255A of the Criminal Procedure Scotland Act 1995 now provides that unless challenged, the age of a person specified in an indictment or a complaint shall be held as admitted.

[21] *Stewart v Glasgow Corporation*, 1958 S.C. 28 at 45. The requirement for corroboration in civil cases was abolished in the Civil Evidence (Scotland) 1988.

[22] At 46.

The operation of an evidential fact to corroborate another item of evi- **8–13** dence is illustrated in *Patterson v Nixon*.[23] This case concerned theft by housebreaking. Patterson had confessed to being near the locus, dressed for housebreaking, but denied that he had actually committed it. This partial confession required corroboration and the police took a tracker dog to the locus. The dog picked up a scent and, when released, went straight to Patterson's house, one of six in a block from which it could have chosen. The dog's behaviour was sufficient to provide the necessary corroboration.

CORROBORATION IN CRIMINAL CASES

Hume[24] described the corroboration rule as a "concurrence of testimonies", **8–14** and explained that "the aptitude and coherence of the several circumstances often as fully confirm the truth of the story as if all the witnesses were deponing to the same facts". The fundamental crucial facts that require to be proven in any crime are the identity of the perpetrator and the actus reus of the crime. When our legal system retained a corroboration rule, the Crown had to prove beyond reasonable doubt that a crime had been committed and that the accused committed it. The facts requiring corroboration obviously varied with the charge.

The classic formulation of the rule of corroboration was provided by **8–15** Lord Justice-Clerk Aitchison in *Morton v HM Advocate*[25]:

"[N]o person can be convicted of a crime or a statutory offence except where the legislature otherwise directs, unless there is evidence of at least two witnesses implicating the person accused with the commission of the crime or offence with which he is charged. This rule has proved an invaluable safeguard in the practice of our criminal courts against unjust conviction, and it is a rule from which the courts ought not to sanction any departure."

Morton was charged with an indecent assault upon a woman whom he had allegedly hustled into a tenement close in order to molest her. He was identified by the victim, both at an identification parade and in court, and she was not cross-examined on her identification. The only other items of evidence were, first, that of a neighbour who had seen the assault from within the close but who could not identify the accused and, second, that of the victim's brother, who spoke only to her distressed state when she arrived home complaining of having been assaulted. Morton was acquitted because there was no corroborated evidence to identify him as the assailant.

The reference to "two witnesses" in Lord Justice-Clerk Aitchison's dic- **8–16** tum had to be interpreted carefully. What was required for corroboration was more than one independent source of evidence, but these did not have to be in the form of *direct* eye witness testimony. For example in *Patterson v Nixon* above, the behaviour of the tracker dog was an item of evidence

---

[23] 1960 J.C. 42. See also *Norval v HM Advocate*, 1978 J.C. 70; *Little v HM Advocate*, 1988 J.C. 16; and *Kennedy v F*, 1985 S.L.T. 22.

[24] II, 384.

[25] 1938 J.C. 50 at p.55.

though it was obviously spoken to in the witness box by the police officer handling the dog.

8–17   When corroboration was required, even a confession had to be corroborated. However, as a confession is one of the most powerful items of evidence against an accused as it is a statement against interest and it is presumed that individuals generally do not make such statements,[26] where the conditions for obtaining a confession were fair to the accused, little other evidence was required for there to constitute a sufficiency of evidence to prosecute. In the course of a trial, evidence may sometimes be led that could corroborate more than one version of events. In *Fox v HM Advocate*[27] evidence in support of the charge of clandestine injury[28] came from the complainer's distress, suggesting her lack of consent to intercourse. Distress was thus positioned as corroboration of a crucial fact, namely the actus reus. The appeal court acknowledged that the distress might have been consistent with alternative accounts put forward by the accused and confirmed that the existence of alternative plausible accounts did not detract from the corroborative *potential* of the Crown's case.[29] This could be an important principle when there is no corroboration requirement and where evidence that is "neutral" and capable of supporting a party's case might supply a sufficiency of evidence to either the defence or the prosecutor.

8–18   The appeal court observed that corroborative evidence was not a competition to be measured according to whose account it best suited. Instead, the question was whether or not it was capable of corroborating another item of evidence. Thereafter it was up to the jury to decide which account they preferred.

FACTS NOT REQUIRING CORROBORATION

Procedural facts

8–19   There are certain procedural facts that must be proved in the course of a criminal trial, but which do not in themselves prove that the crime was committed, or that it was the accused who committed it. Procedural facts did not need to be corroborated. For example, in *Farrell v Concannon*[30] it was held that only one witness was required to speak to the fact that the accused was advised of his rights before consenting to a medical examination. And in *MacLeod v Nicol*[31] the same observation (only one witness required) was offered in respect of all the preliminary procedures in an

---

[26] See Ch.8.

[27] 1998 S.L.T. 335.

[28] historically, a common law crime of having sexual intercourse with a sleeping woman. The crime was replaced by s.1 of the Sexual Offences (Scotland) Act 2009.

[29] Disapproving of the decision in *Mackie v HM* Advocate, 1995 S.L.T. 110, specifically the dictum at 9.118 suggesting that where there were competing accounts, the account with which the corroborating evidence was most consistent should be preferred.

[30] 1957 J.C. 12.

[31] 1970 J.C. 58.

alleged drunken driving charge, up to and including the first positive breath test at the locus.[32]

FACTS WITHIN THE KNOWLEDGE OF THE ACCUSED

Where the Crown allege certain facts rest "peculiarly within the knowledge **8–20** of" the accused,[33] it is settled law that the prosecution evidence need establish only a prima facie case against the accused, and it is then for the accused to produce the evidence which will lead to an acquittal. The clearest examples arise on charges of driving without a licence, or without insurance, and the prima facie case against the accused can legitimately consist simply of one item of uncorroborated evidence. Thus, in *Milne v Whaley*[34] it was held that in such a case, an uncorroborated confession by the accused is sufficient for a conviction.

Where the prosecution adduce as a witness someone who was involved in **8–21** the crime along with the accused (a *socius criminis*) then the evidence of that person does not require corroboration. The trial judge in a trial on indictment is, however, entitled, but not obliged, to warn the jury to treat such evidence with special care.[35]

The next section looks more closely at a number of specific aspects of **8–22** corroboration which give rise to particular issues in practice.

ROUTINE EVIDENCE

The Criminal Procedure (Scotland) Act 1995 contains a range of provisions **8–23** to encourage uncontroversial or routine evidence to be identified by the parties so that either oral evidence may be dispensed with where possible, or the evidence of only one witness required. Thus, in terms of ss.256–258, parties are under a duty to try to agree uncontroversial evidence and, where possible, to prepare a statement of such evidence and serve on the other party—an attempt to limit the disputed issues going to trial and to save time and costs. Evidence which is not in dispute constitutes sufficient evidence of a fact and does not need to be proven with witness testimony.

Routine forensic evidence

Sections 281–282 of the Act provide that the evidence of one pathologist or **8–24** forensic scientist is to be regarded as sufficient to prove any fact or conclusion as to fact contained in any report signed by them and another pathologist or forensic scientist. The signature of a scientist is to be taken as implying that they adopt the findings of junior colleagues who have conducted analyses in the laboratory at earlier stages of an investigation and in

---

[32] The case was decided under s.2 of the Road Safety Act 1967, now s.7 of the Road Traffic Act 1972, and Lord Justice-Clerk Grant described the whole section as containing matters which were "clearly procedural and incidental".

[33] See Ch.14.

[34] 1975 S.L.T. (Notes) 75.

[35] *Docherty v HM Advocate*, 1987 J.C. 81.See too, *O'Donnell (Francis Martin Thomas) v HM Advocate* [2011] HCJAC 84, and discussion of evidence of an accomplice in Ch.12.

accordance with recognised laboratory procedures.[36] The 1995 Act also contains provisions to dispense with corroboration through the use of certification of evidence in cases involving drugs, video surveillance and fingerprints and palm prints. Sections 282–284 detail the procedures that can be used to avoid calling witnesses to court simply to speak to such matters. In terms of s.280, where a certificate is lodged and signed by an authorised person, it is deemed to be sufficient evidence of certain non-contentious issues.[37] In terms of s.281(2), where an autopsy or forensic report is lodged as a production, the Crown, after due notice to the accused and without any objection from him, may call only one pathologist or forensic scientist to give evidence regarding anything contained in their report. At common law it was established that no corroboration was required of the modus of a crime or even, apparently, certain elements of any aggravation of it.[38] However, statutory crimes of an aggravated nature, e.g. hate crimes, may require corroboration.

8–25   Schedule 8 of the Criminal Procedure (Scotland) 1995 Act provides for the admissibility of copy documents and for the certification of documents, primarily business documents, which, if properly authenticated, are admissible as evidence of any fact or opinion of which direct oral evidence would be admissible. "Document" is defined very broadly in para.8 of Sch.8 to include maps, plans, graphs, drawings, photographs, discs, tapes and films. These provisions are a matter of pragmatics and policy—there is no merit in prolonging court proceedings by insisting on proof of uncontested or uncontroversial matters.[39]

IDENTIFICATION OF AN ACCUSED

8–26 The identity of the accused is a crucial fact which, for as long as the corroboration rule prevails, must be proven with two independent items of evidence. As discussed earlier, in *Morton v HM Advocate*,[40] Morton was acquitted because there was no second source of his identity as the perpetrator beyond the complainer's testimony. There was evidence capable of corroborating the fact that an assault had occurred, but not by whom. The rule only comes into play if identification is a live issue. If the accused admits his presence at the locus, or admits the actus reus but denies mens rea, then there will be no need for proof.[41] Once s.57 of the Criminal Justice (Scotland) Bill 2013 is in force, if the facts of the *Morton* case were to recur, then, provided the jury were satisfied that there was a sufficiency of evidence which would include accepting the evidence of the complainer, they would be entitled to deliver a verdict of guilty. The recognised procedure for an eye

---

[36] *Bermingham v HM Advocate*, 2005 J.C. 17.
[37] A wide range of these issues is covered in Sch.9 of the Act and includes matters relating to firearms, drugs, immigration, pollution, and road traffic.
[38] See, e.g. *Yates v HM Advocate*, 1977 S.L.T. (Notes) 42 and *Stephen v HM Advocate*, 1987 S.C.C.R. 570; but see *Lynch v HM Advocate*, 1986 S.C.C.R. 244, in which it was held that corroboration was required of the personal violence necessary to convert theft into robbery.
[39] Acknowledged in the report, *Review of the Practices and Procedure of the High Court of Justiciary*, by the Honourable Lord Bonomy, 2002.
[40] *Morton v HM Advocate*, 1938 J.C. 50.
[41] See *Stewart v HM Advocate*, 1980 S.L.T. 245.

witness to identify the accused is for the witness to point to the accused in court as the person to whom they are referring in their evidence.[42] In *Bruce v HM Advocate*[43] B was charged with wilful fire-raising along with D, and the latter, having pled guilty, then gave evidence implicating B and identifying him. None of the other witnesses in the case was asked to point him out in court, although they referred in their evidence to "the accused James Bruce". In quashing the conviction, Lord Wark on appeal pointed out that,[44] "identification of an accused is not a matter which ought to be left to implication. The proper practice is to have the accused identified directly by persons who are speaking to facts which are material to the charge which is under investigation."

The difficulties facing vulnerable witnesses, especially young children in making a dock identification were illustrated in *P v Williams*,[45] where P was convicted of indecent assault of two child complainers, both vulnerable witnesses. At the trial the children referred to P as, respectively, "Dad" and "Big B". However, neither was asked to identify whether that person was in court. Although P's former partner made a dock identification, the appeal court held that was insufficient. As there was no other corroboration led by the Crown that the man in the dock was the man to whom the children were referring when they used these nicknames, P's convictions were quashed. **8–27**

Sometimes witnesses are unable to identify the accused in court, particularly if a long period has elapsed since the incident. In such situations it is permissible for the prosecution to produce evidence that the accused was identified by the witness on an earlier occasion, for example, at the scene of the crime or at a subsequent identification parade. The leading authority in this area is *Muldoon v Herron*[46] in which three youths were charged with a breach of the peace. Two witnesses—Mr and Mrs Miller—saw the incident and both identified the three accused to the police as soon as they arrived. At the trial, neither was able to identify any of the accused, but both agreed that they had, at the time of the incident, pointed out the culprits to the police. Mrs Miller gave evidence to the effect that the accused in the dock had not been among those whom she had pointed out to the police, but the sheriff disbelieved her. Two police officers gave evidence that the three accused were all among the group identified by both witnesses shortly after the incident and on the basis of this evidence the sheriff convicted. **8–28**

On appeal, the conviction was upheld on the grounds that there were two independent items of identification, namely: (1) the evidence that Mr Miller identified the accused shortly after the incident (that act of identification being spoken to by Mr Miller, and the identification of the accused as being those pointed out coming from the police); and (2) the identical evidence of identification by Mrs Miller, the denial of which on oath by Mrs Miller the court disbelieved in favour of the police officers' confirmation that she had picked them out at the scene. **8–29**

---

[42] A normal requirement confirmed in *Stewart v HM Advocate*, 1980 S.L.T. 245 at 251. For the arrangements for identification by vulnerable witnesses, see Ch.3.

[43] 1936 J.C. 93 at 95.

[44] *Bruce v HM Advocate*, 1936 J.C. 93 at 95.

[45] *P v Williams*, 2005 S.L.T. 508.

[46] 1970 J.C. 30. For the increasing latitude allowed in cases such as this, see *Reilly v HM Advocate*, 1987 S.C.C.R. 68; *Gracie v Allan*, 1987 S.C.C.R. 364; *Nolan v McLeod*, 1987 S.C.C.R. 558; and *Ralston v HM Advocate*, 1987 S.C.C.R. 467.

8–30   *Muldoon* was applied in *Bennett v HM Advocate*,[47] which concerned charges of assault. B was identified by the victim, and by two other witnesses to the assault, during the course of an identification parade. None of the witnesses was able to identify the accused at the trial, and the Crown sought to fill the gap by means of the evidence of one police witness as to what had taken place at the identification parade. On appeal, it was held that in *Muldoon* the evidence of two police officers was enough to complete the chain of identification and provide a corroborated case against the accused. However, in *Bennett* the evidence of the one police officer supplied only one item of evidence and something further was required to identify the accused as the assailant. In the event there was such evidence.

8–31   Although direct evidence of identification is desirable, it is not essential—convictions have been sustained on the basis of indirect or circumstantial evidence.[48] The Court of Criminal Appeal has confirmed that there are numerous ways in which the Crown can seek to prove identification of the accused[49]:

> "...[T]he implication of an accused person in the commission of an offence may be proved in a variety of different ways by direct evidence, or by indirect evidence of different kinds. How the Crown goes about proving that essential feature of a case must be a matter for the exercise of its discretion, in the light of the evidence which may be available to it in the circumstances of any particular case, about which the court will almost certainly have no knowledge."

SUFFICIENCY OF IDENTIFICATION

8–32 In *Howden v HM Advocate*[50] it was held that, provided it could be established beyond reasonable doubt that the offences were both committed by the same person, lack of positive identification on one of the charges was not in itself an impediment to conviction. Howden was convicted of separate charges of attempted robbery of a building society and a bank. He was positively identified as the perpetrator by the building society employees, but the bank employees were unable to make a positive identification. However, the appeal court upheld the trial judge's direction to the jury that if they were satisfied beyond reasonable doubt that the offences were committed by the same person, and that Howden was the perpetrator of at least one of them, then it was not necessary to have a second positive identification.

---

[47] 1976 J.C. 1. See also *Smith v HM Advocate*, 1986 S.C.C.R. 135 for a case in which *Muldoon* was applied even though the witnesses stated in evidence that they were not certain at the time, but had picked out the accused anyway. It was said to be a matter for the jury whether or not they believed the identification evidence to have been positive and unqualified at the time of the parade. See also *Neeson v HM Advocate*, 1984 S.C.C.R. 72, and *Reilly v HM Advocate*, 1987 S.C.C.R. 68 and *Gracie v Allan*, 1987 S.C.C.R. 364 both.

[48] See. e.g. *Langan v HM Advocate*, 1989 S.C.C.R. 379 and *Maguire v HM Advocate*, 2003 S.C.C.R. 758.

[49] *Murphy v HM Advocate*, 2007 S.L.T. 1079 per Lord Osborne at para.48.

[50] 1994 S.C.C.R. 19.

This principle was approved and applied in *Townsley v Lees*,[51] where, in a **8–33** series of three thefts, there was positive identification of only two of the three charges. It was held on appeal that the sheriff had been entitled to convict on all three charges as there was cogent evidence they had all been carried out by the same person.

There has been criticism of these two cases on the basis that they diluted **8–34** the rule that corroboration was required of the crucial fact of identification of a perpetrator.[52] However, although there have been opportunities to refer *Howden* to a larger court for review, the High Court have so far declined to do so.[53]

Identification is not restricted to visual recognition.[54] Where a witness is **8–35** shown a photograph and identifies the accused by name, the witness's evidence is admissible.[55] Separately, an accused may be identified by means of his voice[56] and identification by build may be admissible if taken in conjunction with other positive identification evidence of the accused.[57] A "positive identification" is one that is more than neutral. Thus, a comment from a witness that an accused "doesn't look unlike" a person who had threatened him and stolen his car, was in effect a double negative and was held to be insufficient to constitute a positive identification.[58] It is not necessary for there to be two positive identifications of the accused by eyewitnesses, provided that overall there is sufficient evidence of identification.[59] Identification of an accused can also be made by professional forensic officers relying upon a variety of types of physical evidence, including fingerprints, palm prints, teeth marks, handwriting, ear prints and DNA profiling.[60]

STATUTORY EXCEPTIONS TO THE CORROBORATION RULE

The rules relating to corroboration were largely developed in the common **8–36** law. However, there are numerous statutory exceptions to the general rule, which dispense with corroboration and permit a sufficiency of evidence for the proof of essential facts on the basis of only one source of evidence. These statutory exceptions are preserved in the Criminal Justice (Scotland) Bill, s.58. They vary widely in nature and only a few examples are given here. Some of these exceptions specify that only one witness is required to support

---

[51] 1996 S.C.C.R. 620.
[52] P. Duff, "The Uncertain Scope of Hearsay in Scots Criminal Law Evidence: Implied Assertions and Evidence of Prior Identification" (2005) J.R. 1.
[53] *Gillan v HM Advocate*, 2002 S.L.T. 551.
[54] *Muldoon v Herron*, 1970 J.C. 30, per Lord Cameron at 45.
[55] *Howarth v HM Advocate*, 1992 S.C.C.R. 364.
[56] *McGiveran v Auld* (1894) 21 R. (J.) 69; see also *Burrows v HM Advocate*, 1951 S.L.T (Notes) 69. See too *HM Advocate v Swift*, 1983 S.C.C.R. 204.
[57] *Nelson v HM Advocate*, 1989 S.L.T. 215; *Murphy v HM Advocate*, 1995 S.L.T. 725; and see *Ralston v HM Advocate*, 1987 S.C.C.R. 467, which indicated that if there is at least one emphatic positive identification little else is required.
[58] *MacDonald v HM Advocate*, 1998 S.L.T. 37.
[59] *Kelly v HM Advocate*, 1999 J.C. 35.
[60] See Ch.4.

the prosecution.[61] Others may place the burden of proof on a particular issue with the accused such that the accused has an obligation to produce sufficient credible evidence to satisfy the point and prevent the Crown from discharging their over-arching duty to prove the charge beyond reasonable doubt.[62]

8–37   In those situations, even if the statute appears to place a persuasive burden upon the accused, the evidence produced by the accused does not need to be corroborated and the standard to be reached is on a balance of probabilities.[63] This approach is reinforced by the impact of art.6 and the presumption of innocence, which place serious constraints on the circumstances when a persuasive burden can be imposed upon an accused, let alone a requirement that such a burden be discharged with corroborated evidence. If the burden of proof imposed upon the accused by statute is only evidential, then, provided the evidence put forward is credible, it need not be to any particular standard, nor need it be corroborated. Where the courts are in doubt about the nature of the burden in legislation, there is a tendency to read down the burdens as evidential only.[64]

8–38   In *Templeton v Lyons*[65] Lyons was charged with failing to send his child to school, the charge being brought under an Act which gave the accused the burden of proving any "reasonable excuse" in bar of conviction. Lyons claimed that he was unaware of the truancy, since his wife had intercepted all communications concerning it. Additionally, the attendance officer, who knew him by sight, had on several occasions passed him on the street without comment. In the course of upholding his conviction Lord Wark commented that, "the onus lay upon him to establish by legal proof the excuse which he alleged in explanation of his failure to see that his child attended school, and that he could not do without leading evidence which to some extent corroborated his own evidence".[66] In *Farrell v Moir*[67] the accused was convicted of refusing to give a second breath test or blood or urine sample. He pleaded that there was a "special reason" in terms of s.93(1) of the Road Traffic Act 1972 that he should not be disqualified from driving, in that he had only driven the car because the police had ordered him to move it. There was no corroboration of this claim, but the sheriff ruled that M's uncorroborated evidence (which only had to be proved on a balance of probabilities) was sufficient[68]:

> "The general principle in Scotland is that where there is an onus on a party to prove any essential fact that must be done by corroborated evidence. If this general principle applies to the present case then the

---

[61] See *Sutherland v Aitchison*, 1970 S.L.T. (Notes) 48 applying road traffic legislation which provided only one witness was required to speak to a failure to comply with a traffic sign.

[62] For example, s.51A of the Criminal Procedure (Scotland) 1995, the defence of mental disorder, which has to be established on a balance of probabilities. See Ch.5.

[63] *King v Lees*, 1993 J. C. 19.

[64] *Templeton v Lyons*, 1942 J.C. 102.

[65] *Templeton v Lyons*, 1942 J.C. 102 at 108.

[66] *Templeton v Lyons*, 1942 J.C. 102 at 108.

[67] 1974 S.L.T. (Sh. Ct) 89.

[68] *Farrell v Moir*, 1974 S.L.T. (Sh. Ct) 89 at 90. The sheriff observed that there was no earlier authority directly in point.

accused must fail ... In my opinion in a proof such as this, when the onus is on the accused, his own uncorroborated evidence, if believed, is sufficient."

In *King v Lees* the appeal court confirmed this approach as[69]:

"...[I]n accordance with principle that the evidence led by the accused for this purpose need not be corroborated; all that is required is that the court accepts the evidence led by the accused as being credible and reliable. The law insists upon corroboration where the prosecution require to establish the guilt of an accused beyond reasonable doubt, but different considerations apply where the law imposes a burden upon an accused person to establish a defence; the standard of proof required of him is on a balance of probabilities, and we are not persuaded that there is any requirement for corroboration."

THE *MOOROV* DOCTRINE

As previously discussed, the requirement for corroboration could result in **8–39** harsh consequences. Sexual offences in particular rarely occur in circumstances where there are any independent eye witnesses to the offence. To ameliorate the effects of the rule the common law developed principles to accommodate this. The first of these considered here is that of mutual corroboration which arises when a person is accused of a series of offences which are closely connected "in time, character and circumstance" and have "an underlying unity". This principle was recognised by Hume[70] and became known as the *Moorov* doctrine, having taken its name from the leading case of *Moorov v HM Advocate*.[71] Under this doctrine, the evidence of one witness in a series of two or more separate offences may be capable of providing corroboration for the evidence of a witness in another case or cases where an underlying unity can be proven. In other words, each offence corroborates the other(s) as if the crimes charged were a course of criminal conduct. The general rule is that only the evidence of the greater charge could corroborate the lesser charge and not vice versa.[72]

The accused in *Moorov* was an employer who was alleged to have com- **8–40** mitted separate sexual assaults and indecent assaults involving 21 charges with a total of 19 female employees over a period of four years. He was convicted of seven assaults and nine indecent assaults. Corroborative evidence was only available in three of these charges. On appeal to a full bench of seven judges, the conviction was upheld on nine of the original charges,

---

[69] 1993 J.C. 19 at 23, a decision criticised by David Sheldon in his article, "Hip Flasks and Burdens", 1993 S.L.T. (News) 33.

[70] II, 385, cited in Dickson, *Evidence*, paras 1807–1810.

[71] *Moorov v HM Advocate*, 1930 J.C. 69, approved obiter by the House of Lords in *D.P.P. v Kilbourne* [1973] A.C. 729. *Kilbourne* is primarily concerned with the use of similar fact evidence in English law. For further discussion of the associations between these two authorities see Ch.12.

[72] *HM Advocate v Brown*, 1969 J.C. 72, though Lord Gill suggested, obiter, in *Dean v HM Advocate*, 2007 S.C.C.R. 333 at para 26, that this rule may not apply where there were "compelling similarities".

which stretched over a period of some three years, six of these charges resting on the evidence of a single witness. In explaining the circumstances in which such convictions were possible, Lord Justice-General Clyde pointed out that[73]:

> "Before the evidence of a single credible witness to separate acts can provide material for mutual corroboration, the connection between the separate acts (indicated by their external relation in time, character or circumstance[74]) must be such as to exhibit them as subordinates in some particular and ascertained unity of intent, project, campaign or adventure which lies beyond or behind—but is related to—the separate acts."

Put more briefly, in the words of Lord Sands,[75] "[t]here must be some special circumstances connecting the incidents in order that it may be held that a course of conduct is established".

8–41   In sexual offences there may be little to support the complainer's account and it is only by demonstrating that there has been a course of conduct involving one or more other victims in similar offences that, hitherto, it has been possible to use the testimony of each complainer as corroboration for the other(s). For example, in *Begg v Tudhope*[76] a schoolteacher, Begg, was accused of indecent assaults on two of his female pupils. The evidence against him consisted of the testimony of the two girls themselves, plus independent evidence of the distressed condition of one of the girls shortly after the incident. On appeal it was held that the evidence of the girl's condition (plus a *de recenti* statement made by her to the witness of her condition) was not capable of corroborating her allegation of assault. Nevertheless, the court upheld the convictions because, "as the sheriff accepted the two complainers as credible and reliable ... he was entitled to apply the principle laid down in *Moorov v HM Advocate* ... and hence to find the appellant guilty on both charges".[77]

8–42   The *Moorov* doctrine has been most frequently encountered in cases of sexual assault though, historically, it was not restricted to such cases. For example, it was applied in *McCudden v HM Advocate*,[78] where there were two separate attempts to bribe professional football players; in *HM Advocate v McQuade*,[79] a case involving six charges of assault by razor; and *Harris v Clark*,[80] where there were three charges of reset, The doctrine was also applied in offences involving the obstructive driving of a car, based on two distinct charges of a breach of the peace, and careless driving under the

---

[73] *Moorov v HM Advocate*, 1930 J.C. 69 at 73.
[74] The factors are interchangeable.
[75] *Moorov v HM Advocate*, 1930 J.C. 69 at 89.
[76] 1983 S.C.C.R. 32.
[77] *Begg v Tudliope*, 1983 S.C.C.R. 32 per Lord Stott at 40.
[78] 1952 J.C. 86.
[79] 1951 J.C. 143.
[80] 1958 J.C. 3.

Road Traffic Acts.[81] The resulting conviction was upheld on appeal as the substance of the charges was the same.[82]

It is not strictly necessary for all three elements of time, character and **8–43** circumstance to unite in each case to apply the *Moorov* doctrine. However, where any of them is absent it may be impossible to persuade the trier of fact that there is a sufficient underlying unity for the doctrine to take hold. The mere fact that the crimes libelled against the accused are similar in nature is not per se sufficient for the doctrine to operate.[83] There must be "identity of kind" so that "the crimes are related or connected with each other so as to form part of the same criminal conduct".[84] There is obviously discretion in how that is interpreted.[85]

Time

The time frame between the commission of each of the constituent offences **8–44** charged depends upon the both the character and the circumstances of these offences. One explanation is because "[a] man whose course of conduct is to buy houses, insure them, and burn them down, or to acquire ships, insure them, and scuttle them, or to purport to marry women, defraud and desert them, cannot repeat the offence every month, or even perhaps every six months".[86] For decades a presumption prevailed whereby a period of three years appeared to have been the limit for the offending period, but in regard to which no specific principled basis was offered. In *Coffey v Houston*[87] a male nurse was convicted of indecently assaulting two girls, both aged 11, in hospital wards in separate hospitals. The time gap was two years and two months, which the court said was "comparatively long" but was not fatal to the conviction given the existence of strong links between the offences which were described as "identical assaults". In *Russell v HM Advocate*[88] the accused was charged with lewd and libidinous conduct towards two girls who were in a neighbouring household. The alleged offences were three and a half years apart and this was held to be too long for the operation of the *Moorov* doctrine. The court considered various authorities and noted that "[a]lthough the interval of time between similar offences is not in all cases critical, it is ... a most material consideration. Clearly no hard and fast rule can be laid down as far as time is concerned, but it is significant that we were referred to no case where the doctrine was applied in circumstances where there was an interval of three years or more between two similar offences."[89]

---

[81] *Austin v Fraser*, 1998 S.L.T. 106. See too, *Thomson v HM Advocate*, 1998 S.C.C.R. 657, a case involving two separate robberies, each spoken to by one witness; and *Wilson v HM Advocate*, 2001 S.L.T. 1203.

[82] See Lord Clyde at pp.6–8.

[83] See *Ogg v HM Advocate*, 1938 J.C. 152, *McHardy v HM Advocate*, 1983 S.L.T. 375 and *Tudhope v Hazelton*, 1985 S.L.T. 209.

[84] See *Moorov v HM Advocate*, 1930 J.C. 69 at 73, as applied in *McMahon v HM Advocate*, 1996 S.L.T. 1139.

[85] There are many cases dealing with the question of whether the facts constitute a sufficiency of "underlying unity", e.g. *S v HM Advocate*, 2006 S.C.C.R. 70.

[86] *Moorov v HM Advocate*, 1930 J.C. 69 at 73 per Lord Sands at 89.

[87] 1992 S.C.C.R. 265.

[88] *Russell v HM Advocate*, 1990 S.C.C.R. 18.

[89] *Russell v HM Advocate*, 1990 S.C.C.R. 18 at 24.

8–45   This dictum was applied in *Turner v Scott*,[90] described as "a case on the borderline", where the court held that the *Moorov* doctrine was competent in offences over a period of almost three years, as "there is sufficient coherence in character and circumstance". The Court of Appeal affirmed in *Bargon v HM Advocate*[91] that there is no fixed period after which *Moorov* is inapplicable, but in that case the relevant period between offences was three and seven months and there were said to be considerable differences between the incidents. The courts never provided a rationale for applying a three year limitation to the *Moorov* doctrine, beyond the supposition that any longer period made it difficult to sustain an argument that the conduct in question was "a course of conduct".

8–46   The position was clarified in *Dodds v HM Advocate*,[92] where the offences concerned allegations of rape extending over a period from August 1969 to November 1979. Lord Gill emphasised that there was no maximum interval of time beyond which the doctrine was inapplicable. Where there are "compelling similarities" in offences there was scope to extend the doctrine beyond a three year period.

Character

8–47   Whatever flexibility may have existed on the question of the time frame, in relation to the nature of the offences with which the accused is charged, these have historically had to be substantially similar. For example, in *HM Advocate v Cox*[93] the court refused to apply the doctrine to two charges of incest and a charge of sodomy which were allegedly committed in the family home against stepchildren (two female and one male). The rationale was: (a) that sodomy and incest were not the same crimes; and (b) that the two charges of incest were separated by a period of three years. In similar vein, in *P v HM Advocate*[94] the court affirmed that rape and sodomy were two distinct offences, and where the victims were adults the doctrine could not apply. However, the court conceded that where the victims were young children subjected to rape and sodomy, as in *P v HM Advocate*, then *Moorov* could be applied, as a course of criminal conduct of sexual abuse could be derived from the fact of sexual penetration of each child.

8–48   Making such a distinction between adults and children appeared to some commentators to be illogical, as in cases involving adult victims the fact of sexual penetration is similarly present, and arguably it is the nature of the criminal behaviour that ought to be the focus of the doctrine, not the age of the victims. Aspects of this anomaly may be resolved by the abolition of corroboration, though the success of a prosecution will still depend on whether there is sufficient evidence to persuade the fact-finder of the guilt of the accused.

8–49   *Moorov* requires that the offences charged must be substantially similar, a characteristic that the courts have been willing to interpret as cases which

---

[90] 1995 S.L.T. 200.
[91] 1997 S.L.T. 1232.
[92] *Dodds v HM Advocate*, 2002 S.L.T. 1058, a point Lord Gill repeated in *Dean v HM Advocate*, 2007 S.C.C.R. 303.
[93] 1962 J.C. 27.
[94] 1991 S.C.C.R. 933.

include charges of a different name but with a broadly equivalent nature.[95] As *P v HM Advocate* demonstrates, the important issue is not that "the crimes have a different *nomen iuris*" but that there is an "underlying similarity of the conduct".[96] In *Smith v HM Advocate*[97] two charges of lewd, indecent and libidinous conduct and one of sodomy led to the application of the *Moorov* doctrine because the court held that there was sufficient relation between the offences to provide a connection of the elements of character and circumstance.[98] In *HM Advocate v Brown*[99] the accused was charged with a variety of sexual offences against three stepdaughters (the only witnesses against him), all allegedly committed in the family home within a 21-month period. The time period was held to be short enough to apply the doctrine since only a period of months separated the courses of conduct with each girl. In the case of two of the victims, a course of lewd, etc., behaviour was followed by incestuous intercourse, and it was held that[100]:

> "[T]he evidence in regard to incest can validly be used as corroboration in regard to the charges of lewd practices. The greater here includes the lesser. On the other hand, I do not think the contrary is true. Incest is a very much more serious crime than lewd practices and I think that it would be dangerous to treat evidence that a man had committed lewd practices towards Y as indicative of his guilt of incest with Z . . . On the other hand, as I have already indicated, the *Moorov* doctrine could apply the other way round."

That reference to "the greater here includes the lesser" featured in *Hutchison v HM Advocate*,[101] where it was held that on the basis of *Moorov* an assault charge could provide corroboration for a breach of the peace charge but the reverse was not the case.

Circumstance

In *Hay v Wither*[102] the court had to consider whether there was a sufficient **8–50** connection in character and circumstance in two charges of breach of the peace. In both incidents a teenage boy was sexually accosted in a public place in nearby towns by a man driving a van. It was considered that there was the "necessary nexus" in the offences to apply the *Moorov* doctrine. In contrast, in *Farrell v Normand*[103] two charges of breach of the peace involving young girls in the same geographical area were held not to have sufficient similarities. Only one of the charges concerned indecency and it was considered that the conduct complained of in the other charge could not amount to breach of the peace.

---

[95] e.g. *HM Advocate v WB*, 1969 J.C. 72 and *PM v Jessop*, 1989 S.C.C.R. 324.
[96] per Lord Justice-General Hope in *McMahon v HM Advocate*, 1996 S.L.T. 1139 at 1142.
[97] 1995 S.L.T. 583.
[98] See also *Carpenter v Hamilton*, 1994 S.C.C.R. 108 where a charge of indecent exposure was corroborated by a breach of the peace. But in *Farrell v Normand*, 1993 S.L.T. 793 a charge of indecency was not corroborated by a breach of the peace.
[99] *HM Advocate v Brown*, 1970 S.L.T. 121.
[100] *HM Advocate v Brown*, per Lord Justice-Clerk Grant at 122.
[101] 1998 S.L.T. 679.
[102] 1988 S.C.C.R. 334.
[103] *Farrell v Normand*, 1993 S.L.T.793.

8–51   While each case always has to be determined on its own facts, a detectable shift occurred in the application of the doctrine in recent years, particularly in cases concerning children, that signalled a willingness to apply the doctrine wherever possible. That may owe something to the greater awareness and detection today of child sexual abuse and to improvements in the arrangements for children giving evidence.

8–52   The offences used in order to support *Moorov* prosecutions had to be "live" ones, in respect of which a finding or admission of guilt had not yet been entered.[104] The operation of the doctrine *was also dependent upon* the accused being clearly identified as the suspect in each of the incidents that were conjoined for that purpose.[105]

DISTRESS AS CORROBARATION

8–53 In addition to *Moorov*, another tactic which developed to provide corroboration in sexual offences was the extent to which a victim's distress was able to corroborate the crucial facts. The role of distress in providing corroboration is more complex and constrained than the *Moorov* doctrine. The case law has not produced a consistency of approach that readily permitted a clear exposition of the concept and the development of the principle had an uneven history. It originated in rape prosecutions where there was frequently a defence of consent to the sexual intercourse. Prior to the decision in the *Lord Advocate's Reference (No.1 of 2001)*[106] which changed the definition of the actus reus, the prosecution had to prove that sexual intercourse had occurred against the will of the complainer. A full bench in the *Lord Advocate's Reference (No.1 of 2001)* ruled that the crime of rape was committed if a man had intercourse with a woman without her consent, and in particular held that the use of force was not an essential component of the crime, though its existence obviously implied lack of consent. However, the subsequent decision in *McKearney v HM Advocate*[107] suggested that notwithstanding the *Reference*, the mens rea of rape required corroboration. Remarks by Lord Justice-Clerk Gill (as he then was) in *McKearney* and the later case of *HM Advocate v Cinci*[108] stressed that there were considerable limitations on the use of distress as corroboration. According to Lord Gill, in obiter remarks in *McKearney*, when force ceased to be a part of the definition of rape, then, "the *de recenti* distress of the complainer may tell us about her lack of consent but I fail to see how it tells us anything about the accused's state of mind".[109] In other words, the distress may indicate that a woman did not consent, but it is not evidence that the man knew that, or was reckless as to whether or not she consented. James Chalmers has persuasively argued to the contrary. Chalmers pointed out that to draw a distinction between the role of distress in proving forcible intercourse "and other forms of non-consensual intercourse ... is wholly

---

[104] See *Walsh v HM Advocate*, 1961 J.C. 51.
[105] See *McRae v HM Advocate*, 1975 J.C. 34.
[106] *Lord Advocate's Reference (No.1 of 2001)*, 2002 S.L.T. 466.
[107] *McKearney v HM Advocate*, 2004 J.C. 87.
[108] *HM Advocate v Cinci*, 2004 S.L.T. 748.
[109] *McKearney v HM Advocate*, 2004 J.C. 87, at para.16.

inconsistent with the *Reference* decision". If distress is capable of being used to infer that force was used, then it must also capable of being used to infer lack of consent, which in turn can be used to infer mens rea.[110]

The common law position was overtaken with the enactment of the **8–54** Sexual Offences (Scotland) Act 2009. Although the statutory definition of rape clarifies matters greatly, it does not remove the evidential barriers to proving rape. In particular, the potential ambiguities surrounding distress as an indicator of lack of consent have not altered. On that basis there is every reason to expect that distress will continue to have some evidential role to play in contributing to the sufficiency of evidence in the prosecution of rape. Its historical development is therefore useful.

A line of authority stretched from *Yates v HM Advocate*[111] for the pro- **8–55** position expressed there by Lord Justice-General Emslie that, "evidence as to the condition of the alleged victim of rape is capable of affording corroboration by credible evidence ... that she has been raped".[112] In other words, a victim's distressed condition could corroborate her allegations or rape. In *Gracey v HM Advocate* the appeal court affirmed that[113]:

> "[W]here evidence has been led that a complainer is in a distressed condition after the alleged rape ... it is for the jury to assess the evidence and to determine whether they are satisfied that the complainer was exhibiting genuine distress as a result of the alleged rape, or whether they consider that the evidence of distress has been put on or feigned."

The proposition was frequently challenged, e.g. the retreat from that position following *McKearney* which re-positioned distress as a factor that the jury can take into account but not as evidence of lack of consent as envisaged in *Yates* and *Gracey*, that on its own was capable providing corroboration.[114].

The dicta in cases such as *Yates* and *Gracey* were careful to restrict the use **8–56** of distress as corroboration to cases of rape, where consent was an issue. In *Stobo v HM Advocate*[115] there was a lesser charge of indecent assault and there was considerable evidence from a number of witnesses of the complainer's distress. On appeal, counsel for the appellant argued that distress might be relevant as an adminicle of evidence, but it could never provide corroboration by itself. He criticised the dicta in several cases that suggested distress could corroborate the crucial fact of the commission of the crime. The court declined to accept the grounds of appeal, despite little resistance from the advocate-depute to the main thrust of the appeal. Lord Justice-General Hope observed that, "I am not persuaded that it is accurate to say that the distressed condition of the complainer cannot in law provide corroboration of her evidence about what was done to her".[116] His point was

---

[110] J. Chalmers, "Distress as Corroboration of Mens Rea", 2004 S.L.T. (News) 141.
[111] *Yates v HM Advocate*, 1977 S.L.T. (Notes) 42. See *Stephen v HM Advocate,* 1987 S.C.C.R. 570 and *Moore v HM Advocate*, 1991 S.L.T. 278.
[112] *Yates v HM Advocate*, 1977 S.L.T. (Notes) 42 at 43.
[113] *Gracey v HM Advocate*, 1987 S.C.C.R. 260 AT263.
[114] *McKearney v HM Advocate*, 2004 JC 87.
[115] 1994 S.L.T. 28.
[116] *Stobo v HM Advocate*, 1994 S.L.T. 28.

that distress is circumstantial evidence in the same way that physical injuries or torn clothing would be deemed circumstantial and he did not think it necessary that any such evidence be "unequivocally referable to the crime libelled before it can be said to corroborate the evidence of an eyewitness".[117]

8–57   The leading case on the subject is the five bench decision in *Smith v Lees*[118] which overruled *Stobo*. The charge was lewd and libidinous practices. In a series of careful opinions, the court concluded that the evidential use made of distress in *Stobo* was wrong and did not fit theoretically with the rule of corroboration in Scots law. The court accepted that "in cases of rape where intercourse is admitted, evidence of distress is capable of corroborating a complainer's evidence that she did not consent".[119] However, in situations such as occurred in *Smith*, where a 13-year-old girl complained of a sexual assault, it was held distress could not corroborate the specific acts that had allegedly taken place. Instead, distress could only corroborate the fact that *something* had happened and it could lend support to the credibility of the complainer, but it could not corroborate the crucial facts of the charge. If the corroboration rule is abolished as the Scottish Government proposes, then it will be remain a matter for the fact-finder to determine how much weight to attach to distress evidence and such cases are likely to be ones in which something more than evidence of distress will be required to persuade juries that there is sufficient evidence for a conviction.

8–58   As Chalmers has pointed out, it is unclear how such a distinction can be drawn. If a jury believe the complainer's account that she did not consent, and that her distress was evidence of that, they would also be entitled to infer the accused could not have held an honest belief about her consent. Subsequent cases have emphasised this last point:

> "Distress can, at least in some circumstances, form part of the totality of the circumstantial evidence which would entitle a jury to conclude that an accused had the state of mind requisite for rape."[120]

It is not just in cases of rape that evidence of distress may be used to support an argument of lack of consent. In *Cullington v HM Advocate*[121] evidence of distress was used to corroborate lack of consent in regard to sexual conduct (short of rape) where the accused maintained the conduct was indeed with the complainer's consent. C was charged with indecent assault. The only evidence to corroborate the complainer was the subsequent distress she exhibited to her boyfriend. It was held on appeal that as the accused's evidence was to the effect that the complainer enthusiastically took part in the sexual activity complained of, then, once the jury disbelieved that version, they were left with the complainer's account involving use of force.

8–59   In common with the *Moorov* doctrine, time is of importance and the evidence of distress must not be too remote from the incident which is the

---

[117] *Stobo v HM Advocate*, 1994 S.L.T. 28.

[118] *Smith v Lees*, 1997 J.C. 73.

[119] *Smith v Lees*, 1997 J.C. 73 at 100.

[120] *Spendiff v HM Advocate*, 2005 S.C.C.R. 522 at para.27; *P v HM Advocate*, 2005 S.C.C.R. 764.

[121] *Cullington v HM Advocate*, 1999 G.W.D. 28-1314.

subject of complaint. The greater the passage of time the more difficult it is to argue that the distress was caused by the incident complained of, as opposed to some other subsequent event. Thus, in *Moore v HM Advocate*[122] no corroboration was found in evidence of distress exhibited some 12 to 13 hours after an alleged rape. The court laid emphasis on the fact that during this period the complainer had seen her boyfriend and visited two public houses looking for her handbag without apparently showing signs of distress. However, in *Cannon v HM Advocate*[123] the evidence of a complainer's distress exhibited some 12 hours after a rape was held to be corroborative, because there was evidence that the complainer delayed disclosing her distress until she had the opportunity to speak to a close friend.

If corroborative merit is to be found in the distress, then the court must be **8–60** satisfied that the distress is caused by the offence and no other intervening factor. In *McLellan v HM Advocate*[124] evidence of a child's distress following alleged lewd and libidinous behaviour was held not to be corroborative because it could have been attributable to the child's fear of getting a row from her mother for disobeying an instruction not to go to the house where the alleged assault occurred. Where there is the possibility of a plausible alternative explanation for the distress it is for the jury to determine which explanation is more supported by the facts.[125]

Corroboration in Civil Cases

The requirement for corroboration of the *facta probanda*, or crucial facts, in **8–61** civil cases was removed by s.1(1) of the Civil Evidence (Scotland) Act 1988. The statute enacted the recommendations of the Scottish Law Commission ("SLC") in their Report, *Evidence: Report on Corroboration, Hearsay and Related Matters*.[126] The SLC pointed out that, given modern practice in civil cases[127]:

> "It ... may be inconsistent with justice that a party, though he may have an honest and credible case, must nevertheless necessarily fail if, through circumstances over which perhaps he has no control, corroboration is not available."

Accordingly, it recommended that "[t]he requirement of corroboration in civil proceedings in so far as it still applies should be abolished".[128]

Prior to the Act there had been other inroads made into the general **8–62** rule that corroboration was required. The SLC had in an earlier report, published in 1965,[129] called for the abolition of the corroboration requirement in all civil cases. Political opposition at that stage restricted the

---

[122] *Moore v HM Advocate*, 1990 S.L.T. 278.
[123] *Cannon v HM Advocate*, 1992 S.L.T. 709.
[124] *McLellan v HM Advocate*, 1992 S.L.T.991.
[125] *Anderson v HM Advocate*, 2001 SLT 1265.
[126] *Report on Corroboration, Hearsay and Related Matters*, 1986. Scot. Law Com. No.100
[127] See para.2.8.
[128] See para.2.10.
[129] Scottish Law Commission, Proposals for *Reform of the Law relating to Corroboration*, HMSO, 1967. Scot Law Com. No.4.

recommendation to dispensing with the need for corroboration in cases of personal injury. This became s.9 of the Law Reform (Miscellaneous Provisions) (Scotland) Act 1968, a section replaced by s.1(1) of the 1988 Act, but the history of its interpretation is valuable in demonstrating how the courts interpreted the rule dispensing with the need for corroboration.

CIVIL EVIDENCE (SCOTLAND) ACT 1988

8–63 There is still relatively little reported case law arising from the operation of s.1(1) of the 1988 Act. However, where a pursuer has relied on that section, there is a clear preference for the liberal approach, which was one of two approaches emerging from the earlier provisions in the 1968 Act. By virtue of s.9, and now in terms of s.1(1) of the 1988 Act, the normal rule of evidence requiring that a party provide a corroborated case was dispensed with in claims for damages or *solatium* in respect of personal injuries. The rule applied whether or not the party claiming was the pursuer, and covered any fact in the case which the court is "satisfied" has been established.

8–64 The case law arising under s.9 of the 1968 Act paved the way for interpretive approaches to the equivalent provision in s.1(1) of the 1988 Act. In the first authoritative consideration of s.9, *Morrison v Kelly & Sons Ltd*,[130] the Court of Session ruled that it did not eliminate the need for corroboration in those cases in which it is available. In the opinion of Lord President Clyde[131]:

> "There may be cases where owing to the nature of the circumstances corroboration is unobtainable. Such a case may be an appropriate subject for the application of the subsection [2]. But, where corroboration or contradiction of the pursuer's account of the matter is available, a Court would obviously be very slow indeed to proceed on the pursuer's evidence alone ... How could the Court be satisfied if corroborative evidence was available but without any explanation not produced?"

The ruling might have been regarded by many as a disappointing start for the new section. However, arguably it merely confirmed that a court will always consider the weight of the evidence presented to it and, conversely, the significance of evidence available but omitted. The case itself was not the best candidate for the application of s.9(2) anyway, since the pursuer produced no corroborating evidence and his own testimony was contradicted by every other witness in the case, including two of his own. In rejecting the pursuer's claim on appeal, the court was doing no more than reflect the weight of the evidence.

---

[130] *Morrison v Kelly & Sons Ltd*, 1970 S.C. 65.
[131] *Morrison v Kelly & Sons Ltd*, 1970 S.C. 65 at 79. See also *McGowan v Lord Advocate*, 1972 S.C. 68, in which the only other witnesses in the case apart from the pursuer either were not called or gave evidence contradicting the pursuer. It was held (a) that the pursuer had failed to satisfy the court of his case, and that the question of corroboration did not, therefore, enter into the matter; and (b) that s.9 was in any case primarily intended to cover a case in which there were no eye-witnesses other than the pursuer.

In *McArthur v Organon Laboratories*[132] conflicting testimony from the **8–65** pursuer and a key witness in an action of damages also prevented the pursuer succeeding. The failure of the case was not due to a lack of corroboration, as it was acknowledged that such corroboration was not required. However, because the judge preferred the contradictory testimony of the eyewitness to the accident to that of the pursuer, the burden on the pursuer to prove the case on a balance of probabilities was not discharged.

A subsequent Outer House ruling in *Thomson v Tough Ropes*[133] produced **8–66** a judgment more in keeping with the spirit of s.9. The pursuer claimed damages for injuries sustained in the course of her work, allegedly as the result of defective equipment. Although the judge disbelieved the pursuer's corroborating witness, B, he did believe the pursuer and was at pains not to penalise her because of the poor quality of the evidence from B. Finding that the pursuer's own evidence had established that the accident had occurred as alleged in her averments, Lord Kincraig decided that he could apply s.9 in her favour because:

> "In my opinion, I am entitled to apply s.9 where the accident occurred in the absence of any credible eye-witness other than the pursuer herself. The fact that there was evidence from an unreliable eye-witness who purported to corroborate the pursuer, should not deprive the pursuer of the assistance of s.9."[134]

Similarly, in *Ward v U.C.S. Ltd*[135] the court found in favour of an uncorroborated pursuer even though at the end of the day it found there had been contributory negligence on his part.

In a dissenting judgment in *McLaren v Caldwell's Paper Mill Co Ltd*,[136] **8–67** Lord Stott ruled that s.9 was intended to prevent the unjust situation in which an honest and reliable pursuer was denied a remedy on a technical rule of law. In the case of *McCallum v British Railways Board*[137] the court adopted a liberal approach to s.9. Despite a certain lack of corroboration of some aspects and a failure to call potential witnesses, the appeal court said that, given the essential facts were proven, the pursuer's apparently credible testimony need not be corroborated. The SLC[138] argued that s.9(2) had proved useful and had not led to "a flood of weak claims". It therefore recommended that the principle of the section be extended to all other civil actions and s.1 of the 1988 Act does precisely this.

The cases since the 1988 Act have confirmed that despite the abolition of **8–68** the need for corroboration, the pursuer still has to prove his or her case and where evidence is led that is preferred to the testimony of the pursuer then the case will not succeed. Equally, where witnesses could have been led, but

---

[132] *McArthur v Organon Laboratories*, 1982 S.L.T. 425.
[133] *Thomson v Tough Ropes*, 1978 S.L.T. (Notes) 5. See also *Comerford v Strathclyde Regional Council*, 1987 S.C.L.R. 758.
[134] *Thomson v Tough Ropes*, 1978 S.L.T. (Notes) 5 at 6.
[135] *Ward v U.C.S. Ltd*, 1973 S.L.T. 182.
[136] *McLaren v Caldwell's Paper Mill Co Ltd*, 1973 S.L.T. 158.
[137] *McCallum v British Railways Board*, 1991 S.L.T. 5. The case dealt with an accident and judgment at first instance that predated the 1988 Act.
[138] See para.2.10, *Report on corroboration, Hearsay and Related Matters*, 1986. Scot. Law Com. No.100.

for whatever reason the pursuer chooses not to call them, the court will not necessarily draw adverse inferences. Thus, in *Airnes v Chief Constable of Strathclyde*[139] the failure of the pursuer to call a witness who was present at the time of the alleged assault for which she was seeking an award of damages, was highlighted in the appeal by the defender against a finding of fault. However, the appeal court upheld the award and noted a variety of reasons why it might not be appropriate to call witnesses to an event that occurred some five years previously.

8–69   In terms of s.8(1) of the Civil Evidence (Scotland) Act 1988, decree or judgment in favour of the pursuer in certain family proceedings shall not be pronounced until the grounds of action have been established by evidence. This requirement for evidence applies to actions for divorce; dissolution of civil partnership; separation of spouses or of civil partners; declarator of marriage or of nullity of marriage or of civil partnership; or for parentage or non-parentage.[140] Section 8(3) provides that in an action of divorce, separation or declarator of marriage, or nullity of marriage, the evidence required to establish the grounds of an action "shall consist of or include evidence other than that of a party to the marriage". Section 8(3A) makes equivalent provision for civil partnerships.

8–70   Evidence can come for a source other than another witness, e.g. an extract conviction of a spouse or civil partner's violent behaviour, though even here, a third party will be required to give evidence that the identity of the person to whom the conviction refers is the defender.[141] Section 8(3) avoids using the term "corroboration", but it nonetheless needs to be evidence that is relevant to the pursuer's averments in the pleadings. As the Inner House noted in *Taylor v Taylor*,[142] "recourse to the language of corroboration is not strictly necessary" in a divorce action based on the ground of unreasonable behaviour, but there must nonetheless be sufficient evidence to satisfy the requirements of s.8(3). In *Taylor* family members were able to provide evidence "to establish, along with the evidence of the pursuer, a pattern of behaviour on the part of the defender," a sufficiency which was, in effect, corroborative of "certain specific matters and of the overall pattern and its consequences".[143]

[139] *Airnes v Chief Constable of Strathclyde*, 1998 S.L.T. (Sh. Ct) 15.
[140] See s.8(2) as amended.
[141] *Andrews v Andrews*, 1971 S.L.T. (Notes) 44.
[142] *Taylor v Taylor*, 2000 S.L.T. 1419 at 1423, para.15.
[143] *Taylor v Taylor*, 2000 S.L.T. 1419 at 1423, para.15.

Chapter 9

CONFESSION EVIDENCE

INTRODUCTION

This chapter is concerned with the rules governing the admissibility of **9–01** confession evidence. Scots common law has established a set of principles to govern the admissibility of evidence which is relevant to a case, but which was obtained without lawful authority. Evidence that is unlawfully obtained, such as obtaining a confession by putting a suspect under duress, is not automatically inadmissible in court, but it will only be permitted if the court is persuaded that it is fair and proper to do so. Separate from confession evidence, there is also a set of rules regulating the admissibility of illegally obtained goods or other tangible items, including drugs, stolen goods, or forensic samples. The next chapter focuses on the latter, but the two sets of rules are very closely related. Both serve to uphold fairness and propriety, principles which go to the heart of civil libertarian values and reflect the legal obligation to ensure that an accused person receives a fair trial.

A balance has to be struck between two distinct competing interests: the **9–02** rights of the accused to a fair trial and the interests of the state in prosecuting criminal behaviour and upholding justice. As each case is determined according to its own facts and circumstances, judicial discretion plays an important role in this area. This creates difficulties in defining the precise parameters of evidence which is unlawfully obtained, but which is nevertheless deemed admissible. The case law is not always coherent or consistent and it is often possible to find conflicting lines of authority to support opposing propositions. Unlike the position in English law, there are no general statutory provisions governing the admissibility confession evidence. Instead, the judges have developed guiding principles of admissibility through a very extensive body of case law.

CONFESSION EVIDENCE

Confession evidence plays a very significant role in daily practice within the **9–03** criminal courts. According to Griffiths,[1] "[c]onfession evidence is one of the commonest types of evidence tendered in the Scottish courts and it has a major place in the general law of criminal evidence".

A confession is an exceptionally potent item of evidence because it is a **9–04** statement made by a person against their own interest. People do not generally make statements against their own interests—therefore, if they do, it is

---

[1] D. Griffiths, *Confessions* (Edinburgh: Butterworths, 1994), p.1.

assumed these statements are more likely than not to be true.[2] A confession is described as an extra-judicial admission because it is a statement made outside a court of law. The term "confession" is used to describe any statement of admission made by someone who later becomes the accused in a criminal trial. In civil cases an admission by someone who later becomes a party to a civil action rarely carries such serious consequences as an admission made in the criminal context, but it may still constrain the lines of proof or defence open to such a party.

9–05   When such confessions in criminal cases, or admissions in civil cases, are made formally in court, as part of the judicial process, they are known in both criminal and civil cases as judicial admissions, which are binding upon the maker once they are made.[3] Extra-judicial admissions and confessions do not carry the equivalent weight of judicial admissions. However, when a party has made a confession and then gives sworn evidence in court, their previous confession may clearly have relevance to their credibility if it conflicts with the evidence they now give. Where a party does not give evidence, then their previous admission or confession is admissible as an exception to the hearsay rule.[4]

9–06   In criminal cases, confessions are not the sole evidence in a case, because of the current general rule in Scots law requiring corroboration of crucial facts. If the requirement for corroboration is removed by statute then in law no other evidence may be needed, though if there are reservations concerning the quality of the confession, it would obviously be prudent to produce other evidence to ensure that there is sufficient evidence to take the matter beyond reasonable doubt and warrant a conviction. The circumstances in which the confession was obtained will largely determine its probative value. For example, in *Buick v Jaglar*[5] Sheriff Wilkinson observed:

> "It is true, no doubt, that a statement against interest, made coolly and after reflection, is stronger evidence against its maker than a statement made by a person who is in a greatly distressed condition. It is also no doubt true that such a statement is stronger evidence if it never be contradicted or it be contradicted only after a long interval than if it is contradicted shortly after it is made."[6]

Confessions that have been unfairly obtained are considered inherently unsafe. Even if thought to be true, if there are procedural defects in the manner in which the police have acquired them, such that they jeopardise a fair trial, then they should be considered unsafe and contrary to public policy to rely upon them. When the courts hold a confession to have been unfairly obtained, such that a fair trial is precluded, it will be ruled inadmissible.

---

[2] Dickson, *Evidence*, para.297.
[3] See Ch.15.
[4] See Ch.9.
[5] *Buick v Jaglar*, 1973 S.L.T. (Sh. Ct) 6 at 8.
[6] See also Lord Kincraig in *Liquid Gas Tankers Ltd v Forth Ports Authority*, 1974 S.L.T. (Notes) 35, who approved the statement in Walker and Walker, *Evidence*, 1st edn, pp.27–29, that "in each case the probative weight to be attached to ... an admission must depend upon the circumstances of the particular case".

ADMISSIONS AND CONFESSIONS TO THE POLICE

The decision in *Cadder v HM Advocate* in 2009[7] profoundly altered the law **9–07** and practice within the police station in regard to the detention and questioning of suspects and in the recording of procedures. Cadder was detained by the police in terms of s.14 of the Criminal Procedure (Scotland) Act 1995 on suspicion of serious assault. Although s.14 requires a detainee to provide his name, address, date and place of birth and nationality, he can remain silent in response to further questioning. Cadder was permitted to have a solicitor notified of his detention but he chose not to avail himself of that right.[8] During the subsequent interview by the police he made a number of incriminating admissions which ultimately led to his conviction at trial. He appealed on the basis that as his interview had taken place in the absence of a solicitor, it breached his art.6(3)(c) right to a fair trial.

The Supreme Court held that in the light of the decision of the Grand **9–08** Chamber of the ECtHR in *Salduz v Turkey*,[9] art.6(3) read in connection with art.6(1) of the ECHR required that a person detained under the Criminal Procedure (Scotland) Act 1995 s.14 was entitled to legal advice prior to the start of questioning by the police, unless, in the particular circumstances of the case there were compelling reasons to restrict that right.[10] The Supreme Court further held that the safeguards otherwise available under the Scottish system, which the seven bench decision in *McLeod v HM Advocate*[11] had recently ruled were sufficient to ensure a fair trial in Scotland,[12] were in fact incapable of removing the disadvantage which a detainee would suffer if denied access to legal advice before police questioning. Giving the leading judgment, Lord Hope noted, "[i]t is remarkable that, until quite recently, nobody [including obviously the bench of seven judges in McLean] thought that there was anything wrong with this procedure".[13] However, the Supreme Court considered that *Salduz* did have effect in Scots law.[14] At a stroke the Supreme Court thus overruled the previously established jurisprudence of the High Court of Justiciary, According to Lord Hope the principles of equality of arms and the need to protect a suspect from "abusive coercion" once facing questioning in a police investigation may mean that:

> "[I]n the majority of cases this vulnerability can only be adequately compensated for by the presence of a lawyer whose task it is to . . . help ensure that the right of an accused not to incriminate himself is respected."[15]

---

[7] *Cadder v HM Advocate* [2010] UKSC 43.
[8] *Cadder v HM Advocate* [2010] UKSC 43 at para.5.
[9] *Salduz v Turkey* (2009) 49 E.H.R.R. 19.
[10] *Cadder v HM Advocate* [2010] UKSC 43 at para.41.
[11] *HM Advocate v McLean*, 2010 S.L.T. 73 citing these safeguards as including the opportunity afforded to a suspect in detention to have a solicitor notified of the fact of detention; the need for corroboration of confession evidence.
[12] *McLeod v HM Advocate*, 2010 S.L.T. 73.
[13] *Cadder v HM Advocate* [2010] UKSC 43 at para.4.
[14] *Cadder v HM Advocate* [2010] UKSC 43 at paras 48–50.
[15] *Cadder v HM Advocate* [2010] UKSC 43 at para.33.

The Supreme Court held that, in order to be compliant with art.6, s.14 should be read and given effect so as to preclude, as a general rule, the admission in evidence of any incriminating answers obtained by the police from a detainee who was subjected to questioning without access to legal advice. The repercussions of the *Cadder* decision on the criminal justice system were substantial. In the immediate aftermath of the ruling, all live cases where the Crown relied solely on a "Cadder type" interview and where there was no alternative corroborated evidence to mount a prosecution, had to be abandoned. In total, 1,286 cases were abandoned, of which 80 were the more serious solemn cases, including 9 scheduled for the High Court.[16] In addition, the Criminal Procedure (Legal Assistance, Detention and Appeals) (Scotland) Act 2010 was urgently enacted to enable the Legal Aid Board to fund solicitors to provide legal advice at police stations. Police practice in relation to the conduct of interviews has been transformed and the requirement post-*Cadder* that prior to a police interview a suspect must be given the opportunity to consult with a solicitor will inevitably reduce the likelihood that a suspect will make a voluntary confession, or indeed say anything much at all of evidential value. When we reflect on the 1,286 cases that had to be abandoned post-*Cadder* it gives a sense of the significant scale of statements with evidential value that, hitherto, had been derived from police interviews.

9–09   After the decision *in Cadder v HM Advocate*,[17] revised statutory rights were enacted concerning persons held in custody, whether as suspects detained in terms of s.14 or arrested and not liberated. These include the right, without delay, to access a solicitor (and to have a private consultation).[18] Exceptionally, where necessary, some delay may be permitted, such as in the interests of making a further arrest, or the prevention of crime.[19]

Following *Cadder*, there was a series of Supreme Court cases that became known as the "sons of *Cadder*", which sought to delineate the boundaries of the right to access legal advice before questioning and in turn address some of the unanswered implications of the *Cadder* decision itself. In particular, clarity was required in regard to: when a person could be said to be a suspect; when they could be said to be in police custody; and when police questioning could be said to have started. While each of these might be relatively easily established if the relevant events all took place in the police station, none of the sons of *Cadder* cases did. It is convenient here to discuss these cases using the three categories adopted by White and Ferguson in their analysis,[20] namely: triggering access to legal advice and the right against self-incrimination; possible waiver of the right to legal advice; and the operation of the "the fruit of the poisonous tree" doctrine.

---

[16] The majority of these were crimes of indecency and crimes of violence. For further detail see: *http://www.crownoffice.gov.uk/foi/responses-we-have-made-to-foi-requests* [accessed July 30, 2013].

[17] *Cadder v HM Advocate* [2010] UKSC. 43.

[18] s.15. See Renton & Brown, *Criminal Procedure*, 6th edn.

[19] s.15(1)(b). Renton & Brown, *Criminal Procedure*, 6th edn.

[20] R. White and P. Ferguson, "Sins of the father? The 'sons of Cadder'", 2013 Crim. L.R. 357–368.

When is the right to legal advice triggered?

In regard to when access is triggered, the short answer appears to be when **9–10** the suspect/detainee is in custody. However, determining when a person is in custody is not always straightforward. In *HM Advocate v G*[21] the accused was handcuffed during the course of a search of his flat for drugs and firearms, and while he has was already under arrest for a different offence. His incriminating answers to questions posed during the search were held to be inadmissible as he had been given no opportunity to receive legal advice. The fact his liberty was curtailed by being handcuffed was a clear trigger of his custodial status. In contrast, in *Ambrose v Harris*[22] the accused had been cautioned at the roadside in relation to a drink driving charge and had made statements to police officers that were ruled admissible evidence at his trial. In *HM Advocate v M*[23] the accused was charged with a serious assault and was initially interviewed as a witness at his home under a common law caution. After suspicious responses to questioning (i.e. his admission of involvement in a fight) the interviewed was terminated and continued in terms of s.14 the following night at a police station.

The majority in the Supreme Court (Lord Kerr dissenting) drew a dis- **9–11** tinction between the person who is a suspect and in custody, and who is entitled to legal advice; and the person who has become a suspect but is not yet in custody, perhaps for practical reasons, e.g. they have been asked questions at the scene of a crime. The majority in Ambrose considered that the Strasbourg jurisprudence was not yet unequivocally behind a rule that the suspect who is not yet in custody was entitled to legal advice before being asked questions. While the Court affirmed that the effect of *Cadder* was that "the Lord Advocate had no power to lead and rely on answers by a detainee who was subjected to questioning by the police while he was without access to legal advice",[24] they also found that none of the accused in the cases listed was a detainee as defined by s.14 of the 1995 Act. Instead the common law rules of admissibility would apply—any answers the accused gave to the police before they had access to legal advice would be assessed on the whole circumstances of the case and the extent to which a fair trial was still achievable. Although Lord Hope thought that *Salduz* was ambiguous on whether incriminating statements made before legal advice was available would be admissible,[25] Lord Kerr, dissenting, considered that the circumstances were clearly capable of producing incriminating responses and were inadmissible.[26] In determining the sons of *Cadder* cases, the Supreme Court reviewed the international case law concerning police questioning, suspects' rights and the fair trial. While a resolution has been arrived at meantime, it is not a settled area of law. Lord Kerr's observation in *Ambrose*, that it was not enough for the Court to simply identify the Strasbourg jurisprudence and go no further, but it should instead anticipate Convention development, was not an approach shared by the other judges.[27]

---

[21] *HM Advocate v G*, listed in *Ambrose v Harris* [2011] UKSC 43.
[22] *Ambrose v Harris* [2011] UKSC 43.
[23] Listed in *Ambrose v Harris* [2011] UKSC 43.
[24] *Ambrose v Harris* [2011] UKSC 43.
[25] *Ambrose v Harris* [2011] UKSC 43 at paras 67–72.
[26] *Ambrose v Harris* [2011] UKSC 43 at paras 173–175.
[27] *Ambrose v Harris*, [2011] UKSC 43 at para.130.

The sons of *Cadder* decisions can best be understood as a refinement of the broad right against self-incrimination stressed in *Cadder*, towards a right against *forced* self-incrimination. Whilst *Cadder* certainly reconfigured the territory, there appears to have been a concerted attempt to narrow its effect thereafter.

When is a waiver of the right to legal advice valid?

9–12 The appellant in *McGowan v B* [2011] UKSC 43[28] was detained under s.14 of the 1995 Act on suspicion of housebreaking with intent to steal and associated charges. After being cautioned, both at the locus of the crime and again at the police station, he declined a private consultation with a solicitor, signed a declaration to that effect and verbally confirmed it. Subsequent to this, he was interviewed and made incriminating statements and was then arrested in relation to the housebreaking charge. He was interviewed separately in relation to a drugs charge and again refused the offer of consulting a solicitor.

9–13 The Supreme Court noted that nothing in its own jurisprudence suggested that as a rule, the right to legal advice could only be waived during police interviewing following discussion with a lawyer as to whether to do so. In similar vein, nothing in Scots law prevented waiver (applying Lord Bingham's dictum in *Miller v Dickson*[29] of validity being established so long as the waivers were "voluntary, informed and unequivocal"). Given the possibility of there being a disagreement over how and when the waiver was obtained, Lord Kerr recommended that a record be kept of the reason for waiver. He reiterated this in McGowan[30]:

> "...I consider that such safeguards as are currently available in Scottish law to protect the interests of a suspect are not efficacious to ensure that a decision not to have legal assistance constitutes an effective waiver. In particular, I have pointed out that it is an indispensable prerequisite that there must be some means of ascertaining the reason that a decision not to avail of this fundamental right has been taken."

Lord Kerr made it clear he did not regard this as this "a startling new rule",[31] rather a logical interpretation of existing Strasbourg jurisprudence.[32]

9–14 The Supreme Court did stress, however, that there would be circumstances where access to legal advice prior to waiver was required, e.g. where the suspect was of low intelligence or under the influence of drink or drugs and may not be able to understand the right. The statutory provisions now in place give suspects a right to legal advice before being interviewed and a right to a private consultation, including a telephone conversation with a solicitor.[33]

---

[28] Listed in *Ambrose v Harris* [2011] UKSC 43.
[29] *Miller v Dickson*, 2001 S.L.T. 988.
[30] *Ambrose v Harris* [2011] UKSC 43 at para.130 at para.53.
[31] *Ambrose v Harris* [2011] UKSC 43 at paras 130 at para.61.
[32] *Ambrose v Harris* [2011] UKSC 43 at paras 130 at para.59–61.
[33] Discussed earlier in this chapter.

When might the "fruit of the poisoned tree" doctrine apply?

The fruit of the poisoned tree doctrine is discussed more generally in Ch.10, **9–15** but it arose as part of the post-*Cadder* issues. In *HM Advocate v P*[34] the accused was indicted at the High Court for a charge of assault and rape, was interviewed without access to legal advice and subsequently named a friend who he claimed would "corroborate" his version of events. This friend was then interviewed by the police. In the course of his interview he made a mixed statement,[35] with comments that in part corroborated the account of the accused, but in part also incriminated him. The contentious issue referred by the High Court to the Supreme Court was whether: (1) the suspect's evidence was admissible; and (2) whether the evidence of his friend was admissible. The argument proffered was that as the suspect's evidence was inadmissible by virtue of the *Cadder* decision, the evidence of his friend should also be inadmissible as it was obtained by virtue of the (unlawful) questioning of a suspect who had not had legal advice. The Court relied upon the ECtHR decision in *Gafgen v Germany*[36] in holding that[37]:

"... [T]here was nothing explicit in the Strasbourg jurisprudence to suggest that the leading of the evidence of the "fruits" of an interview where the accused had no access to a solicitor would automatically contravene an accused's article 6 rights."

The application was remitted to the High Court to apply national rules, e.g. *Chalmers v HM Advocate*[38] and *Lawrie v Muir*.[39]

ADMISSIONS AND CONFESSIONS BY WITNESSES IN PREVIOUS CASES

A witness who gives evidence in a case, but not as a party to it, may make **9–16** statements or admissions while on oath in the witness box. Any confessional statement made by that witness is regarded as an extra-judicial admission or confession for the purposes of any later case to which he or she is a party and in which that statement is relevant.[40] Where possible, of course, the witness should be warned before giving such evidence of any privilege against self-incrimination that may apply.[41] In *Banaghan v HM Advocate*[42] B was charged with sending a threatening letter and the Crown were allowed to adduce evidence of the fact that in a previous civil action to which B had not been a party, he had admitted to having been the writer of the letter. In *Edmison*[43] the same rule was applied in regard to a confession of guilt made by Edmison at the criminal trial of another person charged with that offence. It is because of the admissibility of such statements in later cases

---

[34] *HM Advocate v P* [2011] UKSC 44.
[35] See Ch.3.
[36] *Gafgen v Germany* (2011) 52 E.H.R.R.
[37] *HM Advocate v P* [2011] UKSC 44.
[38] *Chalmers v HM Advocate*, 1954 J.C.66.
[39] *Lawrie v Muir*, 1950 J.C.15.
[40] Dickson, *Evidence*, para.288.
[41] See Ch.5 and 13.
[42] (1888) 15 R. (J.) 39; (1888) 1 White 566.
[43] (1866) 1 S.L.R. 107; (1866) 5 Irv 519.

that the need exists for a privilege against self-incrimination. While it would be preferable if a formal record of the admission, such as the transcript or the judge's notes, was available, reliable oral evidence of the making of the statement may be sufficient.[44]

IMPLIED ADMISSIONS AND CONFESSIONS

9–17 At common law an admission or confession may sometimes be implied. This might occur from a person's silence or other reaction when confronted with an allegation that would ordinarily call for some sort of reply, such as a denial. Dickson noted that, "[a]dmissions may be implied from a party remaining silent when statements to his prejudice are made in his presence".[45] However, such a concept is not consistent with modern understandings of fairness. An accused who remains silent in the face of a charge or accusation, or offers a flat denial[46] would still be entitled to the benefit of the presumption of innocence and the right of a person not to make an incriminating statement.

9–18 This does not, however, eliminate the possibility of the court inferring some sort of confession from the fact that an accused reacted in a particular way to a statement made in his or her presence and/or hearing which might be expected to produce a response. For this reason "statements made in the presence of an accused" are regularly admitted as an exception to the hearsay rule in order to cast light on the accused's reaction to them, be it silence or some action, such as bursting into tears or turning pale. For example, in *Annan v Bain*[47] two suspects, who had been chased to a standstill by police officers from the point at which they had abandoned a stolen car, made statements there and then. One of them referred to a "white car" (which only the thieves might have been expected to know) and the other was held to have adopted this reference by remaining silent. It proved crucial in providing corroboration.

9–19 Admissions implied by adoption must be approached with care in regard to the context in which the original statement was made. In *Hipson v Tudhope*[48] Hipson had been a passenger in a stolen car that was pursued by police after it failed to stop. When the police asked whose car it was, another accused, in the presence of H, stated that it was stolen. It was held on appeal that the fact H had not distanced himself from this confession did not amount to a new confession by him. The court said that in view of Hipson's explanation that he did not know that the car was stolen when he accepted a lift in it, he could not be convicted of reset.[49]

9–20 Statute may impose an obligation on a person to reply to police questioning, or be guilty of an offence. The reply may infer guilt. For example, s.172 of the Road Traffic Act 1988 requires a potential witness/accused to

---

[44] See *McGiveran v Auld* (1894) 21 R. (J.) 69 at 72.

[45] Dickson, *Evidence*, para.368. See too, *Larkin v HM Advocate*, 2005 S.L.T. 1087.

[46] See *Robertson v Maxwell*, 1951 J .C. 11 at 14. *Saunders v UK* (1996) E.H.R.R. 313.

[47] *Annan v Bain*, 1986 S.C.C.R. 60. See however *HM Advocate v Davidson*, 1968 S.L.T. 17, where the point was made that the police will not be permitted to force two accused into this sort of confrontation.

[48] *Hipson v Tudhope*, 1983 S.L.T. 659.

[49] See also *Clark v HM Advocate*, 1965 S.L.T. 250.

answer police questions concerning the identity of the driver of a motor vehicle owned by the witness. The answers are subsequently admissible in evidence in court proceedings.

This section was challenged in *Brown v Stott*[50] where the defence argued **9–21** that Brown's obligation to incriminate herself under the road traffic legislation (by identifying herself to the police as the driver of a car when she was suspected of being drunk) was an infringement of her Convention right to a fair trial under art.6. The Judicial Committee of the Privy Council quashed the declaration made by the High Court on the ground that art.6 did not confer absolute rights in circumstances where the state was justified in curtailing the rights of an individual in the broader public interest.[51]

FORM OF CONFESSIONS

There is no distinction made in law between oral confessions and those that **9–22** are in writing or in some other form, such as incriminating behaviour. All such activities are considered statements against interest and are subject to the same rules of admissibility. A written statement may well appear more reliable, but such statements may be challenged on the ground that they did not emanate from the accused, or that they are not in his or her own words. A court will regard as inadmissible a statement that has simply been prepared by a third party for signature by the accused.[52]

In this regard, the English case of *R. v Voisin*[53] provides a vivid illustration **9–23** of how behaviour can be suggestive of guilt. In that case the police were investigating the murder of a woman whose body was found in a parcel with a scrap of paper with words "Bladie Belgiam" written upon it. Voisin was asked to write down these same words and he wrote "Bladie Belgiam". He was subsequently convicted. In *Manuel v HM Advocate*[54] the conduct of Manuel in being able to lead the police to the scene of the crime and point out where a shoe belonging to the victim was buried constituted a confession.

VICARIOUS ADMISSIONS AND CONFESSIONS

As a general rule, an admission or confession made by co-accused A in a **9–24** criminal trial will not be admissible against co-accused B, and similarly in a civil case when A and B are joint pursuers or joint defenders. There are two well recognised exceptions to this general rule. First, where it is shown that the accused were acting in concert, and second, when the statement by A

---

[50] *Brown v Stott*, 2000 S.L.T. 379.
[51] Discussed in Ch.13.
[52] This is often the case with confessions made to police officers. A precognition will also fail the admissibility test: see *Carmichael v Armitage*, 1983 J.C. 8, in which the High Court rejected as inadmissible a declaration made by Armitage before a sheriff which had been prepared for him by his solicitor, as it was more in the nature of a precognition than a statement by the accused himself.
[53] *R. v Voisin* [1918] 1 K.B. 531.
[54] *Manuel v HM Advocate*, 1958 J.C. 41. See, too, *Chalmers v HM Advocate*, 1954 J.C. 66, discussed below as an example of incriminating conduct.

was made in the presence of B and might reasonably be regarded as having required some response from B.

9–25   When the accused act together with a common purpose, they are acting in concert. Before any confession by A will be admissible against B, it must relate to that common purpose. There are relatively few cases on the point,[55] but an example of the principle in operation was *HM Advocate v Docherty*,[56] where the accused was charged with corruption in the public office which he occupied, his alleged corrupter being a person, J, who was dead by the date of the trial. The Crown sought to adduce evidence of incriminating statements made by J in the furtherance of corrupt acts involving Docherty. It was held that if the jury came to the conclusion that Docherty and J were acting in concert, then, since Docherty would be answerable for actions performed by J, it was permissible for the jury to be made aware of J's contemporaneous statements concerning those actions. In short, J's statements were part of the *res gestae* and Docherty was bound by them in so far as the two were acting in concert.

9–26   As noted earlier, a statement made by A in the presence of B may be regarded as having been adopted by B if he fails to dissociate himself from it.[57] However, this will not apply when the second accused has been compelled to listen to the statement in question against his will. In *HM Advocate v Davidson*[58] the accused had been cautioned and charged and placed in a police cell. Shortly afterwards he was brought to the charge bar to hear what a co-accused, C, said when cautioned and charged. He was given no reason for being brought to the bar, and was not warned of what was to happen, or the consequences for him. The subsequent confession by C was inadmissible against Davidson in these circumstances, as it amounted to a breach of Davidson's fundamental right to remain silent after caution and charge.

9–27   Where co-accused A and B are not acting in concert, and A has not made any statement in the presence of B to which a reply could reasonably be expected, the general rule applies—B is not incriminated by anything A says.[59] In *Jones v HM Advocate*[60] the High Court reaffirmed this general principle, emphasising the need for trial judges to make it plain to juries that in normal cases, a confession by one accused is not admissible against any other.

Admissibility of Confessions

9–28   A confession by an accused person carries a great deal of weight. This is so even if the accused subsequently declines to give evidence at their trial. A confession is potentially one of the most powerful items of evidence that can be adduced against an accused. This is because a confession is a statement against interest. One is presumed not to make statements against one's own interest. Therefore, if such a statement is made it is presumed to be true.

---

[55] See, however, *Young v HM Advocate*, 1932 J.C. 63.
[56] 1980 S.L.T. (Notes) 33, citing Walker and Walker, *Evidence*, 1st edn, para.37.
[57] See *Annan v Bain*, 1986 S.C.C.R. 60.
[58] *HM Advocate v Davidson*, 1968 S.L.T. 17.
[59] See, e.g. *Black v HM Advocate*, 1974 J.C. 43 and *Murray v HM Advocate*, 1996 S.L.T. 648.
[60] *Jones v HM Advocate*, 1981 S.C.C.R. 192.

There could, of course, be alternative explanations for the making of a **9–29** statement against interest, such as fabrication or suggestibility, either of which may be motivated by numerous factors. There is a wealth of research evidence to demonstrate this.[61] The primary rule regulating the admissibility of confessions can be reduced to one word—fairness. The test has been described as follows:

> "It is not possible to lay down *ab ante* the precise circumstances in which answers given to the police prior to a charge being made are admissible in evidence at the ultimate trial or where they are inadmissible. This is so much a question of the particular circumstances of each case and those circumstances vary infinitely from one another. But the test in all of them is the simple and intelligible test which has worked well in practice—has what has taken place been fair or not?"[62]

However, the criterion of fairness conceals a great number of complex questions which must be addressed when trying to establish admissibility. At the core of fairness is the attempt to strike the right balance between the public interest in seeing crime controlled and the civil liberties of individuals not to be interrogated in a manner which breaches their rights.

The Fairness Test

It is an essential quality of confession evidence that it has been obtained **9–30** fairly, i.e. given freely and voluntarily, without pressure, inducement or duress. These constituent elements of a fair confession are context dependent. They have to be seen and evaluated by the fact-finder with regard to all the surrounding circumstances. The incriminatory potential of the confession makes it imperative that the law should ensure statements from an accused are genuinely voluntary. If they do not fulfil this criterion then the statement will not be fair and will be inadmissible as evidence. The reforms discussed earlier in the wake of *Cadder v HM Advocate*[63] reinforced the importance of ensuring that confession evidence was not obtained unfairly standing the environment in which incriminating statements might often be obtained. There are long established common law principles which pre-date, but largely reflect, the modern international standards of the fair trial, to which Scots law has always sought to adhere and which remain relevant today.

Is the statement voluntary?

One of the most influential articulations in the modern development of the **9–31** admissibility of confession evidence was expressed by Lord Justice General Thomson in *Chalmers v HM Advocate*.[64] His dicta have stood the test of time and are entirely compatible with the discourse of fairness now associated with art.6 of the ECHR:

---

[61] For discussion see G. Gudjonsson, *The Psychology of Interrogations, Confessions and Testimony* (Chichester: Wiley, 1992).

[62] In *Brown v HM Advocate*, 1966 S.L.T. 105 at 107 per Lord Justice General Clyde.

[63] *Cadder v HM Advocate* [2010] UKSC 43.

[64] *Chalmers v HM Advocate*, 1954 J.C. 66.

"A voluntary statement is one which is given freely, not in response to pressure and inducement and not elicited by cross-examination. This does not mean that if a person elects to give a statement it becomes inadmissible because he is asked some questions to clear up his account of the matter, but such questions ... must not go beyond elucidation."

The common law concept of voluntary has numerous characteristics, all of which are consistent with the principles of a fair trial. Those emerging in the case law include that an incriminating statement must be "freely given" and not the result of pressure from the police. For example, if a suspect was told they would be allowed to go home if information was forthcoming, or, conversely, if they were told that they would be held in custody overnight if information was not forthcoming, that could constitute pressure.[65] A statement that was produced in response to threats or inducements, however subtly implied, could constitute pressure[66] and a statement that was the product of a misunderstanding, even if unintentional,[67] could also constitute pressure. In similar vein, the likelihood of misunderstandings in the questioning process will increase if the suspect has a learning disability.[68]

9–32   To do something voluntarily assumes the suspect is in full possession of their cognitive faculties. For example, a person who is drunk may not be able to make a confession freely. But just because someone has been drinking does not mean their confession is inadmissible.[69] Inappropriate pressure need not be crude or physical. Thus, removing a young person from their bed in the middle of the night, without the involvement of a parent or parental figure,[70] when the circumstances raise no obvious urgency, may well cast doubt on the "voluntary" nature of any subsequent confession.[71]

9–33   The contemporary circumstances where voluntary admissions may take on particular significance are where a suspect waives their right to legal advice prior to police questioning and goes on to make incriminating statements. It is submitted this is now a two stage process. First, the decision to waive one's rights is one that must be voluntary and not made under pressure. Second, subsequent responses to police questioning must also be voluntary and fair. In other words, a waiver of rights at stage one provides no guarantee that the police interview process will be fair. Both art.6 and common law rights are engaged. In *McCann v HM Advocate*[72] the accused was a 16 year old who made incriminating statements to police after waiving his right to legal advice in relation to a robbery and assault. He appealed claiming that due to his age (16) and the influence of drink and drugs he did not recall the interview or being advised about his rights. The trial judge rejected this evidence and preferred the police version of events, finding that the waiver was "unequivocal". The appeal court followed *McGowan v B.*[73]

---

[65] *Black v Annan*, 1996 S.L.T. 284.
[66] *Codona v HM Advocate*, 1996 S.L.T. 1100.
[67] *HM Advocate v McSwiggan*, 1937 J.C. 50.
[68] *Hartley v HM Advocate*, 1979 S.L.T. 26.
[69] *Thomson v HM Advocate*, 1989 S.L.T. 170.
[70] *B v HM Advocate*, 1995 S.L.T. 961 where the accused was said to have impaired mental capacity and to be highly suggestible.
[71] *HM Advocate v B*, 1991 S.C.C.R. 533.
[72] *McCann v HM Advocate* [2013] HCJAC 29.
[73] Listed in *Ambrose v Harris* [2011] UKSC 43.

As there was no rule of law which required a 16 year old to have access to a lawyer, there was a valid waiver. McCann's incriminating statements were therefore admissible. Several points made by the court are worth noting: it was said the appellant appeared to be of normal intelligence; not especially vulnerable; it had not been argued at trial that that he required a parent or carer to explain the significance of waiving his legal rights; and it was accepted his right of access to a lawyer had been explained to him on three occasions in simple language. In the absence of specific evidence of vulnerability the appeal was refused.

In recent years the case law from the ECtHR has sharpened awareness of **9–34** the need for appropriate treatment of vulnerable accused persons in complying with a fair trial.[74] As a result, there has been more effort made to accommodate the vulnerability of young persons under the age of 16 years (and sometimes under the age of 18 years[75]), as well as the vulnerability of those who suffer from learning disabilities, or other intellectual incapacity short of a mental disorder, which might require compulsory intervention under the mental health legislation.[76] Support from the appropriate adult scheme is available in some cities,[77] but is not universally accessible.

Was there any pressure on the accused?

Even in the absence of overt aggression, threats or incentives, a confession **9–35** may be regarded as unfair if there is any suggestion of pressure. In *Balloch v HM Advocate*[78] the accused made a highly incriminating statement to police officers after several hours of questioning. During the interrogation Balloch had come under strong suspicion of guilt and, shortly after being shown, for a second time, the clothing and belongings of the deceased, with whom he had lodged, he confessed. The statement was made without caution and afterwards Balloch was asked if he was sure he was telling the truth. In upholding the trial judge's decision to allow the confession to be put to the jury, Lord Justice-General Wheatley stated that:

> "[A] Judge who has heard the evidence regarding the manner in which a challenged statement was made will normally be justified in withholding the evidence from the jury only if he is satisfied on the undisputed relevant evidence that no reasonable jury could hold that the statement had been voluntarily made and had not been extracted by unfair or improper means."[79]

Threats or inducements will also be classed as unfair, undermining the voluntary nature of the statement and depriving a subsequent confession of any utility that it might have had as an item of evidence. The case law pre-

---

[74] See *T v UK and U v UK*, 2000 30 E.H.R.R.121.

[75] The Victims and Witnesses (Scotland) Bill 2013 proposes make special measures automatically available to children up to the age of 18, rather than 16 as at present.

[76] For example, support at the police interview for vulnerable witnesses with a learning disability may be available through the Appropriate Adult Scheme. See Ch.3.

[77] An appropriate adult is a trained and skilled volunteer who can help to ensure a suspect or witness understands the questions put to them. See: *http://www.scotland.gov.uk/Topics/Justice/law/victims-witnesses/Appropriate-Adult/Guidance* [accessed July 31, 2013].

[78] *Balloch v HM Advocate*, 1977 S.C. 23.

[79] *Balloch v HM Advocate*, 1977 S.C. 23 at 28.

Cadder offers valuable assistance as to the standards expected of fairness, but changes in procedure prompted by *Cadder*, particularly the right to legal advice at the police station, reduce, though do not eliminate, the opportunity for pressure to be put upon an accused person. For example, the greater protection for a suspect, and at an earlier stage in proceedings, should lead to less allegations of improperly obtained evidence at police stations[80] due to threats,[81] tricks[82] or pressure.[83] Similarly, if a suspect is unwittingly tricked or induced into making an incriminating statement then it is unlikely that the statement will meet the test of being voluntary and fair, and will therefore be inadmissible.[84] Where suspects are "encouraged" to make statements, that will be unfair unless they can be shown to be genuinely voluntary.[85]

9–36   Pressure may also be inferred from the circumstances and nature of the police questioning. Unfairness can extend across a broad spectrum of practice:

> "[O]nce a prisoner has been taken into custody and been cautioned and charged and his answer, if any, to the caution and charge noted—after that, so far as investigating the particular charge in respect of which the man has been apprehended, the police are to all intents and purposes *functi*, and they are not entitled to question him with regard to that particular charge."[86]

Vigorous police questioning may produce unfairness, for example third degree forms of interrogation[87] and questions which resemble aggressive assertions of guilt designed to elicit a confession.[88] One stark illustration of this emerged in *Codona v HM Advocate*,[89] where a 14-year-old girl, was accused of murder while acting with others. She was interviewed, in the presence of her father, by two female police officers. The interview was taped and lasted three and a half hours, of which one hour was a break. The tape revealed, however, that the accused was subjected to what was described by the appeal court as police pressure in that the interviewing officers often asked questions simultaneously, and repeatedly told the girl that she was inconsistent and they did not believe her. The appeal court ruled the confession inadmissible as unfair in not having been given voluntarily. Undoubtedly the factors of Codona's age and the length of the interview impinged on the issue fairness. As Sheriff Gordon, as he then was, in his editorial commentary on *Codona* pointedly observed, "it is the job of the police to seek information from the suspect, not to extract a confession".[90]

---

[80] See, for example, *Black v Annan*, 1996 S.L.T. 284,
[81] *Black v Annan*, 1996 S.L.T. 284.
[82] *HM Advocate v Davidson*, 1968 S.L.T. 17.
[83] *Black v Annan*, 1996 S.L.T. 284.
[84] See, e.g. *Tonge v HM Advocate*, 1982 J.C. 130 and *HM Advocate v Campbell*, 1946 J.C. 80.
[85] *Fraser and Freer v HM Advocate*, 1989 S.C.C.R. 82.
[86] *Wade v Robertson*, 1948 J.C. 117.
[87] *HM Advocate v Friel*, 1978 S.L.T. (Notes) 21, and *Boyne v HM Advocate*, 1980 J.C. 47.
[88] *HM Advocate v Mair*, 1982 S.L.T. 471.
[89] *Codona v HM Advocate*, 1996 S.L.T. 1100.
[90] *Codona v HM Advocate*, 1996 S.C.C.R. 300 at 323.

The fairness of the procedures

To a large extent the case law focuses on the procedures surrounding the **9–37** obtaining of a confession and the degree to which these procedures are consistent with a fair trial.[91] In *Chalmers* Lord Justice-Clerk Thomson identified the point at which a person becomes a suspect a particularly significant stage in the police investigative process, for at that point they become entitled to the protection of the courts. He laid down quite strict rules regarding what kind of questions could be asked of a suspect to elicit admissible answers:

> "[T]here comes a point in time in ordinary police investigation when the law intervenes to render inadmissible as evidence even answers to questions which are not tainted by such methods.[92] After that point is reached, further interrogation is incompatible with the answers being regarded as a voluntary statement, and the law intervenes to safeguard the party questioned from possible self-incrimination ... Once [the] stage of suspicion is reached, the suspect is in the position that thereafter the only evidence admissible against him is his own voluntary statement."

The strictness of these rules has been softened, eroded by a series of cases, significantly *Miln v Cullen*.[93] Following a road traffic accident, Cullen was asked whether he was the driver of one of the vehicles involved in the collision. Upon confirming this he was cautioned and charged. At trial the defence objected to this question on the ground of unfairness in that Cullen had not been cautioned prior to answering the question, yet he was clearly under suspicion at the time. Rejecting this argument, Lord Wheatley said[94]:

> "[F]airness is not a unilateral consideration. Fairness to the public is also a legitimate consideration ... it is the function of the court to seek to provide a proper balance to secure that the rights of individuals are properly preserved while not hamstringing the police in the investigation of crime."

The modern test of fairness

As with all areas of law that have evolved within the common law there is a **9–38** large body of authority, and while there is no conflict within the fundamental principle of fairness, the interpretive scope of "fairness" based on the fact-specifics of each case is very broad. The post-*Chalmers* era has yielded significant authorities which appear to erode, or at least re-define what constitutes inadmissibility.[95] Thus, in *Lord Advocate's Reference (No.1 of*

---

[91] *Magee v United Kingdom* (2000) 8 B.H.R.C. 646.

[92] The reference to "such methods" was to bullying, pressure and third degree methods alluded to in an earlier passage in Lord Thomson's opinion.

[93] *Miln v Cullen*, 1967 J.C. 21, a decision cited approvingly by Lord Hope in *Cadder v HM Advocate*, UKSC 43.

[94] *Miln v Cullen*, 1967 J.C. 21 at 29–30.

[95] e.g. *Jones v Milne*, 1975 J.C. 16; *McGlory v McInnes*, 1992 S.L.T. 501; and *Miller v HM Advocate*, 1997 S.C.C.R. 748.

1983),[96] Lord Justice-General Emslie expressed the characteristics determining admissibility of confessions as follows:

> "A suspect's self-incriminating answers to police questioning will indeed be admissible in evidence unless it can be affirmed that they have been extracted from him by unfair means. The simple and intelligible test which has worked well in practice is whether what has taken place has been fair or not ... In each case where the admissibility of answers by a suspect to police questioning becomes an issue it will be necessary to consider the whole relevant circumstances in order to discover whether or not there has been unfairness on the part of the police resulting in the extraction from the suspect of the answers in question. Unfairness may take many forms."

Lord Emslie's "many forms" of unfairness fall broadly into two categories: the effect of any specific characteristics of an accused that might render him or her especially vulnerable; and the procedures surrounding the obtaining of the confession. For a confession to be fairly obtained, it must, as detailed above, have been given voluntarily, and thus the fairness test incorporates the criterion of volition. As will by now be apparent, there is no finite list of criteria that must be satisfied before a statement can be said to be voluntary. However, if challenged, the Crown must be able to demonstrate that the state of mind and physical health of the accused was taken into account and that the police followed the correct procedures.[97]

9–39   These two aspects are illustrated in *HM Advocate v Gilgannon*,[98] a case of attempted rape, where the court rejected the accused's confession to the attempted rape as inadmissible because it was unreliable due to his mental condition. Gilgannon was examined by a police surgeon a few hours prior to the confession. The police surgeon considered him to be mentally subnormal. The police themselves were unaware of this assessment and they simply noted the contents of a statement which Gilgannon volunteered to make. Subsequently, and despite the fact that the police behaviour could not be faulted, the confession was rejected because, as Lord Cameron explained, "it comes as an at least possibly if not probably incomplete narrative from one who is not only mentally subnormal but unable to give a coherent and complete and therefore accurate account of an incident in which he himself played a principal part".[99] Lord Cameron offered a wide definition of the necessary context of fairness governing admissibility of confessions:[100]

> "I am not ... prepared to accept the rigid proposition that the matter of fairness is confined to the detailed circumstances in which the voluntary statement is obtained; that is the questioning itself or the pressures put on the maker of the statement. The mental or physical state of the maker may well be an important and relevant circumstance in determining the issue of admissibility. Once, as here, a suspect is under arrest

---

[96] 1984 J.C. 52 at 58. See too, *Brown v HM Advocate*, 1966 S.L.T. 105.
[97] e.g. *HM Advocate v Jenkinson*, 2002 S.C.C.R. 43.
[98] *HM Advocate v Gilgannon*, 1983 S.C.C.R. 10.
[99] *HM Advocate v Gilgannon*, 1983 S.C.C.R. 10, per Lord Cameron at 12.
[100] *HM Advocate v Gilgannon*, 1983 S.C.C.R. 10, per Lord Cameron at 11.

even before he has been formally charged he is under and is entitled to the protection of the court and therefore it is proper that the circumstances in which the statement is taken should be regarded as well as the manner itself in which the statement is obtained and elicited. The physical or mental state of an accused at the time of making a statement may be such as to make it unfair on him."[101]

In order for a statement to be voluntary and freely given the suspect must understand the question being asked. In *HM Advocate v McSwiggan*[102] a man who was being questioned regarding allegations of incest thought he was being questioned regarding impregnating a woman. His reply to questions was that "he had taken precautions". This response was ruled inadmissible as McSwiggan was said to be "intellectually not that bright" and therefore not capable of appreciating the import of the question or the consequences of his reply.

The next section considers in more detail the fairness of the procedures **9–40** involved in obtaining a confession. These are often determinative in assessing the admissibility of a confession.

Fairness in Procedures

Chalmers v HM Advocate[103] identified three distinct phases in police ques- **9–41** tioning where different aspects of fairness might be a consideration:

(i) Questioning before the accused has become a suspect;
(ii) The need for a caution once suspicion has crystallised upon the accused; and
(iii) Questioning post-caution.

Prior to being charged with an offence, there are two common situations where an accused makes an extra-judicial statement or confession. The first is where the police are simply carrying out inquiries into the offence and the accused has not yet become a suspect. The second is when suspicion has begun to harden against a person, but the position has not yet been reached when the police are ready to caution the suspect and formally charge him or her with the offence. At both stages the accused is entitled to remain silent, unless statutorily detained under the Criminal Procedure (Scotland) Act when a person is obliged to supply certain personal information to verify their identity.[104]

The presumption of innocence is embedded in common law principles and **9–42** embodied in art.6(2), "[e]veryone charged with an offence shall be presumed innocent until proved guilty according to law". Scots law has resisted the sort of inroads to that principle which have been made in English law. The

---

[101] Lord Cameron cited *HM Advocate v Aitken*, 1926 J.C. 83 and *HM Advocate v Rigg*, 1946 J.C. 1 as his authorities.
[102] *HM Advocate v McSwiggan*, 1937 J.C. 50.
[103] *Chalmers v HM Advocate*, 1954 J.C. 66. This must now all be read in light of *Cadder v HM Advocate* and the subsequent case law discussed earlier in this chapter.
[104] ss.13(1A) and 14(10) Criminal Procedure (Scotland) Act 1995.

terms of the English law caution, for example, penalise a suspect who fails to mention at the stage of caution something upon which he or she seeks to rely subsequently at trial. The Scots caution is couched in terms that still entitle a suspect to remain silent. However, an accused's failure at this stage to give an innocent explanation of, for example, recently stolen property in their possession, or to explain there is an alibi, may create problems of credibility at any later trial.[105]

The need for a caution

9–43   Public policy supports the approach that, at least at the early stages of a criminal investigation, the police should not have to contemplate that every person questioned may subsequently turn out to be an accused. Thus, the mere fact that an accused is charged following questioning does not render his or her answers to those questions inadmissible.[106] In *Costello v Mac-Pherson*[107] it was held that police officers were perfectly entitled to stop a person seen carrying goods in suspicious circumstances and question him as to his possession of them. His answers to those questions were admissible. In *Thompson v HM Advocate*[108] while Thompson was being kept at the police station he blurted out, without prompting or caution, "It was her or me". His subsequent full confession, after caution, was held admissible. Generally though, when suspicion has begun to harden on a suspect, the police are expected to administer a caution.[109] Moreover, the effect of *Cadder v HM Advocate*[110] and subsequent case law is that once in custody, a suspect ought to be advised of their right to legal advice before police questioning starts, as well as receiving a caution.

9–44   At common law, although there is no prescribed formula of words for a caution that must be used, it is important to convey certain key information to the suspect.[111] A suspect should be told that they are not obliged to speak, but that if they do, their statement will be recorded and may be used in evidence in any subsequent trial. There is no defined point at which the caution must be administered, indeed it may be prudent to repeat it several times. Where a court subsequently considers that a caution should have been given, in circumstances where it was not, then any incriminating statement made may be ruled inadmissible. In *Tonge v HM Advocate*[112] Tonge and two others were detained under s.2 of the Criminal Justice (Scotland) Act 1980[113] on a charge of rape. At the start of his detention

---

[105] See *Cryans v Nixon*, 1955 J.C. 1.

[106] *Chalmers v HM Advocate*, 66 at 81, per Lord Thomson. See the recent manifestation of this issue in *Gilroy (David) v HM Advocate* [2013] HCJAC 18 where the police did not caution the accused when information was gathered from him as part of a missing person's investigation broad where many people were interviewed in an exercise to trace sightings of the missing person.

[107] *Costello v MacPherson*, 1922 J.C. 9.

[108] *Thompson v HM Advocate*, 1968 J.C. 61.

[109] *Gilroy v HM Advocate* [1213] HCJASC 18.

[110] *Cadder v HM Advocate* [2010] UKSC 43.

[111] The standard form is: "You are not obliged to say anything but anything you do say may be taken down and used in evidence."

[112] *Tonge v HM Advocate*, 1982 J.C. 130. See also *Wilson v Robertson*, 1986 S.C.C.R. 700.

[113] Now s.14 of the Criminal Procedure (Scotland) Act 1995.

Tonge was given the statutory caution then applicable in terms of s.2(7),[114] but he was not given the common law caution. Later, in the course of his detention, and without caution, the investigating officers accused Tonge of the crime, whereupon he made an incriminating statement. The High Court ruled that Tonge's alleged confession should not have been admissible. They found that the allegation made against him amounted to a charge of rape, and that "[t]o charge an accused person without cautioning him is to put pressure upon him which may induce a response".[115] Best practice dictates that all statutory detainees should also receive the full common law caution. Lord Cameron in *Tonge* summarised the requirements of the common law in regard to suspects in a police station[116]:

> "It is of course well established that police officers are entitled to question a suspect as to his possible complicity in a crime which they are investigating, and that his replies will be admissible in evidence if they have not been extracted or compelled by unfair or improper means including threats, intimidations, offers of inducements, or cross-examination designed or intended to extract incriminating replies, but it is equally well recognised that in the case of one on whom suspicion of responsibility or complicity has centred, in order that his replies should be admissible in evidence, it is proper practice that any further questioning should be preceded by a caution in common form."

If a caution is merited but not given, e.g. because suspicion may not have hardened against the accused at that point, statements made by the accused may still be admissible if they are not incriminating and their admissibility does not result in an unfair trial.[117]

The Lord Justice-General Emslie in *Tonge*[118] issued the following **9–45** warning:

> "I would strongly urge police officers throughout Scotland who proceed to accuse a detainee or to question him or to take from him a voluntary statement, to rely not at all upon the efficacy of the warning described in section 2(7), and to appreciate that if any use is to be made in evidence of anything said by a detainee in these circumstances the ordinary rules of fairness and fair dealing which have been developed by the common law should be strictly observed. The wise course will be, inter alia, to administer to the detainee in the events which I have mentioned a full caution in common law terms. The omission to give such a caution will, by itself, at the very least place the admissibility of anything said by the detainee in peril."

---

[114] Namely that he was obliged by law to say nothing apart from giving his name and address. More information is now required in terms of that section, i.e. date of birth, place of birth and nationality.

[115] *Tonge v HM Advocate*, 1982 J.C. 130 at 140.

[116] *Tonge v HM Advocate*, 1982 J.C. 130 at 147.

[117] *Gilroy v HM Advocate*, [2013] HCJAC 18.

[118] *Tonge v HM Advocate*, 1982 J.C. 130 at 145–146.

When an accused is given a caution in relation to one charge and questioned about other related charges, the answers to the related charges will be admissible provided there is no unfairness to the accused.[119]

9–46   So far as concerns the wording of the caution, there are two important constituents, neither of which may be omitted. The accused must be told that they have the right to remain silent. In *HM Advocate v Von*[120] a confession was rejected after the accused was told merely that any answers he gave to police questions might be used in evidence and he was not advised that he need not say anything to incriminate himself. At the same time, informing an accused of the right to remain silent may be insufficient by itself if the accused is not also warned that anything they do say may be noted for any potential evidential significance it may have. The effect of failing to give such a warning will depend on whether unfairness resulted.

9–47   Of course, administering a caution does not relieve police officers of the need for continuing propriety in their behaviour and notification to the suspect that they are entitled to legal advice prior to police questioning. As Lord Justice General, Lord Cooper, stated in *Chalmers*[121]:

> "If under such circumstances cross-examination is pursued with the result, although perhaps not with the deliberate object, of causing [the suspect] to break down and to condemn himself out of his own mouth, the impropriety of the proceedings cannot be cured by the giving of any number of formal cautions or the introduction of some officer other than the questioner to record the ultimate statement."

The need for a charge

9–48   Very shortly after the administration of the caution, and preferably along with it,[122] the accused should be charged. It will otherwise be regarded as unfair for the police to continue to extract incriminating information from an accused once they have collected sufficient information to make them a chargeable suspect.[123] Once a person reaches this stage then, as Lord Cameron pointed out in *HM Advocate v Gilgannon*,[124] the accused acquires new status in which he is "under and ... entitled to the protection of the court". It was, however, suggested in *Johnston v HM Advocate*[125] that to continue to question a suspect prior to a charge is acceptable, even if the suspect has been arrested, provided there is no unfairness. Johnston was arrested at the scene of a crime where a murder had been committed. His answers to police questioning after his arrest both at the locus and later on tape at the police station were held admissible even though he had not been charged, as the appeal court considered that there was no unfairness in the procedures. It was observed that had the police used their powers of

---

[119] *Wilson v Heywood*, 1989 S.L.T. 279, distinguishing *Tonge v HM Advocate*, 1982 J.C. 130, because in that case there had been no common law caution at all of one of the suspects.
[120] 1979 S.L.T. (Notes) 62. See also *HM Advocate v Docherty*, 1981 J.C. 6.
[121] *Chalmers v HM Advocate*, 1954 J.C. 66 at 79.
[122] Certainly not before it: see *Tonge v HM Advocate*, 1982 J.C. 130.
[123] But see *HM Advocate v Penders*, 1996 S.C.C.R. 404, and *Miller v HM Advocate*, 1998 S.L.T. 571 as to the status, if any, of being a "chargeable suspect".
[124] *Advocate v Gilgannon*, 1983 S.C.C.R. 10.
[125] *Johnston v HM Advocate*, 1994 S.L.T. 300.

statutory detention instead of arrest then they would have been entitled to question Johnston for up to six hours.

Statements made after charge

Once a person is formally charged, their immediate reaction to the charge is **9–49** admissible,[126] but no further statements will be admissible unless they are totally spontaneous.[127] In particular, there may be no more police questions designed to elicit new incriminating material from the accused. Where practicable, even a spontaneous statement should be interrupted by a repeated caution and taken down by officers unconnected with the case.[128] Particular care must be taken when the accused has learning disabilities, is mentally impaired or is in some other way vulnerable, and any suggestion that pressure or inducements have been applied to persuade the accused to make further statements will render any such statement inadmissible. Although it is preferable for any reply to caution and charge to be noted verbatim in the notebook of the police officers to whom it is made, oral evidence from those officers as to what the accused said is admissible as direct evidence.[129]

CONFESSIONS OBTAINED THROUGH EAVESDROPPING

If accused persons fall into a trap of their own making then the resulting **9–50** confession will be admissible. This situation arises in cases sometimes described as eavesdropping cases, i.e. when police officers overhear a conversation between an accused and another person, perhaps a co-accused, the conversation will be admissible if it has been made voluntarily and not as a result of any entrapment. Where there is evidence of entrapment then it is likely the confession will be inadmissible.

In *HM Advocate v O'Donnell*[130] an accused in a police cell shouted certain **9–51** incriminating remarks to a co-accused in another cell, which were overheard by police officers. At trial, it was held that the officers could testify as to the contents of the remarks made by the accused. This was considered fair because the remarks had been made voluntarily, no inducement had been offered to the accused to make them, the officers listening in to them had done so spontaneously and had not been deliberately listening in and indeed did not even have any knowledge of O'Donnell's involvement in the case. In coming to this conclusion, the sheriff felt that he could not rely on the conflicting authority of *HM Advocate v Keen*. In *O'Donnell* Sheriff Macphail (as he then was) noted that the decision in *Keen* was unhelpful as the report lacked argument and reasoning.

---

[126] Conveyed to the court by police witnesses who recite to the court what the accused said "when cautioned and charged".
[127] *Wade v Robertson*, 1940 J.C. 117.
[128] *Tonge v HM Advocate*, 1982 J.C. 130; but see also *Aiton v HM Advocate,* 1987 J.C. 41, *Custerson v Westwater*, 1987 S.C.C.R. 389 and *MacDonald v HM Advocate*, 1987 S.C.C.R. 581.
[129] *Hamilton v HM Advocate*, 1980 J.C. 66.
[130] *HM Advocate v O'Donnell*, 1975 S.L.T. (Sh. Ct) 22 at 28.

9–52   *Keen* was not in any event followed in *Welsh and Breen v HM Advocate*.[131] The Thomson Committee[132] preferred the approach taken in *Welsh and Breen* and *O'Donnell*, and recommended that such overheard conversations be put to the accused at judicial examination.[133] The Scottish Law Commission[134] also upheld the view expressed in *O'Donnell*, and it would seem that the courts are no longer prepared to carry fairness to the accused to the length of ignoring safe and highly relevant evidence.[135] The decision in *O'Donnell* was approved in *Jamieson v Annan*[136] where an incriminating conversation between two accused who shouted to each other whilst held in adjoining police cells was admitted as it was regarded as voluntary and spontaneous and absent of any inducement, trap or unfairness.

9–53   Where the police stage-manage a situation, for example by placing two suspects in adjoining cells, because they anticipate incriminating exchanges between suspects, such evidence will be inadmissible. It will breach the common law principle of fairness, and very likely the right to privacy under art.8 of the ECHR, as well as the provisions of the Regulation of Investigatory Powers (Scotland) Act 2000 ("RIPSA"). Such a scenario arose in *HM Advocate v Higgins*[137] where two suspects in an armed robbery were moved to adjoining cells and two police officers posted outside, and out of sight, to record any useful exchanges. Ruling these actions as unlawful, Lord Macphail declared that the police behaviour was a form of covert surveillance in term of s.1(8)(a) of RIPSA, i.e. "carried out in a manner that is calculated to ensure that persons who are subject to the surveillance are unaware that it is or may be taking place". The police had not sought authority for their action, nor apparently had it occurred to them they need do so.

9–54   Lord Macphail acknowledged that lack of authority was not necessarily fatal to admissibility of evidence as fairness was the overall consideration. Nonetheless, he rejected the Crown's argument that it was fairly obtained given the seriousness of the crime, that others as yet unidentified may have been involved, and that a large amount of money was missing[138]:

> "It is important to notice that the surveillance was undertaken after each of the accused had been detained, interviewed under caution, and arrested. Thus they had been and continued to be subject to a rigorous regime, consisting of both statutory and common law rules, governing the detention, treatment and questioning of those in police custody. It was, in my opinion, wholly inconsistent with that regime that they should have been at the same time subject to unauthorised covert

---

[131] November 15, 1973, High Court, unreported but referred to in Macphail, *Evidence*, para.20.22 and *HM Advocate v O'Donnell O'Donnell*, 1975 S.L.T. (Sh. Ct) 22.
[132] Departmental Committee on Criminal Procedure in Scotland, Cmnd. 6218 (1975), para.7.20.
[133] At para.8.18b. Note that s.36 of the Criminal Procedure (Scotland) Act 1995 makes provision for this.
[134] Memo No.46, para.T.45.
[135] By the same token, the courts will also accept as evidence the contents of prisoners' correspondence that has been intercepted: *HM Advocate v Fawcett* (1869) 1 Coup. 183, approved by the Scottish Law Commission, n.63, para.T.46. See also *Ming v HM Advocate*, 1987 S.C.C.R. 110.
[136] *Jamieson v Annan*, 1988 S.L.T. 631.
[137] *Advocate v Higgins*, 2006 S.L.T. 946.
[138] *HM Advocate v Higgins*, 2006 S.L.T. 946 at para.25.

investigation of this nature with a view to their uttering statements that would be admissible against them in court. In the circumstances of this case, where no excuse or explanation has been offered for the failure to observe the requirements of RIPSA, the unauthorised surveillance must be regarded as a serious irregularity which not only cannot be condoned but also points strongly towards the transgression of the principle of fairness."

CONFESSIONS OBTAINED THROUGH ENTRAPMENT

Confession evidence obtained by eavesdropping can be distinguished from **9–55** confession evidence obtained by entrapment. The former is not induced. It is fortuitous (at least from the police perspective), not obtained by design, and is generally admissible. Conversely, when evidence has been obtained in a manner that is calculated, deliberate and deceptive, it is likely to be seen as unfairly obtained and not admissible, unless it has prior authorisation from the State. The Appeal Court held in *Jones v HM Advocate*[139] that if entrapment is alleged it should operate as a plea in bar of trial. Previously, evidence found to have been obtained by entrapment was a treated as a question of admissibility.[140] The approach adopted in *Jones* is to regard entrapment as a type of oppression perpetrated by the police which acts as a bar to trial. The oppression may take various forms including pressure or encouragement or inducement to commit an offence.[141] [142] There is a substantial body of Strasbourg jurisprudence concerning the parameters of evidence obtained in circumstances of entrapment and invoking arts 3, 6 and 8 of the ECHR. Each case has its own jurisdictional influences as the European Court recognises that admissibility of evidence is largely a matter for regulation by national law. However, some common values and principles can be ascertained. One of the leading cases is *Teixeira de Castro v Portugal*[143] where two men, who had been arrested for their suspected involvement in drug trafficking, complained of a breach of art.6(1) because of entrapment on the part of undercover police officers. Although the European Court acknowledged the need for particular measures to combat the fight against organised crime, nonetheless, they stated that the activities of undercover agents must be controlled and the general requirements of fairness demanded by art.6 must be observed. In this case the court held that the police officers had stepped over the bounds of acceptable conduct and had induced the applicant to commit an offence in circumstances where there was no evidence he would otherwise have done so.

---

[139] *Jones v HM Advocate*, 2010 J.C. 255.
[140] see e.g. *HM Advocate v Graham*, 1991 S.L.T. 416.
[141] *Weir v Jessop*, 1991 J.C. 146.
[142] See Renton & Brown, *Criminal Procedure*, 6th edn, para.9-20-1.
[143] *Teixeira de Castro v Portugal* (1999) 28 E.H.R.R. 101.

SURVEILLANCE

9–56 In England it has been argued that the courts are willing to tolerate a measure of deception in police practices where the context is the investigation of organised crime.[144] For operational purposes there are situations in which the police have to work undercover, perhaps using surveillance techniques to gather intelligence about known criminals or criminal activities. Some of these operations require specific authorisation under legislation, an early version of which was the Interception of Communications Act 1985. That Act was a response to a finding in the ECtHR in *Malone v United Kingdom (A/82)*,[145] that UK legislation in the area of secret surveillance of communications was obscure and insufficiently precise. The principal legislation now governing surveillance is contained in the Regulation of Investigatory Powers Act 2000 (extending to England, Wales and Northern Ireland) and the Regulation of Investigatory Powers (Scotland) Act 2000. These two statutes regulate a broad range of surveillance activities, including telephone tapping and other types of bugging devices. Section 1(1) of the Regulation of Investigatory Powers (Scotland) Act 2000 authorises directed surveillance; intrusive surveillance; and the use of covert human intelligence sources, provided the surveillance has previously been authorised and conducted according to the authorisation. In addition there are detailed codes of practice under the legislation.[146]

9–57 To undertake surveillance lawfully the police must first apply for appropriate warrants, and, as with standard search warrants, acting beyond the authorisation warrant may render any evidence obtained inadmissible, but it depends on the context. An authorisation in *Gilchrist v HM Advocate*,[147] which the Crown conceded was invalid due to lack of specification, did not result in the inadmissibility of evidence obtained in the course of a police surveillance operation. It transpired that what was observed took place in public and did not involve any interference with the accused's art.8(1) right to respect for private and family life, home and correspondence. The statutory framework for authorised surveillance complies with art.8(2) which permits interference with the right to private and family life provided such interference is conducted lawfully and for reasons of national security and public safety, including the prevention of crime. A breach of art.8 will not necessarily result in inadmissibility of the evidence or an unfair trial[148]:

> "The lawfulness of interference with private life had to be distinguished from the fairness of using evidence at trial. The way evidence was obtained could infringe art.8, but the leading of that evidence might not be incompatible with art.6."

---

[144] See A. Ashworth, "Police and Deceptive Practices" (1998) 114 L.Q.R., 108, for a review of the position in England. For a UK wide commentary see N. Taylor, "State surveillance and the right to privacy", *Surveillance & Society* 1(1): 66–85. Available at *http://www.surveillance-and-society.org/articles1/statesurv.pdf* [accessed July 31, 2013].

[145] *Malone v United Kingdom* (1985) 7 E.H.R.R. 14.

[146] See *http://www.scotland.gov.uk/Topics/Justice/public-safety/Police/policepowers/17206/7789* [accessed July 31, 2013].

[147] *Kinloch v HM Advocate*, 2013 S.L.T. 133.

[148] *Kinloch v HM Advocate*, 2013 S.L.T. 133 at para.17.

The ECHR gives a significant margin of appreciation to individual states in satisfying Convention rights. Therefore, while surveillance might well interfere with art.8 rights of privacy, such interference may be acceptable if it is "clearly aimed at the 'prevention of crime' and was necessary in a democratic society".[149] The appeal court in *Gilchrist* had no difficulty separating the issue of the invalid RISPA authorisation from the issue of a fair trial and holding that the latter was not in jeopardy merely because of the former.[150] This approach is of course consistent with the common law principles established from *Lawrie v Muir*[151] onwards. The relationship between the common law and Convention rights was reinforced in *Hoekstra v HM Advocate (No.7)*,[152] where Lord Justice-General Cullen, delivering the opinion of the High Court, noted the Strasbourg jurisprudence does not necessarily require the exclusion of illegally obtained evidence for the conditions for a fair trial. Specifically, Lord J-G Cullen[153] cited the judgment in *Schenk v Switzerland*[154]:

"While Article 6 of the Convention guarantees the right to a fair trial, it does not lay down any rules on the admissibility of evidence as such, which is therefore primarily a matter for regulation under national law.

The Court therefore cannot exclude as a matter of principle and in the abstract that unlawfully obtained evidence of the present kind may be admissible. It has only to ascertain whether Mr. Schenk's trial as a whole was fair."

TRIAL WITHIN A TRIAL

Balloch v HM Advocate[155] marked an important procedural departure from **9–58** the hitherto accepted practice by which objections to confessions were considered. *Chalmers v HM Advocate*[156] had laid down a procedure that became known as a "trial within a trial".[157] The procedure was invoked when the defence challenged the admissibility of evidence on the ground of it having been obtained by improper methods. It was the practice for the jury to then be asked to withdraw and for the trial judge alone to hear counsel's arguments and determine the admissibility of the statement by means of a trial within a trial. Only if the evidence was deemed admissible was the returning jury allowed to consider its value as an item of evidence. The

---

[149] *Ludi v Switzerland* (1993) 15 E.H.R.R. 173 at para.39.
[150] *Kinloch v HM Advocate* [2012] UKSC 62 per Lord Hope at para.15.
Ludi v Switzerland (1993) 15 E.H.R.R. 173 was cited approvingly in *Kinloch v HM Advocate* [2012] UKSC 62.
Ludi v Switzerland (1993) 15 E.H.R.R. 173.
[151] *Lawrie v Muir*, 1956 J.C.19.
[152] *Hoekstra v HM Advocate (No.7)*, 2002 S.L.T. 599 at para.31.
[153] *Hoekstra v HM Advocate (No.7)*, 2002 S.L.T. 599 at para.31.
[154] *Schenk v Switzerland*, 1988 13 E.H.R.R. 242 at 265–266, para.46.
[155] *Balloch v HM Advocate*, 1977 S.C. 23.
[156] *Chalmers v HM Advocate* 66 at 80.
[157] A similar procedure operating in English law is usually referred to as voire dire.

practice was frequently criticised in later years[158] and increasingly ignored. *HM Advocate v Whitelaw*[159] epitomises the objections to as trial within a trial. There, Lord Cameron ruled that:

> "Now since the case of *Chalmers* there has been a growing feeling that, as it is both the right and the duty of the jury to hear and pass judgment on all the relevant evidence, evidence as to statements of a possibly incriminating character alleged to have been made by an accused person is prima facie of the highest relevance and the jury's function should not be in fact usurped and, unless it is abundantly clear that the rules of fairness and fair dealing have been flagrantly transgressed, it would be better for a jury seised of the whole evidence in the case and of all the circumstances, under such guidance as they should receive from the presiding judge, themselves to take that decision as to the extent to which, if at all, they will take into account evidence of statements given by a suspect after due caution."

The rationale for avoiding the trial within a trial procedure was explained by Lord Emslie in *Lord Advocate's Reference (No.1 of 1983)*,[160] in which he reminded all trial judges that:

> "[A] judge who has heard all the relevant undisputed evidence bearing upon the admissibility of answers by a suspect, under caution, to police questioning, will normally only be justified in withholding the evidence of the alleged answers from the jury if he is satisfied that no reasonable jury could hold upon that evidence that the answers had not been extracted from the suspect by unfair or improper means."

In other words, judges were to be careful not to usurp the fact-finding function of the jury. Judges remained in charge of determining what evidence was legally admissible, while juries were responsible for deciding how much weight to attach to any individual item of evidence. The difficulty with this approach was identified by Lord Justice-General Rodger in *Thompson v Crowe*[161]:

> "In effect it robs the concept of admissibility of evidence of all real content in those cases where evidence of the statement is actually admitted and the jury are told it is for them to decide whether they can take it into account. But another important consequence of the approach is that the court no longer takes responsibility for decisions on admissibility except in the most extreme cases where the only possible reasonable view is that the evidence is inadmissible."

The court felt that leaving questions of admissibility to the jury was an abrogation of judicial responsibility and therefore the five bench decision in

---

[158] See *Thompson v HM Advocate*, 1968 J.C. 61, and *Hartley v HM Advocate*, 1979 S.L.T. 26.
[159] *HM Advocate v Whitelaw*, 1980 S.L.T. (Notes) 25 at 26, approved in *Tonge v HM Advocate*, 1982 J.C. 130, and *Lord Advocate's Reference (No.1 of 1983)*, 1984 J.C. 52.
[160] *Lord Advocate's Reference (No.1 of 1983)*, 1984 J.C. 52 at 59.
[161] *Thompson v Crowe*, 2000 J.C. 173 at 190.

Thomson v Crowe overruled *Balloch* to return the law to the position that had applied up to the time of *Chalmers*. Lord Justice General Rodger explained[162]:

> "Once again, accordingly, it will be for the trial judge to decide questions of the admissibility of the evidence of statements by the accused, just as it is for the trial judge to decide all other questions of admissibility. The decision will depend, of course, on the facts of the particular case and, where there are conflicts in the evidence about the circumstances, it will be for the trial judge to resolve those conflicts and so to settle the factual basis upon which to take the decision. The judge will exclude the statement if it was taken in circumstances which would render it inadmissible under any rule laid down by the law. In other cases the judge will admit the statement if the Crown satisfies the court that it would be fair to do so, by proving that the statement was made freely and voluntarily and was not extracted by unfair or improper means."

In resolving these conflicts, the trial judge has to determine the issue on a standard of proof that is on a balance of probabilities.[163]

Thomson recounted the history of the trial within a trial procedure, noting **9–59** its importance in upholding the principle against self-incrimination, and concluded that some criticisms of the procedure had been "misconceived". According to the Lord Justice-General, the arguments that the procedure could unduly lengthen trials, inconvenience jurors and distort evidence led for a second time before a jury had to give way to the general duty on a judge to ensure a fair trial.[164] The discharge of that duty might require a trial within a trial to be held to give an accused a proper opportunity to object to the admissibility of certain evidence and to do so without also being obliged to give evidence in the trial as a whole. The impact of *Thomson v Crowe* is to strengthen the role of judicial discretion, especially in determinations over admissibility, a shift which Duff has argued orientates the judicial function more towards the inquisitorial mode.[165]

CONFESSIONS MADE TO OTHER PERSONS

So far it has been assumed that a confession made by an accused person has **9–60** been made to police officers. In fact many officials have the power to interview persons suspected of contravening various statutory provisions. These officials include HM Customs and Excise; HM Inspectors of Taxes and Financial Services Authority; immigration officers; and welfare benefits officers. Accused persons who are assisting the police with their inquiries, or who have been detained pending a court appearance, sometimes make

---

[162] *Thompson v Crowe*, 2000 J.C. 173 at 191–192.

[163] *Platt v HM Advocate*, 2004 J.C. 113.

[164] *Thompson v Crowe* at 198B–E. See too, the 10-point summary of practical conclusions at 202 offering a procedural guide for the future.

[165] P. Duff, "Disclosure in Scottish criminal procedure: another step in an inquisitorial direction?" (2007) 11(3) E &P.153.

statements to persons in authority, such as prison officers or police surgeons. Provided an official is not acting ultra vires, i.e. without the statutory authority to ask the questions, then the principle which applies is exactly the same as that applicable to confessions made to police officers. It is admissible provided it was not obtained unfairly. If an official acts with any trace of impropriety, unfairness or misuse of their powers then any resulting confession will almost certainly be inadmissible.[166]

9–61   In *HM Advocate v Friel*[167] the fairness test, that subsequently became the main test for all confessions per *Lord Advocate's Reference (No. 1 of 1983)*,[168] was applied to questions and answers during an investigation by customs officers. In such investigations the absence of a caution is one factor to be considered in the wider context of fairness. In *Pennycuick v Lees*[169] incriminating answers given by a person being interviewed by Department of Social Security officers were admissible despite the lack of a caution, as the questions were fair and proper and there was no suggestion of unfairness or deception on the part of the interviewers. In contrast, in *Oghonoghor v Secretary of State for the Home Department*[170] the statements of a suspected illegal immigrant were held inadmissible when given in the absence of a caution as to the consequences of the answers. This seems largely to have been due to the assumption in *Oghonoghor* on the part of the interviewer that the accused was an intentional illegal immigrant, although ostensibly the questions were being asked only to establish whether or not she had outstayed her visa.

9–62   Even when a statement is made to a private person such as a friend, the court will wish to ensure that it was fairly made and is therefore voluntary. As Lord Cameron observed[171]:

> "[C]onfessions to a private party will be admissible unless the circumstances in which [it] has been made or extracted are such as to raise doubt as to whether it has been falsely made in order to escape from further pressures or in response to inducements offered, and ... this is an issue which is essentially for the jury to determine upon the evidence laid before them. A case could also be figured when, by arrangement with police officers, a private person could be used to exercise upon a suspect pressures which would be fatal to the admissibility in evidence of a confession extracted by them by the use of such pressures: in such a case it cannot be doubted that any confession so obtained would be inadmissible."

---

[166] *Morrison v Burrell*, 1947 J.C. 43 at 49.
[167] *HM Advocate v Friel*, 1978 S.L.T. (Notes) 21.
[168] *Lord Advocate's Reference (No.1 of 1983)*, 1984 J.C. 52 at 59.
[169] *Pennycuick v Lees*, 1992 S.L.T. 763.
[170] *Oghonoghor v Secretary of State for the Home Department*, 1995 S.L.T. (Notes) 733.
[171] "Scottish Practice in relation to Admissions and Confessions by Persons Suspected or Accused of Crime", 1975 S.L.T. (News) 265 at 268.

STATEMENTS BY ACCUSED PERSONS IN RELATION TO OTHER CHARGES

Renton and Brown explain that where an accused faces more than one **9–63** charge, and the facts that give rise to both charges are the same, an incriminating statement in respect of one charge can be used against the accused as a confession on the second charge provided the first charge is more serious than the second. However, the position remains uncertain when the reverse is true.[172]

In *Willis v HM Advocate*[173] the court admitted, on a charge of culpable **9–64** homicide, an incriminating statement made in respect of a murder charge. However, in *James Stewart*[174] the trial court in a murder trial refused to admit evidence of S's declaration given earlier when the charge was assault to the danger of life. But, in the later case of *HM Advocate v Cunningham*[175] the court saw nothing wrong in allowing in such a statement in similar circumstances. It seems that *Cunningham* has now become the leading authority, since in *McAdam v HM Advocate*[176] the court allowed in evidence statements made by the accused on what was originally a charge of assault to severe injury, even though by the date of the trial the Crown had raised the charge to one of attempted murder. Lord Justice-General Clyde[177] ruled that the important test in such cases was that:

> "[E]ach of the charges must substantially cover the same *species facti*. I say 'substantially' because all the articles which have been stolen may not have been ascertained, when the earlier charge is made, or the full extent of the injuries to the victim may not be known. None the less, justice demands that the jury be informed of the reply given, after caution, to the limited charge originally made."

McAdam was followed in *HM Advocate v McTavish*[178] in which the accused, a nursing sister, had made certain incriminating statements concerning her administration of an injection to a patient at a time when she was charged only with assault. The patient died, and the court held that her statement was admissible on a charge of murder because the *species facti* were substantially the same on the assault charge as they were on the murder charge. The principle laid down in *McAdam* was also approved by the Scottish Law Commission,[179] which added only that the two charges must fall into the same general category (dishonesty, personal violence, etc.).

CORROBORATION OF CONFESSIONS

A confession is one of the most powerful items of evidence against an **9–65** accused, hence the various procedural safeguards described above. As long

---

[172] Renton & Brown, *Criminal Procedure*, para.24–52.
[173] *Willis v HM Advocate*, 1941 J.C. 1.
[174] *James Stewart* (1866) 5 Irv 310.
[175] *HM Advocate v Cunningham*, 1939 J.C. 61, in which *Stewart* was not cited.
[176] *McAdam v HM Advocate*, 1960 J.C. 1, in which both *Stewart* and *Cunningham* were cited.
[177] *McAdam v HM Advocate*, 1960 J.C. 1, at 4.
[178] 1975 S.L.T. (Notes) 27. Note that McAdam's conviction was quashed on other grounds.
[179] Memo No.46, para.T.40.

as Scotland retains its requirement for corroboration, a confession, regardless of how cogent and persuasive it is, still currently requires some other item of evidence in corroboration. As discussed in earlier chapters, abolition of corroboration is likely during 2014 and the comments in this section must be read in that context.[180] The Lord Justice-Clerk Thomson explained in *Sinclair v Clark*[181]:

> "[A]n admission of guilt by an accused is not conclusive against him, unless it is corroborated by something beyond the actual admission. One reason for this rule is to ensure that there is nothing phony or quixotic about the confession.[182] What is required in the way of independent evidence in order to elide such risk must depend on the facts of the case, and, in particular, the nature and character of the confession and the circumstances in which it is made."

The confession itself need only be spoken to by one witness,[183] but an accused cannot in law corroborate their own confession, either by confessing to more than one person, or by repeating it on other occasions.[184] However, the "independent evidence" needed for corroboration is not very demanding. As in *Patterson v Nixon*,[185] it can be the behaviour of a police dog, and, more generally, the cases demonstrate that in practice "very little is required to corroborate a confession".[186]

9–66   The risk of this notion of "very little corroboration" being inappropriately elevated to a rule was highlighted by Lord Justice-General Hope in *Meredith v Lees*[187] when he explained that if that were to happen, "there will be a weakening of the principle that there must be a sufficient independent check of the confession to corroborate it". What constitutes a "sufficient independent check" will depend on the circumstances of the case. *Meredith* was a case involving allegations of lewd, libidinous and indecent practices towards a four-year-old girl. The accused had given the police a detailed confession of his behaviour. Although the child's description of the events lacked specification and her terminology was ambiguous, the court took into account her age and that "she was trying to tell the truth". The accused was convicted and appealed on the ground that the child's evidence did not afford sufficient corroboration of the accused's confession. The appeal court refused the appeal pointing to the consistency of the child's account in relation to time, place and circumstance with that given by the accused, combined with the voluntary and genuine nature of the confession. It was

---

[180] See Ch.8.
[181] 1962 J.C. 57 at 62.
[182] e.g. that the accused has not falsely confessed, as occurred in *Boyle v HM Advocate*, 1976 J.C. 32.
[183] *Mills v HM Advocate*, 1935 J.C. 77.
[184] *Callan v HM Advocate*, 1999 S.L.T. 1102. For examples of civil cases in which self-corroboration was deemed inadmissible, see *Barr v Barr*, 1932 S.C. 696 and *Gibson v N.C.R.*, 1925 S.C. 500.
[185] *Patterson v Nixon*, 1960 J.C.42.
[186] Sheriff Gordon in his commentary on *Cummings v Tudhope*, 1985 S.C.C.R. 125. See too, *Sinclair v Clark*, 1962 J.C. 57, and *Lockhart v Crockett*, 1987 S.L.T. 551.
[187] 1992 J.C. 127 at 131.

held that this consistency constituted sufficient corroboration of the unequivocal confession.

One reason why "very little" corroboration is required is that confessions **9–67** are statements against interest. As Lord Dunpark explained in *Hartley v HM Advocate*,[188] "the confession of guilt by an accused person is prejudicial to his own interests and may therefore initially be assumed to be true". Hartley had confessed to the murder of a small boy by drowning him in a burn. At his trial he denied his confession, and claimed that he had simply been working in the area in a local authority gardening squad. It was held that there was ample corroboration of his confession from the following facts:

(i) his work did not require him to go near the burn, although he had said that it did;

(ii) another young boy described the victim struggling with someone answering Hartley's general description;

(iii) evidence was led to show that his clothing had been in water that day; and

(iv) Hartley stayed off his work for the week following the murder.

Such a collection of cumulative circumstantial evidence may be unexceptionable when dealing with an unequivocal and clear admission of guilt. But great care is obviously required when the circumstances of the confession give rise to doubts, or the accused is of limited intelligence, as was said to be the case in *Hartley*. As Lord Dunpark asserted in that case,[189] one may initially assume that a confession is true, and then "one is not ... looking for extrinsic evidence which is more consistent with his guilt than his innocence, but for extrinsic evidence which is consistent with his confession of guilt". This is arguably much more necessary when there is doubt about the quality of the confession.

The extrinsic evidence in question often comes from information supplied **9–68** by the accused. This may be either by indicating the location of items connected with the crime or by disclosing information that only the perpetrator of the crime, or someone present during the commission of it, could have known. This is acceptable if there is no question of the confession being anything other than freely and frankly given, since it then eliminates the possibility of a bogus confession. It does not, however, guarantee the validity of the confession if it is alleged by the accused that the entire confession—together with the linking facts—was invented by the police.

Extrinsic evidence supplied by the accused suggests inside information. **9–69** This is sometimes described as the "special knowledge" rule, where a confession is almost considered to be self-corroborating. Despite the potential risk of the unreliability of such a confession,[190] the courts regularly accept

---

[188] *Hartley v HM Advocate*, 1979 S.L.T. 26. Lord Grieve, at 31, observed that "[i]t is well settled that where, as here, an accused person has, by means of an unequivocal confession, identified himself with an offence, little is required by way of corroboration to meet the requirements of our law".

[189] *Hartley v HM Advocate*, 1979 S.L.T. 26 at 33.

[190] See Griffiths, *Confessions*, paras 5.63–5.104 for a critical treatment of cases dealing with special knowledge.

such evidence as corroboration. One of the most frequently cited examples of this rule in operation is *Manuel v HM Advocate*.[191] During a confession to a murder Manuel offered to point out to the police the separate spots in a field where he had buried the victim and one of her shoes. His ability to do so later was held to be corroborative of his confession, and this line of reasoning was approved in *Hartley*.

9–70 For a confession to be self-corroborating, it is not necessary for it to contain special knowledge that would only be known to a perpetrator, not least because the perpetrator could have disclosed the details to others. Also, the increasing involvement of the media in serious criminal investigations means that over the course of a police enquiry details of the crime can leak out, whether intentionally or deliberately, into the public domain. This appears to be the position even if the confession contains details inconsistent with the proven facts.

9–71 In *Gilmour v HM Advocate*[192] the accused gave the police a confession to rape and murder containing details which, allegedly, only the real offender could have known. It also contained discrepancies with the proven facts. In his summary to the jury, the trial judge dwelt only on the consistent facts that could be said to corroborate the confession, stating that the inconsistencies had been effectively rehearsed in the defence speech. It was held on appeal that there was nothing wrong with such an approach and that when a confession contains both consistencies and inconsistencies, it is for the jury to decide whether the confession is nevertheless corroborated. At the end of the day, for a court to find that a clear confession has been corroborated, there must be some evidence capable of providing corroboration and a sufficiency of evidence.[193]

---

[191] 1958 J.C. 41. See also *Allan v Hamilton*, 1972 S.L.T. (Notes) 2; *Torrance v Thaw*, 1970 J.C. 58, *Wilson v McAughey*, 1982 S.C.C.R. 390; *McAvoy v HM Advocate*, 1982 S.C.C.R. 263; *Annan v Bain*, 1986 S.C.C.R. 60; *Wilson v HM Advocate*, 1987 S.C.C.R. 217; and *MacDonald v HM Advocate*, 1987 S.C.C.R. 581.

[192] *Gilmour v HM Advocate*, 1982 S.C.C.R. 590.

[193] See *Sinclair v MacLeod*, 1964 J.C. 19; *Cairns v Howdle*, 2000 S.C.C.R. 742.

Chapter 10

EVIDENCE OBTAINED UNLAWFULLY OR IMPROPERLY

INTRODUCTION

The Scots law approach to the issue of admitting evidence obtained without **10–01** lawful authority has been described by one English commentator as "principled"[1] in contrast to the English common law position, which was expressed by Crompton J in *R. v Leatham* in this way "[i]t matters not how you get it; if you steal it even, it would be admissible in evidence".[2] Recent English cases have affirmed this dictum such that evidence obtained through entrapment, invasion of privacy or unlawful searches may still be admissible,[3] although the English judiciary also has statutory powers to exclude evidence recovered by unlawful means if it would be unfair to the defendant to include it.[4]

In Scots law the common law principles governing recovery of tangible **10–02** items of evidence are similar to those governing the obtaining of confessions—in order to be admitted subsequently in court it must be fair to the accused to do so. Thus, the exclusion of evidence that has been obtained unlawfully, e.g. in the absence of a search warrant is not automatic. As with confession evidence, the fundamental concern is to strike a balance between the interests of the accused to a fair trial,[5] and the interests of the State in protecting the public and ensuring the proper administration of justice. Whether or not any individual item duly recovered is admissible all depends on the circumstances of the recovery. Admissibility is a matter of law and there is a great deal of discretion given to the trial judge in determining what constitutes unfairness, such as to exclude the evidence.

In *HM Advocate v McGuigan*[6] the accused was arrested on charges of **10–03** murder, rape and theft. Lord Justice-Clerk Aitchison dismissed objections to the search of the accused's tent in which he had been living, and the removal of various items without a search warrant. In relation to the competing interests in securing fairness he observed[7]:

---

[1] C. Tapper, *Cross and Tapper on Evidence*, 9th edn, at 494–395.
[2] *R. v Leatham* (1861) 8 Cox C.C. 498 at 501.
[3] *R. v Khan (Sultan)* [1997] A.C. 558, H.L.
[4] s.78(1) of the Police and Criminal Evidence Act 1984. For a discussion of comparative approaches to the question of admissibility in this area see S. Kines, "Why Suppress the Truth? U.S., Canadian and English Approaches to the Exclusion of Illegally Obtained Real Evidence in Criminal Cases" (1996) *Res Publica* II (2) 147–162.
[5] That is, a fair trial in terms of both the common law and the ECHR provisions.
[6] *HM Advocate v McGuigan*, 1936 J.C. 16.
[7] *HM Advocate v McGuigan*, 1936 J.C. 16 at 18.

> "[I]t must be obvious that, the accused having been arrested on so grave a charge as murder, it might be of the first importance to the ends of public justice that a search of the tent in which the accused had been living should be made forthwith."

Lord Justice-Clerk Aitchison held the police were acting within their common law powers, given the urgency of the situation. Later, he added obiter, that even had it been otherwise, "an irregularity in the obtaining of evidence does not necessarily make that evidence inadmissible".[8]

10–04   The leading authority of the modern rule is the seven bench decision in *Lawrie v Muir*.[9] In that case, Lord Justice-General Cooper adopted the *McGuigan* approach and cast it in a broader principle that has been applied ever since. The case concerned the inspection of dairy premises occupied by Mrs Lawrie in order to locate stolen milk bottles. Two inspectors under contract to the Scottish Milk Marketing Board ("SMMB") searched the premises of the accused with her permission, but outwith the terms of the search warrant, since the accused was not a SMMB milk distributor. The accused had believed that the warrants covered the search, as did the inspectors, but it was argued that the evidence of the discovery of stolen bottles could not be led because of the false representation of authority. In holding that the evidence was indeed inadmissible, Lord Cooper highlighted the two conflicting interests, which every court must weigh together in every such case, namely:

> "(a) the interests of the citizen to be protected from illegal or irregular invasions of his liberties by the authorities, and (b) the interest of the State to secure that evidence bearing upon the commission of crime and necessary to enable justice to be done shall not be withheld from Courts of law on any mere formal or technical ground."[10]

In referring to Lord Justice-Clerk Aitchison's opinion in *McGuigan*, that an irregularity in recovery of evidence does not necessarily render that evidence inadmissible, Lord Justice Cooper said:

> "Lord Aitchison seems to me to have indicated that there was in his view, no absolute rule and that the question was one of circumstances. I respectfully agree. It would greatly facilitate the task of Judges were it possible to imprison this principle within the framework of a simple and unqualified maxim, but I do not think that it is feasible to do so."[11]

The principles articulated in *Lawrie v Muir* have been applied ever since, but have attracted some criticism.[12] In undertaking this role of balancing the competing interests of the citizen and the state, the underlying principle of

---

[8] *HM Advocate v McGuigan*, 1936 J.C. 16 at 18
[9] *Lawrie v Muir*, 1950 J.C. 19.
[10] *Lawrie v Muir*, 1950 J.C.19 at 26.
[11] *Lawrie v Muir*, 1950 J.C.19 at 27.
[12] Macphail, *Evidence*, para.21.06, who observed that "it seems inconsistent to exclude a confession obtained by illegal means but to countenance the admission of real evidence obtained by illegal means".

"fairness", so dominant in determining the admissibility of confession evidence, also plays an important part. *Lawrie v Muir* has often been applied in cases involving irregularities in the granting of the search warrant. In *Bulloch v HM Advocate*[13] a warrant granted to the Inland Revenue under the Finance Act 1972 was held to have been unlawfully used because it was undated. In *HM Advocate v Bell*[14] items recovered under a warrant were rejected on the ground of irregularity as it was unsigned. In *HM Advocate v Cumming*[15] the warrant granted under the Misuse of Drugs Act 1971, and the evidence obtained under it, was successfully objected to on the ground that it failed to specify the premises to be searched or the officers authorised to search. In *McAvoy v Jessop*[16] the search of a bedsit in a multiple-occupation building was held unlawful as the warrant specified a different bedsit.

Challenges to the validity of search warrants will also now invariably **10–05** make reference to a breach of privacy rights under art.8 of the ECHR.[17] It is not an irregularity in the execution of a search warrant if there are civilian employees of the police present during the search provided such persons are acting under the supervision of the police officer authorised to conduct the search. Many statutory offences now involve being in possession of electronic images or other material, where computer specialists may be necessary at the search to ensure preservation of evidence.[18]

As the case law shows, notwithstanding irregularities, evidence recovered **10–06** under any of the above situations may well be ruled admissible. Separate from the granting of the warrant or whether the police exceeded their powers, where irregularity is claimed, the question of admissibility often centres on one of two situations, either of which can act to excuse the irregularity. These are: (i) the urgency of the situation; and (ii) accidentally stumbling across the goods, as opposed to deliberately embarking upon a fishing expedition.

THE URGENCY OF THE SITUATION

The courts are willing to recognise that it is sometimes expedient for the **10–07** police to seize items of evidence that might otherwise be lost.[19] In *HM Advocate v Hepper*[20] the accused had consented to a search of his house in respect of one charge and in the course of that search a briefcase was found which was taken away in the belief that it related to that charge. It turned out to contain evidence relating to another offence entirely, but the court held that the evidence was admissible on the new charge because the original search had been lawful, the discovery of the briefcase had been incidental and the consideration of urgency justified its removal.

---

[13] *Bulloch v HM Advocate*, 1980 S.L.T. (Notes) 5.
[14] *HM Advocate v Bell*, 1985 S.L.T. 349.
[15] *HM Advocate v Cumming*, 1983 S.C.C.R. 15.
[16] *McAvoy v Jessop*, 1998 S.L.T. 621.
[17] *Birse v HM Advocate*, 2000 J.C. 503.
[18] *Lord Advocate's Reference (No.1 of 2002)*, 2002 S.L.T. 1017, concerning the statutory offence of possession of indecent photographs of children.
[19] *HM Advocate v McGuigan*, 1936 J.C. 16; *Tierney v Allan*, 1990 S.L.T. 178.
[20] *Advocate v Hepper*, 1958 J.C. 39.

10–08   The presence or absence of urgency is a matter for interpretation based upon the facts. Contrast *Hepper* above with *HM Advocate v Turnbull*.[21] Turnbull's premises were searched by the police who had a warrant alleging tax frauds. A large consignment of papers was removed and passed to the Inland Revenue without being examined. On examination, the Revenue found evidence of further offences not covered by the original warrant and further charges were brought against Turnbull as a result. The court rejected the evidence relating to the further offences obtained during the search as it had not been carried out as a matter of urgency. Therefore, it was not a case of evidence accidentally coming to light, but simply a general "fishing expedition". Subsequent cases involving unlawful searches, or lawful searches which exceed their remit, tend to be grouped behind one or other of *Turnbull* and *Hepper*, with the determining criterion being either whether the evidence was recovered as a matter of urgency.

10–09   There are many illustrations of improperly recovered evidence being admitted under the urgency principle. For example in *Burke v Wilson*[22] a number of pornographic videos were recovered during a lawful police search of shop premises for pirate videos. The court held that the pornographic videos were admissible (even though not the subject of the search warrant) as if they had not been seized as a matter of urgency they could easily have been disposed of.

10–10   In *McNeill v HM Advocate*[23] the court used the urgency principle to justify admitting in evidence the fruits of a search of a house in Liverpool under an Excise warrant to search for drugs obtained following the discovery of drugs on a yacht moored in the Clyde. The court was not convinced that the search and seizure of drugs was unlawful, but held that, even if it was, it was justified by the urgency of the situation coupled with the very serious charges involved.

10–11   As Lord Justice-General Cooper acknowledged in *Lawrie v Muir*, the police frequently do not have the luxury of time in which to follow normal procedures, but may have to act in an emergency in order to preserve vital evidence. There is a substantial body of case law to illustrate how the courts appear willing to exercise leniency in the admission of evidence obtained if urgency prevails.[24]

ACCIDENTALLY STUMBLING ACROSS THE GOODS

10–12 The case law draws a distinction between evidence that is stumbled across accidentally—which is generally admissible—and that which is deliberately recovered by a fishing expedition, which is generally inadmissible.[25] In *Leckie v Milne*[26] Leckie was arrested on petition in respect of a charge of theft from a doctor's surgery and the sheriff granted the usual search

[21] *Advocate v Turnbull*, 1951 J.C. 96, following *Fairley v Fishmongers of the City of London*, 1951 J.C. 14; *HM Advocate v Bell*, 1985 S.L.T. 349.
[22] *Burke v Wilson*, 1988 S.L.T. 749.
[23] *McNeill v HM Advocate*, 1986 S.C.C.R. 288.
[24] See, e.g. *Allan v Milne*, 1974 S.L.T. (Notes) 76 and *McHugh v HM Advocate*, 1978 J.C. 12.
[25] *Tierney v Allan*, 1990 S.L.T. 178.
[26] *Leckie v Milne*, 1981 S.C.C.R. 261.

warrant regarding articles connected with that offence. Armed with that warrant, police persuaded D, who lived with Leckie, to allow them to search the house and in the course of that search they discovered evidence which led to Leckie's conviction on new charges of theft from a school and an office. In quashing the convictions, the High Court followed *Turnbull* in holding that the search had been unlawful, being authorised by neither the warrant nor any implied consent from D (who was assumed to have consented only to the extent authorised by the warrant). Noting that the officers who conducted the search were not made aware of the contents of the petition, did not have the warrant with them and appeared simply to have been instructed to search for evidence of theft, the court held that the search was random and the fruits of it were therefore inadmissible.

Examples of accidental recovery of evidence (otherwise improperly **10–13** obtained) include *Drummond v HM Advocate*[27] and *Baxter v Scott*.[28] In the latter case, police officers discovered stolen items while checking the boot of a car belonging to a driver they had arrested. The Crown successfully argued that the police had a general duty to check the contents of vehicles in their temporary custody for dangerous or perishable goods and that stolen goods recovered from such a search were legitimately recovered. In contrast, in *Graham v Orr*[29] some cannabis that was recovered from the parcel shelf of a car, following the arrest of the driver for failing a roadside breath test, was held inadmissible evidence as the police had no common law powers to conduct such a search. The case law indicates that a fine line divides evidence recovered properly from that recovered improperly. It is very much a matter of the specific circumstances of the case.

If the court is not satisfied that there are urgent or accidental circum- **10–14** stances surrounding the recovery of evidence, then the evidence will be inadmissible. In *McGovern v HM Advocate*[30] the court rejected evidence obtained from fingernail scrapings taken from an accused who was under suspicion of safe-blowing, but had not been charged. The necessary evidence could have been obtained quite lawfully, either by applying for lawful warrant or by charging the suspect, but in the absence or either of those procedures, the evidence was deemed inadmissible.

The impact of the human rights legislation will be to ensure that where **10–15** there is a suggestion that evidence has been improperly obtained, any assessment of its propriety will have to take into consideration whether there has been a breach of art.8 of the ECHR. Article 8, which provides for a right to respect for private and family life, home and correspondence, declares that:

> "[T]here shall be no interference by a public authority with the exercise of this right except such as is in accordance with the law and is necessary in a democratic society in the interests of national security, public safety or the economic well-being of the country, for the prevention of disorder or crime, for the protection of health or morals, or for the protection of the rights and freedoms of others."

---

[27] *Drummond v HM Advocate*, 1993 S.L.T. 476.
[28] *Baxter v Scott*, 1992 S.C.C.R. 342.
[29] *Graham v Orr*, 1995 S.L.T. 30.
[30] *McGovern v HM Advocate*, 1950 J.C. 33.

In short, the courts will have to perform precisely the same kind of balancing act of competing interests as that which they have been accustomed to doing, albeit now with the benefit of an additional body of human rights jurisprudence.

SCOPE OF COMMON LAW POWERS

10–16 The common law powers of the police to act without a search warrant in an emergency are not overridden by statutory powers unless the statute in question expressly provides that the common law is overridden.[31] In *Cairns v Keane*[32] Cairns objected to the admission of all evidence relating to the breath and blood samples that had been taken from him while he was suspected of driving while under the influence of alcohol. His objection was based on the grounds that when the breath sample had been taken, the police had been trespassers in his house, having chased him up the drive to his house and in effect made a forced entry to the house behind him. The High Court of Justiciary upheld the sheriff's ruling that the police had common law powers to act in an urgent situation. The statutory provisions did not affect these powers relating to the taking of breath and blood samples.[33]

THE FRUIT OF THE POISONED TREE

10–17 When statements made by an accused are later deemed inadmissible because of the way in which they were obtained, what is the status of any evidence recovered because of that statement? Where further evidence is discovered as a result of inadmissible means, the question arises as to the status of that further evidence. Even although the statements, or information, which led to that discovery are themselves inadmissible, can the additional facts unearthed be admitted? Or, to adopt the terminology of the American courts,[34] may the court consume the fruits of the poisoned tree?

10–18 In Scots law the question has only been partially answered and that is in the context of evidence revealed by inadmissible confessions. The answer in such cases is in the negative. Thus, in *Chalmers v HM Advocate*[35] the accused made a full confession to murder which the court later deemed to be inadmissible. During the course of that confession he offered to take the police to the place where he had hidden the victim's purse and evidence was led to the effect that he had done so. On appeal, it was held that the evidence of the visit to the locus (a cornfield) was inadmissible because it was "part and parcel of the same transaction as the interrogation and if the interrogation and the 'statement' which emerged from it are inadmissible as

---

[31] *MacNeill, Petitioner*, 1984 J.C. 1.
[32] *Cairns v Keane*, 1983 S.C.C.R. 277.
[33] *Cairns v Keane*, 1983 S.C.C.R. 277 at 281.
[34] See, e.g. *Olmstead v U.S.* (1928) 277 U.S. 438.
[35] *Chalmers v HM Advocate*, 1954 J.C. 66.

'unfair', the same criticism must attach to the conducted visit to the cornfield".[36]

The strategic difficulty for the Crown is how to bring to the attention of **10–19** the court an incriminating fact (e.g. that the accused knew where the victim's purse was buried), a fact which only someone involved in the crime might be expected to know, without relating it to the inadmissible statement which led to it. The court in *Chalmers* seemed to be suggesting that the fact that the accused was able to take the police to the locus could not be revealed to the jury because he had first offered to do so during an inadmissible confession. Over the years, the weight of opinion has favoured a more flexible test which would allow the court to make use of the fruit of the poisoned tree, provided that it was not of itself obtained by unfair means and the Crown did not disclose the origin of the information.[37] The rule was clarified in *HM Advocate v P*,[38] and discussed in Ch.9, where it was decided there was no automatic breach of art.6 when the fruits of the poison tree were relied upon.

Macphail, the Thomson Committee and the Scottish Law Commission all **10–20** favoured a more flexible test which would allow the court to make use of the fruit of the poisoned tree provided that it was not of itself obtained by unfair means and the Crown do not disclose the origin of the information.[39] The Scottish Law Commission were of the opinion that this might already be the law. This issue acquired an unexpected prominence due to continuing terrorist activities on mainland United Kingdom in the wake of the 9/11 destruction of the Twin Towers in New York. At its most pointed, the issue that has to be confronted is: when the fruits of the poisoned tree are the results of torture, what status do these fruits have? According to Lord Bingham in the seven bench decision in *A and Others v Secretary of State for the Home Office*[40]:

> "[T]he common law has regarded torture and its fruits with abhorrence for over 500 years and that abhorrence is now shared by over 140 countries which have acceded to the Torture Convention."

Although Lord Bingham was referring to English law, his comments apply to all three UK jurisdictions. The Torture Convention,[41] which the UK has ratified, requires states not merely to refrain from authorising torture but also to suppress and discourage its practice. The Convention prohibits statements obtained by torture to be used as evidence in any proceedings. While this recent affirmation of such a fundamental principle of law is welcome, its implementation is more complex as the circumstances in *A and others* revealed Terrorism and other forms of organised crime pose challenges for policing and the courts. In short, when evidence derives from the

---

[36] *Chalmers v HM Advocate*, 1954 J.C. 66 at 76.
[37] The decision in *Cadder v HM Advocate* [2010] UKSC 43 has thrown this debate into sharper relief.
[38] *HM Advocate v P* [2011] UKSC 44.
[39] The Thomson Committee (Cmnd. 6218), para.7.26; Machpail, *Evidence*, para.21.04; and the Scot. Law. Com. Memorandum No.46, para.U.02;
[40] *HM Advocate v Bell*, 2005 U.K.H.L. 71 at para.51; 2006 2 A.C. 221.
[41] The United Nations Convention against Torture and Other Cruel, Inhuman or Degrading Treatment or Punishment, 1984.

security services its origins are not readily identifiable. The intelligence services gather information from sources whose identity may not be known or disclosed. It may be very difficult to ascertain whether or when courts are being presented with evidence from the poisoned tree, or to guarantee that evidence which has been unlawfully obtained by torture is totally absent from UK courts.

CIVIL ACTIONS

10–21 The sole test of the admissibility of illegally obtained evidence in civil cases has traditionally been simply that of whether or not it is relevant. The leading case is *Rattray v Rattray*[42] in which a letter, sent by the defender to the co-defender in a divorce action based on adultery, was stolen from the Post Office by the pursuer and used by him in evidence. Theft of a letter from the Post Office was a criminal offence and the pursuer was successfully prosecuted. On appeal in the civil case, although it was held that there was insufficient evidence of adultery, the majority court ruled that the letter had been rightly admitted in evidence. The justification of admissibility despite the fact of the theft was stated by Lord Trayner thus, "the policy of the law in later years (and I think a good policy) has been to admit almost all evidence which will throw light on disputed facts and enable justice to be done".[43]

10–22   This observation was essentially obiter, and there was dissenting opinion, notably from Lord Young, but the case has set an uncomfortable precedent for later courts to follow.[44] Any application of this principle to criminal cases was eliminated by *Lawrie v Muir*[45] and it is only in civil cases that it is still possible to cite *Rattray* as authority for the alarming suggestion that even evidence obtained by criminal means is admissible. However, later courts have felt obliged to follow *Rattray* because it was a ruling by a full court of the Second Division and no other opportunity to reverse or reconsider the full implications of it has occurred before that court since. In some cases the courts have expressed discomfort but have been unable to extricate themselves from the rules of precedent and *stare decisis*. Thus, in *McColl v McColl*[46] Lord Moncrieff was clearly unhappy at having to follow the authority of *Rattray* to admit in evidence a letter from the defender to the paramour which had been intercepted by criminal means. Similarly, in *Duke of Argyll v Duchess of Argyll*[47] Lord Wheatley admitted that, "I must confess that I find the reasoning of Lord Trayner [in *Rattray*] ... difficult to follow ... but ... I feel bound by the decision if unconvinced by the reasoning in that case".

10–23   Certainly, in so far as evidence has been obtained by underhand means that fall short of being criminal, the courts appear to admit it routinely

---

[42] *Rattray v Rattray* (1897) 25 R. 315.
[43] *Rattray v Rattray* (1897) 25 R. 315 at 318–319.
[44] The precise grounds for doubting the binding nature of the case as a later authority are explained by Macphail, *Evidence*, para.21.08.
[45] *Lawrie v Muir*, 1950 J.C. 19.
[46] *McColl v McColl*, 1946 S.L.T. 312.
[47] *Duke of Argyll v Duchess of Argyll*, 1962 S.C. 140, at 141–142.

without objection being taken. In *MacNeill v MacNeill*[48] and *Turner v Turner*,[49] for example, no objection was raised to the use in evidence of letters passing between defenders and paramours which had been intercepted by both pursuers. And in *Watson v Watson*[50] it was held that the pursuer might found upon a torn-up draft letter by the defender to the paramour which he found.

In the notorious case of *Duke of Argyll v Duchess of Argyll* certain diaries **10–24** were admitted in evidence which belonged to the Duchess and which were acquired by the Duke by theft. Because adultery was historically treated as a quasi-criminal offence,[51] Lord Wheatley felt himself entitled to treat *Lawrie v Muir* as applicable to a modern divorce case, and he added that:

> "There is no absolute rule, it being a question of the particular circumstances of each case determining whether a particular piece of evidence should be admitted or not. Among the circumstances which may have to be taken into account are the nature of the evidence concerned, the purpose for which it is used in evidence, the manner in which it was obtained, whether its introduction is fair to the party from whom it has been illegally obtained and whether its admission will in fairness throw light on disputed facts and enable justice to be done."[52]

The principle of subjecting illegally obtained evidence in civil cases to the same tests as that in criminal cases has found favour with other commentators.[53] It is largely the principle that now governs the position in England, where the court has discretion to exclude evidence that has been obtained improperly, subject to the overriding objective of the interests of justice.

---

[48] *MacNeill v MacNeill*, 1929 S.L.T. 251.
[49] *MacNeill v MacNeill*, 1930 S.L.T. 393.
[50] *Watson v Watson*, 1934 S.C. 374.
[51] At the time the standards of proof of crime and adultery were the same, namely beyond reasonable doubt.
[52] *Duke of Argyll v Duchess of Argyll*, 1963 S.L.T. (Notes) 42 at 43.
[53] See, e.g. Macphail, *Evidence*, para.21.14; Wilkinson, *Scottish Law of Evidence*, at 118; The Law of Evidence, 1980, Scot. Law. Com, Memorandum No.46.

Chapter 11

HEARSAY

INTRODUCTION

11–01 The hearsay rule has been defined as "[a]n assertion other than one made by a person while giving oral evidence in the proceedings is inadmissible *as evidence of any fact asserted*".[1] It is a common law rule and there are numerous exceptions to the general rule formulated both within common law and by statute, many of which demand complex and technical interpretation. In criminal cases the rule operates generally so as to restrict evidence given by a witness in court to an account of what *he* or *she* perceived with one of their senses, i.e. what they saw, smelt, heard or touched. Evidence is also restricted to statements of fact and therefore evidence from a witness of their opinion is normally inadmissible unless the witness is an expert witness.

11–02 The hearsay rule renders inadmissible any statement by A which simply repeats something A was told by B, whether or not B is called as a witness. To take a simple example, when an assault is witnessed by A, it is A who is required to give evidence of what was seen, and not B to whom the incident was recounted. The purported evidence of B is hearsay and, in accordance with the general rule, is inadmissible. Nor is the ban restricted to oral accounts that are passed on in this fashion. The hearsay rule applies also to entries in documents whose authors are not available as witnesses to speak to such entries, although, as we shall see, there is a wide range of statutory exceptions to this application of the rule. The remainder of this chapter considers in more detail the nature of a statement described as hearsay and then the various exceptions to the hearsay rule. The chapter is largely concerned with criminal cases because s.2 of the Civil Evidence (Scotland) Act 1988 abolished the hearsay rule in civil cases. However, the impact of that abolition is considered. The dangers of hearsay evidence are recognised internationally[2] and form a specific element of art.6 of the ECHR. Article 6(3)(d) states:

> "Everyone charged with a criminal offence has the following minimum rights:
> . . .
>
> (d) to examine or have examined witnesses against him and to obtain the attendance and examination of witnesses on his behalf under the same conditions as witnesses against him . . ."

---

[1] Cross and Tapper, *Evidence*, 7th edn (Oxford: Oxford University Press, 1990) at 42 (emphasis added) cited approvingly in *Morrison v HM Advocate*, 1990 J.C. 299 at 312.
[2] *Subramaniam v Public Prosecutor* [1956] 1 W.L.R. 65 at 970 on appeal from Malaya.

This provision has generated considerable case law which is discussed in the course of this chapter.

HEARSAY EVIDENCE DISTINGUISHED FROM ORIGINAL EVIDENCE

When a witness speaks to a statement in court simply to prove the fact that **11–03** it was made, such a statement is known as "original evidence" (sometimes termed "primary evidence") and is distinguishable from hearsay, which is the admission of a statement as evidence of the truth of its contents. Provided a party seeks only to prove the fact that a statement was made, i.e. regardless of whether or not it is true, the fact will be admissible in court. As the Judicial Committee of the Privy Council observed in *Subramaniam v Public Prosecutor*[3]:

> "Evidence of a statement ... is hearsay and inadmissible when the object of the evidence is to establish the truth of what is contained in the statement. It is not hearsay and is admissible when it is proposed to establish by the evidence, not the truth of the statement, but the fact that it was made."

The facts of *Subramaniam* provide a helpful illustration of this distinction. He was charged with being in possession of firearms without lawful excuse. His defence was one of duress. Subramaniam claimed that Malayan terrorists had threatened to kill him if he refused to keep the arms for them. It was held that, regardless of whether or not the terrorists meant to carry out those threats, Subramaniam could testify to the fact that the threats were made.

The Scottish case of *McLaren v McLeod*[4] offers another illustration. **11–04** McLaren was charged with brothel keeping. Evidence was admitted of a conversation overheard by police officers in the premises in question between two women who were not called as witnesses. It was held that evidence of the fact of the conversation was relevant and admissible in that it proved that the conversation occurred and therefore it cast light on the nature of the premises and the purpose for which they were being used. Such evidence would not have been admissible had its purpose been to prove the truth of the substance of the conversation.[5]

The distinction between a hearsay statement and original evidence is not **11–05** always easy to draw, as the case law illustrates. Thus, in *Ratten v R*[6] the Judicial Committee of the Privy Council admitted evidence of a telephone call by a murder victim, shortly before her death, in which she asked for police assistance. The Privy Council held that evidence of the telephone call was not hearsay, because it was original evidence of: (i) the fact that it was not the only call from the house that day, as the accused claimed; and (ii) the

---

[3] [1956] 1 W.L.R. 965 at 969, on appeal from Malaya.
[4] *McLaren v McLeod*, 1913 S.C. (J.) 61.
[5] For a critique of the interpretation of the rule here and the status of implied assertions generally, see P. Duff, "The Uncertain Scope of Hearsay in Scots Criminal Evidence" (2005) *Juridical Review*, 1.
[6] In *Ratten v R* [1972] A.C. 378.

victim's state of emotion or fear. The second finding can only be relevant if it is regarded as implying that the victim was indeed under threat. This virtually amounts to using the statement as evidence of the truth of its implied contents. In *Ratten*, the court noted obiter that had the call been regarded as hearsay, it would have been admissible under one of the exceptions to the rule, namely the res gestae exception, dealt with below.[7]

THE RATIONAL OF THE GENERAL RULE

11–06 Lord Normand in *Teper v R.*[8] summarised the rationale for the hearsay rule as follows:

> "The rule against the admission of hearsay evidence is fundamental. It is not the best evidence and it is not delivered on oath. The truthfulness and accuracy of the person whose words are spoken to by another witness cannot be tested by cross-examination, and the light which his demeanour would throw on his testimony is lost."

This rationale, which the courts have frequently endorsed, comprises five separate elements, listed here, together with a brief critique of each:

11–07 (1) Hearsay statements are not the best evidence. They may, however, be the best which is now available, hence the exception which is permitted when the maker of the original statement is now dead. However, even if it is the only evidence available, if it is to be admissible it must still be compatible with art.6 and the right to a fair trial. In some cases, a hearsay statement may even constitute the best evidence possible. As the House of Lords observed in *Waugh v British Railways Board*[9] in regard to a report made by eyewitnesses concerning a railway accident, some of whom were available to testify in the subsequent civil action arising from it:

> "It is clear that the due administration of justice strongly requires disclosure and production of this report. It was contemporary. It contained statements by witnesses on the spot. It would be not merely relevant evidence but almost certainly the best evidence as to the cause of the accident."

11–08 (2) The maker of a hearsay statement is not on oath when he or she makes it. The argument that hearsay evidence lacks the solemnity of the oath in underlining to a witness the seriousness of testimony in court is no longer as convincing as it once might have been. In an increasingly secular society, the significance of the oath, with its dependency on a belief in religious retribution, is rapidly diminishing and retaining the offence of perjury for those

---

[7] It would also be admissible in Scotland both as a statement by a deceased person and as res gestae. See below.
[8] *Teper v R* [1952] A.C. 480 at 486; and for a wider discussion see the Scottish Law Commission's *Report on Hearsay Evidence in Criminal Proceedings*, 1995. Scot Law Com. No.149.
[9] *Waugh v British Railways Board* [1980] A.C. 521 at 531. This is an "eyewitness" exception to the general privilege that operates *post litem motam*.

who lie in the witness box would arguably be just as effective. A separate argument against the need for an oath is that a statement made by a person close in time to the events to which it relates may well be more reliable than one recounted months later in court, irrespective of whether or not the latter is made on oath. This consideration underlies the exception to the general rule permitted in those cases in which the statement is part of the res gestae.

(3) There is a risk that a hearsay statement will lose its accuracy through **11–09** repetition and therefore renders hearsay evidence inherently unreliable. That may be so, but it is a factor the court can take into account through the degree of weight it attaches to the evidence. If the statement in question was made in writing close to the events which it describes, that may enhance its reliability, hence the exception to the rule permitted in the case of public and business records.

(4) There is a risk that hearsay evidence will be manufactured. Whilst this **11–10** is a possibility, it is one that applies to all evidence.

(5) The court is unable to observe the demeanour of the original witness **11–11** whose evidence is given as hearsay through another witness in court, and their words cannot be tested in cross-examination. The argument that hearsay should be excluded because it prevents effective observation of demeanour or cross-examination, merit the same response as the third point, namely that of the weight attaching to such evidence. If the consequence of being unable to interrogate a witness about hearsay testimony is that the particular witness cannot provide a meaningful answer, or is forced to dissemble or remains silent in response to searching questions, then the cross-examination has been effective. The point has been made—the witness cannot say, because his or her knowledge is limited. Moreover, questions as to that person's demeanour, i.e. their physical or emotional state, can be asked of the witness now testifying.[10]

In the past 20 years or so, much of the rationale underlying the hearsay **11–12** rule has been critically questioned.[11] The relevance of the hearsay rule to the modern law of criminal evidence has been examined by the law commissions in both English and Scottish jurisdictions.[12] The statutory reform enacted in Scotland in 1995 is discussed later in this chapter. The modern rules on hearsay are often more notable for the breadth of the exceptions that exist to the general rule described above. Many of these exceptions are now embodied in statute having started life as common law rules. However, the rules are not exclusively statutory. Some common law rules remain in regular use and we start by considering those.

---

[10] Arguably, replicating the function of *de recenti* evidence, res gestae evidence and distress as corroboration. See Ch.8.
[11] See, for example, A. Zuckerman, "Law Commission's Consultation Paper No.138 on Hearsay: The Futility of Hearsay" (1996) Crim. L.R. 4; J. Spencer, "Hearsay Reform: A bridge not far enough?" (1996) Crim. L.R. 29; and P. Duff, "The Uncertain Scope of Hearsay in Scots Criminal Evidence" (2005) *Juridical Review*, 1.
[12] Law Commission Report 245, Cm.3670 (1997) *Evidence in Criminal Proceedings: Hearsay and Related Topics* (1995). *Report on Hearsay Evidence in Criminal Proceedings*, 1995. Scot.law.Com. No.149.

Common Law Exceptions to the Hearsay Rule

11–13 In the five bench House of Lords decision in *Myers v DPP*[13] Lord Reid noted[14] "the law regarding hearsay evidence is technical, and I would say absurdly technical".[15] In many respects, *Myers* exemplifies the lack of any principled basis for the development of the law. The case concerned the falsification of registration plates, and other identifying chassis and engine numbers of stolen cars, in order to re-sell them for profit. The hearsay point arose because it was not possible to identify, let alone trace, the employees of the car manufacturers who had recorded the original plates and other identifiers of the stolen cars. The court felt obliged to hold that in the absence of these witnesses, merely having another employee of the manufacturers give evidence about the procedures that workers would have followed in recording the identifying numbers was inadmissible as hearsay. The House of Lords was clearly discomfited by the effect of holding that the records were hearsay, but the majority could not find scope to interpret the common law in such a way as to bring the evidence within the ambit of the existing exceptions. It fell to parliament to do that in subsequent legislation.[16]

11–14 The exceptions to hearsay have emerged and evolved in response to expediency rather than principle, which gives the impression that hearsay evidence was sometimes permitted simply because it was the best available, even if it fell short of the best evidence rule. In regard to common law exceptions, Lord Reid also noted in *Myers*[17]:

> "By the nineteenth century many exceptions had become well established, but again in most cases we do not know how or when the exception came to be recognised. It does seem, however, that in many cases there was no justification either in principle or logic for carrying the exception just so far and no farther. One might hazard a surmise that when the rule proved highly inconvenient in a particular kind of case it was relaxed just sufficiently far to meet that case, and without regard to any question of principle."

The remainder of this chapter is devoted to an examination of the main exceptions to the hearsay rule as currently recognised by the criminal courts, dealing first with common law and then statutory situations where hearsay is admissible. The main common law exceptions to hearsay are discussed before considering the statutory framework which is now in place.

Confessions

11–15 As discussed in Ch.9, confession evidence is one of the most significant exceptions to the hearsay rule, permitting its repetition in court by a third

---

[13] *Myers v DPP* [1965] A.C. 1001.
[14] *Myers v DPP* [1965] A.C. 1001at 1019.
[15] *Myers v DPP* [1965] A.C. 1001 at 1019.
[16] Criminal Evidence Act 1965.
[17] *Myers v DPP* [1965] A.C. 1001 at 1020.

party, commonly a police officer. Thus, the question often posed to officers by the prosecution as to whether the accused person made any reply to caution and charge can be read out from the officer's notebook without infringing the rule of hearsay. This exception also permits any incriminatory or exculpatory statement from the accused to the police to be led before the trier of fact, even where the accused exercises their right not to give evidence in court. Prior to the ruling in *Cadder*,[18] the great majority of trials contained some evidence based on the interview of the accused by the investigating police officers.

STATEMENTS THAT ARE RES GESTAE

Davidson has observed that the development of the hearsay rule across most **11-16** adversarial systems is uneven and contested,[19] arguably no more so than in the formation and re-formation of the res gestae exception. A statement that is res gestae is a set of words that is so closely connected to a fact or facts in issue that it is said to form part of the disputed facts, and is therefore admissible in evidence. It has been defined as follows[20]:

> "Evidence is admissible of a statement made contemporaneously with an action or event which is, or forms part of, the fact or facts in issue by a person present at that action or event. The res gestae may be defined as the whole circumstances immediately and directly connected with an occurrence which is part of the facts in issue."

Thus, in the case of *Ratten v R.* discussed earlier, the words heard and subsequently narrated by the telephone operator in the emergency call, were in effect res gestae as they were so closely connected to the fact of the disputed call and the shooting incident. The res gestae exception is justified on the ground that it represents the spontaneous reaction of the person who made the statement. The statement was made before any opportunity existed for reflection and is therefore likely to be a genuine indication of what really happened. The exception covers not only statements but other physical reactions, such as fainting or vomiting. Res gestae statements include the express and implied assertions, not only of the participants in the incident themselves, but also of those observing it.

In *O'Hara v Central S.M.T. Co*,[21] a civil personal injuries action involving **11-17** a bus, where the account of a pedestrian some few minutes after the accident as to what had occurred was (perhaps surprisingly) considered by the Court to be res gestae. Lord President Normand made the following obiter comments:

> "The principle on which evidence of res gestae, including hearsay evidence, is admitted is that words and events may be so clearly interrelated that the truth can only be discovered when the words

---

[18] *Cadder v HM Advocate* [2010] UKSC 43.
[19] Davidson, *Evidence*, especially paras 12.08–12.25.
[20] Wilkinson, *Scottish Law of Evidence*, p.39.
[21] *O'Hara v Central S.M.T. Co*, 1941 S.C. 363.

accompanying the events are disclosed. But it is not essential that the words should be absolutely contemporaneous with the events (see, e.g. *AB v CD*[22]). What is essential is that there should be close association, and that the words sought to be proved by hearsay should be at least *de recenti* and not after an interval which would allow time for reflection and for concocting a story. So a long narrative is never allowed to be proved as part of the res gestae. In most of the cases which are reported the words which were allowed to be proved by hearsay evidence were uttered by the party injured or by the party accused in a criminal case."[23]

This dictum was doubted in *Cinci v HM Advocate*,[24] Lord Justice-Clerk Gill noting:

"I doubt whether the logic of the res gestae principle can admit of such a modification to it. In my view, a statement cannot be both part of the res gestae and *de recenti*. If the words spoken, though closely related to the event, are not part of the event, they cannot be treated as part of the res gestae. It may of course be difficult to define exactly when the event ceases...In *O'Hara v Central SMT Co*, in my view, the event had certainly ceased when the pedestrian made the admission in the presence of the driver and the conductress."

These reservations Lord Gill expressed in *Cinci* were obiter and both he and Lord Kirkwood acknowledged the court had not had a full citation of authority. There are arguments that can be made in favour of a broader approach to res gestae, such as that adopted in *O'Hara*, but these have yet to be aired before the High Court.[25]

11–18   Among the more obvious examples of res gestae statements are the screams and protests of a rape victim, or the use of nicknames in an unguarded moment by members of a gang of hooded, armed robbers.[26] In *Murray*[27] the accused was charged with the rape of a girl who was described in the indictment as "of weak and imbecile intellect" and was thus deemed incompetent as a witness because of her disability. It was held that her mother might testify as to "the first statement or exclamation she made" when she returned home, which was described as a cry of distress.[28]

---

[22] *AB v CD* (1848) 11 D 289.

[23] *O'Hara v Central S.M.T. Co*, 1941 S.C. 363 at 381.

[24] *Cinci v HM Advocate*, 2004 J.C. 103 at 107.

[25] See, for example the arguments presented in *R. v Andrews*, [1987] A.C. 281. For a discussion, see F. Davidson, "Res Gestae in the Law of Evidence" (2007) 11 Edin. L.Rev. 279.

[26] Thus, if one of the accused has the same nickname, the use of it by one of the gang to another may be employed in Evidence to identify the accused by implication, even if the person who uttered it has never been traced. The statement will be spoken to by the person (e.g. the victim) who heard it being made.

[27] *Murray* (1866) 5 Irv 232.

[28] Although the cry did not strictly accompany the assault, and was therefore more like a *de recenti* statement (for which see below), the circumstances were such that the court felt itself entitled to regard it as being part of the res gestae.

"The statement must be sufficiently close in time to the incident as to form part of it, and must relate to it in some material way. This accords with the rationale of the exception, namely that the statement should be spontaneous and erupt instinctively from the maker in the heat of the moment—described in some jurisdictions as 'an excited utterance'."[29]

Separate from the issue of contemporaneity, English law has recognised the context in which a statement may form part of the res gestae, i.e. "in such conditions (always being those of approximate but not exact contemporaneity) of involvement or pressure as to exclude the possibility of concoction or distortion".[30]

The phrase "exact contemporaneity" has given rise to a range of inter-   **11–19** pretations. Any time lapse may be critical to admissibility. In *Teper v R*[31] the evidence from a police officer who repeated in court the words of a witness (who could not be traced), implicating the accused in an alleged arson attack, was held on appeal not to be part of the res gestae, and thus hearsay and inadmissible. Lord Normand in *Teper* described the basic requirements that had to be met before any statement could be regarded as part of the res gestae:

"It is essential that the words sought to be proved should be, if not absolutely contemporaneous with the action or event, at least so clearly associated with it, in time, place and circumstances, that they are part of the thing being done, and so an item or part of real evidence and not merely a reported statement."[32]

Applying that to the statement to the facts in *Teper*, he ruled the words could not be part of the res gestae[33]:

"The words were closely associated in time and place with the event, the assault. But they were not directly connected with that event itself. They were not words spontaneously forced from the woman by the sight of the assault, but were prompted by the sight of a man quitting the scene of the assault, and they were spoken to for the purpose of helping to bring him to justice."

Although *Murray*[34] suggested the courts will allow some latitude of time, where the statement in question, although not precisely contemporaneous with the incident to which it relates, is, nevertheless, clearly made under the continuing psychological pressure of that incident, more recent dicta have decidedly shifted away from such an interpretation.[35]

---

[29] e.g. US Federal Rules of evidence.
[30] *Ratten v R.* [1972] A.C. 378 at 391. See too *R v Andrews* [1987] A.C. 281.
[31] *Teper v R* [1952] A.C. 480.
[32] *Teper v R* [1952] A.C. 480 at 487.
[33] *Murray* (1866) 5 Irv. 232.
[34] *Murray* (1866) 5 Irv 232.
[35] *Cinci v HM Advocate*, 2004 J.C. 103.

DE RECENTI STATEMENTS

11–20 Res gestae statements are distinct from, but may be connected to, statements made *de recenti*. Whereas the former are part of the commission of the crime, the latter, a *de recenti* statement, is one which is made shortly after the incident to which it relates. On those relatively rare occasions when *de recenti* statements are admissible, such as to support lack of consent by the victim in a rape case, they serve only to enhance the credibility of the maker as a witness, and are not evidence of the truth of their contents.[36] It is the fact that the earlier statement was made which is important. As discussed in Ch.8, *de recenti* statements acquire a particular significance in cases of alleged rape or sexual assault as complainers in these cases often find their credibility comes under attack in cross-examination in court. The admission of such previous consistent statements that were made *de recenti* is an example of the general rule that original (hearsay) evidence will be admitted when it is relevant.

11–21   The following are therefore the main points of distinction between res gestae and *de recenti* statements:

(1) Statements made res gestae are part of the incident to which they refer, whereas statements *de recenti* occur shortly afterwards.

(2) Statements made res gestae may be admitted as evidence of the truth of their contents; statements made *de recenti* merely enhance the credibility of the maker, who is now a witness.

(3) Statements made res gestae are admissible regardless of who made them; statements made *de recenti* are only admissible when the maker is now a witness giving evidence which is consistent with that contained in the *de recenti* statement.

(4) *De recenti* statements in criminal cases are almost certainly restricted, under modern law, when used to show consistency in a complainer's denial of consent in a sexual assault case.

STATEMENTS BY DECEASED PERSONS

11–22 In *William Thyne (Plastics) Ltd v Stenhouse Reed Shaw (Scotland) Ltd*[37] a company sued its insurance brokers for alleged negligence. The pursuers were under-insured at the time of a fire and the defenders sought to adduce an internal memorandum from the manager of the relevant office, now deceased, concerning the instructions given to him by the pursuers. They were refused leave to do so because the memorandum had been sent after it was known that the pursuers were holding them responsible for their losses. As such, it "was not a spontaneous account of events written at the time, but a considered version of them after intimation of a prospective claim, and must give rise to a reasonable suspicion that it was a one-sided version of the

---

[36] See *Morton v HM Advocate*, 1938 J.C. 50; *Cinci v HM Advocate*, 2004 J.C. 103.
[37] *William Thyne (Plastics) Ltd v Stenhouse Reed Shaw (Scotland) Ltd*, 1979 S.L.T. (Notes) 93.

truth".[38] Because of the danger of bias creeping in, the courts will likewise reject any statement by a person now deceased that takes the form of a precognition. This is because such statements are not the original words of the witness, but have been "filtered through the mind of another", i.e. the precognoscer who is conducting the interview.[39]

In *Moffat v Hunter*[40] the court admitted as evidence statements by a **11–23** person (now deceased) who had been a witness to a road accident. The statements had been given in his own words to an insurance inspector. The inspector did not proceed by question and answer, but simply collected the witness's verbatim statement. He had done so five months before the writ was issued and the witness had no clear idea of the insurance company's interest in the case. It was held that in the circumstances, it was not "tainted by interest" and was not a precognition.

Similarly, in *HM Advocate v Irving*[41] the High Court admitted statements **11–24** made to the police by the victim in a theft and rape case, who died shortly afterwards, because it was held that her statements were in the form of a straightforward complaint and not by way of precognition. But in *Thomson v Jamieson*[42] the court rejected a statement made by the (now deceased) driver of a car which had been in collision with the pursuer's motorcycle because it was made to a claims inspector employed by an insurance company at a time when a claim was in prospect, and took the form partly of a question-and-answer session. That was enough, said the court, to make it inadmissible on the ground that it was "akin to a precognition".

The common law also recognised exceptional circumstances in which even **11–25** a statement originally made in the form of a precognition could be admissible after the maker is dead. An example of these exceptional circumstances was the dying declaration or deposition of a witness in a criminal case who had material evidence to give in the case.[43]

The other possible main exception arises when the statement in question **11–26** has been given in the form of evidence in another case. In such cases, the statement could be challenged on the basis it derives only from examination and cross-examination and is therefore akin to a precognition, but it has the perceived advantage of having been given on oath. It is therefore arguably the best evidence now available. The authorities are divided as to whether or not the fact that the witness has not been cross-examined by the opposing party in the present case is fatal to its admissibility,[44] but the Scottish Law Commission[45] recommended that this should affect only the weight to be attached to it. The Commission also recommended[46] that if a deceased

---

[38] *William Thyne (Plastics) Ltd v Stenhouse Reed Shaw (Scotland) Ltd*, 1979 S.L.T. (Notes) 93.
[39] *Kerr v HM Advocate*, 1958 J.C. 14, per Lord Justice-Clerk Thomson at 19. See too, *Young v N.C.B.*, 1960 S.C. 6. But see the more recent discussion as to what constitutes a precognition in *HM Advocate v McSween*, 2007 S.L.T. 645.
[40] *Moffat v Hunter*, 1974 S.L.T. (Sh. Ct) 42.
[41] *HM Advocate v Irving*, 1978 J.C. 28.
[42] *Thomson v Jamieson*, 1986 S.L.T. 72. See also *Hall v Edinburgh Corporation*, 1974 S.L.T. (Notes) 14; *Pirie v Geddes*, 1973 S.L.T. (Sh. Ct) 81; and *Ferrier's Exr v Glasgow Corporation*, 1966 S.L.T. (Sh. Ct) 44.
[43] Walker and Walker, *Evidence*, 3rd edn, para.15.5.1. See also Macphail, *Evidence*, para.19.33.
[44] See Macphail, *Evidence*, para.19.32 and *Hogg v Frew*, 1951 S.L.T. 397.
[45] See para.T.11, *The Law of Evidence*, 1980 Scot. Law Com. Memorandum No.46.
[46] See para.T.10,

person's statements are to be admitted, the fact that they are in the form of a precognition should go only to their weight.

STATUTORY EXCEPTIONS TO THE HEARSAY RULE

11–27 Significant changes were made to the hearsay rule following the Scottish Law Commission's *Report on Hearsay Evidence in Criminal Proceedings*, in 1995.[47] The Commission's recommendations encompassed many of the principles underlying the common law and these were largely embodied in the Criminal Procedure (Scotland) Act 1995. Sections 259 and 260 of the Act set out the statutory exceptions which permit hearsay evidence to be admissible in court.

THE STATUTORY FRAMEWORK

Section 259

11–28 In terms of s.259(1), provided the trial judge is satisfied as to four conditions then in certain circumstances, specified in s.259(2), hearsay evidence is admissible and indeed must be admitted. There is no residual judicial discretion to exclude it.[48] These four conditions are:

    (i)   that the witness is unavailable;
    (ii) that had the maker of the statement given evidence the statement would not be hearsay;
    (iii) that the maker of the statement was competent at the time the statement was made;
    (iv) that the statement can be proved without recourse to hearsay.

Section 259(2) then specifies the five separate grounds (a) to (e) under which testimony other than oral testimony can be received. These grounds are as follows:

(a) The witness is now dead or unfit or unable to give evidence

11–29 At common law, statements by persons now deceased were treated as admissible as evidence of the truth of their contents in certain limited circumstances.[49] The rationale of the rule was that it was the best evidence available to the court of the matters contained in such statements. Following the amendments to the law in 1995, there was some uncertainty as to whether the common law continued to co-exist with the legislation. The position was clarified in *HM Advocate v Malloy*[50] where the High Court held that ss.259(2) and s.262(4) were to be interpreted as abrogating the common

---

[47] *Report on Hearsay Evidence in Criminal Proceedings 1995*. Scot. Law Com. No.149.
[48] A series of cases in 2003 illustrates this: *N v HM Advocate*, 2003 S.L.T. 761; *McKenna v HM Advocate*, 2003 S.L.T. 769; and *Daly v HM Advocate*, 2003 S.L.T. 773.
[49] *Lauderdale Peerage Case* (1885) 10 App. Cas. 692 at 707; *HM Advocate v Irving*, 1978 J.C. 28.
[50] *HM Advocate v Malloy* [2012] HCJ 124 at para.17.

law exceptions to the inadmissibility of hearsay evidence, which were thus replaced exclusively with the statutory provisions. The only common law exceptions that now remain are those not brought within the compass of ss.259(2) and 262(4).

The subsection also permits hearsay from a witness who, "by reason of his **11–30** bodily or mental condition", is unfit or unable to give competent evidence.

In *HM Advocate v Patterson*[51] a key prosecution witness died prior to the **11–31** trial. The Crown applied to have a previous statement made by the deceased admitted as evidence. The defence objected on the ground that the deceased was a known alcoholic and therefore not a competent witness in terms of s.259(1)(c). This argument was rejected by the appeal court which stated that unless a witness was either permanently or temporarily insane, or unable to understand the difference between truth and falsehood, then they would be deemed competent. The condition of alcoholism did not, in itself, render a witness incompetent.

In *HM Advocate v Nulty*[52] the Crown deserted a rape trial and subse- **11–32** quently raised a fresh prosecution. By the time of the second trial the complainer was mentally ill and unfit to give evidence. The Crown then sought to use as evidence the complainer's previous statement, which had been recorded on tape. The defence objected to the admission of the tape recording arguing that it would contravene the accused's right to a fair trial in terms of arts 6(1) and 6(3)(d) of the ECHR. This argument was rejected by the appeal court which ruled that there was no overall unfairness to the accused as there were two other safeguards available, namely the require-ment for corroboration of the complainer's evidence, and the provisions of s.259(4), which permits a party to challenge the reliability and credibility of any hearsay evidence. In arriving at its decision the court endorsed the approach articulated by the ECtHR in numerous cases (e.g. *Doorson v Netherlands*[53]), that the question of fairness must be looked at in the round:

"No violation of Article 6(1) taken together with Article 6(3)(d) of the Convention can be found if it is established that the handicaps under which the defence laboured were sufficiently counterbalanced by the procedures followed by the judicial authorities."

The question of the fairness of admitting hearsay was also raised in *HM Advocate v Beggs (No.3)*[54] where the accused was charged with assault, sodomy and murder. The defence objected to the Crown's request to lead evidence of a witness statement from P, who had died by the date of the trial, in which P described an incriminating conversation with Beggs. In the statement P, who was gay, claimed Beggs had told him that he liked "to cruise early morning in an attempt to pick up young guys in his car". Lord Osborne held that this evidence would have been admissible as evidence

---

[51] *Advocate v Patterson*, 2000 J.C. 137.
[52] *HM Advocate v Nulty*, 2000 S.L.T. 528.
[53] *Doorson v Netherlands* (1996) 22 E.H.R.R. 330.
[54] *HM Advocate v Beggs (No.3)*, 2002 S.L.T. 153.

from P had he been alive, thus satisfying s.259(1)(b). No Convention rights were breached by admitting P's hearsay statement as there were other safeguards, such as the need for corroborated evidence of the crimes charged,[55] the protection of s.259(4), and given that Beggs had not contended that anything in P's statement was untrue.[56]

(b) that the witness is outwith the UK and it is not practicable to secure his attendance or obtain evidence by alternative means

11–33   This exception is essentially to meet the practical and expedient needs of the criminal justice process. It is both inconvenient and potentially unjust to have to delay proceedings simply on account of an absent witness, if the evidence that witness is to give is available in an appropriate form. In *Aslam v HM Advocate*[57] the appeal court upheld a decision by a sheriff to refuse an application by the Crown to lead, as hearsay evidence, the statement of a witness alleged to be abroad. The sheriff had not been satisfied that the witness was in fact abroad. The appeal court stated that such decisions were a matter for the discretion of the judge at first instance.

(c) that the witness has been sufficiently identified, but cannot be found

11–34   This is another provision to promote expediency. The subsection requires that all reasonable steps be taken to find the witness.[58]

(d) that the witness declines to give evidence having been advised that it might be incriminating

11–35   The purpose of this provision was to ameliorate the effects of the decisions in *Perrie v HM Advocate*[59] and *McLay v HM Advocate*[60] cases where statements made to third parties by an incriminee were deemed hearsay and inadmissible. Such statements are sometimes described as implied assertions and, arguably, not hearsay at all.[61] The position now is that such statements can be led.

(e) that the witness refuses to take the oath or to give evidence

11–36   This provision was intended in part to address the difficulties experienced by vulnerable witnesses, especially young children, who might be so intimidated by the court process that they become mute or have limited recall of events once in the witness box.[62] The first application under this subsection was in *Macdonald v HM Advocate*,[63] a case involving various charges of

---

[55] If the corroboration rule is abolished, as the Scottish Government proposes, then the loss of this safeguard will have to be carefully assessed to ensure that here is a sufficiency of evidence and that the admissibility of the uncorroborated statement is compatible with a fair trial.

[56] *Advocate v Beggs* (No.3) at 162J–163B.

[57] *Aslam v HM Advocate*, 2000 J.C. 325.

[58] See *Hill v HM Advocate*, 2005 J.C. 259 in regard to what might be "reasonable" steps.

[59] *Perrie v HM Advocate*, 1991 J.C. 27.

[60] *McLay v HM Advocate*, 1994 S.L.T. 873.

[61] See SLC Report no.149 at para.5.12. For discussion, see P. Duff, "The Uncertain Scope of Hearsay in Scots Criminal Evidence" (2005) *Juridical Review*, 1.

[62] See letter by Iain MacPhail (later Lord) to the editor, 1999 S.L.T. (News) 75.

[63] *Macdonald v HM Advocate*, 1999 S.L.T. 533.

shamelessly indecent conduct towards several children. During the trial, an eight-year old girl in the course of answering questions put to her by the prosecutor, became upset, then broke down and became unable to answer further questions. The prosecutor successfully applied to the court to regard the child's conduct as a "refusal to give evidence" in terms of s.259 and to lodge as evidence the child's previous statement to a police officer. On appeal, it was held that the trial judge had erred in his interpretation of the statute as it only takes effect once a witness has been directed by the judge to give evidence and refuses to do so. In this case the absence of a specific direction from the sheriff to the witness to answer questions was fatal to the admissibility of the previous statement. The requirement for the trial judge in terms of s.259(2)(e)(ii) to "direct the witness to give evidence" needs to be interpreted in the context of vulnerable witnesses, whose inability to answer questions may well be to do with fear, anxiety and distress, as opposed to a lack of co-operation. For such witnesses to be "directed" to answer may not be conducive to achieving their best evidence. Of course it all depends upon how a judge goes about "directing" a witness to answer, but one can see that, applied insensitively, such an instruction might be counter-productive.

Section 260

In terms of s.260, it is now possible for a prior statement of a witness to be **11–37** admissible at a trial provided three conditions are met. These are:

(i) that the statement is contained in a document (but is not a precognition);
(ii) that the witness adopts the statement as his or her evidence; and
(iii) that at the time the statement was made the maker was a competent witness.

This provision reflects the decision in *Jamieson v HM Advocate*,[64] the ratio of which the Scottish Law Commission recommended be embodied in statute.[65] In *Jamieson* the appeal court upheld the decision of the trial judge to admit in evidence a statement made by a witness to police officers, the terms of which she was unable to recall in court, although she was able to recall having given the police such a statement and acknowledged its accuracy at the time. Jamieson extended the application of the principle in *Muldoon v Herron*[66] where evidence from police officers was permitted to fill the gap in a witness's memory and where the witness confirmed that she had made an earlier statement that represented her evidence. As Lord Hope explained in *Jamieson*[67]:

"Where a person identifies the alleged culprit to the police officers, he is in effect telling them what he saw. He is making a statement to the police officers which is a statement of fact and ought, if possible, to be spoken to by the witness in the witness-box. But if he is unable to

---

[64] *Jamieson v HM Advocate*, 1994 J.C. 251.
[65] Scottish Law Commission, *Evidence: Report on Hearsay Evidence in Criminal Proceedings*, HMSO, 1995. Scot. Law Com. No.149.
[66] *Muldoon v Herron*, 1970 J.C. 30.
[67] *Jamieson v HM Advocate*, 1994 J.C. 251 at 258.

recollect what he said to the police when he comes to give evidence, the gap in his recollection can be filled by what the police said he said to them at the time. This evidence, when taken with the witness's own evidence that he made a true statement at the time to the police, is held to be admissible because there are two primary sources of evidence. One is the evidence of the police officers as to who was in fact identified and the other is the witness's own evidence that he identified the culprit to the police. The consistency between these two pieces of evidence provides the link between them and completes the chain. As Lord Cameron said in *Muldoon* at 46, neither of these facts proves identity, but both are elements in the structure of evidence from which identification may be held proved."

One of the recommendations in the *Review of the Law and Practice of Disclosure Report* by Lord Coulsfield[68] was to remove the requirement that witnesses had to rely upon memory recall while giving evidence in court. The report acknowledged this made the task of being a witness an unnecessary memory test at a time when many witnesses would already be unnerved at the mere prospect of appearing in court. The recommendation that witnesses should be able to refer to copies of their prior statements in all cases where these statements have been available to the Crown and the defence[69] was enacted in s.85 of the Criminal Justice and Licensing (Scotland) Act 2010.[70]

STATEMENTS BY A CO-ACCUSED

Section 261(2) of the Criminal Procedure (Scotland) Act 1995

11–38 If certain conditions are met, s.261 permits one co-accused to lead evidence of incriminating statements made by another co-accused. Notice must be given in terms of the intention to found upon the prior statement of a co-accused[71] and such statements will only be admitted if they would also be admissible for use by the Crown.[72] Where one or both co-accused rely upon the defence of incrimination, both accused (or all accused if there are more than two) are entitled to a fair trial and careful consideration must be given to how hearsay evidence can be admitted whilst preserving the rights of all the accused to be vindicated. For example, if a statement had been unlawfully obtained it would endanger the fair trial of the maker if a co-accused could rely upon it.[73] In jury trials the judicial directions must be carefully crafted to avoid a miscarriage of justice.[74] The complexity and lack of certainty concerning the interpretation of these statutory provisions have been criticised.[75]

---

[68] Scottish Government, 2007.
[69] Recommendation 2. See para.5.4.2.
[70] Inserted as s.261A as an amendment to the Criminal Procedure (Scotland) Act 1995.
[71] s.259(5) of the Criminal Procedure (Scotland) Act 1995.
[72] *McIntyre (Ian Wayne) v HM Advocate*, 2009 S.L.T 716
[73] *Brand v HM Advocate*, 2012 S.L.T. 952.
[74] *Taylor v HM Advocate*, 2011 S.C.L. 628
[75] See Case Comment, SCL, October 2012, 855–870; Renton and Brown, 6th edn, 24–24 to 24–26.1.

IMPACT OF ECHR

Decisions by the courts to admit hearsay evidence have been the subject of **11–39** numerous challenges with reference to Convention rights. Objections to the admissibility of hearsay usually centre on the perceived prejudice to a fair trial if the maker of the statement admitted in evidence is not in court to be "examined" as envisaged by art.6(3)(d), which provides that an accused person has the right "to examine or have examined witnesses against him. . .". This is often referred to as "a right of confrontation"[76] which might suggest that hearsay evidence would be inadmissible, if the maker of the statement is not in fact present in court to be confronted.[77] However, this provision within art.6 has not been interpreted by the courts as precluding the use of hearsay evidence.[78]

A second objection is the inherent unreliability of hearsay evidence. **11–40** Where a conviction is based "to a decisive extent" on hearsay statements that may preclude a fair trial.[79] The ECtHR has upheld objections to hearsay evidence if it is the *only*, or substantial, evidence against the accused, whist affirming that the issue is whether the trial as a whole is fair.[80] The Scottish courts have confirmed that there is no fundamental objection under the ECHR to the concept of the admissibility of hearsay evidence.[81] However, as noted earlier, the corroboration rule has often been cited as an important counter-balancing safeguard of a fair trial in circumstances where hearsay evidence is admitted. Were the corroboration rule to be abolished there would need to be sufficient remaining safeguards to ensure art.6 compliance. Separately, the Grand Chamber decision in *Al-Khawaja and Tahery v United Kingdom*[82] may herald a shift in emphasis on the fair trial and hearsay evidence. Although it was based on an English appeal, it obviously has ramifications for Scots law. The case concerned allegations of sexual assault by two complainants, one of whom had committed suicide by the time of the trial. Her police statement was read out to the jury and the Chamber held here that there had been a breach of the applicants' right to a fair trial under art.6(1) and art.6(3)(d) as the conviction was entirely reliant upon the two hearsay testaments which had been admitted in evidence. In previous English cases the Supreme Court had chastised the ECtHR, with Lord Phillips offering an especially strong critique of the Chamber's approach[83] in noting that s.2 of the HRA required the UK Courts to take account of ECtHR jurisprudence but not to blindly follow it if it was felt

---

[76] M. Redmayne, "Confronting confrontation" in P. Roberts, and J. Hunter (eds.), *Criminal evidence and human rights: imagining common law procedural traditions* (London: Hart Publishing).

[77] That is the position adopted in the USA: 6th Amendment to the U.S. Constitution. For a critique of confrontation see; M. Redmayne, "Confronting confrontation" in: P. Roberts, and J. Hunter, (eds.) *Criminal evidence and human rights: imagining common law procedural traditions*, (London: Hart Publishing).

[78] *HM Advocate v Bain*, 2002 S.L.T. 340.

[79] *Kostovski v Netherlands*, 1990 E.H.R.R. 434;

[80] *Kostovski v Netherlands*, 1990 E.H.R.R. 434, *Unterpertinger v Austria*, 1991 13 E.H.R.R. 175; *Asch v Austria* (A/203A) (1993) 15 EHRR 597; and *Van Mechlen v Netherlands*, 1998 25 E.H.R.R. 647. See Ch.3. in regard to the testimony of anonymous witnesses.

[81] *McKenna v HM Advocate*, 2000 J.C. 291.

[82] *Al-Khawaja and TaherY v United Kingdom* (2012) 54 E.H.R.R. 23.

[83] *R v Horncastle* [2009] UKSC 14.

that the decision did not take account or appreciate an aspect of English law. He further critiqued the Chamber's reasoning noting that their jurisprudence on the issue of art.6 compatibility with hearsay evidence "lacked clarity" and that the "sole or decisive" rule on which the chamber's judgment hinged had been introduced into that jurisprudence "without discussion of the principle underlying it or full consideration of whether there was justification for imposing the rule as an overriding principle applicable equally to the continental and common law jurisdictions".

11–41   The Grand Chamber of the ECtHR subsequently took heed of the Supreme Court's analysis in the case of *Al Khawaja and Tahery v United Kingdom* (2012) 54 E.H.R.R 23 finding that the admission of a statement by a witness who did not attend the trial and whose evidence was the sole or decisive basis for a conviction would not necessarily breach the ECHR art.6(1) and art.6(3)(d). However, there did have to be sufficient counterbalancing factors, including strong procedural safeguards, to offset the prejudice to the defendant of not being able to cross-examine the absent witness. Interestingly, the Court of Appeal has recently held in the case of *R. v Riat (Jaspal)* [2012] EWCA Crim 1509 that when determining whether hearsay evidence should be admitted, in the event of a conflict between the European Court of Human Rights judgment in *Al-Khawaja v United Kingdom* (2012) 54 E.H.R.R 23, the UK courts were under a duty to follow the Supreme Court decision in *R. v Horncastle* and apply the provisions of the Criminal Justice Act 2003, even where the evidence was sole or decisive. Although this all pertains to English law it should resonate in Scotland given the forthcoming abolition of corroboration which may open the way to more art.6 challenges in the context of hearsay evidence.

ABOLITION OF HEARSAY IN CIVIL CASES

11–42 In regard to civil cases, s.2 of the Civil Evidence (Scotland) Act 1988 abolished the hearsay rule for all civil proceedings covered by the Act, including consistorial causes. This permits evidence to be led of any statement made by a person other than in a court of law, provided that statement would have been admissible had the person making it done so in the form of sworn testimony. The Civil Evidence (Scotland) Act 1988 resulted from the Scottish Law Commission's *Report on Corroboration, Hearsay and Related Matters*.[84] The purpose of the legislation was to promote the inclusion of all relevant evidence and to reduce the effect of exclusionary rules that prevented the court from considering evidence that might be of assistance in reaching decisions. Section 2(1) of the Act provides:

> "In any civil proceedings—
>
> (a) evidence shall not be excluded solely on the ground that it is hearsay;
> (b) a statement made by a person otherwise than in the course of the proof shall be admissible as evidence of any matter contained in the statement of which direct oral evidence by that person would be admissible; and

---

[84] *Report on Corroboration, Hearsay and Related Matters*, 1986 Scot. Law Com No.100.

(c) the court, or as the case may be, the jury, if satisfied that any fact has been established by evidence in those proceedings, shall be entitled to find that fact proved by evidence notwithstanding that the evidence is hearsay."

The conditions for the operation of s.2 are simply that the statement must be relevant and the maker must have been a competent witness. At the same time, s.2 continues to permit evidence of the making of such statements where this is relevant as original evidence. Statements include all "representations (however made or expressed)", but precognitions are expressly excluded from the operation of s.2. Five aspects of evidence are briefly considered.

(1) The evidence of children

A number of cases emerging in the aftermath of the legislation involved **11–43** children and threw up particular difficulties.[85] Section 24 of the Vulnerable Witnesses (Scotland) Act 2004, abolished the requirement that the court had to rule that the child was a competent witness before they could give evidence.[86] The section applies to both criminal and civil cases. Although the child witness is no longer subjected to a competency test, it will still be of value to the court if there is some evidence on the level of understanding of the child when the statement was first taken. As Lord Bonomy commented, obiter, in *MT v DT*[87]:

"[W]hen a child's statement is taken in a 'formal' setting such as by a police officer, it is likely to assist a court considering the statement later if the interviewer has been able to explore the child's understanding in the course of the interview."

Pre-dating the 2004 Act, the five bench court in *MT v DT*[88] decided that s.2(1)(b) did not embody a competency test[89] and therefore there was no requirement in civil proceedings to demonstrate competency, either at the time of the making of the statement, or at the time of the court hearing. Instead, it was implicit within the 1988 Act that the maker of a statement was a competent and admissible witness and thus, unless there is a separate reason for inadmissibility, any hearsay statement subsequently admitted in the court proceedings will be deemed competent.[90]

In *MT v DT* the central issue was at which of two dates a child, whose **11–44** evidence was critical to the findings of fact in an action by a father for

---

[85] e.g. *M. v Kennedy*, 1993 S.C. 115 and *F v Kennedy (No.2)*, 1993 S.L.T. 1284. For discussion of some of these cases, see the articles by L. Edwards, "Better Seen and Not Heard", 1993 S.L.T. 9, and D. Sheldon, "I Heard it on the Grapevine", 1993 J.L.S.S. 292.

[86] See Ch.3.

[87] *MT v DT*, 2001 S.L.T. 1442 at 1460L.

[88] *MT v DT*, 2001 S.L.T. 1442 over-ruling in full *F v Kennedy (No.1)*, 1992 S.C. 28; and in part *L v L*, 1996 S.L.T. 767.

[89] In contrast to its criminal counterpart contained in s.259(1)(c) of the Criminal Procedure (Scotland) Act 1995.

[90] It was observed in *MT v DT* that dicta in earlier cases had caused difficulties in that counsel and solicitors had felt obliged to bring children to court for the purposes of determining competency even if there was no actual intention to take the child's evidence.

contact with his daughter, should have been determined a competent witness. Was it at a date in August 1998 when she had made certain statements to a female police constable, or was it at the dates of the proof in 1999? In previous cases, it had been suggested that competency should be determined as at the date of the making of the statement. This raised the practical problem of how competency would be established in retrospect.[91] In 1990 the Scottish Law Commission had recommended the date of the proof was more appropriate for assessing competency,[92] which is in effect the current position—their evidence is now evaluated on the strength of what evidence is led at the proof.

(2) Sufficiency and hearsay

11–45 With the abolition of the need for corroboration in civil cases, coupled with the abolition of the rule against admitting hearsay, it is theoretically possible for an uncorroborated pursuer to succeed on the basis of hearsay evidence alone. However, there must still be sufficient evidence to found a case and, as was pointed out in *Gordon v Grampian Health Board*,[93] the court has discretion as to how much weight to attach to uncorroborated hearsay evidence. In that case, a reparation action against employers, the only evidence was from the pursuer who relied on a hearsay statement from a colleague. That colleague was cited as a witness but not actually called because the pursuer believed she might be a "hostile witness". The sheriff held that "although there was a bare sufficiency of evidence for the pursuer" he was not satisfied that she had proved her case on a balance of probability. As Sheriff Graham Johnston observed in his commentary to the reported case, while "the Act may well have abolished the *necessity* of corroboration to prove an essential fact, it does not abolish the *desirability* of leading evidence to back up the credibility of a party".[94]

(3) Expert witnesses

11–46 As discussed in Ch.4, expert witnesses have numerous privileges, one of which is the right to cite and rely upon the work of other authors in support of, or opposition to, the opinions they are presenting to the court. Section 2(1)(b) operates so as to permit the oral evidence of experts who speak to written reports as part of their testimony, but who may not be the authors of these reports.[95]

(4) Documentary evidence under statute

11–47 On a strict application of the rule against hearsay, all entries in documents would be essentially hearsay in nature, since they represent merely what someone has recorded on an earlier occasion. An entry in a document cannot therefore be evidence of the truth of the facts which it records, and even if the person who made the entry is called, he or she may well not be the person with the knowledge of the truth of the facts recorded. For example,

---

[91] See *Sanderson v McManus*, 1997 S.C. (HL) 55, per Lord Hope at 60B–C.

[92] *The Evidence of Children and Other Potentially Vulnerable Witnesses*, Report 125.

[93] 1991 S.C.L.R. 213.

[94] At 214.

[95] *Smith's Exrs v Upper Clyde Shipbuilders Ltd (in liquidation)*, 1999 G.W.D. 33-1597.

the Registrar of the Register of Births, Deaths and Marriages simply records information provided by another person. However, rigid adherence to this principle would make proof of many facts impractical, or at best would delay the process of justice to intolerable lengths. For this reason, Parliament has on many occasions, and for many different purposes, decreed that entries in documents may be adduced as evidence of the facts that they contain, subject to certain safeguards.

The Civil Evidence (Scotland) Act 1988 makes substantial provision for **11–48** the certification of certain types of documents being provable in evidence without the need for a witness to speak to them. Thus, s.5 admits, for the purposes of any "civil proceedings", a document suitably docqueted and purportedly signed by "an officer of the business or undertaking to which the records belong". Such a statement can be received in evidence without being spoken to by a witness. In terms of s.6, a copy document is similarly admissible if it purports to be authenticated by the person making it. Documents and records are defined in s.9 of the Act and include tapes, disks and computer records.

Apart from these major statutory provisions, other statutes render **11–49** admissible, for the limited purposes specified in each statute, various other records, mainly of a public nature. For example, s.41 of the Registration of Births, Deaths and Marriages (Scotland) Act 1965 renders extracts or abbreviated certificates issued by the relevant registrar evidence of the facts they record, although it is necessary in practice to produce other evidence in order to identify the persons named in the record. Entries in the Registers of Sasines, Inhibitions and Adjudications, the Books of Council and Session and court records are all admissible under statutes applicable to them. There is also general authority for the statement that all public records may be regarded as evidence of the facts which are recorded in them, as may official records kept by a public officer.[96]

Despite the broad terms of s.2, there is still a prohibition, contained in s.9 **11–50** against evidence given in precognitions. Whereas a statement is written or prepared by a witness, a precognition "is usually not an account of what the witness has actually said but is the precognoscer's reconstruction or interpretation".[97] As such, it is considered to be of less value that a direct account in a statement expressed in the witness's own words. In *Anderson v J.B. Fraser & Co. Ltd*[98] it was held that what was said to a precognoscer could be distinguished from what was recorded in a precognition. It is competent therefore to lead evidence from a precognoscer as to what the witness said, but not what was recorded. However, the weight to be attached to such statement may be limited.[99]

(5) Ancient rights and "pedigree" cases

According to Stair[100] and Erskine[101] evidence of reputation is admissible in **11–51** questions of ancient rights. In cases involving marriage, legitimacy, pedigree

---

[96] Dickson, *Evidence*, paras 1104, 1204 and 1209.
[97] Wilkinson, *Scottish Law of Evidence*, at p.39.
[98] *Anderson v J.B. Fraser & Co. Ltd*, 1992 S.L.T. 1129.
[99] *Cavanagh v BP Chemicals Ltd*, 1995 S.L.T. 1287.
[100] Stair, IV, xliii.
[101] Erskine IV, 2, 7.

and ancient rights, the common law has long recognised exceptions to the general rule against hearsay. Evidence in such cases was permitted under the best evidence rule, on the ground that the events into which the court was then inquiring occurred so long ago that no witnesses remained who could testify in court. The exception was most clearly developed in those cases involving marriage and legitimacy.[102] The import of the common law rules here has been weakened by the provisions of the 1988 Act and, most recently, by s.3 of the Family Law (Scotland) Act 2006 which abolishes cohabitation by habit and repute.

---

[102] *De Thoren v Wall* (1876) 3 R. (H.L.) 28. See too, *Brook's Executrix v James*, 1971 S.C. (H.L.). The application of the exception to peerage cases was recently confirmed in *Viscountcy of Dudhope and Earldom of Dundee*, 1986 S.L.T. (Lyon Court) 2.

Chapter 12

CHARACTER EVIDENCE

INTRODUCTION

For the purposes of the Scots law of evidence, a person's character includes **12–01** not only "their known disposition from previous actions, but also their general reputation in society".[1] The term "reputation" has been criticised as out-dated and "ludicrously weak material" upon which to base a criminal conviction, given that reputation may be erroneous or ill-motivated.[2] However, whatever description one attaches to character it will be subject to that same, quite legitimate, objection that persons can attract fame or notoriety on an entirely inaccurate basis, which is doubtless one of the reasons why evidence of character is considered collateral. In modern times, references to "bad character" tend to refer to previous convictions or some form of dishonest behaviour, such as propensity to lie.

According to Dickson, character evidence is a collateral issue in all but a **12–02** minority of cases and thus, as a general rule, is inadmissible.[3] However, as is frequently the case with the rules of evidence, it is the exceptions to that general rule that give rise to complexities of interpretation and application. When one sees reference in official reports and legislation to "good" character and "bad" character it might be assumed that these are readily identifiable categories, but they are of course highly contestable and not easily defined.

In evidence law, collateral matters are excluded from proof because they **12–03** are too peripheral to the main issue to be worth devoting court time to determine, and/or because they may be a distraction from the main issue if they are more prejudicial than probative. As the Lord President explained in *A v B*[4] the reason for excluding collateral issues is that:

"...[I]t is better to sacrifice the aid which might be got from the more or less uncertain solution of collateral issues, than to spend a great amount of time, and confuse the jury with what, in the end, even supposing it to be certain, has only an indirect bearing on the matter in hand."

There are some situations where the character of one of the parties is *the* issue in a trial or proof. In such circumstances character will no longer be collateral, but will be provable as a main issue. An obvious example is in a defamation claim where it is the reputation of the pursuer which is the main

---

[1] Wilkinson, *Scottish Law of Evidence*, p.22, citing *R. v Rowton* (1865) 34 L.J.M.C. 57.
[2] P. Roberts, *Criminal Evidence* (2004) at 503.
[3] Dickson, *Evidence*, para.6.
[4] Lord President Robertson in *A v B* (1895) 22 R. 402 at 404 (also reported as *Simpson v Melvin*, 1895 S.L.T. 515).

issue. In *C v M*[5] the defender was allowed to adduce evidence to show that the pursuer was well known for having "a loose and immoral nature",[6] but could only cross-examine as to credibility in regard to *specific* acts of adultery as fair notice of those allegations had been given.

12–04   A person's character may be a main issue in a criminal action, as, for example when an accused is charged with driving while disqualified as a result of a previous conviction. In civil actions it may be competent to adduce evidence of bad character to justify one's actions. In *Wallace v Mooney*[7] the pursuer sued Mooney, a police constable, for an assault arising from his forcible ejection from a racecourse. Mooney had instructions to remove all persons of bad character and it was held that he could adduce evidence of Wallace's bad character to justify his actions.

12–05   In the vast majority of cases, however, both civil and criminal, a person's character, using the term in its broadest sense, is not the central issue. As a collateral issue, it is something that may only be proved where it is felt that it has a material bearing on at least one of the main issues, permitting it to be treated as an exception to the general rule against admissibility.

12–06   These exceptional circumstances can be grouped into six broad categories:

1. Similar fact evidence in criminal cases.
2. Similar fact evidence in civil cases.
3. Character of complainer.
4. Character of witness.
5. Character of a criminal accused.
6. Character of other persons.

SIMILAR FACT EVIDENCE IN CRIMINAL CASES

12–07 Similar fact evidence has been defined as, "evidence of the character or of the misconduct of the accused on other occasions ... tendered to show his bad disposition, (which) is inadmissible unless it is so highly probative of the issues in the cases as to outweigh the prejudice it may cause".[8]

12–08   According to the Scottish Law Commission, the expression "similar fact evidence" is not a term of art in Scots law.[9] None the less, they use the term in their report to mean "evidence that the accused has, before or after the facts alleged in the instant charge, acted in a similar way to that charged". It would accordingly include evidence of the accused person's previous convictions.[10] The Law Commission reported on *Similar Facts and the Moorov*

---

[5] *C v M*, 1923 S.C. 1.
[6] An example of a description that demonstrates the problematic nature of definitions of character. It will be apparent that depending on the century and society one chooses, conceptions of "morality" and "immorality" vary greatly.
[7] *Wallace v Mooney*, (1885) 12 R. 710.
[8] Cross and Tapper, *Evidence*, 9th edn, p.335.
[9] Scot Law Com. para.1.6
[10] Scot Law Com. para.1.6. For discussion see P. Duff, "Towards a unified theory of 'similar facts evidence' in Scots law: relevance, fairness and the reinterpretation of *Moorov*", 2002 J.R. 133 at 133.

Doctrine in 2012.[11] The Report was critical of the haphazard development of these evidential doctrines and made a substantial number of clarifying and rationalising recommendations which have not yet been taken forward. The Report acknowledges that some of the recommendations will be controversial, but the analysis is essential reading for anyone trying to make sense of the interplay evident across the various concepts and practices that have evolved in the case law over the decades.

The acceptance of similar fact evidence in criminal cases is an exception to **12–09** the general rule that a person's previous behaviour is not relevant to the assessment of their guilt or innocence in a criminal trial. The rationale behind admitting similar fact evidence is that it may be reasonable to take into account a person's behaviour on a previous occasion provided:

> "[I]t be relevant to an issue before the jury, and it may be so relevant if it bears upon the question whether the acts alleged to constitute the crime charged ... were designed or accidental, or to rebut a defence which would otherwise be open to the accused."[12]

The origins of similar fact evidence are located in the Australian case of *Makin v Attorney-General for New South Wales*.[13] Mr and Mrs Makin were charged with the murder of a baby that been unofficially fostered by them in return for money and whose body had been found buried in the back yard of their house. Their defence was that the baby had died accidentally or of natural causes.

In order to rebut this defence the prosecution led evidence of three **12–10** separate discoveries of corpses. First, the discovery of the bodies of three other babies at the Makins' house; second, evidence of the remains of another seven babies at a house previously occupied by the Makins; and third, the remains of two more babies at yet another house the Makins had occupied. The prosecution also adduced evidence from a number of women who had given up their babies to the Makins for fostering and had never seen the babies again. The accused had initially insisted that they had only fostered one baby. On appeal to the Privy Council, it was held that the prosecution could adduce this similar fact evidence of past misdeeds to negative the defence put forward by the accused and to challenge their assertion of accidental or natural death.

In cases such as *Makin*, the admissibility of evidence of previous misdeeds **12–11** of the accused is admitted on two grounds. First, because of the similarity of circumstance, which is highly suggestive of the accused's guilt of the offence with which he or she is now charged; and second, because it negatives some innocent explanation of the present charge which the accused is putting forward. The first of these must be treated with care as often such evidence is highly relevant to the case in hand but nonetheless is excluded due to its prejudicial effect, especially where there is a risk of a jury attaching too great a probative value to it.[14]

---

[11] Scottish Law Commission, *Similar Facts and the Moorov Doctrine*, 2012 Scot Law Com. No. 229.
[12] *Makin v Attorney-General for New South Wales* [1894] A.C. 57 at 65.
[13] *Makin v Attorney-General for New South Wales* [1894] A.C. 57 at 65.
[14] See *D.P.P. v Kilbourne* [1973] A.C.729 and *D.P.P. v Boardman* [1975] A.C. 421.

12–12   The rule emerging from *Makin* has had a complex history under English law[15] and has only made rare appearances in Scotland.[16] It was referred to in submissions in the Scottish case of *HM Advocate v Joseph*.[17] In *Joseph* details of a fraud committed by the accused abroad were held to have been properly libelled in an indictment in Scotland in order to show the fraudulent intent with which the present offence had been committed. Lord Murray declared that it was settled that:

> "[E]vidence in regard to another incident of a similar character may be admitted in proof of a crime charged notwithstanding that this evidence may incidentally show, or tend to show, the commission of another crime, provided there be some connection or 'nexus' which in the opinion of the court is sufficiently intimate between the two 'incidents'."

This reference to a nexus between incidents is, of course, similar to the rationale of *Moorov v HM Advocate*.[18] The link between the present charge and the previous act must be as strong as that required for the operation of the *Moorov* doctrine, although that may not be very much.[19] There is, however, one key distinction. Under the *Moorov* doctrine, two or more similar charges on the same complaint or indictment are spoken to by only one witness (in respect of each charge) in order to produce a corroborative course of criminal conduct. In the *Makin* type of case, reference is being made to behaviour on the part of the accused that is *not* now charged[20] largely to rebut some defence that the accused is raising to the present charge. Thus, in *Joseph* Lord Murray stated[21]:

> "I am of opinion that it is the law in Scotland, as in England, that it is open to the prosecution to prove any facts relevant to the charge, notwithstanding that they may show or tend to show the commission of another crime, if they show or tend to show that the act charged was *done of design and did not arise by accident, or if they tend to rebut a defence of innocence.*"

The concept of similar fact evidence has developed much more substantially in English law compared to Scots law. There is a range of dicta to the effect that it is not possible to have a definitive list of categories when similar fact evidence will be relevant. Nor is it possible to define the degree of probative value required before similar fact evidence will be admissible, beyond stating that it "requires a strong degree of probative force".[22] This "strong degree" might be derived from evidence of conduct that offers such "striking

---

[15] For which see Cross and Tapper, *Evidence*, 9th edn at 335–347, and *R. v Selvey*, 1970 A.C. 304.

[16] See P. Duff, "Towards a Unified Theory of 'Similar Fact Evidence'" (2002) Juridical Review 143; and F. Raitt, "The Evidential Use of Similar Facts" (2003) 7 Edin. L. Rev. 174.

[17] 1929 J.C. 55. See too *Nelson v HM Advocate*, 1994 J.C. 94 at 101.

[18] 1930 J.C. 68, considered in Ch.8.

[19] See *Reynolds v HM Advocate*, 1995 S.C.C.R. 504.

[20] And may never have been charged, as in *Makin*.

[21] *HM Advocate v Joseph*, 1929 J.C. 55 at 57 (emphasis added).

[22] *D.P.P. v Boardman* [1975] A.C. 421.

similarity" to other crimes committed by the accused that it would offend against common sense to exclude it from probation.[23]

For example, evidence that *only* shows the accused to be of bad dis- **12–13** position will be inadmissible. To be admissible the evidence must do more than infer that the accused has a propensity to commit a crime of the type charged. Thus, in *R. v B*[24] evidence produced at trial of pornographic magazines in B's possession was held by the House of Lords to be improperly admitted insofar as it was intended to suggest B had committed the indecent assaults of his two grandsons with which he was charged. The magazines and other related evidence merely proved propensity to commit the crime, which did not meet the criterion for admissibility of similar fact evidence.[25]

Remarkably, the rule appears to have featured little in Scots law since **12–14** *Joseph*, and when it has, the evidence has been adduced to show motive or intention.[26] In any future case in Scotland there could be recourse to English authorities, where, as already noted, it has arisen frequently, although care would be required as the rule has evolved so differently in the two jurisdictions.[27] The modern test in England now has a statutory framework to replace the common law.[28] However, the older cases are likely to continue to contribute to interpreting the new provisions, not least because the statutory tests adopt the approach developed in the common law.[29] The English approach to admissibility of similar fact evidence can be broadly stated as dependent on its relevance and its probative value.[30] Given that similar fact evidence is potentially very prejudicial, it will only be admissible if the nexus between the present crime and the previous act is sufficiently strong. The evidence must obviously be relevant to an issue before the jury and it will not be admitted if its prejudicial value outweighs its probative value. The consideration of this balance between prejudice to the accused and probative value occurred in *R. v Z*.[31] In this case Z was charged with rape. He had faced four previous allegations of rape. On three of these occasions he had been acquitted and on one occasion he had been convicted. In each case he had put forward a defence that the woman had consented to sexual intercourse, or at least that he had believed that she had consented. The Crown wished to bring evidence from those four complainants to negate Z's defence, arguing that such evidence was admissible under the similar facts rule. The trial judge accepted the evidence came within the scope of the

---

[23] *D.P.P. v Boardman* [1975] A.C.421.

[24] [1997] 2 Cr. App. R. 88, CA.

[25] See *HM Advocate v Pritchard* (1865) 5 Irv 88 for a case in which it was held that an accused's previous misconduct gave rise to a motive for murder, and was admissible as evidence of such.

[26] See, in particular, *Griffen v HM Advocate*, 1940 J.C. 1, and also, *Booth v Tudhope*, 1986 S.C.C.R. 638 and *McIntosh v HM Advocate*, 1986 J.C. 169. See too, F. Davidson, *Evidence*, paras 10.18–10.19.

[27] See Cross and Tapper, *Evidence*, 9th edn, at 335–347. Also, *D.P.P. v Boardman* [1975] A.C.421; *R. v Wilson*, 1973 58 Cr.App.Rep. 169; and *Thompson v R.* [1918] A.C. 221.

[28] ss.101 and 103 of the Criminal Justice Act 2003.

[29] For a detailed analysis see P. Roberts and A. Zuckerman, *Criminal Evidence*, 2nd edn (Oxford: Oxford University Press, 2004).

[30] See Roberts and Zuckerman, *Criminal Evidence*, 2nd edn (Oxford: Oxford University Press, 2004).

[31] *R. v Z* [2000] 3 All E.R. 385.

similar facts rule, but held that evidence of the three acquittals was inadmissible due to the double jeopardy rule.[32] The House of Lords ultimately ruled in favour of the Crown. The basis of their ruling was that evidence of the previous acquittals was being led, not to put the accused on trial on a second occasion, or to seek to punish the accused, but to demonstrate his behaviour towards other complainants on previous occasions as that was relevant to his defence of consent. There was therefore no infringement of the double jeopardy rule and the testimony was admissible as similar fact evidence.

Similar Fact Evidence in Civil Cases

12–15 There is no equivalent rule to *Makin* in civil cases, and the general rule is that what may or may not have happened in other incidents is of no relevance in the present action, not even if it sheds light on the character of one of the parties. As noted above, in *A vB*,[33] a pursuer seeking civil damages for rape was not allowed to adduce evidence of the defender's alleged attempts to rape two other women, on the ground that such evidence was collateral and irrelevant. It was considered by the court that the allegations were being presented, not because these other women were complaining of rape, but "merely in order to lend some probability to the pursuer's case".[34]

12–16 Similarly, in *H v P*,[35] where the main issue in a slander action was whether or not H had committed adultery with P, it was held that P could not lead evidence to show "instances of H's unchastity with other men" as such evidence relating to third parties was irrelevant. In both cases, however, it was held that such questions might be put to test the party's credibility as a witness, provided that fair notice had been given. This remains the case today, although doubts have been expressed about the current value of such a practice,[36] and the Scottish Law Commission has recommended the abolition of cross-examination on issues of chastity which cannot be tested by evidence in chief.[37]

12–17 There is authority to the effect that a party's behaviour on a previous occasion may be relevant to the case in hand, and provable in chief, when it appears to form a "course of conduct" with the behaviour currently in issue. *Whyte v Whyte*[38] is regarded as an early example of this principle in action, when, in an action for divorce on the grounds of adultery with a female servant, Mrs Whyte was allowed to adduce evidence of her husband's indecent behaviour with another female servant. However, in *A v B*[39] the

---

[32] The effect of the double jeopardy rule is that a person cannot be tried twice for the same offence. See the Double Jeopardy (Scotland) Act 2011. The trial judge in *R v Z* ruled the previous conviction evidence did not of itself establish "a sufficiently cogent picture" (at 389) to be admitted as similar fact evidence.

[33] *A v B* (1895) 22 R. 402.

[34] *A v B* (1895) 22 R. 402at 404.

[35] *H v P* (1905) 8 F. 232.

[36] See Macphail, *Evidence*, para.16.05, and *Duff v Duff*, 1969 S.L.T. (Notes) 53.

[37] Memo No.46, para.Q.04.

[38] *Whyte v Whyte* (1884) 11 R. 710.

[39] *A v B* (1895) 22 R 402.

court considered *Whyte* should have a narrow application, and be confined to matrimonial cases.[40]

The rule has been applied beyond matrimonial actions—in *Knutzen v* **12–18** *Mauritzen*,[41] an action for damages against for the delivery of poor quality goods, the pursuer was allowed to adduce evidence that another delivery from the same consignment, made by the defender to a third party, was also of poor quality. Although *Knutzen* did not relate strictly to a question of character, the principle involved is the same. Where the similar fact (or similar act) belongs in what may fairly be called the same course of conduct with an alleged act into which the court is now inquiring, it may be sufficiently relevant to transform itself from a mere collateral issue into a main issue which may be proved by evidence in chief.

THE CHARACTER OF A WITNESS—ISSUES OF CREDIBILITY

Previous sections have been largely concerned with the character of parties **12–19** to litigation. The character of a witness is also treated as collateral and irrelevant, unless the character issue goes to the heart of the dispute and satisfies the test of relevancy.[42] In sexual offences the historical tendencies to disbelieve complaints of sexual assault made by women and children still resonate today and commonly lead to applications to introduce evidence of bad character such as dishonesty,[43] or previous false complaint.[44] Deep rooted acceptance of false complaints in rape cases[45] are still apparent today,[46] despite empirical research evidence that the rate of false complaints is no different from false complaints in the reporting of crimes generally.[47] The further belief that rape complaints are easily made, despite the accepted low reporting rate[48] and high attrition rate,[49] in part explains the doubts that still attach to a rape witness's veracity or credibility, and which make the character of sexual offences an area which produces exceptions to the general rule that character is collateral. As one of the main purposes of cross-examination is to test the credibility of a witness and the reliability of their evidence, it is therefore unsurprising, if disappointing, that the courts regularly have to deal with applications to introduce evidence attacking the

---

[40] See too *Roy v Pairman*, 1958 S.C. 334, in which P's admitted act of intercourse with R after she had become pregnant was held to be admissible on the issue of his alleged intercourse with her *before* conception.

[41] *Knutzen v Mauritzen*, 1918 1 S.L.T. 85. See also *Morrison v McLean's Trs* (1862) 24 D. 625.

[42] Dickson, *Evidence*, para.6.

[43] *Cumming v HM Advocate*, 2003 S.C.C.R. 261 HCJ.

[44] *CJM v HM Advocate*, 2013 S.L.T. 380.

[45] Attributed to Lord Chief Justice Sir Matthew Hale from the 17th century, "rape...is an accusation easily to be made and hard to be proved, and harder to be defended by the party accused, tho never so innocent".

[46] System Three survey (February 2008)—TNS System Three survey of 986 Scots for the Scottish Government

[47] P. Rumney, "False Allegations of Rape" (2006) 65 Camb L.J. 128.

[48] *Report by Baroness Stern CBE of an Independent review into How Rape Complaints are Handled By Public Authorities in England and Wales* (London: Home Office, 2010).

[49] *Report by Baroness Stern CBE of an Independent review into How Rape Complaints are Handled By Public Authorities in England and Wales* (London: Home Office, 2010) found that on average across al jurisdictions just 12 out of 100 cases prosecuted resulted in a conviction.

character of the complainer. The courts may allow questioning on aspects of a witness's character that have a direct bearing on their credibility, if it is in the wider interests of justice.[50] Sometimes such attacks may focus solely on the reliability of a witness's observation or recollection, but at other times the attacks may go directly to credibility.

12–20 However, in observance of the general rule that character is collateral, there are limits. Witnesses may be asked questions that are designed to undermine their credibility and show that they are of such poor character generally that they should not be believed.

Three situations are considered here:

12–21 (i) The older authorities cite a previous conviction for perjury as a specific example of relevant bad character that may be used to discredit a witness,[51] but in general, extracts of previous convictions of a witness cannot be produced.[52] Nor will a party seeking to test the credibility of a witness be permitted to make "vague suggestions against the character of a witness by a series of insulting questions".[53]

12–22 (ii) One of the most important impediments to a witness's credibility could be the fact that he or she has some sort of personal interest in the outcome of the case. This may be in the form of a personal relationship, present or former, to one of the parties or the accused, or it may be that the witness has a financial stake in the subject matter of the action. As a general rule, the relationship of a witness to a party in an action does not disqualify them from testifying.[54]

12–23 (iii) If, during a criminal trial, it is alleged that a witness giving evidence in the trial also took part in the criminal activities with which the accused is now charged then that person acquires the status of a *socius criminis*[55] and their character becomes under scrutiny. In a jury trial, the presiding judge is entitled to draw the jury's attention to the potential doubt over the credibility of the evidence of any *socius criminis*. However, such a warning is not obligatory.[56] Where a witness appears reluctant to testify due to intimidation then it may be necessary to adduce evidence of that intimidation to explain to the trier of fact the behaviour of the witness while testifying.[57]

---

[50] e.g. *Green v HM Advocate*, 1983 S.C.C.R. 42; *Marshall v Smith*, 1983 S.C.C.R. 156; and *Williamson v HM Advocate*, 1979 J.C. 36.

[51] Walker and Walker, *Evidence*, 3rd edn, para.12.13.2 and Dickson, *Evidence*, para.1618. Not even this may be proved by additional evidence when denied by the witness: see *Carey v Tudhope*, 1984 S.C.C.R. 157.

[52] See *Kennedy v HM Advocate* (1896) 23 R. (J.) 28, and *Dickie v HM Advocate* (1897) 24 R. (J.) 82 at 83.

[53] e.g. as in *Falconer v Brown* (1893) 21 R. (J.) 1 at 4.

[54] Evidence (Scotland) Act 1840, s.1; Criminal Procedure (Scotland) Act 1995, s.265(3).

[55] Defined in *Wallace v HM Advocate*, 1952 J.C. 78, per Lord Keith at 83 as being anyone who has been convicted of, or pleaded guilty to, the offence with which the accused is charged or who gives Evidence, on his own admission, as an accomplice in that crime.

[56] In *Docherty v HM Advocate*, 1987 J.C. 81, the practice of giving what is usually referred to as the *cum nota* warning was stated to be a matter of discretion for the trial judge. Corroboration is not required if the witness is believed. Note that an accused still on trial cannot be treated as *socius criminis*.

[57] *Manson v HM Advocate*, 1951 J.C. 49.

THE CHARACTER OF THE COMPLAINER

On some occasions, the character of the victim of a crime can be a material **12–24** issue, whether the victim is called as a witness-complainer or not. This could arise, for example, when an accused on an assault charge pleads self-defence or an alleged murderer pleads provocation. The general rule in all such cases is that if the character in question is materially relevant to the defence, then it is admissible.

Evidence of a psychiatric illness

In *Green v HM Advocate*[58] the appellant and another had been convicted of **12–25** rape. Their defence was consent and there was evidence that the complainer had been sniffing glue on the day of the incident, which might have affected the reliability of her evidence. Subsequent to their convictions, a successful application was made to have the appeal court to consider fresh evidence, not available at the trial, relating to the complainer's character.[59] The appeal court heard that she had on previous occasions made false allegations of rape, was suffering from a psychiatric disturbance which led her to fantasise and had admitted to a third party that the present allegations were false. It was held that this fresh evidence cast such grave doubts on the credibility of the complainer and had such serious implications for the original defence of consent, that the accused must be acquitted on the grounds of a miscarriage of justice.

When the character evidence consists of the victim's behaviour at the time **12–26** of the alleged offence, then no special notice is required, but if the accused intends to attack his victim's character on general grounds, then it is.[60]

Evidence of a violent disposition

It is generally stated that while accused persons can lead evidence of specific **12–27** acts of violence by the victim on the occasion into which the court is now inquiring and evidence concerning the victim's character generally, they cannot cite specific acts of violence on other occasions.[61] However, there are circumstances where the courts will permit character evidence of the victim if it is directly relevant to the accused's defence. In *HM Advocate v Kay*[62] the accused was charged with the murder of her husband. The indictment also libelled previous indications of malice and ill-will on the part of Kay towards the deceased. Her special defence of self defence took the form of a belief on her part that she was about to be assaulted by the deceased and she was allowed to lead evidence of previous assaults upon her by the deceased. Lord Wheatley[63] ruled that:

---

[58] *Green v HM Advocate*, 1983 S.C.C.R. 42. See also *Marshall v Smith*, n.34, but see *Allison v HM Advocate*, 1986 J.C. 22.

[59] The application was in terms of s.106(3) of the 1993 Act.

[60] See Walker and Walker, *Evidence*, 3rd edn, para.7.7.1, and *Dickie v HM Advocate* (1897) 24 R. (J) 82.

[61] Walker and Walker, *Evidence*, 3rd edn, para.7.7.1.

[62] *HM Advocate v Kay*, 1970 J.C. 68.

[63] *HM Advocate v Kay*, 1970 J.C. 68 at 69.

"I consider that it would be unfair to allow detailed evidence by the Crown in support of that part of the indictment which alleges that the accused had previously evinced malice and ill will towards the deceased, without allowing the accused the opportunity of proving in turn by detailed evidence that she had reason to apprehend danger from the deceased."

Kay was described by Lord Justice Clerk Ross, in *Brady v HM Advocate*,[64] as "a very special case" where evidence of specific acts of violence was permitted because "the indictment libelled previous malice and the accused was pleading self defence". Is this such a "very special" set of circumstances? One might argue that to lead evidence of the violent disposition of a complainer is highly relevant, and not merely collateral, to any plea of self-defence. It is certainly so when the accused knows, from personal experience, that the complainer has a history of violence. Although *Kay* is regarded as having a restricted application, the Scottish Law Commission has approved the ruling and proposed widening it as follows[65]:

"We do not see how an accused can readily prove that the victim was a violent person unless he is permitted to cite specific violent actings on the part of that person ... The arguments against allowing such evidence are that it prolongs criminal trials and can also confuse juries. We do not consider either of these arguments sufficiently weighty to justify the status quo, and propose that in cases of murder or assault the accused should be entitled by citing specific acts of violence to prove that the injured person was of a violent or quarrelsome disposition."

This argument is equally applicable to battered women who kill their violent partners or ex-partners and are thought to be suffering from battered woman syndrome.[66] Such women find the traditional defence of self defence unsuitable for their particular circumstances as they rarely satisfy the elements of the defence, namely a fear of danger to life or limb, no means of escape and a proportionate response. There is a substantial body of research that explains one of the long term effects of being subjected to abuse within intimate relationships is the loss of self-esteem and a "learned helplessness".[67]

12–28   Prolonged domestic abuse has a deep psychological impact which prevents women from having the capability to decide to leave, quite apart from the usual disadvantage they suffer from being physically weaker than their abusive partner. Instead, if there comes a breaking point, perhaps after years of abuse, when they snap and react violently, they are unable to use the mitigatory plea of provocation as they cannot satisfy the essential elements of that plea, namely a sudden loss of control from an immediate

---

[64] 1986 S.L.T. 686 at 687.
[65] Memo No.46, para.Q.05. See also *HM Advocate v Cunningham* (1974), unreported, cited in Macphail, *Evidence*, para.16.07, in which an accused in a similar position to *Kay* was allowed to prove the deceased's previous conviction for culpable homicide, and evidence in chief was permitted of previous assaults by the deceased upon the accused.
[66] See, for example, *R. v Ahluwalia* [1992] 4 All E.R. 889, and *R. v Thornton (No.1)* [1992] 1 All E.R. 306.
[67] L. Walker, *The Battered Woman Syndrome* (New York: Springer, 1984).

provocation. Their subsequent defence is frequently therefore based upon a plea of diminished responsibility.[68] It is essential to the success of this defence and to explain the state of mind of the accused that evidence is admitted regarding the alleged violent character of the deceased.

Character of complainer in sexual offences

One of the most controversial applications of the law in relation to the **12–29** character of a complainer is the use made of sexual character evidence in rape or sexual assault prosecutions. A person's sexual morality is irrelevant in most cases except, it seems, in certain sexual offences where examination may be permitted in assessing whether or not a complainer's morality affects their credibility. At common law an accused could attack his victim's general reputation for chastity.[69] According to Dickson,[70] this represented the only exception to the general rule forbidding character evidence and was justified:

> "...[W]hile so much depends on the truth of her statements, and there is so great risk of her story having been concocted in a fit of jealousy, or with the view of extorting money, or covering her shame when discovered in a voluntary connection, that a full inquiry into her character is requisite to enable the jury to estimate her credibility."

There is now an extensive academic literature critiquing many of the assumptions about rape complainers and challenging the assumption that a complainer's previous sexual history necessarily had any relevance to the allegations under investigation, especially if these allegations related to a later date and with a different person.[71] Historically, in practice, counsel had considerable license to use a complainer's sexual history and sexual behaviour to suggest to the jury that there were grounds to believe the complainer was someone who was likely to have consented to sexual intercourse.[72] Juries were then invited to determine that what occurred between the parties was consensual sex rather than rape. As consent to sexual intercourse is the defence most commonly relied upon by men accused of rape, casting doubt on the complainer's credibility is an inevitable tactic.[73] Legislation was introduced in 1985 to restrict the type of sexual character evidence that could be introduced in court.[74] [75] It was

---

[68] See, *Galbraith v HM Advocate (No.2)* 2002 J.C. 1.

[69] *Dickie v HM Advocate* (1897) 24 R. (J) 82.

[70] Dickson, *Evidence*, para.1622.

[71] e.g. A. McColgan, "Common law and the Relevance of Sexual History Evidence" (1996) 16 Oxford Journal of Legal Studies, 275; Temkin, *Rape and the Legal Process*, 2nd edn (Oxford: Oxford University Press, 2002).

[72] J. Temkin, "Prosecuting and Defending Rape: perspectives from the Bar" (2000) 27(2) *Journal of Law and Society* 219.

[73] B. Brown, M. Burman and L. Jamieson, *Sex Crimes on Trial* (Edinburgh: Edinburgh University Press, 1993).

[74] The Law Reform (Miscellaneous Provisions) (Scotland) Act 1985, s.36, amending s.141 of the Criminal Procedure (Scotland) Act 1975.

[75] Brown et al., *Sex Crimes on Trial* (Edinburgh: Edinburgh University Press, 1993).

intended to regulate questioning in rape cases that appeared to relate only to the general sexual character of the complainer.[76] These provisions were subject to an over-arching discretionary consideration, namely that trial judges could admit character evidence if it was in the interests of justice to do so.

12–30   Research carried out in 1992 found that in 32 per cent of sexual offence trials the defence made an application to lead evidence of the previous character of the complainer and in 85 per cent of these cases the applications were at least partially successful. The research also found that there was a high incidence (24 per cent of cases) of breach of the prohibition against leading character evidence.[77] Section 36 was therefore re-enacted as s.274 of the Criminal Procedure (Scotland) Act 1995 but placed within a stronger regulatory regime. However, the scope of s.275 retained the level of judicial discretion in the original 1985 legislation, effectively neutralised the potential "restraining provisions of s.274".[78]

12–31   The reforms in the 1995 legislation failed to allay criticisms. The treatment of rape and sexual assault complainers is frequently cited as one explanation for the under reporting of such offences and for the proportionately poor rate of convictions, as compared to other offences.[79]

12–32   The Scottish Government embarked upon a further series of reforms including the Sexual Offences (Procedure and Evidence) (Scotland) Act 2002 which made major changes to the provisions in the Criminal Procedure (Scotland) Act 1995. It did so largely by substituting new versions of ss.274 and 275 and by requiring advance written notice if the defence of consent was to be relied upon. Accused persons are now also required to apply in advance to the court if they wish to introduce evidence of the complainer's character, including sexual history. Considerable detail has to be given in the application of the evidence sought to be admitted or elicited and the proposed inferences which the applicant aims to submit to the court concerning what should be drawn from that evidence.

STATUTORY RESTRICTIONS OF QUESTIONING ON CHARACTER

12–33 Section 274 provides:

"(1) . . .the court shall not admit, or allow questioning designed to elicit, evidence which shows or tends to show that the complainer—

(a) is not of good character (whether in relation to sexual matters or otherwise);
(b) has, at any time, engaged in sexual behaviour not forming part of the subject matter of the charge;

---

[76] J. Temkin, "Prosecuting and Defending Rape: perspectives from the Bar" (2000) 27(2) *Journal of Law and Society* 219.
[77] Brown et al., *Sexual History and Sexual Character Evidence in Scottish Sexual Offence Trials*, 1992, Scottish Office Central Research Unit Papers.
[78] Brown, et al, *Sex Crimes on Trial* (Edinburgh: Edinburgh University Press, 1993).
[79] Brown et al., *Sexual History and Sexual Character Evidence in Scottish Sexual Offence Trials*, 2002, Scottish Central Research Unit Papers.

(c) has, at any time (other than shortly before, at the same time as or shortly after the acts which form part of the subject matter of the charge), engaged in such behaviour, not being sexual behaviour, as might found the inference that the complainer—

    (i) is likely to have consented to those acts; or
    (ii) is not a credible or reliable witness; or

(d) has, at any time, been subject to any such condition or predisposition as might found the inference referred to in subparagraph (c) above."

Section 275(1) provides a set of exceptions to the restrictions under s.274. The court may allow questions on character if satisfied:

"(a) the evidence or questioning will relate only to a specific occurrence or occurrences of sexual or other behaviour[80] or to specific facts demonstrating—

    (i) the complainer's character; or
    (ii) any condition or predisposition to which the complainer is or has been subject;

(b) that occurrence or those occurrences of behaviour or facts are relevant to establishing whether the accused is guilty of the offence with which he is charged; and

(c) the probative value of the evidence sought to be admitted or elicited is significant and is likely to outweigh any risk of prejudice to the proper administration of justice arising from its being admitted or elicited."

It was stated in the five bench decision in *CJM v HM Advocate* that[81]:

"[W]hen considering a s.275 application, it is necessary for the court to determine at the outset whether the evidence proposed to be adduced is admissible at common law. If it is not admissible at common law, for example because it concerns a collateral issue, then s.275 cannot render it admissible, since the provision was designed to restrict evidence and not to remove common law prohibitions."

The term, "the proper administration of justice" in s. 275(1)(c) is defined in s. 275(2)(b) as including the following two considerations:

"(i) appropriate protection of a complainer's dignity and privacy..."

The criterion, "the proper administration of justice", gives the court a wide discretion to allow, to limit, or to refuse the extent of questioning on the complainer's character. In order to gauge the effectiveness of the reforms in the Sexual Offences (Procedure and Evidence) (Scotland) Act 2002, the

---

[80] Specificity is essential—general evidence as to credibility will not satisfy the subsection: *MacKay v HM Advocate*, 2005 J.C. 24.
[81] *CJM v HM Advocate*, 2013 S.L.T. 380 at para.10.

(then) Scottish Executive commissioned research to establish the use of sexual history and sexual character evidence in trials prior to the new legislation, and its use after the Act came into force. The research, published in late 2007, suggested the legislation had not achieved its aims.[82] The initial applications to introduce sexual character evidence indicated a marked increase.[83] [84]

12–34   The early case law after the reforms suggested a liberal interpretation of the exceptions in s.275.[85] The first two appeals under the new legislation were upheld against the rulings of the court at first instance to exclude character evidence and the Crown offered no opposition to the appeals. However, the legislation is now applied more strictly.[86]

12–35   The provisions of the Human Rights Act have so far impacted on this area of the law in three principal ways. First, there is far greater recognition of the rights flowing from the ECHR to complainers and other witnesses in terms of arts 3, and 8. Article 3 accords the right not to be subjected to inhuman or degrading treatment; and art.8 is the right to a private and family life. Both lie behind the statutory requirement in ss.274 and 275 of the Criminal Procedure (Scotland) Act 1995 which, as already noted, requires judges to take account of "the appropriate protection of a complainer's dignity and privacy" in determining applications to ask questions on sexual history or behaviour. At common law judges ought to take the dignity and privacy of all witnesses into account in ensuring they receive appropriate treatment during cross-examination and in all other aspects of the trial process.[87] Thus, excessively intrusive, or irrelevant cross-examination relating to sexual history of a type that humiliates and degrades witnesses could contravene the Act and the common law.[88] It also underpins the rationale for s.288C of the 1995 Act which prohibits an accused from representing himself in the conduct of his defence at trial. Either he instructs counsel to conduct his defence or, failing which, the court will appoint counsel.

12–36   Second, there have been several unsuccessful appeals arising from rulings from trial judges to exclude sexual history evidence, which the appellants claimed were breaches of art.6. For example, in *Moir v HM Advocate*[89] the appeal court rejected the appellant's claim that being required to give advance notice of questioning placed unfair restrictions on the conduct of the cross-examination and created an inequality.

12–37   Third, the Judicial Committee of the Privy Council (the role of which is now performed by the UK Supreme Court) considered the effect on a fair

---

[82] M. Burman, L. Jamieson, J. Nicholson, and O. Brooks, *Impact of Aspects of the Law of Evidence in Sexual Offence Trials: An Evaluation Study*, Scottish Government, 2007.

[83] Burman, Jamieson, Nicholson, and Brooks, *Impact of Aspects of the Law of Evidence in Sexual Offence Trials: An Evaluation Study* (Scottish Government, 2007).

[84] Burman, Jamieson, Nicholson, and Brooks, *Impact of Aspects of the Law of Evidence in Sexual Offence Trials: An Evaluation Study* (Scottish Government, 2007).

[85] See *Kinnin v HM* Advocate, 2003 S.C.C.R. 295, and *Cumming v HM Advocate*, 2003 S.C.C.R. 261.

[86] See, e.g. *Abbas v HM Advocate* [2013] HCJAC 55.

[87] See *SN v Sweden*, App 34209/96, July 2, 2002, unreported.

[88] *Moir v HM Advocate*, 2005 J.C. 102. See e.g. *R. v Brown* [1998] 2 Cr. App. Rep. 364.

[89] *Moir v HM Advocate*, 2005 J.C. 102.

trial of s.275A of the 1995 Act in *DS v HM Advocate*.[90] That section provides that where an application to cross-examine a complainer on sexual character is granted the Crown must lay before the court any relevant previous convictions of the accused. The Privy Council ruled that the production of an accused's previous conviction does not breach his right to a fair trial under art.6 because the court will only admit a previous conviction if satisfied that the three statutory tests set out in ss.274 and 5 are met. As Lord Hope opined[91]:

> "The important point to notice is that such questioning or the admission of such evidence will only be permitted if the court has been persuaded that it passes those three tests. The purpose of section 275 is to ensure that the accused will receive a fair trial, notwithstanding the restrictions that are imposed by section 274. The three tests are designed to achieve that purpose consistently with the proper administration of justice which, as section 275(2)(b) makes clear, includes the appropriate protection of the complainer's dignity and privacy. A court which is satisfied that all three tests are met will have concluded that the questioning or evidence relates only to specific matters which are relevant to establishing whether the accused is guilty and are of significant probative value."

THE CHARACTER OF A CRIMINAL ACCUSED

12–38 The character of a criminal accused obviously raises special issues. On the one hand, it is crucial to a fair trial that the court, and particularly a jury, should not be influenced in its decision as to the accused's guilt of the offence now charged by hearing evidence of the accused's misdeeds on previous occasions. Historic misdeeds are not necessarily a guide to current culpability. On the other hand, it is equally important that an accused should not be allowed to make false claims to having a good character, or to malign the character of those who are testifying against him or her, without the court being advised of their true character. At the same time, there may be some incident in the accused's past which it may be logical to draw to the attention of the court, given the nature of the present charge, whether the accused has put character in issue or not.

12–39 At common law, it is always open to an accused to put their own character in issue. This will normally take the form of evidence of good character, which an accused is entitled to raise as an issue.[92] This right predates the Criminal Evidence Act 1898 which first made the accused a competent witness in their own defence. Good character evidence may take the form not only of testimony by the accused, but also of testimony from other character witnesses called by the defence.[93]

12–40 There is, however, a risk attaching to the defence strategy of raising character as an issue. If an accused person gives evidence of their own

---

[90] *DS v HM Advocate*, 2007 S.C. (P.C.) 1.
[91] *DS v HM Advocate*, 2007 S.C. (P.C.) 1at para.28.
[92] Dickson, *Evidence*, para.15.
[93] Or conceivably from prosecution witnesses, by means of cross-examination.

character then the prosecution have a statutory right to cross-examine on that matter. If, on the other hand, the accused declines to go into the witness box, but arranges for other witnesses to speak to their good character, then the normal rule is that, while the prosecution can cross-examine, they have no separate right to lead evidence which they may have concerning the accused's character. The presiding judge, but not the prosecution, may however comment on an accused's failure to testify.[94]

12–41　　On rare occasions it may be necessary for an accused person to use their *bad* character in their own defence, as, for example where an alibi defence consists of the fact that the accused was in prison at the material time. The choice of raising bad character is that of the accused and, as discussed below, it must not be elicited as a result of a prosecution attack on character.[95]

12–42　　Until fairly recently, the main problem concerning the character of an accused person related to the restrictions placed upon the prosecution against cross-examining on character when the accused had chosen to testify. A number of cases have seen a gradual erosion of these restrictions and where the prosecution successfully argue that an accused's character is relevant to the issues in hand, then they have been allowed to adduce evidence of character in chief, regardless of whether or not the accused chooses to give evidence. Additionally, there is the situation where one accused attacks the character of a co-accused in order to exculpate themselves. These and other issues are considered next.

Prosecution Evidence in Chief of the Character of the Accused

12–43　　The general rule is that the prosecution may not, in the course of their own evidence in chief, lead evidence of the bad character of the accused as evidenced by past misdeeds, or by any other inference.[96] This rule is embodied in statute in s.101(1) (solemn proceedings) and s.166(3) (summary proceedings) of the 1995 Act which provide that no reference should be made to previous convictions of an accused in the course of a trial.[97]

12–44　　The apparent strictness of these rules is, however, tempered by a line of cases in which previous convictions have been placed before the court accidentally, and it has been held that no substantial prejudice occurred to the accused and that the conviction could stand. Thus, in *HM Advocate v Corcoran*[98] Lord Anderson ruled that:

"Where a witness in good faith, and in answer to a competent question fairly put by the prosecutor, incidentally discloses the existence of a prior conviction, I do not think that a contravention of the statute takes place."

---

[94] Criminal Procedure (Scotland) Act 1995, s.266.
[95] See *Carberry v HM Advocate*, 1975 J.C. 40 at 46.
[96] Dickson, *Evidence*, para.15. Neither may a co-accused: see *Slane v HM Advocate*, 1984 S.L.T. 293.
[97] And see *Forsyth v HM Advocate*, 1992 S.L.T. 189 where there was held to have been a miscarriage of justice though not based on statutory provisions.
[98] *HM Advocate v Corcoran*, 1932 J.C. 42 at 49.

This view was endorsed obiter in *Carberry v HM Advocate*,[99] while in *Johnston v Allan*[100] the same view was taken of a previous conviction contained on a computer printout from the DVLC which was handed to the sheriff in error, with no improper motive on the part of the fiscal depute.

These rulings appear to proceed upon the basis that there was no delib- **12–45** erate attempt by the prosecution to prejudice the accused and that there was no active intent to lay the previous conviction before the court. However, in most cases this will not reduce the prejudicial effect for the accused and the more important question on appeal should be whether or not this prejudice was material. Thus, where a schedule of previous convictions, including some for dishonesty, was placed before a sheriff and the sheriff indicated he had grave concerns about the situation but nonetheless proceeded to continue with the trial, the appeal court quashed the subsequent conviction.[101] The court considered that a reasonable bystander would have inferred that justice could not be seen to be done.

The consequences of a deliberate breach of either section will normally be **12–46** an acquittal on appeal, or a desertion of the diet *ex proprio motu* by the presiding judge. An example of this was *Smith v HM Advocate*[102] in which a police witness, asked in chief if he recognised the accused, not only acknowledged him but gratuitously informed the court that he knew him as a housebreaker. The subsequent conviction was quashed.

In *Cordiner v HM Advocate*[103] the appellant was convicted on an indict- **12–47** ment libelling three charges. On the date upon which one of these was alleged to have occurred, the appellant had been serving a prison sentence in respect of a previous conviction and he intimated this to the Crown in his special defence of alibi. The Crown could have readily confirmed this. Instead, they allowed the special defence to be read to the jury and then later in the trial withdrew the only charge to which it related. On appeal the convictions *quoad* the remaining charges were quashed, the Crown having conceded that forcing the appellant to disclose his prison sentence was equivalent to the prosecution having laid a previous conviction before the court.

Separate from those cases examined above in which breach of the sections **12–48** was held to have been accidental, there are three competent exceptions to the statutory rule contained in the 1995 Act.

---

[99] *Carberry v HM Advocate*, 1975 J.C. 40 at 46; this case is considered below.
[100] *Johnston v Allan*, 1984 S.L.T. 261; see also *O'Neill v Tudhope*, 1984 S.L.T. 424 and *Moffat v Smith*, 1983 S.C.C.R. 392.
[101] *McKee v Brown*, 2001 S.C.C.R. 6.
[102] 1975 S.L.T. (Notes) 89. See also *Graham v HM Advocate*, 1984 S.L.T. 67, in which an accused charged with assaulting his wife and various other offences was acquitted on appeal after a police witness read out a reply to caution and charge which consisted of the words: "That cow's got me the jail again!" The appeal court went so far as to accuse the fiscal depute of having engineered the breach of the statute without justification. See also *McCuaig v HM Advocate*, 1982 J.C. 59 and *Binks v HM Advocate*, 1984 J.C. 108.
[103] *Cordiner v HM Advocate*, 1978 J.C. 64; N.B. however that the defence must make timeous objection to any breach of the section: *Jackson v HM Advocate*, 1982 J.C. 117.

(1) When disclosure of convictions is competent in support of a substantive charge

12–49   Provisos to both ss.101(2)(b) and 166(8)(b) of the 1995 Act allow previous convictions to be disclosed in circumstances in which it is competent to do so "in support of a substantive charge".[104] This is because in certain exceptional circumstances, the Crown cannot effectively libel the charge(s) against an accused without making reference to a previous conviction. For example, a charge of driving while disqualified by its very nature implies a previous motoring offence and the Crown cannot obtain a conviction without proving both the disqualification and the offence which gave rise to it.[105] In such cases, because the disclosure of the conviction is a pre-requisite of the current charge, it is regarded as an essential exception to the general rule. Disclosure should be achieved with the minimum of prejudice to the accused, reflecting the wording of the proviso to each of the sections, which refers to such evidence being led "in support of" the charge.[106]

12–50   Two examples of this exception in operation are *Varey v HM Advocate*[107] and *Murphy v HM Advocate*.[108] Varey was charged with prison-breaking and the indictment libelled the length of the sentence he had been serving and the offence for which it had been imposed. Despite a defence challenge, the court held that the indictment was relevant, since it was essential to the Crown case to prove the date and length of the sentence and the fact that such detention proceeded upon lawful cause. In *Murphy* the accused was charged with perverting the course of justice. He had given his solicitor false information concerning his private life. That information was then used in mitigation of sentence on two separate occasions. Murphy had previous convictions, which he had admitted on each occasion. The Crown called as witnesses the sheriff and justice who had sentenced him on each occasion to testify that but for the false representations the sentences would have been more severe. It was held that disclosure of the previous convictions was admissible as the Crown could not competently narrate the charges without including reference to these convictions.

12–51   The right to adduce evidence of an accused's previous convictions in support of a charge may also occasionally be found in statute. For example, s.19 of the Prevention of Crimes Act 1871 allows a prosecutor who has proved an accused's possession of stolen property to adduce evidence of previous convictions implying dishonesty, if they are less than five years old, in support of the mens rea of guilty knowledge.

(2) Where disclosure of convictions is relevant to a defence raised by the accused

12–52   On rare occasions, the Crown cannot adequately rebut a defence put forward by the accused without revealing that he or she has previous

---

[104] See *Russell v HM Advocate*, 1993 S.L.T. 358, a case decided under the previous statutory provisions.
[105] *Moffat v Smith*, 1983 S.C.C.R. 392.
[106] The difficulty in *Moffat v Smith* (1983 S.C.C.R. 392) was the fact that, although obliged to libel one previous conviction, the Crown had inadvertently proved two.
[107] *Varey v HM Advocate*, 1986 J.C. 28.
[108] *Murphy v HM Advocate*, 1978 J.C. 1.

convictions and in such cases it seems that they may be permitted to do so. For example, in *Carberry v HM Advocate*[109] a statement led in evidence in which the accused admitted to being "in Barlinnie" was held in the particular circumstances of the case to be admissible.[110]

The principle embodied in ss.101 and 166 extends to exclude disclosure of **12–53** A's previous convictions by a co-accused B. This was established in *Slane v HM Advocate*,[111] in which Slane was on trial with two others. During the course of the Crown case, counsel for a co-accused, M, asked a Crown witness questions expressly designed to show that Slane had a criminal record. It was held that, although this was not technically a breach of s.160, it was contrary to its spirit, since "those accused of crime are entitled to enjoy the presumption of innocence throughout their trial and ... information as to their criminal past should not be disclosed to the court or the jury".[112] Holding that, ordinarily such an "inexcusable" breach of professional ethics would give rise to a miscarriage of justice, the appeal court nevertheless upheld the resulting conviction because of the weight of the other evidence against Slane.

(3) Where s.275A of the Criminal Procedure (Scotland) Act 1995 applies

Section 10 of the Sexual Offences (Procedure and Evidence) (Scotland) Act **12–54** 2002 amended the Criminal Procedure (Scotland) Act 1995 by inserting a new s.275A to permit disclosure of an accused's previous convictions where the court has allowed questioning under s.275 of the complainer in a rape or sexual offences trial.

As any such questions would be designed to impugn the character and **12–55** credibility of the complainer, this amending provision is intended to create an equivalence of focus on the credibility of the accused and his propensity to commit crimes.[113] The previous conviction can only be disclosed if there is a substantial sexual element in regard to the offence of which he was convicted. The section also details the grounds for objection that can be raised against disclosure.

CROSS-EXAMINATION OF THE ACCUSED ON ISSUES OF CHARACTER

The character of an accused person may not normally be the subject of **12–56** comment from the Crown or a co-accused except in various statutorily defined circumstances.

The accused who gives evidence

Section 266(3) provides that an *accused who gives evidence* is not protected in **12–57** cross-examination from questions which "would tend to incriminate him as to the offence charged". However, he is protected from questions that

---

[109] *Carbery v HM Advocate*, 1975 J.C.
[110] See too, *Gemmill v HM Advocate*, 1979 S.L.T. 217.
[111] *Slane v HM Advocate*, 1984 J.C. 60 —the first direct case on the point; see Sheriff Gordon's commentary at 1984 S.C.C.R. 77 at 80.
[112] *Slane v HM Advocate*, 1984, J.C. 60 at 79.
[113] See *DS v HM Advocate*, 2007 S.C. (P.C.) 1.

suggest his bad character, *unless* he has already put his own good character in evidence, or has impugned the character of the complainer or other prosecution witnesses.[114] In the event of the latter situation, s.266(4)(b) permits the prosecution the option of cross-examining the accused as to character:

> "(4) An accused who gives evidence on his own behalf in pursuance of this section shall not be asked, and if asked shall not be required to answer, any question tending to show that he has committed, or been convicted of, or been charged with, any offence other than that with which he is then charged, or is of bad character, unless—
>
> (a) the proof that he has committed or been convicted of such other offence is admissible evidence to show that he is guilty of the offence with which he is then charged; or
> (b) the accused or his counsel or solicitor has asked questions of the witnesses for the prosecution with a view to establishing the accused's good character or impugning the character of the complainer, or the accused has given evidence of his own good character, or the nature or conduct of the defence is such as to involve imputations on the character of the prosecutor or of the witnesses for the prosecution or of the complainer; or
> (c) the accused has given evidence against any other person charged in the same proceedings."

Before an accused can be asked questions about his bad character the court must give permission.[115] Thus, an accused person has to be carefully advised about their choices in answer to charges. First, if the accused elects to give sworn evidence in their own defence they forfeit the normal privilege against self incrimination which is granted to an ordinary witness. Second, if the accused raises the issue of their own good character, or maligns the character of Crown witnesses, they discard any protection against disclosure to the trial court of previous convictions, or misdemeanours.[116] Sections 101(2) and 166(8) of the 1995 Act expressly permit this. Evidence tending to impugn the accused's credibility as a witness will invariably also suggest guilt of the charge, as the two are inextricably linked.[117]

The accused who does not give evidence

12–58 Even where an accused does not testify it is still possible for them to put their own good character in evidence, or impugn the character of the complainer, or other prosecution witnesses through examination and cross-examination of other witnesses. It is then open to the prosecutor to lead evidence that the accused has committed other offences, or is otherwise of

---

[114] s.266(4)(b).
[115] s.266(5).
[116] s.266(4).
[117] *Stirland v D.P.P.* [1944] A.C. 315; 2 All E.R. 13.

bad character,[118] provided the court consents to the introduction of such evidence.[119]

The prosecution can only cross-examine on character if the accused has **12–59** brought themselves within one of the circumstances listed above. Character in these circumstances is not confined to previous convictions, but is interpreted more broadly. As noted, it is proper practice for prosecutors to seek the leave of the court before introducing character evidence.[120] In all cases except under s.266(4) the prosecution must seek the leave of the court, outwith the presence of the jury, before proceeding to cross-examine the accused as to character. But a co-accused against whom evidence has been given is not affected by these restrictions.[121]

If a prosecutor raises character evidence inappropriately, i.e. is in breach **12–60** of s.266(4), it will normally lead to a successful appeal in a solemn case if not carefully corrected by the trial judge when charging the jury, and will be almost certainly fatal in a summary trial. In *McLean v Tudhope*[122] McLean was charged with a breach of the peace, and in the course of being cross-examined he stated that he was an honest man. Without seeking the leave of the court, the fiscal depute then referred to a previous conviction and in re-examination McLean was obliged to give details of it by way of a damage limitation exercise. On appeal, it was held that since the case turned on credibility, the reference to the previous conviction required the conviction to be quashed.[123]

The four principal situations envisaged by s.266(4) are now considered.

(1) Subsection(4)(a): Accused's character relevant to the charge

There are circumstances in which, notwithstanding the general rule against **12–61** adducing evidence of the accused's character in chief, the prosecution may rely on such evidence when it is "relevant" to the charge that the accused now faces. Subsection (4)(a) allows the Crown to cross-examine the accused along these lines. It has been held in the English case of *Jones v D.P.P.*[124] (interpreting similar provisions) that the words "tending to show" must be interpreted as meaning "tending to show for the first time". The effect of this is that, for example, if the court becomes aware of a previous conviction by other means,[125] then the accused may be cross-examined on it.

Thus, in cases such as *Varey v HM Advocate*[126] and *Murphy v HM* **12–62** *Advocate*,[127] the prosecution could not only adduce evidence of the accused's

---

[118] s.270(1).

[119] s.270(2) and (3).

[120] *O'Hara v HM Advocate*, 1948 J.C. 90. This case was over-ruled in relation to other aspects by *Leggate v HM Advocate*, 1988 S.L.T. 665.

[121] See *McCourtney v HM Advocate*, 1977 J.C. 68 at 72.

[122] *McLean v Tudhope*, 1982 S.C.C.R. 555.

[123] The fact that McLean had apparently put his character in issue appears not to have been considered: see Sheriff Gordon's comment on the case, *McLean v Tudhope*, 1982 S.C.C.R. 555 at 557.

[124] *Jones v D.P.P* [1962] A.C. 635; which considered the equivalent provisions in English law; followed in *Dodds v HM Advocate*, 1988 J.C. 21.

[125] e.g. if the accused makes reference to it, or even if a prosecution witness refers to it by accident: see *HM Advocate v Corcoran*, 1932 J.C. 42.

[126] *Varey v HM Advocate*, 1986 J.C. 28 at 79.

[127] *Varey v HM Advocate*, 1986 J.C. 28 at 80.

previous convictions in chief, but could cross-examine on them if the accused has chosen to give evidence.[128] When similar fact evidence is relevant in terms of the rule in *Makin v Attorney-General for New South Wales*[129] that could bring it within the ambit of permitted cross-examination under subs.(4)(a).

(2) Subsection (4)(b): Accused gives evidence "of his own good character"

12–63 When an accused sets out to establish his or her good character, either by cross-examining witnesses for the prosecution concerning it or by giving such evidence on oath, then the Crown are entitled, with the leave of the court, to counter such evidence.[130] The Crown may cross-examine the accused as to character to show that the position is other than the accused would have the court believe. It is uncertain whether or not, if the accused denies the accusations made against him, the Crown may go on to prove them by recalling a witness or calling fresh evidence altogether. Section 266(4)(b) only operates when the accused gives evidence. Section 270 of the Criminal Procedure (Scotland) Act 1995 covers the situation where the accused declines to go into the witness box, but nonetheless makes good character an issue. In the event that the accused attacks Crown witnesses in cross-examination or seeks to set up his or her good character through defence witnesses called for this purpose, the Crown can retaliate by leading evidence of the accused's previous misconduct including previous convictions.

12–64 Problems can arise when good character evidence is obtained by co-accused A from co-accused B or from B's witness. B may then wish to cross-examine A as to B's good character. Since A has "set up" his character it is only fair to allow B to set the record straight by cross-examining A as to his misdeeds in the past. This is particularly true where the two are running what is popularly known as a "cut-throat" defence (i.e. each is incriminating the other) and the issue of credibility is crucial. There is, not surprisingly, no direct authority on the point, since in most such cases each accused will go on to give evidence against the other, and thus invoke subs.(4)(c).

(3) Subsection (4)(b): "Nature and conduct of defence involves imputations on character of prosecutor, prosecution witnesses or complainer"

12–65 The basic rules of fair play suggest that when the accused sets out, either in chief or in cross-examination,[131] to impugn the character of the prosecutor[132] or the Crown witnesses or the complainer,[133] then the court should also be advised of any stains on the accused's own character. At the same time, an accused is entitled to a fair opportunity to develop a genuine defence and that may, incidentally, involve imputations against the prosecution witnesses. A balance has to be struck between these two considerations. The

---

[128] As in *Carbery v HM Advocate*, 1975 J.C. and *Gemmill v HM Advocate*, 1979 S.L.T. 217.
[129] *Makin v Attorney-General for New South Wales* [1894] A.C. 57 at 65.
[130] See Walker and Walker, *Law of Evidence in Scotland*, paras 13.4.2–13.14.4.
[131] There are no restrictions on the form that such evidence can take.
[132] See *HM Advocate v Grudins*, 1976 S.L.T. (Notes) 10.
[133] The addition of the complainer to this list is an extension of the statutory provisions as contained in ss.141 and 346 of the 1975 Act.

circumstances in which an accused can lose the statutory immunity against attacks on character were clarified by *Leggate v HM Advocate*.[134]

12–66 *Leggate* was a full bench decision that overturned a line of case authority from *O'Hara v HM Advocate* in 1948,[135] including a five bench decision in *Templeton v McLeod*.[136] Until *Leggate*, the practice was to grant an accused whose defence necessarily involved casting aspersions on the character of Crown witnesses some degree of statutory immunity.[137] This immunity protected the accused against a character attack and/or the disclosure of previous convictions, if the accused gave evidence. The appeal court in *Leggate* decided that when an accused attacks the character of a Crown witness, even if this is necessary to establish his defence, he does not retain any immunity from attack on his own character. It was recognised that there might be situations where this was unduly prejudicial to an accused so the trial judge has discretion to ameliorate the consequences of an attack on character. Section 266(5) requires the prosecution to apply to the court for permission to cross-examine on character. The application must be made outwith the presence of the jury. The judge can refuse leave to cross-examine the accused on character.

12–67 *Leggate* was decided with more than a glance southwards to the very solid body of English case law that had developed. However, all the old English cases were swept away by the Criminal Justice Act 2003, which introduced a more liberal framework for the admissibility of bad character evidence. However, some of these English cases are mentioned here as they shed light on the origins and rationale of the Scottish position. The Scottish Law Commission were asked by the Scottish Government, in January 2008, to review specific aspects of the law of evidence, including bad character and double jeopardy, and proposals for reform are already in legislation, e.g. the Double Jeopardy (Scotland) Act 2011, or are in progress. In the meantime, the English case law pre-2003 remains of some interpretive relevance to Scots law.

12–68 The issue in *Leggate* was the effect of s.266(4) which, it will be recalled, provides that the accused shall not be asked any question "tending to show" that he has committed, been convicted of or even charged with previous offences.

12–69 In *Maxwell v D.P.P.*[138] it was held that even though the accused may throw away his immunity by giving evidence of the type prescribed by (a), (b) and (c) of subs.(4), the prosecution may even then only adduce such evidence of his character as is relevant in the circumstances. In particular, the House of Lords doubted whether there would be many cases in which the fact that the accused had been charged with a previous offence but acquitted would be relevant to the present charge.

12–70 The search for a balance between permitting an accused to develop a genuine defence and preventing an accused making imputations against Crown witnesses produced a confusing and often contradictory series of

---

[134] *Leggate v HM Advocate*, 1988 J.C. 127.
[135] *O'Hara v HM Advocate*, 1948 J.C.90.
[136] *Templeton v McLeod*, 1985 J.C. 112.
[137] *Maxwell v D.P.P* In terms of ss.141(1)(f) and 346(1)(f) of the 1975 Act.
[138] [1935] A.C. 309. See *Lowson v HM Advocate*, 1943 J.C. 141, and *Lindie v HM Advocate*, 1974 S.L.T. 208; 1974 J.C. 1.

cases in England. These culminated in *Selvey v D.P.P.*[139] where the House of Lords refused to exclude the possibility of cross-examination on character of an accused who could not mount a fair defence without impugning the character of prosecution witnesses.

12–71   In *HM Advocate v Grudins*[140] it was held that subs.(4)(b) does not apply[141] and the accused does not lose the statutory protection when the character which is being attacked is not that of a witness. In *Grudins* the accused on a murder charge did not lose her immunity when she attacked the character of the deceased. The wording of subs.4(b) indicates that the statutory protection is not lost if the accused attacks the character of a defence witness who proves "hostile".

(4) Subsection (4)(c): "Accused gives evidence against a co-accused"

12–72   Section 266(4)(c) applies in respect of any two accused who appear on the same complaint or indictment, regardless of the charges against them. When subs.(4)(c) comes into play an accused may be cross-examined as to character not only by the prosecution but also by a co-accused. When one co-accused attacks the character of another co-accused or the witnesses of a co-accused, then, by virtue of subs.(4)(c) the statutory protection for the attacker will be lost.

12–73   In *Murdoch v Taylor*[142] the House of Lords, in an English case, held that giving "evidence" against a co-accused could consist of either giving evidence which supports the prosecution's case against him in some material respect, or giving evidence which undermines the defence being put forward by that co-accused. In addition, it held that such evidence could be given either in chief or in the course of being cross-examined, and that it was not necessary for the accused to have any hostile motive, since the test of whether or not evidence is given "against" a co-accused is objective and not subjective.

12–74   Both rulings were adopted in *Burton v HM Advocate*.[143] The court added that there was no distinction to be drawn between the case in which an accused gave evidence against a co-accused expressly, and that in which an attack on the co-accused might be inferred from the evidence given, or arose by implication. An accused who has been incriminated by a co-accused has a right to cross-examine that accused on the incriminating evidence.[144] This may entail a second cross-examination. Evidence by one co-accused is evidence *in causa* generally and may be used against another co-accused even if not intended for that purpose.[145]

12–75   Once an accused has given evidence against a co-accused in terms of subs.(4)(c), the judge has no discretion to exclude the disclosure of that accused's bad character.[146] This is because when one accused gives evidence

[139] *Selvey v D.P.P* [1970] A.C. 304.
[140] *HM Advocate v Grudins*, 1976 S.L.T. (Notes) 10.
[141] Or at least the equivalent statutory provisions in force at that time.
[142] *Murdoch v Taylor* [1965] A.C. 574.
[143] *Burton v HM Advocate*, 1979 S.L.T. (Notes) 59. Some doubts were cast, obiter, on the accuracy of the first interpretation in *Sandlan v HM Advocate*, 1983 J.C. 22.
[144] *Sandlan v HM Advocate*, 1983 J.C. 22.
[145] *Todd v HM. Advocate*, 1984 S.L.T. 123.
[146] *McCourtney v HM Advocate*, 1977 J.C. 68.

against another, he "is in the same position as a witness for the prosecution so far as the co-accused is concerned, and nothing must be done to impair the right of a person charged to discredit his accusers".[147]

Section 266(5) also permits a prosecutor, with leave of the court, to dis- **12–76** close a previous conviction of the accused, if the latter has led evidence to try to establish good character. In *Barr v HM Advocate*,[148] the accused had said during cross-examination that he was "totally against ... any drugs like that", referring to heroin. The prosecutor was then granted leave to introduce evidence of Barr's previous conviction for cannabis use. On appeal against conviction, the court considered that the accused's comment did constitute evidence of his own good character. However, the trial judge had exercised her discretion incorrectly in granting leave to reveal a conviction for cannabis use, in particular when the advocate-depute had not disclosed to the court the details of that conviction prior to introducing it in evidence. The trial judge was under a continuing duty to ensure fairness to the accused and granting leave in this case was a disproportionate response to the comment the accused had made in evidence.

CHARACTER OF OTHER PERSONS

Occasionally it can become important for the court to consider the character **12–77** of a person who is not a party to the case, or a witness, or the victim of a crime. If such evidence is relevant, it is possible it may be admitted. In *Gracie v Stuart*,[149] a reset trial, it was held that the Crown could prove that the person from whom the accused admitted having obtained a stolen watch was in fact a dealer in stolen watches. In *MacPherson v Crisp*,[150] a charge of brothel-keeping, the Crown were allowed to show that two women, not cited as witnesses, but who had been observed entering the accused's premises, were known to be prostitutes.

---

[147] Cross and Tapper, *Evidence*, 9th edn, at 373–374.
[148] *Barr v HM Advocate*, 2006 J.C. 111.
[149] *Gracie v Stuart* (1884) 11 R. (J.) 22.
[150] *MacPherson v Crisp*, 1919 J.C. 1.

Chapter 13

PRIVILEGE

INTRODUCTION

13–01 When a witness has a privilege against answering a certain question or a series of questions, it means that the law recognises their right not to answer such questions. Even if the questions are relevant and competent, and the witness is otherwise compellable, if the response belongs to a category of information regarded in law as privileged the witness can decline to divulge information. Historically, a spouse or civil partner had a privilege against being compelled to disclose the contents of communications during the marriage or civil partnership as such communications were accorded a privileged status. That rule has been abolished, making spouses and civil partners both competent and compellable witnesses for each other.[1] However, if the couple were co-accused, the rules concerning co-accused persons prevail and they would not be compellable.[2]

13–02 If a witness is able to claim a privilege against answering questions then the normal penalty for refusing to answer a competent question as a compellable witness, namely, a charge of contempt of court, cannot be enforced. Information withheld under a privilege is frequently highly relevant to the matters under consideration by the court. Thus, the recognition of a legal privilege is clearly a matter of balancing the policy of confidentiality in limited circumstances, against the interests of justice.

13–03 The general rule is that the privilege is that of the witness who is being called upon to testify and they are entitled to waive that privilege if they wish. If the witness does waive the privilege, the other party has no right to object, but may object if the privilege is wrongfully upheld, depriving that party of vital evidence which it was intended to lead.[3] There is a lack of clear authority as to whether information that a privileged witness would give as evidence remains privileged if that evidence emanates from a third party into whose hands the information has fallen. There appears to be no general rule, but the courts will take account of factors, including whether the information was acquired lawfully, is already in the public domain and the balance between any privacy rights under art.8 of the ECHR and the wider interests of justice.[4]

---

[1] Criminal Procedure Scotland Act 1995, s.264(1) as amended by the Criminal Justice and Licensing (Scotland) Act 2010, s.86(1).
[2] Criminal Procedure Scotland Act 1995, s.264(2).
[3] *Kirkwood v Kirkwood* (1875) 3 R. 235 at 236.
[4] For discussion see Walker and Walker, *Evidence*, 3rd edn, paras 9.10.1 and 10.3.2; and Davidson, *Evidence*, paras 13.02–13.05.

PRIVILEGE AGAINST SELF-INCRIMINATION: THE ACCUSED

It is a fundamental proposition within Scots law that a person cannot be **13–04**
forced to incriminate themselves. This is a principle affirmed in the ECHR,
now incorporated into domestic law by the Human Rights Act 1998. In
Saunders v United Kingdom the European Court of Human Rights stated
that "the right not to incriminate oneself, like the right to silence, was a
generally recognised international standard which lay at the heart of the
notion of a fair procedure under Article 6 of the convention".[5] This right is
not explicit in terms of art.6, but as the *Saunders* judgment reinforced, it is
integral to fair treatment.

An untrue answer can lead to a perjury charge.[6]   **13–05**

As discussed in Ch.12, there is a statutory exception to this privilege in   **13–06**
circumstances where an accused elects to give evidence at their own trial.
Since 1898 an accused person has possessed the right to give sworn testimony at their own trial, a right which is now to be found in s.266(1) of the
Criminal Procedure (Scotland) Act 1995. However, an accused is not
granted the same degree of privilege against self-incrimination that applies
to witnesses who are not charged with criminal offences. An accused person
cannot be selective about the answers they give to questions. Either they
decline to go into the witness box, which they are perfectly entitled to do or,
if they chose to give evidence-in-chief, they must answer all questions put to
them in cross-examination. They cannot refuse to answer such questions on
the basis they might be incriminatory as to the offence charged.

That said, an accused is entitled to be protected from questions that are   **13–07**
designed to show the commission of offences beyond those charged. Sections 266(3) and (4) of the Criminal Procedure (Scotland) Act 1995 which
regulate the position:

> "(3) An accused who gives evidence on his own behalf in pursuance of
>   this section may be asked any question in cross-examination not-
>   withstanding that it would tend to incriminate him as to the offence
>   charged.
>
> (4) An accused who gives evidence on his own behalf in pursuance of
>   this section shall not be asked, and if asked shall not be required to
>   answer, any question tending to show that he has committed, or
>   been convicted of or been charged with, any offence *other than that
>   with which he is then charged*...[emphasis added]"

These provisions offer a shield to the accused against certain incriminating
answers. To this extent an accused is treated more favourably than normal
witnesses who may, subject to the general privilege, be asked questions that
impugn their credibility as a witness.[7]

---

[5] *Saunders v United Kingdom* (1996) 23 E.H.R.R. 313.
[6] *Graham v HM Advocate*, 1969 S.L.T. 116.
[7] For a discussion of the circumstances in which an accused may forfeit the shield of subs.(4),
see Ch.12.

PRIVILEGE AGAINST SELF-INCRIMINATION: WITNESSES OTHER THAN THE
ACCUSED

13–08 It is not only an accused person who has a privilege against self-incrimination. All witnesses in civil and criminal cases have a privilege against
answering in court a question that might incriminate them in respect of
certain matters. The privilege is against answering the particular question
that has such an effect—the general rule does not prevent the question being
posed in the first place. In general, it is for the witness to claim the privilege
when the question is put. However, there are two statutory exceptions to this
general rule, in terms of which the question may not even be asked. These
are s.2 of the Evidence (Further Amendment) (Scotland) Act 1874, which
deals with questions which tend to show that the witness has been guilty of
adultery; and s.266 of the Criminal Procedure (Scotland) Act 1995, which
applies to questions asked of an accused in a criminal trial. Macphail suggested[8] that a new statutory rule should be enacted which prevented the
question even being asked. There can be difficulties in avoiding questions
that raise issues of privilege. First, a questioner may not always be aware
that the question has incriminatory implications. Second, a witness may not
realise that they have a privilege against answering a particular question. It
is therefore regarded as the duty of the judge to advise the witness of the
privilege when a particular question seems likely to lead towards an incriminating answer.[9]

13–09   At present there is no procedure for determining whether an answer is
genuinely incriminatory. Thus, if all that is required is that the witness states
an objection, without need for further inquiry, then many awkward questions may be avoided by the unscrupulous or the unwilling witness. As was
observed by Lord Stephen in *R. v Cox and Railton*,[10] "the secret must be told
in order [that the court may] see whether it ought to be kept".

13–10   A witness may not succeed in claiming a privilege against answering a
particular question, perhaps because of a lack of awareness of the existence
of the privilege, or because the answer is denied privilege by the trial judge.
Additionally, a witness may elect to waive the privilege. In such circumstances, the answer given becomes admissible for all purposes, even if the
witness is a party to the action.[11] For example, in *O'Neill v Wilson*[12] it was
affirmed that a failure to warn a witness of their privilege does not affect
liability to subsequent prosecution. However, if a statement were forced
from a witness by a denial of the privilege, it would be classed as "invo-
luntary" and therefore inadmissible as a confession.

13–11   The privilege as originally formulated seems very wide in its application,
but in practice it is most commonly encountered in circumstances where
answering questions would incriminate the witness in regard to a criminal

---

[8] Macphail, *Evidence*, Ch.18.05.
[9] Lord President Inglis in *Kirkwood v Kirkwood* (1875) 3 R. 235 at 236.
[10] (1884) 14 Q.B.D. 153 at 175.
[11] Lord President Inglis in *Kirkwood v Kirkwood*, n.1.
[12] 1983 J.C. 42. In *Graham v HM Advocate*, 1969 S.L.T. 116, it was held that a witness who is
   not advised of his privilege, and who then goes on to give a false answer to the question,
   cannot hide behind the failure to advise him of his privilege in any subsequent perjury trial.

offence. In particular, the following limitations on the privilege are recognised.

(1) It is not applicable when the witness is no longer at risk of conviction **13–12** of the offence revealed by the answer, if given. If, for example, an accused has already pled guilty, or been convicted of the offence in question, or has been granted immunity by the Crown because he or she is to be used as a *socius criminis* witness by them, then the witness may no longer refuse to testify as to guilt.[13] A finding of not guilty will also rob the witness of privilege because the matter is then res judicata and a desertion *simpliciter* by the Crown will presumably have the same effect.

(2) A witness cannot, in all probability, claim the privilege against **13–13** answering a question that will reveal the commission of an offence under foreign law. Although many consider that in principle the privilege should extend to such questions, the point remains unsettled under Scots law.[14] The House of Lords in the English appeal case of *Rio Tinto Zinc v Westinghouse Electric Corporation*[15] allowed the privilege to be invoked against disclosure of documents which might expose the defenders to various fines under EC Regulations.[16]

(3) With the exception of adultery,[17] the privilege may not be claimed in **13–14** respect of any question the answer to which might expose the witness to a civil action. This creates an area of uncertainty in those cases in which a future action, although civil in form, can result in penalties that are quasi-criminal in nature. An example is the system of fines which operates as the penalty for breaches of EC Regulations and, as the *Rio Tinto Zinc* case shows, the English courts are prepared to extend a statutory privilege in such circumstances. Although there does not appear to be any Scots authority on this specific point, s.2 of the Evidence (Further Amendment) (Scotland) Act 1874 preserves the privilege in statutory form, in "any proceedings", and prevents such questions even being asked of the witness. There has been little reported interpretation of this provision, and it has not been consistent. In an undefended divorce action in the sheriff court on the grounds of the defender's adultery, the sheriff-principal found that there could be no objection to the use of affidavits in which both the defender and the paramour admitted adultery, on the ground that the witnesses were not warned of their privilege to decline to swear the affidavits.[18]

(4) A number of statutory exceptions remove the privilege where wider **13–15** public interests in securing justice outweigh an individual's right to privacy

---

[13] *MacMillan v Murray*, 1920 J.C. 13.
[14] See, for example, Macphail, *Evidence*, Ch.18.13 who conceded the practical difficulty of the presiding judge having to become acquainted with the law in question.
[15] [1978] A.C. 547.
[16] See also *HM Advocate v Entwhistle* (1980) unreported, per Macphail, *Evidence*, Ch.18.13A, in which a witness in the High Court was allowed the privilege against answering questions that might render him liable to prosecution in England. See too the discussion in Davidson, *Evidence*, at paras 13.12–13.14.
[17] There is consensus that this exception is anachronistic: Macphail, *Evidence*, para.18.18; Davidson, *Evidence*, para.13.17; Walker and Walker, *Evidence*, 3rd edn, para.12.13.3.
[18] *Sinclair v Sinclair*, 1986 S.L.T. (Sh. Ct) 54. For a contrary decision see *Cooper v Cooper*, 1987 S.L.T. (Sh. Ct) 37, where there were additional procedural reasons for rejecting the affidavits. To avoid ambiguity, best practice would be to include an acknowledgement of the privilege in the body of any sworn documents agreed by the parties relating to the court case as discussed in Walker and Walker, *Evidence*, 3rd edn, para.12.13.1.

from self-incrimination. For example, the common law protection against self-incrimination has been modified by s.172(2)(a) of the Road Traffic Act 1988. This section provides that a person requested by the police must supply details of the driver of a vehicle. The question of whether this provision in effect compelled a person to make an incriminating statement, and thus was incompatible with the Human Rights Act 1998, was tested in *Brown v Stott*.[19] Brown was questioned by police whilst under suspicion of having stolen a bottle of gin from a supermarket. The officers smelt alcohol on her breath and asked her how she had got to the supermarket. She explained she had driven her car there. Her admission, as required by the statute, was subsequently challenged at trial on the ground that it breached the Convention right to a fair trial contained in art.6 of the ECHR. On appeal the High Court held that the only way of rendering s.172 compatible with art.6 was to declare that the Crown had no power to lead and rely on evidence of the accused which she was compelled to make under the section.[20] The Lord Advocate appealed to the Judicial Committee of the Privy Council, which reversed the decision and upheld Brown's conviction.[21]

13–16   While the Privy Council acknowledged that there was a general right not to incriminate oneself, the court did not interpret this as an absolute right[22]:

> "Limited qualification of these rights is acceptable if reasonably directed by national authorities towards a clear and proper objective and if representing no greater qualification than the situation calls for."

According to Lord Bingham, the admission of being the driver of a car was not in itself an offence unless some other proven facts pointed to an offence having been committed. Moreover, all car drivers understood they were subject to a "regulatory regime" that was necessary given the potential of cars to cause grave injury. In those two contexts, the requirement of s.172 was not disproportionate.

13–17   In a similar vein, Lord Kirkwood argued[23] that while the right to a fair trial under art.6 was absolute (the question of what is "fair" being the issue) the right implied in art.6 not to incriminate oneself was not absolute:

> "It is a right which is capable of being limited by law to some extent, always provided that the limitation is shown to be necessary to protect the legitimate interests of the community."

There was no suggestion of coercion or compulsion in seeking an answer to the question posed under the road traffic legislation. Lord Kirkwood therefore considered the statutory provision met the test of proportionality required by the jurisprudence of the ECtHR. A balance had to be struck between the general interests of the community to be protected against drunk drivers and the rights of a suspect to a subsequent fair trial. This is an argument that has broad potential appeal in assessing all manner of ECHR

---

[19] *Brown v Stott*, 2001 S.L.T. 59.
[20] *Brown v Stott*, 2000 S.L.T. 379.
[21] *Brown v Stott*, 2001 S.L.T. 59.
[22] *Brown v Stott*, 2001 S.L.T. 59 per Lord Bingham at 70.
[23] *Brown v Stott*, 2001 S.L.T. 59 at 85.

challenges to regulatory regimes, such as other road traffic measures, including speed cameras, and the extensive use of CCTV in public places.

Another quite common example of encroachment of the protection **13–18** against self-incrimination arises in s.47(3) of the Bankruptcy (Scotland) Act 1985. In terms of this section, a bankrupt person must answer "all lawful questions" which may be put to them in their public examination, even if the responses are incriminatory. However, the apparent lack of privilege here is ameliorated by the saving proviso that the bankrupt person's answers may not be used against them in any subsequent criminal proceedings. Many other statutes contain similar provisions where it is felt that public interest outweighs private privilege.[24]

When a witness claims the privilege against self-incrimination, no adverse **13–19** inferences should arise.[25] But it is always possible that asserting a privilege may impact upon the credibility of the witness, since, according to Dickson, "an innocent man is far more likely to answer with an indignant denial than to avail himself of his privilege".[26]

COMMUNICATIONS DURING MARRIAGE/CIVIL PARTNERSHIP

There are statutory provisions dating from the 19th century that accord **13–20** privilege to certain communications between spouses. The privilege appears to emanate from a respect for the marital state.

Civil cases

In civil cases, s.3 of the Evidence (Scotland) Act 1853, grants a privilege **13–21** against disclosing marital communications. It states:

> "[N]othing herein contained shall in any [civil] proceeding render any husband competent or compellable to give against his wife evidence of any matter communicated by her to him during the marriage, or any wife competent or compellable to give against her husband evidence of any matter communicated by him to her during the marriage."

The privilege is that of the witness spouse alone, and he or she is free to waive it if so desired.[27] Macphail recommended the abolition of this provision.[28] The privilege appears to apply to any form of communication, written, oral or other.[29] Where the issue in dispute is the behaviour of one spouse towards, another the privilege does not apply. For example, in *Mackay v Mackay*[30] a letter written by a husband confessing to adultery was

---

[24] See, e.g. Explosive Substances Act 1883, s.6(2), and Representation of the People Act 1983, s.141.

[25] Macphail, *Evidence*, para.18.05.

[26] Dickson, *Evidence*, para.1790.

[27] See *HM Advocate v HD*, 1953 J.C. 65, a criminal case, but it is suggested the principle would also be applicable to civil cases.

[28] Macphail, *Evidence*, para.4.06.

[29] See Walker and Walker, *Evidence*, 3rd edn, para.13.10.2.

[30] *Mackay v Mackay*, 1946 S.C. 7.

held not to be privileged, thus allowing the wife, who would not otherwise have been competent, to relate its contents.

13–22   In criminal cases, the privilege against disclosing marital communications was removed by an amendment[31] to s.264(1) of the Criminal Procedure (Scotland) Act 1995, which now states "[t]he spouse or civil partner of an accused is a competent and compellable witness for the prosecution, the accused or any co-accused in the proceedings against the accused".

13–23   Even if a particular witness claims a privilege, the court can hear the same evidence that is covered by the privilege if given by an alternative source, e.g. a witness who overheard the privileged conversation, or a third party who intercepted a privileged letter.[32] The privilege relates only to the spouse as a witness and not to anyone else. It is unclear whether or not the privilege ends with the marriage and whether, for example, a former spouse can claim the privilege in respect of a communication made during the existence of the marriage. Dickson[33] claims that the privilege survives death or divorce, but modern commentators challenge this view on the grounds both of utility and the wording of the relevant sections.[34]

13–24   Couples who chose to cohabit have no privilege in respect of their communications. This position is in keeping with many other aspects of legal benefits and protections available to spouses and civil partners but not to those who cohabit.

LAWYER–CLIENT PRIVILEGE

13–25   Communications passing between a legal adviser and a client are privileged, i.e. have confidential status, and do not have to be disclosed in evidence. It is a privilege recognised since Stair[35] and the rationale is because "it is essential for the administration of justice that persons should be able to consult their legal advisers freely without the subject matter of their discussions being under risk of disclosure".[36]

13–26   The privilege reflects the fundamental relationship of trust between legal advisers and their clients and thus the need for confidentiality in their dealings.[37] Communications in the normal course of business are protected—the privilege is not confined to circumstances where litigation is in contemplation. The privilege, or confidentiality, is limited to qualified legal advisers.[38] It does not extend, for example, to accountants giving legal advice in the course of their work. The Supreme Court decision in *R (Prudential Plc and another) v Special Commissioner of Income Tax and*

---

[31] Amended by s.86(1), Criminal Justice and Licensing (Scotland) Act 2010.

[32] See Walker and Walker, *Evidence*, 3rd edn, para.13.10.2.

[33] Dickson, *Evidence*, para.1660.

[34] See, Wilkinson, *Scottish Law of Evidence*, p.103; Clive, *Husband and Wife*, 4th edn (Edinburgh: W. Green, 1997) para.18–017; Macphail, para.4.10; Davidson, *Evidence*, at 637. See too the position in England, *R. v Ash* (1985) 81 Cr.App.Rep. 294.

[35] Stair, IV, xliii.

[36] Wilkinson, *Scottish Law of Evidence*, 18, p.94.

[37] See too the statutory protection available to "licensed providers" of legal services: Legal Services (Scotland) Act 2010, s.75(2).

[38] Dickson, *Evidence*, para.1665.

another[39] ruled by a majority of 5:2 that the legal advice privilege does not apply to legal advice given by professionals other than qualified lawyers. The European Court of Justice has also ruled that in-house lawyers in competition investigations are not protected by legal professional privilege.[40]

Although it is often referred to as "the solicitor and client privilege", it is **13–27** more extensive, covering solicitors and advocates, and their clerks and other staff.[41] The privilege belongs to the client, so that the legal adviser may disclose the communication if authorised to do so by the client. In addition, by virtue of s.1 of the Evidence (Scotland) Act 1852, the privilege is lost if the client calls that legal adviser as a witness.[42] This section applies to both civil and criminal proceedings, but the position in criminal proceedings is reinforced by s.265(2) of the Criminal Procedure (Scotland) Act 1995. This section provides that where a solicitor, who is or has been an agent for an accused, is called to testify, the accused cannot insist on the confidentiality of certain matters on the grounds of agent-client privilege.

The choice rests with the client. If the client wishes to preserve the con- **13–28** fidentiality of the relationship with their legal agent then they have to forego the opportunity of citing the agent as a witness. If the priority is to have the agent as a witness then confidentiality is lost.

The absolute nature of the privilege was affirmed in the English case of *R.* **13–29** *v Derby Magistrates' Court, Ex p. B*[43] where the House of Lords declined to permit a person accused of murder access to solicitors' files that might have assisted him in the preparation of his defence. Refusal was on the ground that these files were confidential between the solicitor and his client (a person previously acquitted of the murder) and the privilege attaching to that relationship was paramount. Lord Taylor observed[44]:

> "Legal professional privilege is thus much more than an ordinary rule of evidence ... It is a fundamental condition on which the administration of justice as a whole rests."

In order to cover a particular communication the privilege must have been made in circumstances in which the relationship of legal adviser and client was at least in contemplation between the parties. It is uncertain what the precise position is when a solicitor receives the communication and then declines to act. In *HM Advocate v Davie*[45] such evidence was admitted under reservation, although it was unnecessary to consider the point on appeal. However, doubts have been expressed as to whether this represents Scots law,[46] and it does not apply in England, where the privilege is invoked as soon as the relationship is fairly in contemplation.[47]

---

[39] *R (Prudential Plc and another) v Special Commissioner of Income Tax and another*, 2013 UKSC 1.
[40] *AKROS Chemicals v Commission* [2011] 2A.C. 338.
[41] Macphail, *Evidence*, para.18.20.
[42] *Whitbread Group Plc v Goldapple Ltd*, 2003 S.L.T. 256.
[43] *R. v Derby Magistrates' Court, Ex p. B* [1995] 4 All E.R. 526.
[44] *R. v Derby Magistrates' Court, Ex p. B* [1995] 4 All E.R. 526 at 540–541.
[45] *HM Advocate v Davie* (1881) 4 Coup 450.
[46] Macphail, *Evidence*, para.18.21. See too, R. Black, *"A Question of Confidence"* (1982) 27 J.L.S.S. 299, 389.
[47] *Minter v Priest* [1930] A.C. 558.

13–30   The privilege ends when the relationship ends and communications made afterwards are not covered. However, communications made during the relationship continue to attract the privilege.[48] The privilege survives the death of the legal adviser and, in some cases, the death of the client.[49] When the communication relates to some item of property in which the client's executors have an interest, it seems that the privilege transfers to the executors, but cannot be invoked to deny a third party rights in the succession.[50]

There are various limitations to the extent of the privilege:

13–31   (1) It has been stated that the privilege covers not only those matters formally communicated by the client to the legal adviser operating in that professional capacity, but also to observations noted by the legal adviser during consultation, such as blood-stained clothing.[51] It certainly can be argued that to draw a distinction between information that is conveyed orally and that which is conveyed through physical presence is illogical, not least in circumstances where both sets of information could generate incriminating inferences. However, an oral communication is deliberate and purposeful while one's appearance may simply be incidental.

13–32   (2) The privilege does not apply when the very matter into which the court is inquiring is whether or not the communication was made. Thus, in *Anderson v Lord Elgin's Trustees*[52] the question arose as to whether or not the pursuer had delayed in bringing his action, as the defenders averred, and it was held to be competent to adduce correspondence between the defenders and their solicitors which referred to an earlier claim.

13–33   (3) The privilege will not cover communications that reveal the true nature of the relationship between the parties where this itself is in dispute. In *Fraser v Malloch*,[53] for example, the pursuer raised an action against a solicitor who had acted for a client in a previous action, claiming that the solicitor had done so without instructions. The pursuer was allowed to recover correspondence passing between the solicitor and the alleged client in order to shed further light on the relationship.

13–34   (4) The privilege will not cover communications which have passed between a solicitor and a client who is alleged to have performed some illegal act, when it is also alleged that the solicitor was directly involved in the performance of the illegal act. In *Micosta S.A. v Shetland Islands Council*[54] the pursuers brought an action against the local authority for alleged abuse of statutory powers. They successfully obtained commission and diligence to recover certain documents, amongst which was a sealed envelope containing correspondence that had passed between the defenders and their law agents. Although the pursuers alleged the documents related directly to the alleged abuses, and were indicative of the defenders' state of mind at the time, the court sustained the defenders' arguments that the correspondence was privileged and could not be opened up. The court

---

[48] Dickson, *Evidence*, para.1664.
[49] Walker and Walker, *Evidence*, 3rd edn, para.10.2.3.
[50] See *Mackenzie v Mackenzie's Trs*, 1916 1 S.L.T. 271.
[51] Walker and Walker, *Evidence*, 3rd edn, para.10.34. See too, Davidson, *Evidence*, paras 13.25–13.26 and Wilkinson, *Scottish Law of Evidence*, p.95.
[52] (1859) 21 D. 654. See also *Kidd v Bunyan* (1842) 5 D. 193.
[53] (1895) 3 S.L.T. 211 (O.H.).
[54] *Micosta S.A. v Shetland Islands Council*, 1983 S.L.T. 483, especially at 485.

stressed that such privilege would not apply if the legal advisers had been directly involved in the action complained of[55]:

> "[T]he only circumstances in which the general rule will be superseded are where fraud or some other illegal act is alleged against a party and where his law agent has been directly concerned in the carrying out of the very transaction which is the subject-matter of inquiry."

This statement from Lord President Emslie was clarified in *Kelly v Vannet*[56] in respect of the question whether the law agent had to be *aware* that they were involved in the performance of an illegal act. It appears not, as the court in *Kelly* relied upon a passage in Dickson which declared that no confidentiality attaches to a crime where the legal adviser is associated as either "an innocent instrument" or "an accomplice".[57] If that seems an onerous responsibility placed upon legal advisers it acts as a reminder that those who take instructions from clients must exercise judgement consistent with the prudence required of a skilled professional legal adviser.[58] This is especially so in a world where the potential for deception and illegal activities through identity fraud and money laundering are not infrequent practices, for which solicitors' law firms can unwittingly present as the ideal cover.

Paterson and Ritchie raise the further issue of what precisely constitutes **13–35** "fraud or some other illegal activity" (to quote *Micosta*). They argue that the Outer House decision in *Conoco(UK) Ltd v The Commercial Law Practice*,[59] which favoured the public policy interest for disclosure over confidentiality, is a much broader interpretation of the principle than the ruling in *Micosta*.

A distinction is drawn between a communication made in the furtherance **13–36** of an unlawful purpose, which is not privileged, and a request for legal advice afterwards on possible defences to a particular action, which is privileged. Requests for advice as to the legality of a contemplated course of action will also attract the privilege.

(5) In terms of s.47(3) of the Bankruptcy (Scotland) Act 1985, a bankrupt **13–37** person must answer all questions posed during his public examination and cannot generally claim privilege on the grounds of confidentiality against disclosure of communications with another person. However, the bankrupt person need not disclose matters communicated with his or her legal adviser, unless that adviser is also called for examination.[60]

There are many statutory provisions, including s.37(6) of the Restrictive **13–38** Trade Practices Act 1976 and s.3(2) of the Data Protection Act 1984, that preserve the legal adviser/client privilege even though it might be argued that it is in the public interest that all the client's dealings be brought into the open. However, Macphail pointed out that EC Regulations are not so

---

[55] *Micosta S.A. v Shetland Islands Council*, 1983 S.L.T. 483 at 485 per Lord President Emslie.

[56] *Kelly v Vannet*, 1999 J.C. 109.

[57] *Kelly v Vannet*, 1999 J.C. 109 at 115–116.

[58] A. Paterson and B. Ritchie, *Law, Practice and Conduct for Solicitors* (Edinburgh: W. Green, 2006).

[59] *Conoco (UK) Ltd v The Commercial Law Practice*, 1997 S.L.T. 372.

[60] McBryde, *Bankruptcy*, para.11–24.

protective and that on at least one occasion the legal adviser/client privilege has been waived aside in the interests of the enforcement of the Treaty of Rome.[61]

13–39   There remains the question of whether or not the court may make use of privileged communications that have become available from another source, such as the overheard conversation or the intercepted letter.[62] There is no direct Scottish authority on the position when the information is obtained illegally, although Macphail argued that such material should be subject to the normal rules relating to illegally obtained evidence.[63]

13–40   In *McLeish v Glasgow Bonding Co. Ltd*[64] privileged information that became available to a third party through an innocent mistake was held admissible for the purposes of cross-examination, not least because the release of the information had not occurred at the point of transmission between legal adviser and client.

COMMUNICATIONS *POST LITEM MOTAM*

13–41 A communication *post litem motam* is a communication made in circumstances in which a party anticipates or is contemplating litigation. Any such communication, whether directly between legal adviser and client or with a third party in connection with litigation, is generally privileged. This privilege is wider than the legal adviser/client privilege in terms of who is affected and it is not limited simply to situations in which a writ has been issued. However, the privilege is narrower than the legal adviser/client privilege in the sense that while the latter covers all communications made at any time, for a communication to be *post litem motam*, it must be made when litigation is at least in contemplation. Or, as explained in *Admiralty v Aberdeen Steam Trawling and Fishing Co*,[65] not "merely after the summons has been raised, but after it is apparent that there is going to be a litigious contention".

13–42   Lord Hunter, in *Marks & Spencer v British Gas Corporation (No.1 Corp)*,[66] drew a distinction between communications which are made *post litem motam* and those which are not, in this way:

> "[T]he contrast is between reports which are designed to put the person concerned in possession of the true facts, on the one hand, and reports made in contemplation of judicial proceedings, on the other."

---

[61] Macphail, *Evidence*, para.18.20. See too *AM & S Europe Ltd v Commr of the European Communities* [1983] Q.B. 878.

[62] For general principle of illegally recovered evidence, see *Duke of Argyll v Duchess of Argyll*, 1963 S.L.T. (Notes) 42, following, reluctantly, *Rattray v Rattray* (1897) 25 R 315. See discussion in Ch.10.

[63] Macphail, *Evidence*, para.18.22.

[64] *McLeish v Glasgow Bonding Co. Ltd*, 1965 S.L.T. 39.

[65] *Admiralty v Aberdeen Steam Trawling and Fishing Co*, 1909 S.C. 335 at 340.

[66] *Marks & Spencer v British Gas Corporation (No.1 Corp)*, 1983 S.L.T. 196 at 197; see too *Komori v Tayside Health Board*, 2010 S.L.T. 387 in regard to recovery of hospital medical records.

However, this is not an entirely satisfactory distinction because arriving at a position where you are "in possession of the true facts" may not be achievable without enquiries and investigations of a depth that permit you to decide whether these is a viable cause of action. The privilege needs to operate from the outset of any enquiry into the facts if Lord President Cylde's dictum in *Johnstone v National Coal Board*[67] is to be satisfied:

"[A]fter an accident and even before any claim has been made, each party having a possible interest should be entitled to pursue his own investigations into the cause of the accident, free from the risk of having to reveal his information to the other side."

A communication *post litem motam* does not cease to have confidential status on the completion of the case for which it was prepared.[68]

There is one type of post-accident report which forms an exception to the **13–43** general privilege normally afforded to statements *post litem motam*. There is no privilege attached to a report made to an employer by an employee who was present at the scene of an accident, if the report is made at, or about, the time of the accident. This is so even though it may be very likely that litigation will result and where the accident has been reported along with a list of potential witnesses. As Lord Johnston explained[69]:

"I can conceive that injustice might be done if, in a case like this, defenders were to be allowed to secure the monopoly of obtaining the names of persons present and therefore witnesses of the accident, names which in many cases—e.g. in the present, where the pursuer was rendered insensible—their opponent could not get unless the persons themselves came forward, possibly at some interval, and said they had been present."

This exception to the general rule can also be justified by the principle of contemporaneity similar to the underlying rationale for admitting *de recenti* statements:

"[I]f such a report is made as part of routine duty, and as a record of the reporter's immediate reaction before he has had the time, opportunity or temptation to indulge in too much reflection, it may well contain an unvarnished account of what happened and consequently be of value in the subsequent proceedings as a touchstone of truth."[70]

---

[67] *Johnstone v National Coal Board*, 1968 S.C. 128 at 133, quoting Lord Walker in *Young v N.C.B.*, 1957 S.L.T 266 at 268 and adopted in *More v Brown & Root Wimpey Highland Fabricators Ltd*, 1983 S.L.T. 669 at 670 where the privilege operated to prevent the pursuer recovering photographs taken by the defenders' safety officer shortly after the accident. See too *Anderson v St Andrews Ambulance Association*, 1942 S.C. 555 at 557; and *Hepburn v Scottish Power*, 1997 S.C. 80.

[68] *Hunter v Douglas Reyburn & Co. Ltd*, 1993 S.L.T 637.

[69] *MacPhee v Glasgow Corp*, 1915 S.C. 990 at 992.

[70] Lord Justice-Clerk Thomson in *Young v N.C.B.*, 1957 S.L.T 266 at 270. This rationale was also approved in *More v Brown & Root Wimpey Highland Fabricators Ltd*, 1983 S.L.T. 669, in which the exception was affirmed as still representing the law of Scotland.

Macphail criticised the exception as anomalous.[71]

13–44   A party who seeks to rely on one item in a course of correspondence, or other communications passing between themselves and another party, may thereby be taken to have waived any privilege which might otherwise be claimed in regard to the entire course of correspondence.[72] If a party were permitted to be selective about the item or items in regard to which they sought privilege there would be an obvious risk of distortion and an unfair advantage might result.[73]

COMMUNICATIONS IN AID OF SETTLEMENT OF LITIGATION

13–45 A general privilege exists in respect of communications passing between the parties to an action and their respective solicitors with a view to settling the action out of court. These communications may also be covered by the solicitor/client privilege. This is true even if the communication consists of, or includes, an admission. The privilege was said by Dickson to arise from "mutual concessions".[74] It is clearly in everyone's interests that extra-judicial settlements should be encouraged in this manner. The result of the existence of the privilege is that concessions may be offered by either or both parties to a dispute without fear that they may be used against them in court should the attempted settlement fail.[75]

13–46   The existence of the privilege explains the tendency of solicitors attempting to settle a dispute to head their correspondence "without prejudice", a phrase which in recent years has evolved into a much more substantial disclaimer intended to cloak the author(s) in privilege. The effect of the phrase has been considered in two Outer House decisions. In *Bell v Lothiansure Ltd*[76] Lord McCluskey held that the general rule applied and that nothing written or said under the cloak of "without prejudice" should be looked at unless both parties consented.

13–47   Privilege covers only those matters that are the subject of the negotiations in hand, and does not extend to any other matter appearing in the correspondence:

> "[T]he words 'without prejudice' inserted in correspondence may not cover with the cloak of confidentiality all portions of a particular letter which do not strictly relate to a proposed settlement ... Nevertheless,

---

[71] See Macphail, *Evidence*, para.18.26. A proposal to abolish this exception was, however, rejected by the Scottish Law Commission (Memo No.46, para.S.26).

[72] *Wylie v Wylie*, 1967 S.L.T. (Notes) 9. The privilege waived was both solicitor/client and *post litem motam*.

[73] See *Marks & Spencer v British Gas Corporation (No.1)*, 1983 S.L.T. 196, in which the defenders were not allowed to waive confidentiality on part only of a report when this was not clearly severable from the rest of the report. In England there is recent authority that privilege may be claimed for part only of a document: *G.E. Capital Corporate Finance Group Ltd v Bankers Trust Co.* [1995] 2 All E.R. 993.

[74] See Dickson, *Evidence*, para.305.

[75] Both the Civil Evidence (Family Mediation) (Scotland) Act 1995 and the Industrial Tribunals Act 1996 grant privilege re certain statements made to mediators and ACAS officers, respectively.

[76] *Bell v Lothiansure Ltd*, 1990 S.L.T. 58.

they do cover actual negotiations and, in particular, negotiation figures for a settlement.".[77]

The privilege may be invoked by either party to the dispute, whether that party was the maker or the recipient of the communication.

In *Daks Simpson Group Plc v Kuiper*, Lord Sutherland,[78] in distinguishing **13–48** *Bell*, said that, "if offers, suggestions, concessions or whatever are made for the purposes of negotiating a settlement, these cannot be converted into admissions of fact". However, he went on to say that if someone made a clear and unequivocal admission or statement of fact, then "I see no objection in principle to a clear admission being used in subsequent proceedings".[79] Both this case and *Gordon v East Kilbride Development Corporation*[80] suggest a fairly strict approach will be taken to the application of the privilege. In *Gordon* Lord Caplan observed that the privilege should only apply "where the communication in question is clearly eligible for it".[81]

The phrase "without prejudice" may not, in any event, cover the entire **13–49** correspondence between the parties if such correspondence shows that one of the parties was prepared to settle on terms which have subsequently been awarded by the court. In such circumstances Macphail has argued that fact should be disclosed to the court when determining expenses.[82] The aim of disclosure would be to focus the parties' minds and encourage settlement of the action.

FAMILY MEDIATION

A particular statutory privilege arises in certain family proceedings where **13–50** mediation has taken place. Section 1(1) of the Civil Evidence (Family Mediation) (Scotland) Act 1995 accords a broad privilege to "what occurred during family mediation". The ethos of the Act is to encourage a frank exchange of views in mediation without concern that anything revealed can be used subsequently in court proceedings. Various exceptions are set out in s.2.

OTHER CLAIMS TO PRIVILEGE

There are many other professional relationships whose communications are **13–51** perceived as "confidential", but that does not mean they will give rise to any rule of privilege. Such communications include those between doctors and their patients, counsellors and psychotherapists,[83] accountants or financial advisers and their clients. However, none of these relationships gives rise to

---

[77] *Ware v Edinburgh District Council*, 1976 S.L.T. (Lands Tribunal) 21.
[78] *Daks Simpson Group Plc v Kuiper*, 1994 S.L.T. 689 and see *Richardson v Quercus*, 1999 S.L.T. 596.
[79] *Ware v Edinburgh District Council*, 1976 S.L.T. (Lands Tr) 21 at 24.
[80] *Gordon v East Kilbride Development Corporation*, 1995 S.L.T. 62.
[81] *Gordon v East Kilbride Development Corporation*, 1995 S.L.T. 62 at 692 at 64C.
[82] See Macphail, *Evidence*, para.18.28.
[83] Though the Supreme Court of the United States has recognised confidential communications between clients and psychotherapists as privileged: *Jaffee v Redmond*, 116 S Ct 1923.

a claim for privileged status in a court of law. With a few rare additions,[84] the Scottish courts recognise only those privileged communications already discussed in this chapter. Two other areas worth examining where claims of privilege may been proposed but not accepted, are journalists and clergy.

Journalists

13–52   Journalists frequently rely on unidentified sources to provide "scoops", whistle-blowing revelations or even prosaic reportage. Understandably, they wish to protect their sources, not least in the interests of future goodwill and information flow. The legal position of a journalist who is called as a witness is that they may remain silent until ordered by the court to speak. Thereafter, they must either disclose the communication or face a charge of contempt of court. This is so even though the breach of confidence may thereby expose the witness to civil legal action for breach of confidence.

13–53   The consequence of a refusal to disclose a confidential source was apparent in *HM Advocate v Airs*,[85] where the court fined a journalist working for the *Daily Record* £500 for contempt of court when he refused to disclose details of a conversation he had allegedly had with one of the accused in the so-called Tartan Army trial. It was held that, except in the rare instance in which a judge may excuse a witness from answering on the ground of conscience (unlikely to occur when the evidence is highly material to the case), no one could be excused from the duty to answer a competent and relevant question. In the words of Lord Justice-General Emslie[86]:

> "Now that all possible causes of misapprehension have been dispelled, any witness, including any journalist witness, who declines to answer a competent and relevant question in court must realise that he will be in contempt and be liable to incur severe punishment."

With the advent of the Human Rights Act 1998 this view may have to be tempered in future cases where journalists claim a privilege. In 1995 the European Court of Human Rights found the United Kingdom to be in breach of the Human Rights Convention for imposing a fine on a journalist who refused to reveal his source of information.[87] The English courts deal with claims of privilege from journalists on a regular basis and there is a limited privilege offered to journalists (applicable to Scotland) through s.10 of the Contempt of Court Act 1981.[88]

13–54   The possible consequence of a civil claim for breach of confidence arose in *Santa Fe International Corp. v Napier Shipping S.A.*[89] In this case the pursuers were suing for alleged infringement of a patent and called for recovery of certain documents which had passed between the defenders and third parties. The defenders refused, on the ground that to do so would reveal

---

[84]   e.g. the exceptions set out in the Bankers' Books Evidence Act 1879.

[85]   *HM Advocate v Airs*, 1975 S.L.T. 177.

[86]   *HM Advocate v Airs*, 1975 S.L.T. 177at 181.

[87]   The case of the journalist Bill Godwin, reported in *The Scotsman,* March 28, 1995.

[88]   See *John v Express Newspapers* [2000] 1 W.L.R. 1931 and *R. v Central Criminal Court, Ex p. Bright* [2001] 1 W.L.R. 662 for insight into the English approach to this issue. See, too, Cross and Tapper, *Evidence*, pp.465–467.

[89]   *Santa Fe International Corp. v Napier Shipping S.A*, 1985 S.L.T. 430.

certain technical information which they were bound by contract with those third parties not to reveal. They argued that disclosure would render them liable to an action for breach of contract. In holding that the defender must yield up the documents, it was emphasised by the court that except in "special circumstances" private promises of confidentiality must yield to the public interest in justice and truth.[90]

Clergy and penitent

No privilege attaches to information communicated in a confessional setting **13–55** between clergy or equivalent spiritual mentors and penitents. Although a few instances have been cited in the literature,[91] there is no established rule recognising confessional-type communications. The Scottish Law Commission has suggested that each case be considered on its merits but declined to recommend that the privilege be formally recognised through the exercise of a general judicial discretion to uphold confidences except where the interests of justice dictate otherwise.[92]

Public Interest Immunity

In an adversarial system founded upon oral testimony it is logical that there **13–56** are few exceptions to the general rule that a witness need not have to disclose information. One such exception, noted earlier, is the privilege occasionally accorded to information that need not be revealed if a wider public interest prevails over individual rights to have such information disclosed. Historically, this type of situation was known as Crown privilege when it was a rule most often invoked by Ministers on behalf of Her Majesty's Government. Today it is known as public interest immunity ("PII") and it extends beyond government departments to encompass local authorities, police authorities and similar pubic bodies. In PII cases the person or body holding confidential information may claim an immunity against disclosing it in a court of law. The underlying rationale of the immunity is that in some circumstances private justice should be subordinated to national security interests, or to the proper functioning of the State. The appropriate procedure is for the public officer responsible for authorising or withholding disclosure to grant a certificate, or other document, which informs the court of the general ground upon which immunity is being claimed.

The development of the law across the United Kingdom has been uneven. **13–57** In the English case *Duncan v Cammell Laird & Co. Ltd*,[93] which occurred during the Second World War, the Minister of Defence successfully resisted the production of plans of a British submarine in an action for damages by the relatives of those who had died in it. The court agreed that the Minister who claimed Crown privilege had ultimate discretion and his certificate was conclusive. However, this approach was not adopted unequivocally as part of the law of Scotland. In *Glasgow Corporation v Central Land Board*[94] the

---

[90] *Santa Fe International Corp. v Napier Shipping S.A*, 1985 S.L.T. 430 per Lord Hunter at 432.
[91] Macphail, *Evidence*, paras 18.38 and 18.39.
[92] Memo No.46, para.S.32.
[93] *Duncan v Cammell Laird & Co. Ltd* [1942] A.C. 624.
[94] *Glasgow Corporation v Central Land Board*, 1965 S.C. (H.L.) 1.

House of Lords held that the Scottish courts have the power to go behind a ministerial certificate and decide for themselves whether or not a particular item of evidence is deserving of immunity, after weighing private interests against public ones. In *Conway v Rimmer*[95] the House of Lords agreed that the correct approach was for the court—not a Minister—to evaluate the competing public interests involved. These twin interests are, first, the public interest in refusing to disclose documents in order to prevent harm to the national interest or to the proper functioning of the public service and, second, the public interest in producing the documents to enable the proper administration of justice.

13–58   The effect of *Conway* was to bring the law of England into harmony with that of Scotland. English authority since 1968 has therefore possessed additional weight in Scotland.[96] However, as the Scottish Law Commission has observed, "[a]lthough this power to overrule ministerial directions is now recognised in both jurisdictions, courts on both sides of the Border have been slow to exercise it".[97]

13–59   There are two types of case in which the immunity may be claimed. The first arises when the document or information called for contains items which it is believed should be withheld (the so called "contents" cases). The second arises where the document itself, while perhaps not containing anything immediately sensitive, belongs to a class of documents which is normally withheld (the "class" cases). Both are, however, subject to the same tests and in recent years there has been an expansion in the type of document or other information that may be subject to the immunity. There is also authority to support the position that "the categories of public interest are not closed and must alter from time to time whether by restriction or extension as social conditions and social legislation develop".[98]

13–60   In *D v N.S.P.C.C.* immunity was successfully sought against disclosing the identity of the person who had made a complaint to the N.S.P.C.C. concerning D's ill-treatment of his child. A similar ruling was made in *Rogers v Secretary of State for Home Dept*[99] in which the pursuer sought damages for defamation in respect of a report on him sent by the police to the Gaming Board. The court refused to order the disclosure of the report on the ground that its production might jeopardise the working of the public service.

13–61   The distinction between the categories of classes and contents is becoming of less significance. The approach adopted currently in England is that each application for immunity should be determined on its merits and not depending on whether it belongs to a particular class of documents.[100] Although there is little authority in Scotland, in *Strathclyde Regional Council v B*[101] a local authority was unsuccessful in its claim to the immunity in relation to a social work file. The success of a claim for privilege will depend largely upon the extent to which the party seeking disclosure can

---

[95] In *Conway v Rimmer* [1968] A.C. 910 at 990, in which the English authorities are extensively reviewed.

[96] See Macphail, *Evidence*, para.18.54.

[97] *Law of Evidence*, Memo No.46, S.39.

[98] *D. v N.S.P.C.C* [1978] A.C. 171 at 230.

[99] *D. v N.S.P.C.C* [1973] A.C. 388.

[100] *R. v Chief Constable of West Midlands, Ex p. Wiley* [1995] 1 A.C. 274.

[101] Unreported, per Macphail, *Evidence*, para.18.54C.

show that the information required is vital to the case. The stronger the private interest in disclosure, the stronger must be the public interest against it. In *Park v Tayside Regional Council*[102] a foster mother, who claimed she had contracted hepatitis B from a child she had fostered, sought to recover hospital and social work records relating to the child. Noting that there had been no case in Scotland in which public interest privilege had been extended beyond departments of national government or of the Lord Advocate, Lord Sutherland went on to say that in this case, "the public interest in seeing justice done far outweighed the public interest in favour of confidentiality".[103]

The nature of the remedy sought, and the moral worthiness of the party **13–62** seeking disclosure, may also have a bearing on the outcome.[104] In particular, courts in recent years have been reluctant to go behind the certificate claiming immunity in cases in which a former accused person or suspect is seeking a civil remedy against a police authority. Thus, in *Friel, Petitioner*[105] the "victim" of a lawful, but fruitless, police search for stolen goods tried to bring a civil action against the person who had informed on him to the police. To do this Friel required to know the identity of the informant and he petitioned the court for an order for recovery of the relevant police records. This was opposed by the Chief Constable and the Lord Advocate on the ground that the document in question fell within a class of documents which must be withheld in the interests of crime detection. Against this it was argued that if such claims were upheld, members of the public in Friel's position would find themselves denied access to the courts. It was held that in such cases the Lord Advocate's objection to disclosure could only be overridden by another, more pressing public interest, e.g. the interests of justice to the individual. Denying the petitioner the possibility of bringing a civil action for malicious slander was not considered to outweigh the general public interest in law enforcement.

Friel was followed in *P. Cannon (Garages) Ltd v L.A.*[106] when the court **13–63** refused to order the production of a blood sample taken from an alleged drunken motorist, or of his relevant certificates, for use in a civil action by the owner of a car damaged in the resulting accident. Here again it was held that the private interest involved did not generate sufficient public interest to outweigh the public interest in the administration of criminal justice.[107]

The immunity applies in both civil and criminal cases, but in the latter the **13–64** interests of justice to the individual accused must weigh heavily against any routine denial of information simply because that information belongs in a class which is normally immune. For example, *Rogers v Secretary of State*

---

[102] *Park v Tayside Regional Council*, 1989 S.L.T. 345.
[103] *Park v Tayside Regional Council*, 1989 S.L.T. 345 at 348D.
[104] Compare, e.g. *Norwich Pharmacal Co. v Customs and Excise Commrs* [1974] A.C. 133 with *Alfred Crompton Amusement Machines Ltd v Customs and Excise Commrs* [1974] A.C. 405, the difference between which appears to have been the fact that in the first case, the party whose identity would have been revealed by disclosure was himself a wrongdoer, while in the second he was not.
[105] *Friel, Petitioner*, 1981 S.L.T. 113, also reported sub. nom. *Friel v Chief Constable of Strathclyde*, 1981 S.C. 1.
[106] *P. Cannon (Garages) Ltd v L.A.*, 1983 S.L.T. 50.
[107] See too *Alexander v Palombo*, 1984 S.L.T 3.32.

for Home Department[108] observed obiter that the police would not be entitled to protect the identity of an informer when his or her identification might establish the innocence of an accused. A conviction in these circumstances, i.e. the refusal of a police officer to disclose the identity of an informer, was quashed in *Thomson v Neilson*.[109]

13–65   The interests of justice to the individual also played a prominent role in the *Matrix Churchill* trial mentioned in Ch.1. The defendants were prosecuted in 1992 for alleged breaches of export regulations during the Iran/Iraq war which occurred in the 1980. If convicted they would almost certainly have been imprisoned. Their defence was that the relevant government departments were well aware of their activities and in effect condoned them as two of the defendants who worked for the export company were also agents for MI5 and MI6. The trial collapsed after the judge's partial quashing of the public interest immunity certificates claimed by various government ministers and after one of the ministers confirmed under cross-examination the accuracy of the defendants' claims.[110] In cases such as these, there are obviously competing interests between the needs of the individual and the wider interests of the state. Challenges under the public interest immunity regime will now make greater use of ECHR case law under art.6, though this is an area where the ECtHR would likely give a significant margin of appreciation to the protection of State interests.[111] The constitutional role of the Lord Advocate was discussed in *Al Megrahi v HM Advocate*[112] where it was acknowledged that since devolution in 1998, the Lord Advocate's authority is confined to public interest immunity claims in Scottish criminal proceedings, and he or she has no authority outside Scotland, Therefore, where issues concern UK interests, the appropriate UK government minister will, therefore, have responsibility for certifying the wider UK public interest claims for immunity.

[108] 1973 A.C. 388.
[109] *Thomson v Neilson* (1900) 3 F. (J.) 3.
[110] See I. Leigh, "Matrix Churchill, Supergun and the Scott Inquiry" (1993) *Public Law*, 630 and also the series of articles after the publication of Sir Richard Scott's *Report into the arms to Iraq affair* (1996) *Public Law* 357–527.
[111] *Edwards v UK*, 1993 T.L.R. 20 and *Rowe and Davis v UK*, 2000 T.L.R. 147.
[112] *Al Megrahi v HM Advocate*, 2008 S.L.T. 333. See F. Davidson, "Public interest immunity: *Al Megrahi v HM Advocate*" (2008) Edin. L.R. 472.

Chapter 14

JUDICIAL NOTICE

INTRODUCTION

Judicial notice is one of three forms of evidence without proof considered in **14–01** this and the following chapter. In the adversarial process a court cannot generally find as a fact something which has not yet been proven. However, there are important exceptions to this rule, namely, the doctrine of judicial notice; judicial admissions and agreements; and the principle of res judicata. Each of these rules serves to expedite the process of proof as each rule sets out criteria which, if met, obviate the need for witnesses to be called.

JUDICIAL NOTICE

According to Cross and Tapper,[1] "[w]hen a court takes judicial notice of a **14–02** fact ... it declares that it will find that the fact exists, or direct the jury to do so, although the existence of the fact has not been established by evidence". Judicial notice is permissible whenever the points in issue "are matters which can be immediately ascertained from sources of indisputable accuracy, or which are so notorious as to be indisputable".[2] This sets up two categories of judicial knowledge: that which is "immediately ascertainable"; and that which is so well-known as to be "indisputable". These are sometimes described, respectively, as judicial notice after inquiry and judicial notice without inquiry. These are dealt with in turn.

JUDICIAL NOTICE AFTER ENQUIRY

When a matter is noted *after* judicial inquiry, it is one in which a judge has **14–03** referred to some other source for verification of what is argued to be within judicial knowledge. Certain information may be incontrovertible, but not committed to memory. Thus, while a judge is presumed to "know" the Scots law on any matter which may be placed before the court, that does not preclude the judge consulting authoritative books on the subject, or perusing case reports or statutes. A judge may not of course simply read a textbook and judicially note its findings.[3] When judicial notice is taken after inquiry, the court is merely refreshing its memory on some point which it is

---

[1] Cross and Tapper, *Evidence*, 11th edn, p.67. This definition is an equally valid description of the process under Scots law. The terminology, also used under Scots law, whereby a fact that is within judicial knowledge is judicially noted.
[2] Walker and Walker, *Evidence*, 3rd edn, para.11.6.1.
[3] *Davie v Magistrates of Edinburgh*, 1953 S.C. 34.

deemed to know anyway. The position is different if the subject is the province of a specialist and is contested, since, as indicated above, the more appropriate course is to hear expert testimony and receive it as oral evidence.[4]

14–04   Given that there is a dividing line between being reminded of the obvious, and taking unchallenged expert opinion as if it were fact, which books may the courts use in order to assist them in the pursuit of judicial knowledge? It is now well established that they may employ a dictionary, as in *Inland Revenue Commrs v Russell*[5] where, by reference to the *Oxford Dictionary*, the Court of Session satisfied itself that a person could be the "stepchild" of another for the purposes of the Finance Acts, even though that person's natural parents were still alive. No doubt other unimpeachable sources of pure reference may also be employed without any great danger, for example ordnance survey maps for measurements of distance, and marine charts for ocean depths. However, although a text may be commonly regarded as a reference book, that does not necessarily raise its contents to the status of being within judicial knowledge. For example, the courts have held that the fact that there is a Highway Code is within judicial knowledge, but the stopping distances given in it are not and cannot be referred to without leading evidence.[6] The geography of Great Britain is considered to be within judicial knowledge, and thus waters "adjacent to Scotland" discernible in a prosecution concerning unlawful fishing.[7]

14–05   Judges may still on occasion consider it appropriate to form their own opinions, for example in regard to the normal, or likely, period of human gestation. In *Preston-Jones v Preston-Jones*[8] Lord Normand observed:

> "If the only period to be considered were the period of gestation, I have myself no doubt that ordinary men and women would unhesitatingly say that a 360-days gestation is beyond the limits of what is possible, and a court of law would so decide without evidence. So far at least judicial knowledge may be allowed to reach."

The only matters which should be judicially noted, even after inquiry, are undisputed items of common knowledge. Care should therefore be taken before assuming that any standard work of reference necessarily constitutes "common knowledge" and can substitute for expert testimony. With this caveat, some of the items that are most frequently judicially noted after inquiry are considered.

Acts of Parliament

14–06 In terms of s.3 of the Interpretation Act 1978, the provisions of Acts of Parliament need not be proved in court, but may be judicially noted. It provides "[e]very Act is a public Act to be judicially noticed as such, unless

---

[4] *McTear v Imperial Tobacco Ltd*, 2005 2 S.C. 1, discussed in Ch.4.
[5] 1955 S.C. 237. See also *Edinburgh Corporation v Lord Advocate*, 1923 S.C. 112.
[6] *Cavin v Kinnaird*, 1994 S.L.T. 111. See also Macphail, *Evidence*, Ch.11.35A.
[7] *Enriquez v Urquhart*, 2001 S.L.T. 1320.
[8] [1951] A.C. 391 at 46. But see *Williamson v McLelland*, 1913 S.C. 678, in which the court ignored the expert medical evidence in order to rule that a child born to a woman only 306 days after intercourse with the pursuer could not be his.

the contrary is expressly provided by the Act". A similar provision operates for the Acts of the Scottish Parliament.[9] By virtue of the decision in *Pepper v Hart*,[10] the courts are permitted to examine *Hansard* and the Official Report,[11] or the relevant debates where the construction of a statute is ambiguous or obscure or the literal meaning would lead to an absurdity. In addition, since 1999, all public Acts are accompanied by a set of Explanatory Notes. Although these Notes are not authoritative, they may well be useful in legal argument as an aid to identifying what the Government intended when promoting the Bill.[12]

Statutory Instruments

There is authority for the practice of treating a statutory instrument[13] as the equivalent of an Act of Parliament and therefore within judicial knowledge,[14] but Macphail has argued that the authority for such an assumption is challengeable and suggested that the position should be clarified by statute.[15] Where delegated legislation (which includes statutory instruments) is relied upon in any prosecution there is no ambiguity. Section 279A(3) of the Criminal Procedure (Scotland) Act 1995 provides that if any "order by any of the departments of state or government or any local authority or public body made under powers conferred by any statute, a print or copy of any such order is produced, it is to be admitted as evidence without the need for any other proof". **14–07**

Section 279A(3) does not *require* the order to be produced—a party may choose to rely upon the common law authorities. In terms of s.279A(4), a party may challenge any such order on the grounds that it was made ultra vires of the authority that made it, or on any other competent ground. **14–08**

What constitutes Scots law in relation to judicial knowledge?

Judges, sheriffs and stipendiary magistrates of the Scottish courts must take judicial notice of all Scots law, from whatever source.[16] This includes the judgments of the UK Supreme Court and its predecessor the House of **14–09**

---

[9] Scotland Act 1998, s.28(6).

[10] *Pepper v Hart* [1993] A.C. 593.

[11] The Scottish Parliament's record of proceedings.

[12] According to the website *http://www.opsi.gov.uk/acts.htm* [accessed July 12, 2013], "the purpose of these Explanatory Notes is to make the Act of Parliament accessible to readers who are not legally qualified and who have no specialised knowledge of the matters dealt with. They are intended to allow the reader to grasp what the Act sets out to achieve and place its effect in context." The Explanatory Notes are invaluable and often provide information that is not apparent from the statute alone.

[13] Which term has since 1948 included Orders in Council (Statutory Instruments Act 1946, s.1(1)) and Acts of Sederunt and Adjournal (Statutory Instruments Act 1946, s.1(2)). Acts of Sederunt and Adjournal passed prior to that date also appear to have had statutory effect, first under the Act 1540, c.10, and then under the Rules Publication Act 1893, s.4.

[14] *Sharp v Leith* (1892) 20 R. (J.) 12; and *Hutchison v Stevenson* (1902) 4 F. (J.) 69.

[15] *Evidence*, Ch.11.02. See too, Walker and Walker, *Evidence*, 3rd edn, para.19.8.1.

[16] Walker and Walker, *Evidence*, 3rd edn, at para.11.7.2, "Scots law, including Scottish judicial decisions in the House of Lords and the lower courts, and the practice and procedure of the Scottish courts, are within judicial knowledge, and Evidence regarding these matters is excluded". See also Macphail, *Evidence*, Ch.2.02.

Lords,[17] not only on points of Scots law for which it is the Supreme Court in civil matters, but also on points from other jurisdictions that are the same as Scots law. Since the enactment of the Scotland Act 1998 there was a final right of appeal from the High Court of Justiciary in Edinburgh to the Judicial Committee of the Privy Council whose decisions were binding in all legal proceedings other than those before the Judicial Committee itself.

14–10   Since that Act came into force the Scottish courts have had to take account of the judgments of the European Court of Human Rights on matters relating to the interpretation of the European Convention on Human Rights. From the implementation in 1999 of the devolution arrangements under the Scotland Act 1998, acts of the Scottish Government (successor to the Scottish Executive) and legislation from the Scottish Parliament have been subject to legal challenge on the basis that they are incompatible with Convention rights. From October 2, 2000 the Human Rights Act has had wider application and all public authorities, including the courts themselves, are bound to give effect to the Convention rights embodied in the Act, whether the legal context involves legislation emanating from Westminster or Holyrood, or the common law.

14–11   It is the duty of all those who appear in the courts to bring to the courts' attention *all* the relevant law on the matter in hand, whether it is favourable to their case or not. The judgment of the House of Lords in *Glebe Sugar Refining Corporation v Greenock Harbour Trustees*[18] reinforced this duty:

> "It is not, of course, in cases of complication possible for their Lordships to be aware of all the authorities, statutory or otherwise which may be relevant to the issues which in the particular case require decision. Their Lordships are therefore very much in the hands of counsel, and those who instruct counsel, in these matters, and this House expects, and indeed insists, that authorities which bear one way or the other upon matters under debate shall be brought to the attention of their Lordships by those who are aware of these authorities. This observation is quite irrespective of whether or not the particular authority assists the party which is so aware of it."

EU law

14–12   By virtue of the European Communities Act 1972, s.2(1) the Scottish courts must take notice of legislation emanating from the European Community, and European Union. Section 3(1) of the 1972 Act requires all Scottish courts to treat questions of community law as questions of law, and not questions of fact which require to be proved as items of foreign law (see below). Section 3(2) also requires such courts to take judicial notice "of the

---

[17] For the precise historical status of the House of Lords in this context, see *Trs of Orr-Ewing v Orr-Ewing* (1884) 11 R. 600, in which it was also established that the Scots courts must defer to rulings of the House in English or Irish cases in which the point of law involved is analogous to the law of Scotland. The same applies to the rulings of the Judicial Committee of the Privy Council of a similar nature.

[18] 1921 S.C. (H.L.) 72 per the Lord Chancellor, Lord Birkenhead at 73–74.

Treaties, of the Official Journal of the Communities and of any decision of, or expression of opinion by, the European Court".[19]

The Civil Jurisdiction and Judgments Act 1982 requires the courts to take **14–13** judicial notice of the EC Convention which gave rise to that Act, which has the force of law in Scotland.[20] A similar provision is laid down in s.3(2) for decisions of the European Court regarding the Conventions listed in s.1(1) of the Act.

Foreign law

Foreign law, i.e. the law of any jurisdiction outwith Scotland, including **14–14** English law, is regarded in the Scots courts as a question of *fact* to be proved like any other.[21] There is a rebuttable presumption of law to the effect that foreign law[22] is the same as Scots law on any given point. The burden of proving that the foreign law is in fact different rests upon the party relying on that assertion.[23] The same party must also prove what that law is and must do so by means of evidence.[24] A variety of methods is available.[25] Customary international law is not foreign law, but is part of the law of Scotland.[26]

There are some exceptions to this general rule that foreign law has to be **14–15** proved.

(1) The UK Supreme Court in civil cases is the highest Scottish court[27] **14–16** and it may judicially note the laws of all the jurisdictions that send it appeals.[28] When hearing a Scottish appeal it is also competent for the Supreme Court to note judicially and incorporate in its judgment a point of English law that does not conflict with Scots law.

(2) Scottish courts may be required by a statute to take judicial notice of **14–17** foreign law, mainly English. Thus, in *Commrs for the Special Purposes of the Income Tax v Pemsel*[29] it was held that when dealing with income tax cases,

---

[19] subs.(2). Even those instruments not published in the Official Journal may be proved, per subss.(3), (4) and (5), by production of a certified true copy.

[20] s.2(1).

[21] *Duffes v Duffes*, 1971 S.L.T. Notes 83.

[22] *Trs of Orr-Ewing v Orr-Ewing*, (1884) 11 R. 600.

[23] P. Beaumont and P. McEleavy, *Anton's Private International Law*, 3rd edn (Edinburgh: SULI/W. Green, 2011) p.1228 para.27.171; see also *Bonnor v Balfour Kilpatrick Ltd*, 1974 S.C. 223 and *Emerald Stainless Steel Ltd v South Side Distribution Ltd*, 1982 S.C. 61.

[24] P. Beaumont and P. McEleavy, *Anton's Private International Law*, 3rd edn (Edinburgh: SULI/W. Green, 2011), para.27.173 "[t]he rule that foreign law must be proved by evidence is always applicable in the Scottish courts". Since any point of law discovered is for the purposes of that case a fact, it may not be founded on as a precedent for any future action: see *Killen v Killen*, 1981 S.L.T. (Sh. Ct) 77. Where the court merely wishes to make use of a foreign jurisdiction's law and practice to aid in the construction of a contract governed by the provisions of a European directive, proof of that foreign law by expert evidence is not necessary: see *Roy v M. R. Pearlman Ltd*, 1999 S.C. 459.

[25] e.g. remit of consent to a foreign lawyer, the hearing of expert testimony, or a stated case to a Dominions court.

[26] *Lord Advocate's Reference (No.1 of 2000)*, 2001 J.C. 143 at para.23 per Lord Prosser.

[27] The highest court since October 1, 2009 when it assumed the judicial authority previously afforded the House of Lords. See the Constitutional Reform Act 2005.

[28] *Elliot v Joicey*, 1935 S.C. (H.L.) 57.

[29] [1891] A.C. 531.

the Scottish courts are obliged to apply the English law of charities.[30] A final illustration—when sitting in their capacity as judges in the Courts-Martial Appeal Court, Scottish judges are required to adopt the criminal law and procedure of England, as well as its laws of evidence.[31]

The limits of judicial knowledge

14–18 Judicial knowledge does not include a judge's own personal experience of a particular matter where direct evidence is available which might have a bearing on the subject. Judicial notice is restricted to matters that are beyond dispute and not those that are in issue between the parties. The function of judicial knowledge is only to note the existence of a matter beyond dispute, not to usurp the function of evidence on a contested matter.

14–19 Judges should not rely upon their own knowledge[32] or substitute it for that of an expert.[33] In *Kennedy and Others v Smith*[34] it was held that a judge might not form his own unaided opinion of the likely effect of one and a half pints of lager on a man who was not a regular drinker and who had been drinking on an empty stomach. In *Davie v Magistrates of Edinburgh*[35] an expert witness gave evidence on the effect of shock waves in blasting operations and made reference to a section of a pamphlet that he claimed supported his view. The Lord Ordinary rejected the expert testimony, and in doing so adopted other parts of the same pamphlet to which the expert had not referred. In disapproving this course of action, the Court of Session ruled that,[36] "the Court cannot ... rely upon such works for the purpose of displacing or criticising the witness's testimony".

14–20 Judges have sometimes attracted criticism by adopting the role of a witness, e.g. examining productions or scenes of incidents for themselves and forming their own conclusions. While a court may "take a view" of something in order more easily to understand the evidence which they are about to hear, it is not competent for this to occur independently of such evidence. Otherwise, in effect the court is simply substituting its own view for that of the witness.[37]

14–21 Finally, a matter which may be judicially noted without difficulty in a particular locality, or at a particular time, may require further inquiry, or even expert testimony, in a different locality or only a few years later. For example, in *Oliver v Hislop*[38] the accused was charged with an offence under a local statute which made it an offence to be caught salmon fishing by

---

[30] Similarly in *Scottish Burial Reform Society v Glasgow Corporation*, 1967 S.C. (H.L.) 116, when dealing with a claim for rate exemption under the 1962 Act, Lord Reid observed (at 122) of the effect of s.4: "It is well settled that that means that we have to apply the English law of charities". These provisions are unaffected by the Charities and Trustee Investment (Scotland) Act 2005.

[31] See Courts-Martial (Appeals) Act 1968, s.2(1)(b) which provides for the appointment of Scottish judges to sit in such appeals. And, see *Hendry*, 1955 S.L.T. (Notes) 66.

[32] *Black v Ruxton*, 1998 S.L.T. 1282.

[33] *Gibb v Edinburgh and District Tramways*, 1912 S.C. 580 at 583; *Herkes v Dickie*, 1958 J.C. 51; *Knox v Lockart*, 1985 S.L.T. 248; and *Gray v HM Advocate*, 1 2005 J.C. 233 at para.28 per Lord Eassie.

[34] 1976 S.L.T. 110.

[35] *Davie v Magistrates of Edinburgh*, 1953 S.C. 34.

[36] *Davie v Magistrates of Edinburgh*, 1953 S.C. 34 at 41.

[37] See e.g. *Hattie v Leitch* (1889) 16 R. 1128 and *McCann v Adair*, 1951 J.C. 127.

[38] 1946 J.C. 20.

means of a "cleek". The sheriff felt he could not note judicially what a cleek was, as no evidence was led on that point, nor on whether it was indeed a cleek that had been found in the accused's possession. Lord Justice-Clerk Cooper noted that a Border sheriff ought not to need evidence "as to the meaning of the terms which have been employed in the statutory regulation of the river for a period of close on ninety years".[39]

JUDICIAL NOTICE WITHOUT ENQUIRY

The sort of facts that the courts will judicially note without inquiry include **14–22** significant calendar dates, historic events, matters of geography, economics and current affairs. The courts may take judicial notice of matters of contemporary custom[40] and professional, economic and commercial practice.[41] They have noted the fact that witnesses in criminal trials are often subject to intimidation,[42] that the state makes financial provision for the maintenance of adults with disabilities,[43] that children may be oblivious to, and need protection from, dangers which would be apparent to adults.[44]

In *Doyle v Ruxton*[45] an appeal based on a conviction of the offence of **14–23** liquor trafficking, the appellant challenged the sheriff's claim of judicial knowledge that brands of liquor, including McEwan's Export, Guinness, and Carlsberg Special Brew, were of sufficient alcoholic strength to require a licence. The appellant argued that expert evidence should have been led as to the nature of the contents of the bottles and cans. In dismissing the appeal the court noted the widespread media advertising of such products and commented, "we found the argument that judicial knowledge did not extend to these matters somewhat unattractive and unrealistic".[46] Where information is broadly within the public domain, it can reasonably be assumed to be within judicial knowledge. Thus, in *Birse v HM Advocate*[47] the appeal court observed, "[f]or many years now it has been common knowledge, even among Judges, that the smoking of cannabis can produce an unusual and distinctive smell".

When a court applies the doctrine of judicial notice the matters in ques- **14–24** tion are said to be within judicial knowledge. Sometimes solicitors or counsel invite the court to take judicial notice of certain matters but in very obvious situations, e.g. widely accepted political or historical facts, the judge may simply take note of these facts when assessing evidence of which they are part and not even formally note that this is what has been done.

The concept of judicial notice has to be seen in the broader context of the **14–25** contingency of knowledge discussed in Ch.4. Knowledge is rarely a

---

[39] At 24.
[40] See, e.g. *Read v Bishop of Lincoln Read v Bishop of Lincoln* [1892] A.C. 644 per Lord Halsbury at 653; *MacCormick v Lord Advocate*, 1965 S.C. 396 per Lord Russell at 415;
[41] *Naismith v Assessor for Renfrewshire*, 1921 S.C. 615 at 624; *Taylor v Wylie & Lochhead*, 1912 S.C. 978 at 983; *Lord Advocate's Reference No.1 of 1992*, 1992 S.L.T. 1010.
[42] *Manson v HM Advocate*, 1951 J.C. 49 at 52.
[43] *McLelland v Greater Glasgow Health Board*, 1999 S.C. 305.
[44] *Taylor v Glasgow Corporation*, 1922 S.C. (H.L.) 1.
[45] 1999 S.L.T. 487.
[46] *Doyle v Ruxton*, 1999 S.L.T. 487 at 490 F–G.
[47] 2000 J.C. 503 at para.8.

permanent state of affairs so cannot necessarily create precedents. What constitutes a fact today and is recognised as knowledge, may be replaced tomorrow by understandings based upon new data and research findings. While some areas are probably more stable than others—for example, maths, archaeology and mediaeval literature—no area is immune from challenge. In contemporary times even areas of knowledge which were once considered settled, such as the Darwinian theories of the origin of the species, have been attacked as false by proponents of creationism and intelligent design. Some disciplines are, however, clearly more likely to be in a constant state of development, none more so than medicine, bio-technology, environmental sciences and forensic science.[48]

14–26   No discipline can claim to be based upon absolutely fixed knowledge, or knowledge that is capable of only one interpretation. In terms of the law of evidence, where parties are in agreement about facts the position is straightforward. However, if grounds exist for contesting a fact, it is unlikely to be appropriate to invoke the doctrine of judicial notice. Instead, the parties will usually turn to expert evidence to support their arguments.

---

[48] See LJ Gage's comments about the contingent state of medical and scientific knowledge in *Shaken Baby Appeals* [2005] EWCA Crim 1980 at para.270.

Chapter 15

JUDICIAL ADMISSIONS AND RES JUDICATA

INTRODUCTION

Judicial admissions and res judicata are two other forms of evidence without **15–01** proof. As with judicial notice discussed in Ch.14, the effect of judicial admissions is to relieve one or both parties of the need to lead any evidence on the fact or facts admitted. This helps to reduce delays in the process of proof and to focus attention on the issues in dispute. Judicial admissions must be taken subject to any explanations or qualifications which accompany them.

JUDICIAL ADMISSIONS AND AGREEMENTS

If one party in judicial proceedings makes formal admissions to averments **15–02** (i.e. claims) made by another party, then there is no need to lead evidence to prove these averments that would otherwise require proof before becoming a finding of fact. A matter which has been judicially admitted is one which is to be taken as proved just as if a witness had given unchallenged evidence on the point. Walker and Walker have explained[1] "judicial admissions are in themselves, and without anything more, conclusive against the party making them, for the purposes of the action in which they are made".

There are numerous specialised texts which discuss civil advocacy, **15–03** pleadings and procedure in greater detail, and these are recommended for further consultation.[2] The focus here is on some of the more relevant evidential aspects of pleadings. The rules of procedure are different for civil and criminal law and are considered in turn.

Judicial admissions in civil cases

Scots law has specific procedures for the form required of written pleadings **15–04** in civil proceedings.[3] There are detailed rules of procedure laid down for both the sheriff courts and the Court of Session. In the course of a civil action, there are basically three procedures in which a fact or set of facts may be judicially admitted by one of the parties: (i) in the closed record adjusted between the parties[4]; (ii) through an oral admission at the bar; and

---

[1] *Law of Evidence in Scotland*, para.48(a), quoting Stair, IV, xlv, 5 and Erskine, IV, ii, 33.
[2] For example, Maxwell, *Practice of the Court of Session*; Macphail, *Sheriff Court Practice*, 3rd edn; and McLaren, *Court of Session Practice*. Walker and Walker, *Evidence*, 3rd edn, Ch.11.
[3] For full details of the rules of procedure see *Parliament House Book* (Edinburgh: W. Green).
[4] i.e. the final set of written pleadings upon which parties proceed to proof.

(iii) in a minute of admissions. It is also possible a party may be implied to have admitted a fact, either by remaining silent when it is arguable that he or she should not have done, or by virtue of a partial averment in the written pleadings. The Scottish Civil Justice Council and Criminal Legal Assistance Act enacted in 2013 established a new body known as the Scottish Civil Justice Council with powers generally to keep the justice system under review and more specifically to review the civil practices and procedures in both the Court of Session and the sheriff court.[5] Modernisation of the pleading procedures is anticipated to satisfy the principles underpinning the new Council regarding fair, accessible and efficient access to justice,[6] with practice and procedure that is as clear and easy to understand as possible,[7]

(i) Admissions in the closed record

15–05 "The closing of the record marks the borderline between pleading and Proof."[8] The closed record is the final statement of the written pleadings of the parties of those matters which require to be litigated. The written pleadings will consist of a series of averments, i.e. claims, by each party which will be either admitted or denied by the other party. An averment has no factual significance unless and until it is proved, whereas, as already explained, an admission on record is equivalent to proof.[9] In other words, what party A chooses to concede in the closed record in response to averments from party B will be held as proved against A. However, what a party avers, with no admission from the other party, must be proved.[10]

15–06 The art of drafting pleadings demands skill and forethought. Solicitors and counsel must accurately identify the precise grounds of claim, as the closed record provides the basis for the evidence that can be led, though the court has discretion to permit the record to be amended in certain circumstances. If sufficient care in the drafting is not taken then a party may be held to have made an admission by implication—either by remaining silent when a denial was called for, or by making an ambiguous averment which is capable of being interpreted as consistent with an averment made by the other party. The dangers of the consequences of sloppy drafting are well-known,[11] and the courts vary in the strictness of their approach to "improperly drawn pleadings".[12]

(ii) Oral admissions at the bar

15–07 Counsel or solicitors frequently make admissions orally at the bar. Although such admissions are not as formal as those contained in the closed record, they have the same effect. The other party is therefore relieved of the

---

[5] s.2(1).

[6] s.2(3)(a).

[7] s.2(3)(b).

[8] Maxwell, *Practice of the Court of Session*, p.202.

[9] Lord Sorn in *Lee v NCB*, 1955 S.C. 151 at 160.

[10] See *Stewart v Glasgow Corporation*, 1958 S.C. 28.

[11] *Wilson v Clyde Rigging and Boiler Scaling*, 1959 S.C. 328 at 332. But see *Dobson v Colvilles Ltd*, 1958 S.L.T. (Notes) 30.

[12] *Lord Advocate v Gillespie*, 1969 S.L.T. (Sh. Ct) 10 at 12. See too *Ellon Castle Estates Co. v MacDonald*, 1975 S.L.T. (Notes) 66, followed in *EFT Finance Ltd v Hawkins*, 1994 S.L.T. 902.

duty of proving the point and the fact admitted finds its way into the formal record of the proof, either in the form of a minute noted by the court as being of consent, or in the notes of evidence. Whereas an admission contained in the closed record will be regarded as final, and as the equivalent of proof, oral admissions at the bar may be rescinded if they are proved to be incorrect.[13]

(iii) Minute of admissions

Minutes of admissions, whether lodged by one party or jointly, are **15–08** encouraged in litigation as a means to record admissions, expedite proceedings and filter out non-contentious matters. For example, in actions for personal injuries, this could include the medical evidence if perhaps the extent of the injuries is not disputed, but the cause of them is. In actions of divorce or separation, or dissolution of civil partnership, agreements between the parties on questions relating to children or the financial arrangements may be incorporated in a joint minute. Generally, whatever is jointly admitted will normally be taken as final, with no opportunity of reopening the issue. However, in family cases, the court has statutory powers in some instances to set aside, or vary, an agreement or any term in an agreement made by the parties to resolve questions relating to the children or to financial provision.[14]

Judicial admissions in criminal cases

There are three contexts in which a judicial admission arises in a criminal **15–09** case:

    (i)   a plea of guilty;
    (ii) in a joint minute between the prosecution and the defence; and
    (iii) in the course of a special defence, which may or may not include a partial admission as to the actus reus.

There are also certain statutory situations in which an accused who fails to challenge an assertion is taken to have admitted it by implication.

(i) Plea of guilty

"A plea of guilty is a solemn judicial confession of fact, and if accepted, may **15–10** result in an immediate conviction."[15] The procedural and evidential consequences of a plea of guilty vary between solemn and summary cases.

(a) Solemn cases

    Section 77(1) of the Criminal Procedure (Scotland) Act 1995 states that if **15–11** the accused pleads guilty and the plea is accepted by the Crown, then a written copy of the plea should be signed by the accused and countersigned

---

[13] See *Whyte v Whyte* (1895) 23 R. 320.
[14] In addition to this general power, the court can set aside or vary an agreement in terms of s.16(1)(a) and s.16(3) respectively of the 1985 Act. See *Milne v Milne*, 1987 S.L.T. 45 and *Horton v Horton*, 1992 S.C.L.R. 197.
[15] Macphail, *Evidence*, para.2.26.

by the trial judge. If the plea is to only part of the indictment and the Crown are not prepared to accept it, then the non-acceptance is also recorded.[16] There is no obligation on the Crown to accept any plea of guilty, not even one which covers the entire indictment,[17] but they cannot thereafter make any evidential use of the fact that the accused was prepared to plead guilty.

15–12   In solemn cases if the Crown accepts a partial plea of guilty in respect of an indictment which contains more than one charge, and proceeds to trial on the remaining charges, they cannot make use of that plea of guilty as evidence against the accused on the remaining charges.[18] In *Walsh* the accused was charged on indictment with the theft of three cars and at the trial diet he tendered a plea of guilty to the third charge and pleas of not guilty to the first two. The jury was then empanelled and the sheriff clerk read out all three charges to them. In charging the jury, the sheriff directed them formally to find Walsh guilty on the third charge, and consider whether or not it was relevant to the issue of his guilt on the remaining charges, using the *Moorov* doctrine to provide corroboration.[19] Walsh was convicted on all three charges and appealed. On appeal, it was held that the jury should not have known about Walsh's plea of guilty, that the third charge should not have been read out to them and that they should not have been directed to find him guilty. Irrespective of the operation of the *Moorov* doctrine, it was held that the sheriff had misdirected the jury by suggesting that a plea of guilty to charge 3 was of evidential value on charges 1 and 2, and the convictions were therefore quashed.

15–13   Macphail has argued that the operation of the rule is unrealistic in cases in which the *Moorov* doctrine might otherwise be applied.[20] He accepted that in general it is undesirable for a jury to be influenced by being made aware of the accused's plea of guilty to one or more other charges. However, he noted that the effect of *Walsh* is to make it prudent for the Crown to decline partial pleas when they intend to invoke the doctrine. It can be argued that outcome is not in the interests of the efficient administration of criminal justice as matters might be taken to trial that would not otherwise need to be.

15–14   The effect of a plea of guilty, once signed and countersigned, is as if a formal finding of guilt had been made following trial. The court may proceed to pass sentence following the prosecution's summary of the circumstances of the offence and the defence plea in mitigation, though in practice where the plea is only partial sentencing is likely to be deferred until the end of the trial on the remaining charges.[21]

(b) Summary cases

15–15   In summary cases, if the prosecutor accepts a plea of guilty the court can proceed immediately to sentence, following the usual representations by the fiscal and the defence agent.[22] As in solemn cases, there is no obligation on

---

[16] s.77(2) Criminal Procedure (Scotland) Act 1995.
[17] *Peter and Smith* (1840) 2 Swin. 492. See also *Strathern v Sloan*, 1937 J.C. 76 at 80.
[18] *Walsh v HM Advocate*, 1961 J.C. 51.
[19] For discussion of the *Moorov* doctrine see Ch.8.
[20] Macphail, *Evidence*, para.2.28.
[21] See s.77.
[22] See s.144.

the prosecutor to accept any guilty plea, and, although the offer of a plea and its rejection will be recorded, the prosecutor may not thereafter make any evidential use of it.[23]

In summary cases, if the prosecutor accepts a partial plea of guilty to **15–16** certain charges on a complaint and proceeds to trial on the remainder, they may make use of these guilty pleas to prove the guilt of the accused on the remaining charges.[24]

It was held in *Tudhope v Campbell*[25] that an accused person may withdraw **15–17** a plea of guilty before the conviction and sentence have been recorded, if they can show their plea was as a result of trickery, coercion or a genuine misunderstanding due to a lack of legal representation.

Joint minutes

In both solemn and summary proceedings, there are provisions to permit the **15–18** lodging of joint minutes of admissions.[26] The purpose is again to speed up the court process by not having to spend time proving non-contentious matters. Joint minutes are frequently used in regard to non-contentious aspects of medical or forensic evidence, or even the entire evidence of a witness, such as a police scenes-of-crime photographer. The intention behind the 1995 provisions is to go further than agreements relating to formal or expert evidence. It is to seek and obtain evidence from a legally represented accused, which, at the pre-trial stage at least, appears uncontroversial. Both the prosecution and defence can use s.256, but the latter may be reluctant to agree anything other than the most non-contentious evidence on the basis that the accused is entitled to put the Crown to the test.

Section 257 places a duty on the Crown and the defence to identify facts **15–19** which are unlikely to be disputed and which if admitted would avoid the need for oral evidence. Section 258 entitles a party who considers there are facts which are unlikely to be disputed, to serve on the other party a statement setting out those facts. If unchallenged by the receiving party within seven days, the facts "shall be deemed to have been conclusively proved".[27] Any document admitted through the joint minute procedure is deemed proven. Only represented accused have the duty to agree evidence. Although unrepresented accused are entitled to take advantage of s.256, this inevitably imposes additional work on the prosecutor who has the responsibility of preparing these minutes.

A minute of admissions or agreement will be strictly construed. In *Evans v* **15–20** *Wilson*[28] a failure to lodge productions referred to in a minute of agreement (namely, a doctor's and an analyst's certificates in a trial for alleged drunken driving) led to the conviction being quashed.

---

[23] By virtue of s.146(8) of the 1995 Act it is not necessary for the prosecutor to prove the accused's guilt of those charges to which he has pled guilty.

[24] *McColl v Skeen*, 1980 S.L.T. (Notes) 53 at 54.

[25] J.C. 24.

[26] s.256.

[27] s.258(3).

[28] *Evans v Wilson* 1981 S.C.C.R. 60.

Implied admissions created under statute

15–21 Section 280(9) of the Criminal Procedure (Scotland) Act 1995 provides that at any trial, it is presumed that the person who appears in answer to the complaint is the person originally charged by the police, and any contrary assertion must be disposed of by way of a preliminary plea. This provision operates as a link in a chain corroborating the identification of the accused. By virtue of s.138(4) and Sch.3 of the Criminal Procedure (Scotland) Act 1995, certain offences when libelled against the accused may contain implicit terms regarding the commission of the offence. Any objection taken to these require to be by way of preliminary plea prior to the recording of the plea to the charge.[29]

Res Judicata

15–22 The rule of evidence known as res judicata prevents a matter that has already been adjudicated being adjudicated on a subsequent occasion. The rule was summarised by Dickson[30] thus:

> "When a matter has been the subject of judicial determination by a competent tribunal, the determination excludes any subsequent action in regard to the same matter between the same parties on the same grounds."

It operates as a procedural bar to any further court action on the matter, and "is based upon considerations of public policy, equity and common sense, which will not tolerate that the same issue should be litigated repeatedly between the same parties on substantially the same basis".[31]

15–23 The rule is most frequently encountered in civil cases, although it applies in criminal cases as a plea in bar of retrial for the same offence. There is also a limited form of res judicata applicable between civil and criminal cases. The rule is one that has considerable overlap with the law of procedure and specialist texts on that subject will provide a more detailed study. The remainder of this section focuses on the principal aspects of the plea as they intersect with the rules of evidence.

General rule in civil cases

15–24 The conditions to be satisfied before a plea of res judicata will be accepted in a civil action were summarised in *Esso Petroleum Co v Law*.[32] "There must have been an antecedent judicial decree of a competent tribunal, pronounced *in foro contentioso* between the same parties (or their authors) relative to the same subject-matter and proceeding on the same grounds."

15–25 This decision embodies five separate elements for a res judicata plea:

---

[29] See Renton and Brown, *Criminal Procedure*, 6th edn.

[30] Dickson, *Evidence*, para.385.

[31] Lord President Cooper in *Grahame v Secretary of State for Scotland*, 1951 S.C. 368 at 387.

[32] 1956 S.C. 33, per Lord Carmont at 38; see also Maxwell, *Practice of the Court of Session*, 196.

   (i)   an antecedent decree pronounced *in foro contentioso*;
   (ii) a competent antecedent tribunal;
   (iii) the same subject matter;
   (iv) the same grounds of action (media concludendi); and
   (v) the same parties.

(i) Antecedent decree in foro contentioso

A decree *in foro* is any decree pronounced in a cause after defences have **15–26** been lodged. It includes every kind of decree—interlocutory, interim and final—other than a decree of dismissal[33] or a decree in absence.[34] A decree in absence is one in which there has been no appearance for the defender, or where, despite an initial appearance, defences are never lodged. Such a case is not regarded as a defended one.[35] It does not constitute a decree *in foro* and it cannot constitute the basis of a later plea of res judicata.[36] However, once the defender has entered an appearance *and* lodged defences, any resulting decree (including one granted by default) will be regarded as *in foro* and a suitable base for a subsequent plea of res judicata.[37] A decree of absolvitor will also be sufficient to support the plea.[38] A decree *in foro* may be set aside where it is obtained by fraud or collusion between the parties.[39]

(ii) Competent antecedent tribunal

Before a plea of res judicata will be upheld, it must be shown that the decree **15–27** *in foro* founded upon was issued by a "competent tribunal". This will normally be a court of law, i.e. in Scottish civil cases, the sheriff court,[40] the Court of Session and the House of Lords and, since 2009, the Supreme Court. A ruling by a "tribunal" in the narrow sense of the word[41] may be sufficient to found a plea of res judicata in the mainstream civil courts, but tribunals generally have exclusive jurisdiction over the matters remitted to them, subject to an appeal on a point of law only.[42]

---

[33] *Duke of Sutherland v Reed* (1890) 18 R. 252. *Waydale Ltd v DHL Holdings (UK) Ltd*, 2000 S.C. 172 reviewed the authorities in regard to the effect of a decree of dismissal and affirmed the rule that such a decree left it open to a party to bring a fresh action whereas a decree of *absolvitor* did not.

[34] Maxwell, *Practice of the Court of Session*, p.617. It was observed in *Gibson & Simpson v Pearson*, 1992 S.L.T. 894 that a decree in absence might found a plea of *res judicata* if personal bar operated. For the purposes of the sheriff court, a decree *in foro* has been defined by W. J. Dobie (*Sheriff Court Practice*, (Edinburgh: William Hodge & Co. 1948) p.249) as "[a] decree granted after both parties have been heard, and where both have been represented in the course of the process", a definition adopted in *McPhee v Heatherwick*, 1977 S.L.T. (Sh. Ct) 46 at 47, for which see also below.

[35] *Esso Petroleum v Law*, 1956 S.C. 33.

[36] *Lockyer v Ferriman* (1876) 3 R. 882 per Lord Gifford at 911–912.

[37] *Forrest v Dunlop* (1875) 3 R. 15. See also Maxwell, *Practice of the Court of Session*.

[38] Maxwell, *Practice of the Court of Session*. See *Hynds v Hynds*, 1966 S.C. 201, per Lord Cameron at 202 and *Waydale Ltd v DHL Holdings (UK) Ltd*, 2000 S.C.at 183.

[39] See *Lockyer v Ferriman* (1876) 3 R.882 at 911.

[40] *Murray v Seath*, 1939 S.L.T. 348 at 352 confirmed the competency of the plea of *res judicata* in the Court of Session when founding upon a sheriff court decree.

[41] i.e. a judicial body such as an employment or mental health tribunal, which exists outside the traditional court structure.

[42] The legislation that establishes such tribunals normally provides that cases before a tribunal cannot be raised elsewhere. Thus the scope for a res judicata plea is very limited.

15–28   A foreign decree may found a plea of res judicata in the Scottish courts.[43] There are various statutes which permit foreign decrees to be enforced in the Scottish courts.[44] The effect of such statutory provisions is that the party against whom the judgment operates will normally be unable to contest the obligation thus created and will be bound by the original judgment. The practical outcome is the same as a plea of res judicata by the enforcing party.[45]

(iii) Same subject matter

15–29   For res judicata to operate the matter to be litigated must have been litigated between the same parties on a previous occasion. The "sameness" relates not to the facts to be proven, but to whether there is "a difference in the matter to be litigated".[46] Thus, the same facts may be deployed in justification of a matrimonial interdict as may later be used in a divorce action. This is no res judicata as the remedy sought on each occasion relates to a different subject matter.

15–30   To illustrate, in *Ryan v McBurnie*[47] there had been an earlier action between the driver of a car and the operators of a bus, arising from a collision between the two vehicles, which had led to the award of damages to the car driver. A passenger in the bus then raised an action for damages against the car driver, who pleaded res judicata on the general ground that the matter in issue (i.e. the liability for the accident) had already been litigated. It was held that the two actions were different, since the first dealt with the injuries of the car driver (and the duty of care of the bus driver to him) while the second dealt with the injuries of the passenger (and the duties of care of both drivers to her).[48] The subject-matter here is not confined to the narrow legal remedy sought by the pursuer but to the broader issue— what did the previous case decide?[49]

(iv) Same grounds of action

15–31   The *media concludendi* of a case may be defined as "the grounds of action in fact and law",[50] or "the reality and substance of the thing disputed between

---

[43] P. Beaumont and P. McEleavy, *Anton's Private International Law*, 3rd edn (Edinburgh: SULI/W.Green, 2011) para.9.64.

[44] See, e.g. the provisions of the Foreign Judgments (Reciprocal Enforcement) Act 1933.

[45] NB that s.10 of the Presumption of Death (Scotland) Act 1977, which makes provision for the recognition in Scotland of a declaration by a foreign court that a person domiciled or habitually resident in that country is dead, only states that such a declaration shall be "sufficient evidence of the facts so declared". The presumption is clearly rebuttable and there can be no question of it being *res judicata* of any action in Scotland relating to the same death (e.g. in respect of Scottish property).

[46] *Hynds v Hynds*, 1966 S.C. 201 at 203–204. See too, *Rorie v Rorie*, 1967 S.L.T. 75, in which *Hynds* was followed, in a case in which the earlier sheriff court action had been for adherence and aliment, rather than separation and aliment.

[47] 1940 S.C. 173.

[48] See also *Mitchell's Trs v Aspin*, 1971 S.L.T. 29, in which it was held that the issues created by the liferent of a share in an estate enjoyed by one daughter of the testator were not the same issues as arose in the case of another liferent enjoyed by another daughter.

[49] *Glasgow and South Western Ry. v Boyd and Forrest*, 1918 S.C. (H.L.) 14 at 30. See too *Grahame v Secretary of State for Scotland*, 1951 S.C. 368 at 387.

[50] Maxwell, *Practice of the Court of Session*, at 197.

the parties".[51] As such they represent the narrow factual issues raised by a case. They are distinguishable from the subject matter of a case, in that while the latter deals with the overall legal relationship between two or more parties (e.g. whether A is entitled to a divorce from B; whether C is liable to pay damages to D and so on), the *media concludendi* are the facts in issue in each case.

An earlier case will only be res judicata of a second case when both the **15–32** subject matter and the *media concludendi* are the same. As Lord Kinnear in *North British Ry. Co. v Lanarkshire and Dunbartonshire Ry. Co*[52] noted:

> "...[I]n order to support a plea of res judicata it is necessary to show not only that the parties and the subject-matter in two suits are identical, but also that the two suits present one and the same ground of claim, so that the specific point raised in the second has been as directly raised in the pleadings and concluded by the judgment in the first."

There is a line of authority[53] which suggests that res judicata can apply in cases where the *media concludendi* of the second case *could* have been raised by the pursuer in the previous action, but were not. The rationale is to encourage drafters to plead each issue of law which can reasonably be raised, otherwise a later court may uphold a plea of res judicata, not on the *media concludendi* which were raised, but on ones which might have been. The *media concludendi* will not be regarded as identical if the present claim introduces new facts (*res noviter*) which were not available to the pursuer in the previous action. This is to be distinguished from the effect of another procedural bar known as "competent and omitted". This plea prevents a pursuer from putting forward, as a new *medium concludendi,* a ground of action which could have been pled (but was not) in an earlier case between the same parties in which the pursuer was the defender. The purpose of the doctrine "is to avoid endless litigation".[54]

(v) Same parties

A prerequisite of a successful plea of res judicata is that the subsequent **15–33** action now litigated involves the same parties in their same capacities. If, for example, a previous action was by A against B, then it will be res judicata of any subsequent action by A against B, or B against A. However, it will not operate so as to prevent a subsequent action by A against C, or B against D, unless the new party is in some way *legally* associated with the former one. Thus, in *Glasgow Shipowners v Clyde Navigation Trustees*[55] a shipowners' association was prevented by a res judicata plea from reopening an issue with the trustees as the issue had been dealt with in an earlier action where

---

[51] *Glasgow and South Western Ry. Co. v Boyd and Forrest*, 1918 S.C. (H.L.) 14e per Lord Shaw at 31.

[52] (1897) 24 R. 564 at 57. See too, *Matuszczyk v National Coal Board* 1955 S.C. 418 which held that common law negligence and breach of statutory duty leading to common law liability to an employee involve the same *media concludendi*

[53] Commencing with *Glasgow and South Western Ry. v Boyd and Forrest*, 1918 S.C. (HL) 14.

[54] *Rorie v Rorie*, 1967 S.L.T 75 at 78 per Lord Milligan. See also article by P. Beaumont, "Competent and Omitted", 1985 S.L.T. (News) 345.

[55] *Glasgow Shipowners v Clyde Navigation Trustees*, 1885 12 R 695 per Lord Shand at 701.

the interests of the shipowners had been represented by the trustees themselves.

15–34   A judgment "in rem" is res judicata of a second action and operates against all potential future litigants to the same issue. This is in contrast to a judgment in personam which affects only the parties to it. A judgment in rem is, "[a] judgment of a court of competent jurisdiction determining the status of a person or thing, or the disposition of a thing".[56] A judgment in rem offers "conclusive evidence for and against all persons whether parties, privies or strangers, of the matters actually decided".[57]

15–35   Examples of judgments in rem are decrees of divorce or nullity of marriage,[58] declarators of death and the award of confirmation on the estate of a deceased. A decree for the reduction of a deed or contract operates as a judgment in rem, rendering the deed void so far as concerns not only the parties to it, but also anyone else having an interest in the subject-matter.

15–36   Where, however, a previous finding is not in rem and the parties to the present case are not the same as those in the previous case, the doctrine of res judicata will not be extended so as to debar a party from re-opening an issue which has not previously been litigated and by which that party is not bound. This rule is evident in road traffic accidents, which sometimes give rise to multiple claims. Where there has been a decree in an earlier court establishing the proportions of liability for the accident, that finding will not be res judicata in another case arising from that accident that involves different parties.[59]

Statutory interventions

15–37   Two statutory creations mitigate the operation of the res judicata rule. Section 11(1) of the Law Reform (Miscellaneous Provisions) (Scotland) Act 1968 permits findings in certain earlier civil proceedings to give rise to presumptions in subsequent civil cases. The first creation concerns a finding of adultery in any matrimonial proceedings,[60] or of paternity of a child in affiliation proceedings in any court in the United Kingdom. In each of these, the court findings are admissible as evidence of the adultery or of fatherhood, as the case may be.[61] Section 11(2) makes the finding in each case probative "unless the contrary is proved", which clearly places a persuasive burden on the party seeking to disprove the point, who may not necessarily be the party to whom the finding relates. A finding from an earlier hearing can have evidential effect in a subsequent case in which the parties are different. If, for example, A is found to have been in an adulterous relationship with Mrs B in an action for divorce raised by B, Mrs A may then rely upon that finding in her action for divorce against A.

---

[56] Halsbury's *Laws of England* (Hailsham, ed.), Vol. 13, p. 405.
[57] *Lazarus-Barlow v Regent Estates Co. Ltd.* [1949] 2 K.B. 465 at 475.
[58] See, e.g. *Administrator of Austrian Property v Von Lorang* 1926 S.C. 598 at 622, 1927 S.C. (H.L.) 80; and *Murray v Murray* 1956 S.C. 376.
[59] See *Anderson v Wilson*, 1972 S.C. 147.
[60] s.11(6) extends "matrimonial proceedings" to proceedings in the English, Welsh or Northern Irish courts.
[61] Law Reform (Miscellaneous Provisions) (Scotland) Act 1968, s.11(1).

RES JUDICATA IN CRIMINAL CASES

In a criminal case the two parties—the Crown and the accused—and the **15–38**
media concludendi, i.e. the guilt or innocence of the accused, are always the
same. The res judicata rule is thus limited to the question of whether, when a
previous trial of A is followed by another trial, the subject-matter is the
same and has been fully litigated. If so, then res judicata will apply and the
accused is said to have "tholed his assize".[62]

Has the matter been fully litigated?

In a criminal case, the matter has been fully litigated if it results in a finding **15–39**
of guilt, a formal admission of guilt or a finding of not guilty or not proven
in a court of competent jurisdiction.[63] Desertion of the criminal charges
simpliciter, whether on the Crown's motion or from the court *ex proprio
motu*, will also be treated as res judicata.[64] When the accused pleads not
guilty, but is found guilty after trial, then he need not have been sentenced
for res judicata to apply.[65] When an accused pleads guilty before the trial has
commenced,[66] a different rule apparently applies and the accused has not
tholed his assize until he has been sentenced.[67] In fact, it may now be the case
that the principles of res judicata do not apply until that sentence has
actually been recorded, following the ruling in the High Court in *Tudhope v
Campbell*.[68]

Subject-matter must be the same

Macdonald[69] states that before the plea of tholed assize will be upheld, the **15–40**
previous trial "must have been for the same crime, depending upon the same
evidence, and not for what is truly another crime". Lord Justice-Clerk
Grant in *HM Advocate v Cairns*[70] interpreted this as meaning, "[i]t is identity
of the charges and not of the evidence that is the crucial factor". In that
case, the accused had on an earlier occasion stood trial on a charge of

---

[62] See generally Renton and Brown, *Criminal Procedure*, 6th edn, paras 9–08 to 9–12.1.

[63] i.e. it must be a district court, a sheriff court or the High Court, and must be acting within its jurisdiction.

[64] NB not a desertion *pro loco et tempore*, which is a desertion of the diet but not of the right of the prosecutor to raise the charge(s) again; see Renton and Brown, *Criminal Procedure*, 6th edn, para.10–15 and *Herron v McCrimmon*, 1969 S.L.T. (Sh. Ct) 37 at 39. However, formal intimation of abandonment has the same effect as a Crown desertion *simpliciter;* see Renton and Brown, *Criminal Procedure*, 6th edn, paras 9–32 to 9–34; *Thom v HM Advocate*, 1976 J.C. 48; *H. v Sweeney*, 1983 S.L.T. 48; and *Lockhart v Deighan*, 1985 S.L.T. 549.

[65] Lord Justice-General Emslie in *Dunlop v HM Advocate*, 1974 J.C. 59 at 67. See *Milne v Guild*, 1986 S.L.T. 431 applying the rule at least in relation to summary cases.

[66] i.e. before the jury is sworn in, or before the first witness is called in a summary case; see Renton and Brown, *Criminal Procedure*, 6th edn, para.18–67 (solemn cases) and Criminal Procedure (Scotland) Act 1995, s.152 (summary cases). This will also include a plea of guilty at a specially convened diet under s.76 of the Criminal Procedure (Scotland) Act 1995.

[67] Renton and Brown, *Criminal Procedure*, 6th edn, para.9–27; see *Herron v McCrimmon*, 1969 S.L.T. (Sh. Ct) 37 at p.39.

[68] 1979 J.C. 37 at 41.

[69] *Criminal Law of Scotland*, 5th edn, p.272. Lord Justice-General McNeill in *Fraser* (1852) 1 Irv 66 at 73 gave as his test whether or not the present charge was one that the accused was "in jeopardy of" at the previous trial.

[70] 1967 J.C. 37 at 41.

murder by stabbing M and following his own sworn testimony, in which he denied the stabbing, the charge was found not proven. The Crown then served an indictment for perjury upon him, libelling that he had falsely denied the stabbing at the earlier trial. The defence objected to the new indictment on the ground that Cairns had already stood trial (tholed his assize) on the question of the stabbing. It was held that the new indictment was competent and that res judicata was not applicable, because the two charges (i.e. murder and perjury) were wholly different in nature and the two crimes were allegedly committed on different dates and at different places.

15–41   It is also well established that the same facts may give rise to different charges in different trials where events have occurred which alter the nature of the crime. For example, when a trial for assault is followed by the death of the victim, an accused may be re-indicted for murder or culpable homicide.[71] However, unless there has been some material change of circumstance that gives rise to a charge which was not available to the prosecution at the earlier trial, they cannot bring a second charge after the completed trial for the first, "for the same facts, under a new denomination of the crime".[72] For example, having failed to secure a conviction for robbery against D, the prosecution cannot recharge him with separate charges of assault and theft arising from the same alleged incident. On the other hand, where an indictment is dismissed as irrelevant for lack of specification, a fresh indictment libelling the same offences may be competent, and not res judicata, provided there is a material difference in the way the charges are expressed.[73]

15–42   The Court of Criminal Appeal has statutory power to set aside the verdict of the trial court and grant authority to the Crown to bring a new prosecution.[74] A plea of tholed assize is not then available to the defence. In summary cases, however, no sentence may be passed on conviction in the retrial which could not have been passed on conviction in the earlier proceedings. Where a new prosecution proceeds under these statutory provisions either party can lead evidence which it was competent to lead in the earlier proceedings.[75]

15–43   Note there was a significant shift in policy with the Double Jeopardy (Scotland) Act 2011. Although that legislation gives statutory confirmation that no person can be retried for the same crime,[76] in certain circumstances it also permits a fresh prosecution for the same crime on two conditions. First, that the High Court has, on the application of the Lord Advocate, set aside

---

[71] See, e.g. Macdonald, *Criminal Law of Scotland*, 5th edn (Edinburgh: W. Green, 1948). See also, *Stewart* (1866) 5 Irv 310 and *O'Connor* (1882) 5 Couper 206.

[72] Hume, II, 466. See *HM Advocate v M*, 1986 S.C.C.R. 624 above, in which the material difference between the first indictment and the second was said to be a narrower latitude of time, and a different wording of the charges. A plea of tholed assize was rejected.

[73] *HM Advocate v M*, 1986 S.C.C.R. 624 where the Lord Justice-Clerk said at p. 630 that the test for res judicata is "whether the second libel is identical with the previous libel at the instance of the same prosecutor and charges the accused with precisely the same crime".

[74] ss.118 (solemn) and s.185 (summary) proceedings of the Criminal Procedure (Scotland) Act 1995.

[75] ss.119(6) and 185(6) respectively.

[76] s.1.

the acquittal[77] and, second, that the High Court has granted authority to bring a new prosecution.[78] The necessary circumstances are that the court[79]:

> "(a) is satisfied that the acquitted person or some other person has (or the acquitted person and some other person have) been convicted of an offence against the course of justice in connection with the proceedings on the original indictment or complaint, or
> (b) concludes on a balance of probabilities that the acquitted person or some other person has (or the acquitted person and some other person have) committed such an offence against the course of justice."

Private prosecutions

A plea of res judicata does not operate so as to prevent a private prosecution **15–44** in those cases in which the Crown have simply thrown in their hand by means of a desertion *simpliciter*, or given formal intimation of abandonment. Such an action operates as a personal bar only against the Crown and no one else.[80]

Although private prosecutions are extremely rare, they are still compe- **15–45** tent. The most recent successful example was the highly publicised case of *H. v Sweeney*,[81] in which three youths were indicted by the Lord Advocate in the High Court on charges of rape and assault. Subsequently, relying on the advice of a psychiatrist who stated that the complainer would be unable to withstand the rigours of a trial for several months, the Lord Advocate sent a letter to each accused informing them that no further proceedings were to be taken against them.

The complainer subsequently applied to the High Court with a bill for **15–46** criminal letters to allow her to raise a private prosecution on the same charges. *Sweeney* was the first occasion since 1829 that an application for leave to prosecute privately had been made in a case in which the Crown had formally abandoned charges against an accused.[82] In granting the bill, and allowing the private prosecution to proceed, Lord Justice-General Emslie ruled[83] that "the only effect of desertion of a diet simpliciter on the prosecutor's motion is to disable that prosecutor from taking fresh proceedings against the accused upon the same charge or charges". Lord Cameron added[84] that "the abandonment of the prosecution by the Crown in no way excluded the right of a private prosecutor to seek at the hands of this court the issue of criminal letters in her own name".

---

[77] s.2.
[78] s.2(2) (a).
[79] s.2(3) (a)
[80] Where desertion simpliciter is by the court *ex proprio motu*, it binds all future parties.
[81] *H. v Sweeney*, 1983 S.L.T 48.
[82] In all other such cases, the Crown had simply declined to proceed at all.
[83] *H. v Sweeney*, 1983 S.L.T 48 at 55. Earlier Lord Elmslie impliedly equated desertion simpliciter with the formal abandonment which had occurred in this case, and the two may therefore be taken as having the same effect so far as concerns a subsequent right of private prosecution.
[84] *H. v Sweeney*, 1983 S.L.T 48 at 52.

15–47   A more recent application for a private prosecution in 1995 was unsuccessful and reinforced the very substantial obstacles facing a complainer in such circumstances.[85]

RES JUDICATA: CIVIL AND CRIMINAL CASES INTER SE

15–48   The older authorities[86] acknowledged that the doctrine res judicata could not operate between civil and criminal cases since the parties to each action are different and the same issues do not arise in the same cause of action. The older cases also follow the same theme, allowing in civil actions what were in substance retrials of issues which had already been considered in criminal cases. Thus, in *Wood v North British Ry. Co.*[87] a cab operator who had been convicted of a breach of the peace by resisting his removal from Edinburgh Waverley Station was allowed to raise an action for damages for assault and illegal arrest against the police officer responsible for his removal. The court rejected the defence averment of res judicata. Lord Traynor, in *Wilson v Bennett*,[88] explained that, "a conviction or judgment in a criminal court is not a res judicata effectual to bar an action or claim in a civil action arising, or alleged to arise, out of the same circumstances".

15–49   Separately from a res judicata plea, sometimes an earlier conviction before a criminal court may have evidential relevance in a later civil action. These circumstances fall into two broad categories. First, where the earlier action does, as an exception to the general rule, operate so as to resolve the matter for all time. Second, where the earlier action creates a presumption of guilt.

Finding of guilt res judicata of later civil action

15–50   The main exceptions to the general rule are statutory, but even at common law there is some authority for regarding a previous finding of guilt as being res judicata of a particular issue where it is re-raised in a later civil action between the same parties. Since it is rare for a private individual to be a party to a criminal case, such cases will clearly not arise often, but where they do, all the necessary ingredients are present for a successful plea of res judicata.

15–51   In *Young v Mitchell*[89] a servant brought a criminal complaint of illegal dismissal against his former employer under the Master and Servant Act of 1867. The charge was found not proven. The servant then raised a civil action based on precisely the same facts, but the court dismissed the action holding that the criminal case was res judicata of any subsequent civil action.[90]

---

[85] *C v Forsyth*, 1995 S.L.T. 905

[86] e.g. Hume, 1171, 479 and Dickson, *Evidence*, para.3.5.

[87] (1899) 1 F. 562. See also *Faculty of Procurators of Glasgow v Colquhoun* (1900) 2 F. 1192.

[88] (1904) 6 F. 269 at 271.

[89] (1874) 1 R. 1011—see the Lord President's comments at 1013. See also *Kennedy v Wise* (1890) 17 R. 1036.

[90] Circumstances which Walker and Walker, *Evidence*, 3rd edn, para.11.53 regarded as "rare", and limited to cases in which "the proceedings in the criminal court were of a quasi-civil character and the parties in both proceedings were the same".

Convictions as evidence in subsequent civil proceedings

Statute also makes it competent for a complainer in an assault case, which **15–52** has resulted in a conviction, to raise a civil action for damages in compensation for the same assault and to argue that the conviction is res judicata of the fact of the assault. Section 10 of the Law Reform (Miscellaneous Provisions) Act 1968 provides that:

> "In any civil proceedings the fact that a person has been convicted of an offence by or before any court in the United Kingdom or by a court-martial there or elsewhere shall...be admissible in evidence for the purpose of proving, where to do so is relevant to any issue in those proceedings, that he committed that offence, whether he was so convicted upon a plea of guilty or otherwise and whether or not he is a party to the civil proceedings."

Section 10(2)(a) creates a rebuttable presumption of guilt, placing a persuasive burden on the person concerned of proving that, despite the conviction, they are in fact innocent. Although not settled, it is likely that the standard of proof borne by a person in these circumstances is on a balance of probabilities.[91] Documents, such as complaints, indictments and charge-sheets, are admissible to show the whole circumstances of the offence.[92]

Section 12 of the Law Reform (Miscellaneous Provisions) Act 1968 makes **15–53** specific provision for the use of convictions in defamation actions:

> "In an action for defamation in which the question whether a person did or did not commit a criminal offence is relevant to an issue arising in the action, proof that, at the time when that issue falls to be determined, that person stands convicted of that offence shall be conclusive evidence that he committed that offence; and his conviction thereof shall be admissible in evidence accordingly."

The obvious use for this provision arises when, say, a newspaper publishes an item describing someone as "a convicted thief", or even simply "a thief", and the person concerned challenges the writer to prove that he actually committed the offence.[93] In recognition of some high profile English cases, the Law Reform Committee, in its 15th Report,[94] recommended a corresponding change in the law, which in Scotland found expression in s.12.

The effect of s.12 is that a conviction is regarded in later defamation **15–54** proceedings[95] as conclusive of guilt of the offence to which it relates. As with s.10, once the conviction itself has been proved, previous documentation

---

[91] See Ch.2 and *King v Patterson*, 1971 S.L.T. (Notes) 40. See also Macphail, *Evidence*, para.11.08, and the English cases quoted there.

[92] s.10(2)(b), e.g. in the case of an "assault", that it was in fact an assault by a man upon his wife, which may be an essential factor in a separation or divorce action. This provision may be even more important when the convicted person is not a party to the present proceedings.

[93] See, e.g. *Hinds v Sparks* [1964] Crim. L.R. 717 and *Goody v Odhams Press* [1967] 1 Q.B. 333.

[94] Another recommendation of the committee, that acquittal of an offence should be regarded as conclusive evidence of innocence, was rejected.

[95] But no other type of action, e.g. damages for unlawful arrest.

relating to the conviction is also admissible.[96] The conviction may be by any court in the United Kingdom, or any court-martial.[97]

15–55 The rationale for authorising the production of documents, such as copy complaints, is that it is not always obvious from the bare record of a conviction to appreciate what exactly the accused did. For example, an extract conviction for a breach of the peace encompasses a wide range of criminal behaviour. Where a newspaper article refers to a person as being a "Peeping Tom"[98] the journalist may find it difficult to defend a defamation action without access to supplementary papers beyond an extract conviction. The latter may show only that the pursuer committed a breach of the peace, but with no further specification.[99]

15–56 Frequent use is made of s.10 in personal injuries claims arising from road accidents in which the defender has been convicted of a motoring offence arising from the same accident; and in matrimonial actions where, for example, a pursuer in a divorce action cites violent behaviour towards her by her spouse and convictions exist. The pursuer may still face difficulties in identifying the precise nature of the offence and showing that the person named in the conviction is the defender.[100] The pursuer still requires to link the present defender with the previous accused and to demonstrate that the two incidents are the same. In some cases it may be easier to prove *de novo* that the defender committed the act(s) in question. Given the lower standard of proof in civil cases, this should not be too onerous.

---

[96] s.12(2).
[97] subs.(3). NB that certified copies are allowed under subs.(2) by virtue of subs.(4).
[98] A species of breach of the peace identified in *Raffaelli v Heatly*, 1949 J.C. 101.
[99] *Levene v Roxhan* [1970] 1 W.L.R. 1322.
[100] e.g. *Caldwell v Wright*, 1970 S.C. 24 and *Andrews v Andrews*, 1971 S.L.T. (Notes) 44.

Chapter 16

THE CRIMINAL TRIAL

INTRODUCTION

This chapter is concerned with the process by which evidence is heard in the **16–01** criminal trial. Although this is a book on evidence, the rules of procedure play a significant role in determining how evidence is led, so some account here of procedure is unavoidable. Specialised texts will provide the reader with more detailed analyses of trial procedure and advocacy techniques.[1]

The rules of evidence apply in the separate contexts of solemn proceedings **16–02** where the trier of fact is a jury, and summary proceedings where the judge is the trier of fact. The presence of a jury places a duty upon the presiding judge to offer guidance to the jurors and to ensure fairness. The actual order in which the evidence is heard is the same in both types of case and begins when the Crown call their first witness. Unlike the system in England and Wales, there are no opening speeches by either the prosecution or the defence.

In virtually all criminal trials the persuasive burden of proof is on the **16–03** Crown and it is therefore the obligation of the Crown to lead their witnesses first. Each witness for the Crown is examined in chief by the prosecutor, i.e. the procurator fiscal or the advocate depute, after which the witness is available for cross-examination by the defence. Before leaving the witness box, the prosecutor has an option to re-examine the witness to clarify any ambiguities in the evidence led so far. After leading all their witnesses, but before closing the Crown case, the prosecutor will place before the court any record of judicial examination of the accused[2] and any joint minute agreed with the defence.

After the Crown has closed their case, it is the turn of the defence to call **16–04** their witnesses, beginning always with the accused if he or she is to give evidence. The roles are then reversed, with the defence agent examining the witnesses in chief and the Crown subjecting them to cross-examination, the defence having the right to re-examine where appropriate. Once the defence has led their last witness and has no further evidence, the normal procedure is for the Crown to sum up their case, leaving the defence to conclude with a summary of the defence case. In solemn trials, the presiding judge is then responsible for giving the charge to the jury, summarising the law and the available evidence, before the jury retire to reach a verdict. In summary trials the sheriff or justice (in district court cases) may adjourn to consider the evidence before coming to a conclusion.

---

[1] Renton and Brown's, *Criminal Procedure*, 6th edn.
[2] Criminal Procedure (Scotland) Act 1995, ss.35–39.

JUDICIAL QUESTIONING

16–05 At any stage of a trial the judge can intervene to ask questions, either to clarify a matter which remains obscure, or perhaps to open up another line of inquiry which seems pertinent. Little formal objection is likely to be raised to such a course in a summary criminal trial, but where the judge is sitting with a jury, impartiality must be observed to avoid any grounds for an appeal.[3] The parties ought to be offered an opportunity to cross-examine on any new points raised by questions from the bench.[4] The role of the judge in overseeing fairness and in acting at all times with impartiality is an important ingredient of fulfilling art.6 of the ECHR, the right to a fair trial. Where a trial judge's interventions and conduct render a trial unfair it will almost certainly lead to a quashed conviction. The reasoning of the European Court of Human Rights in the English case of *CG v United Kingdom*[5] regarding the parameters of judicial intervention in adversarial proceedings would be equally applicable to proceedings in the Scottish courts.

EXAMINATION IN CHIEF

16–06 Examination in chief is the process whereby counsel or the solicitor for a party elicits from a witness called by that party evidence which it is believed will be favourable to that party's case. As the Crown prosecutes in the public interest, they have a duty to elicit *all* evidence having a bearing on the case and not just that which is apparently favourable to them. Lawyers prepare for examination and cross-examination on the basis of the precognitions and statements of the witnesses. However, the information provided by witnesses at a preceding stage do not always live up to their early promise. Lawyers can deploy various tactics to overcome the gap between the testimony that lawyers anticipate a witness will give in the witness box, and that which they actually give. These include: (i) leading questions; (ii) refreshing memory from notes taken contemporaneously; and (iii) reminding the witness of statements made by them on a previous occasion.

(i) Leading questions

16–07 A leading question is one that either suggests the desired answer, or takes for granted a crucial fact that has yet to be proved. For example, if, in an assault charge the witness complainer is asked by the prosecutor, "After you came out of the pub, he hit you, didn't he?" that is a leading question because it suggests a desired answer. To avoid a leading question the witness could simply be asked, "What happened after you came out of the pub?" Equally, if before the fact of assault is established by evidence, the same

---

[3] See *Elliot v Tudhope*, 1988 S.L.T. 721 where 28 questions asked by the sheriff were for clarification and did not amount to oppression such as to constitute a miscarriage of justice. Significantly, none of the questions raised new material.

[4] See e.g. *McLeod v HM Advocate*, 1939 J.C. and *Livingstone v HM Advocate* (Court of Criminal Appeal 2213174) reported in *Tallis v HM Advocate*, 1982 S.C.C.R. 91 in Sheriff Gordon's commentary and *Nisbet v HM Advocate*, 1979 S.L.T. (Notes) 5.

[5] (2002) 34 E.H.R.R. 31.

witness is asked, "What did you do after he hit you?" that is a leading question which takes for granted a crucial fact which has yet to be proved.

Generally, leading questions are permissible when put to a witness in **16–08** cross-examination, but they ought not to be asked of a witness called on behalf of one's own party. In practice however, it is acceptable for the agent calling a witness to lead them through the introductory and non-controversial part of their evidence—name, address, occupation, presence at the locus, etc. Exceptionally (and normally by prior agreement between the agents) a witness may be led through all, or a large portion of, the evidence, where it is uncontroversial and the parties have not arranged in advance for a joint minute to cover it. A typical example is expert opinion evidence or the technical evidence of a police photographer speaking to photographs taken of the locus, or of a casualty doctor speaking to injuries sustained by a road accident victim.

When a leading question is improperly put, an objection should be made. **16–09** However, the damage may well have been done if the witness has given the desired answer before any objection. Walker and Walker[6] suggest that the form of the question and answer should be recorded in order to assist an appeal court to assess the reliability of that evidence. The question of the weight to be attached to a witness's testimony is left to the judge at first instance, who can make allowances for the fact that the witness was led.

(ii) Refreshing memory

It remains an expectation within the adversarial that when a non-expert **16–10** witness gives oral testimony, the witness will be able to speak from memory of something which they personally experienced. Given that months and possibly years may pass before a witness is called upon to give an account in court of an incident which they experienced in the past, it is quite reasonable that the witness is allowed to refresh their memory by reference to notes they made at or shortly after the time of the incident.[7] There is therefore now a statutory right for all witnesses to access any previous statements made by them which have been made available to both the Crown and defence.[8] Police officers are permitted to refer to their notebooks in order to testify as to precisely what the accused said when cautioned and charged.

The documents from which the witness refreshes their memory do not **16–11** become documentary evidence in the case—rather they become part of the witness's oral testimony. As Lord Justice-General Clyde explained in the leading case of *Hinshelwood v Auld*[9]:

> "If ... when he gives his evidence, he requires to look at the notes in order to enable him to give his account of what occurred, then the notes become part of his oral evidence. They are—so to speak—read into his oral testimony, as a material part of the foundation on which that testimony rests."

---

6 Walker and Walker, *Evidence*, 3rd edn, para.12.5.3.
7 See, e.g. Walker and Walker, *Evidence*, 3rd edn, para.12.7.1.
8 s.85 of the Criminal Justice and Licensing (Scotland) Act 2010.
9 1926 J.C. 4 at 7–8; *Deb v Normand*, 1997 S.L.T. 107.

If a witness does rely on notes to refresh memory and give oral testimony, then the notes must be made available to the other party.[10] If notes are available but not relied upon in testimony there is no need to produce them.[11]

16–12   The type of note to which a witness may validly refer in the course of oral testimony must serve simply to *refresh* memory and may not be used as a total substitute for it.[12] If the witness has no recollection of the events in question then they should not be giving oral testimony at all. Where the note is being used to refresh the witness's memory, and is incorporated into their oral testimony, it is proper practice for it to lodged as a production,[13] though it need not be in a form that would make it admissible per se. A note that represents a witness's only recollection of events must be lodged to even have a chance of being considered admissible.[14]

(iii) Previous consistent statements

16–13   Because of the primacy of oral testimony, previous consistent statements have limited status as evidence but can sometimes serve useful purposes. In criminal cases, there is a general prohibition against the admissibility of previous statements other than in specific exceptional circumstances. The reasoning is twofold. First, if the witness reads out or affirms the contents of the previous statement, it simply duplicates their present testimony and the latter is always to be preferred. Second, if someone else relates the previous statement, it would usually fall foul of the hearsay rule. The position varies depending on whether or not the previous statement is consistent with what the witness is now saying in the witness box. In both cases, there is a recognition that evidence is always admissible of the fact that a statement was *made*, as opposed to evidence of the contents of that statement, and it is also admissible "of the attitude or reaction of the accused at the time it was made".[15] This reflects the distinction made in the hearsay rule regarding original evidence and hearsay evidence.

(a) De recenti statements

16–14   A previous statement may be admitted if it has been made *de recenti*, i.e. a statement by the complainer made about the incident or against the accused shortly after the event, and usually to a close trusted friend or relative. *De recenti* statements mostly arise in assault cases, particularly sexual assault. For example, the Crown offered a *de recenti* statement as corroboration in *Morton v HM Advocate*[16] where the accused was accused of dragging his victim up a close and sexually assaulting her. Shortly after the assault, the victim allegedly went home while in a distressed condition and told her

---

[10] At 8. See also *Niven v Hart* (1898) 25 R. (J.) 89. See too *Deb v Normand*, 1997 S.L.T. 107.

[11] *Deb v Normand*, 1997 S.L.T. 107.

[12] Dickson, *Evidence*, para.1778. See also *HM Advocate v McPherson* (1845) 2 Broun 450; and *McGowan v Mein*, 1976 S.L.T. (Sh. Ct) 29.

[13] See *Hinshelwood v Auld*, 1926 J.C. 4. See too the Criminal Procedure (Scotland) Act 1995, s.157, which states that such statements are not documentary evidence, and need not be lodged as productions, in summary cases.

[14] *HM Advocate v McPherson* (1845) 2 Broun 450 at 452–453.

[15] *Morrison v HM Advocate*, 1990 J.C. 299 at 313.

[16] 1938 J.C. 50, considered more fully in Ch.8.

brother of the assault. Lord Justice-Clerk Aitchison[17] explained the purpose of *de recenti* evidence:

> "[T]he Court will allow the evidence of complaints or statements *de recenti* made by the injured party, for the limited purpose of showing that the conduct of the injured party has been consistent and that the story is not an afterthought, and, in the case of assaults upon women, to negative consent. A complaint *de recenti* increases the probability that the complaint is true and not concocted, and the absence of complaint where sexual offences are alleged is always a material point for the defence. But it must be clearly affirmed that the evidence is admissible as bearing on the credibility only, and the statements of an injured party, although made *de recenti* of the commission of a crime, do not in law amount to corroboration ... A statement of the injured party *de recenti* is nothing but the statement of the injured party, and is not evidence of the fact complained of."

Such statements are only admissible if they are made as soon after the alleged assault as is reasonable in the circumstances.[18] Davidson makes the point that a complainer could be expected to use the first opportunity of encountering a "natural confidante" to make a *de recenti* statement and cites some older authorities where *de recenti* statements have been admitted as evidence after as much as 24 and 48 hours have elapsed.[19] Although such time lapses may seem to run counter to the concept of "recent" statements, there is now a great deal of empirical psychological and psychiatric research to support the wide range of behaviours and responses that are typical of victims of violent crime, especially sexual offences. These responses include shock-induced delay in reporting and fear of disbelief, which may be counter-intuitive for the average trier of fact.[20]

The *de recenti* rule is illustrated in *Begg v Tudhope*,[21] which demonstrated **16–15** that one potential use for such a statement is to supply the credibility required of a victim in order that her statement may be used as a foundation for the application of the *Moorov* doctrine. The potential of *de recenti* statements are significant, such that the defence are likely to use the absence of an early complaint to attack the credibility of the complainer. However, as explained above, the range of responses to assault means that victims of such crimes are not necessarily all motivated to lodge instant complaints. One should therefore be cautious about the inferences to be drawn from the lack of an early complaint.

---

[17] *Morton v HM Advocate*, 1938 J.C. 50 at 53.
[18] See *Anderson v McFarlane* (1899) 1 F. (J.) 30, and *Hill v Fletcher* (1847) 9 D. 7. Although both these cases were civil cases they involved allegations of a criminal offence.
[19] *Evidence*, at 571, n.526 and the cases discussed there.
[20] See A. Burgess and L. Holmstrom, Lynda L. "Rape trauma syndrome" (1974) 131 *American Journal of Psychiatry*, 981.
[21] 1983 S.C.C.R. 32. Here, there was an attempt to use the girl's complaint to a teacher shortly after the alleged event as corroboration of her oral testimony, on the grounds that it was admissible as part of the res gestae.

(b) Reply to caution and charge

16–16 It is normal practice for police officers to relate to the court what, if anything the accused said when cautioned and charged.

(c) Mixed statements

16–17 A mixed statement is one containing both exculpatory and incriminatory elements. In such circumstances the prior statement can be admitted, but must then be admitted in full so that the court can have regard to the whole contents of the statement,[22] and the judge should direct the jury accordingly.[23] As the court explained in *Morrison*,[24] "it would be unfair to admit the admission without also admitting the explanation"[25] and it is then for the jury to decide which, if any, parts of the statement they accept as true.

(d) Evidence of previous identification

16–18 A previous statement may be admitted when a witness at a trial identifies the accused in court and states that they identified the accused on an earlier occasion, e.g. at an identification parade. When the witness identifies the accused again when in the dock, then the evidence of the previous identification might seem superfluous but it is a practice that "has existed without objection for many years"[26] and may serve to bolster the witness's reliability.

16–19 If a witness who has picked out the accused in an identification parade is unable subsequently to identify that accused in court as the person the witness believes committed the crime, the law permits other witnesses (usually police officers) to give evidence that on an earlier occasion the witness did identify the accused. Provided the witness confirms that an identification was made earlier, then there is considered to be corroboration of the identification of the accused.[27] The rule also extends to identification by description given previously to the police.[28]

(e) Adoption by witness of previous statement

16–20 There are occasions when a witness under oath is unable to recall what they said in a previous statement. In such circumstances the witness will be permitted to adopt the contents of that previous statement provided they are able to say that it was true when they made it, and they would have been a competent witness when the statement was made. This is the principle that emerged from *Jamieson v HM Advocate (No.2)*.[29] Following a Scottish Law Commission recommendation,[30] the ratio in *Jamieson* acquired statutory form as s.260 of the Criminal Procedure (Scotland) Act 1995.

---

[22] *Morrison v HM Advocate*, 1990 J.C. 299 (a seven bench decision).
[23] *McGowan v HM Advocate, Harris v HM Advocate*, 2006 S.C.C.R. 186.
[24] *Morrison v HM Advocate*, 1990 J.C. 299.
[25] *Morrison v HM Advocate*, 1990 J.C. 299 at 313. See too, *Hoy v HM Advocate*, 1997 S.L.T. 26, *R v HM Advocate* [2010] HCJAC 97.
[26] Macphail, *Evidence*, para.19.60.
[27] *Muldoon v Herron*, 1970 J.C. 30.
[28] *Frew v Jessop*, 1990 S.L.T. 396.
[29] 1994 S.C.C.R. 610.
[30] Report No.149, *Report on Hearsay Evidence in Criminal Proceedings*, published in 1995, at paras 7.39–7.40.

In *Jamieson* a witness stated at the trial that she could not remember **16–21** details of an assault. During her examination-in-chief by the Crown she acknowledged that she had made an earlier statement to the police about the incident and that the prior statement was a true statement. A police officer to whom the witness had given the original statement then gave evidence regarding its content. The accused was convicted. He appealed on the ground that the police officer's evidence was inadmissible hearsay.

The appeal court applied the principle in *Muldoon v Herron* which they **16–22** declared to be "of wider application and ... not confined to identification evidence".[31] The court considered there were two separate and primary sources of evidence.[32] First, the evidence of the police officer of what the witness told him. Second, the evidence of the witness that she had made a statement to the police officer, and that what she said to him at the time was true.

CROSS-EXAMINATION

The purpose of cross-examination was described *Hartley v HM Advocate* as **16–23** follows[33]:

"[Cross-examination] consists in questioning an adverse witness in an effort to break down his evidence, to weaken or prejudice his evidence, or to elicit statements damaging to him and aiding the case of the cross-examiner."

Cross-examination is designed to challenge and test the evidence given by a witness for the other party, thus presenting the position of one's own party in more favourable light. It is also used to lay the ground for a line of argument that is to be developed later by putting certain questions to a witness under cross-examination and giving the witness an opportunity to respond.[34]

Cross-examination is both a skill and an art and there are many books **16–24** devoted to the techniques of advocacy.[35] In the hands of a good cross-examiner a great deal of useful evidence can be elicited. Various professional codes of conduct set out how cross-examiners can behave effectively and ethically to ensure proper treatment of witnesses whilst securing appropriate evidential outcomes.[36]

---

[31] *Muldoon v Herron*, 1970 J.C. 30 per the Lord Justice-General at p.618.
[32] *Muldoon v Herron*, 1970 J.C. 30 at 618 E-F.
[33] 1979 S.L.T. 26 per Lord Avonside at 28.
[34] See *Lee v HM Advocate*, 1968 S.L.T. 155 at 157.
[35] There are both classic tests such as E. Du Cann, *The Art of the Advocate*, and skills texts such as N. Shaw, *Effective Advocacy* (1996); M. Hyam, *Advocacy Skills*, 4th edn (1999).
[36] See the Code of Conduct for Criminal Work in *Parliament House Book* (Edinburgh: W. Green) F839. It exhorts solicitors "at all times to comply with good professional practice and the ethics of the solicitors' profession as set out in practice rules, other codes of conduct and textbooks on professional ethics". Advocates are under a similar obligation.

THE RIGHT TO CROSS-EXAMINE

16–25 The general rule is that every party may cross-examine every witness who is called by the other party, and may also, if wished, examine that witness in chief.[37] Thus, the opposing party is both permitted to treat a witness called by the other side as a witness of his or her own, or has a right to cross-examine every such witness. In terms of the legislation, it is necessary for the witness to be called and sworn in before the opposing party has this right. In criminal trials the defence may call, and examine in chief, any witness who appears on the Crown witness list, but who is not actually called by the Crown.[38] In *McLeod v HM Advocate*[39] it was held that the party against whom such evidence operates should, in such a case, have a further right to cross-examine.

16–26 Where there is more than one accused, the evidence of each accused is admissible against the others.[40] Therefore, "once one of the accused goes into the witness-box in support of his separate defence, the door opens for a general cross-examination by his co-accused for the purpose of vindicating their own separate defences".[41]

16–27 The Crown have a right to cross-examine a co-accused after the remaining accused have done so.[42] Exactly the same procedure is observed in regard to the remaining witnesses called for each accused, so that, as Macphail explained,[43] "in the trial of X, Y and Z, X and each of his witnesses are in turn examined by X's advocate then cross-examined by Y, Z and the prosecutor. Accused Y is then examined by his own advocate and crossed by X, Z and the prosecutor."

16–28 The order in which each of the accused is allowed to take part in this rotating system seems to be the order in which each appears on the complaint or indictment, and "this is determined by the Crown on what may be alphabetical, chronological or tactical grounds; or it may be simply a matter of chance".[44] The presiding judge has a discretionary right to alter this order, in the interests of justice or clarity.[45]

IMPLICATIONS OF FAILURE TO CROSS-EXAMINE

16–29 It is not essential to cross-examine every witness in a criminal trial and it will be a question of tactics as to when one chooses not to cross-examine. The burden of proof is on the Crown to prove the accused guilty beyond reasonable doubt, and defence lawyers are not obliged to cross-examine all or any of the Crown witnesses, but failure to cross-examine prevents the

---

[37] s.263 of the Criminal Procedure (Scotland) Act 1995.

[38] Section 67(6) of the Criminal Procedure (Scotland) Act 1995 allows any party (including a co-accused) to examine *in causa* any witness listed by another party. See *Todd v HM Advocate*, 1984 S.L.T. 123 and *Hunter v HM Advocate*, 1984 S.L.T. 434.

[39] 1939 J.C. 68. Macphail argues that the same rule should apply in civil cases.

[40] *Young v HM Advocate*, 1932 J.C. 63.

[41] At 74. See s.266 of the Criminal Procedure (Scotland) Act 1995.

[42] *Young v HM Advocate*, 1932 J.C. 63.

[43] Macphail, *Evidence*, at para.825..

[44] Macphail, *Evidence*, at para.825..

[45] *Sandlan v HM Advocate*, 1983 S.L.T. 519.

defence undermining the credibility or reliability of the Crown witnesses.[46] It is a matter of professional judgment as to how best to conduct a case on behalf of a client.[47]

The question of the evidential significance of a failure on the part of the **16–30** Crown to cross-examine defence witnesses arose in *Young v Guild*[48] when neither the accused nor his witness (his wife) were cross-examined by the procurator fiscal. On appeal, it was argued that this failure amounted to an acceptance by the Crown of the defence version of events (an assault) and that the Crown should not then have sought a conviction. It was held that, while such a failure might well have "an impact on the weight and value of the evidence", it could not operate as a bar to conviction. The court took its lead from *McPherson v Copeland* and ruled[49] that:

> "It was for the sheriff to decide at the end of the day on all the evidence before him whether a conviction should result or not. If the unchallenged evidence of the appellant and his wife had even cast a reasonable doubt in his mind about convicting, that would have been enough to warrant an acquittal."

PREVIOUS INCONSISTENT STATEMENTS

As discussed earlier, in criminal cases there is a general prohibition against **16–31** the admissibility of previous statements other than in specific circumstances. In contrast, where there is a suggestion that the witness made a previous statement that is *inconsistent* with the evidence now produced in court, s.263(4) of the Criminal Procedure (Scotland) Act 1995 states that the witness may be challenged about a previous statement that is in different terms. Evidence can then be led at the trial, under very constrained parameters,[50] to show that a different statement was made previously and the witness then cross-examined regarding the apparent inconsistency.

The fact that a witness has made a statement on a previous occasion that **16–32** is inconsistent with the one now given in evidence in court may be used to suggest that the witness is unreliable. A party seeking to prove a witness's previous inconsistent statement must first lay a basis for this by putting to the witness the fact that it was made, and to whom, and give them the opportunity to confirm or deny that fact—to use the terms of the statute, to detail what was said "on any specified occasion". Only if it is denied can the evidence of the previous inconsistent statement be led.[51] As is the position

---

[46] *McPherson v Copeland*, 1961 J.C. 74.
[47] *Anderson v HM Advocate*, 1996 J.C. 29.
[48] *Sandlan v HM Advocate*, 1985 S.L.T. 519.
[49] *McPherson v Copeland*, 1961 J.C. 74 at 360.
[50] See *Paterson v HM Advocate*, 1998 J.C. 182. For discussion see Davidson, *Evidence*, para.12.135.
[51] *Mactaggart v HM Advocate*, 1934 J.C. 33, and *Paterson v HM Advocate*, 1998 J.C. 182. Presumably if the witness admits they made a previous inconsistent statement then their "correct" testimony can be clarified there and then.

with previous consistent statements, this rule does not extend to precognitions.[52] The fact of a previous inconsistent statement can form the basis of a charge of perjury.[53]

CROSS-EXAMINATION AS TO CREDIBILITY

16–33 The previous section considered previous inconsistent statements as a means of attacking the credibility of a witness. The Scottish Law Commission canvassed views on whether a prior inconsistent statement might be admissible, not just of the fact it was made, but of its content.[54] They reported, "the weight of opinion was against such a radical reform of the law".[55] One compelling reason against admitting such a statement was the consideration that an "accused could be convicted on the basis of prior statements attributed to witnesses by police officers, even though the witnesses denied having made such statements".[56]

16–34   Cross-examination should not be used to mount a general attack upon the character of a witness because the general rule, discussed in Ch.12, is that character evidence is collateral evidence and not relevant to the essential facts. However, a cross-examiner may pose questions designed to undermine the credibility of a witness and suggest that they are so unreliable that they should not be believed. Evidence suggesting some dubiety about the witness's credibility is regarded as an exception to the general rule that credibility is collateral. But the party attacking credibility is normally only permitted to raise the suggestion that the witness is not to be believed and leave it at that.[57] It is not permissible to pursue the point and rebut any denial with additional evidence.

If a witness has a personal interest in the outcome of a case, then that may well affect their credibility but it does not generally disqualify them from testifying.[58]

RE-EXAMINATION

16–35 The purpose of re-examination is to give the party adducing the witness:

> "[A]n opportunity of clearing up difficulties or ambiguities which may have emerged from cross-examination or to seek to repair the damage which cross-examination may have done."[59]

---

[52] Precognitions given on oath before a sheriff are statements that can be put to a witness. See *Coll, Petr*, 1977 J.C. 29, in particular Lord Justice-Clerk Wheatley at pp.32–33; and the discussion in *HM Advocate v McSween*, Scot Courts, June 15, 2006 at paras 8–19 per LJ-C Cullen.

[53] See, e.g. *Dorona v Caldwell*, 1981 S.L.T. (Notes) 91, and *Low v HM Advocate*, 1987 S.C.C.R 541.

[54] Report No.149, *Report on Hearsay Evidence in Criminal Proceedings*, 1995.

[55] At para.8.11.

[56] At para.8.11.

[57] as in *Falconer v Brown* (1893) 21 R. (J.) 1.

[58] Criminal Procedure (Scotland) Act 1995, s.265(3).

[59] Wilkinson, *The Scottish Law of Evidence*, p.161.

The normal rules of examination-in-chief should be observed in re-examination. Re-examination should be confined to matters already covered in cross-examination. There should be no leading questions. If the judge gives permission to the examiner to raise new matters, further cross-examination should also be permitted.[60] This would satisfy the principle of equality of arms intrinsic to a fair trial, as well as the general rule that evidence against an accused (from whatever source it originates) is something upon which the accused should always have the right to cross-examine.

OBJECTIONS TO EVIDENCE

At any stage of a trial or proof, the flow of examination and cross-examination may be interrupted by an objection by one of the parties to a question being asked of the witness, or to an entire line of questioning which is being embarked upon. Two questions then arise under the law of evidence. First, if a party does not object immediately have they, by implication, accepted the admission of that evidence? Second, must a trial judge make a decision there and then, or can evidence be allowed in under reservation of the question of its admissibility? **16–36**

(1) Implied acceptance by silence

In summary cases s.192(3) of the Criminal Procedure (Scotland) Act 1995 provides that in a case in which the accused is legally represented, no appeal may be based on the admission or rejection of an item of evidence unless the appropriate objection "shall have been timeously stated" at the trial. The High Court in *Skeen v Murphy*[61] explained the effect of this rule, "unless objection to the ... admission of evidence is timeously taken, it cannot be subsequently taken, and, if not, such evidence becomes part of the evidence *in causa*". However, failure to object to evidence that is per se incompetent[62] would not bar an appeal. **16–37**

Although there is no equivalent of s.192(3) in solemn cases, the best practice is for counsel to object timeously.[63] The wrongful admission of **16–38**

---

[60] Walker and Walker, *Evidence*, 3rd edn, para. 12.2.1, and Macphail, *Evidence*, Ch.8.34. See too *McLeod v HM Advocate* 1939 J.C. 68.

[61] 1978 S.L.T. (Notes) 2. This was a Crown appeal in which the High Court held that the defence failure to object to the late service of the analyst's certificate, etc. in a drink driving case was fatal to the suggestion that the sheriff could not consider them in evidence. The section clearly covers appeals against acquittal as well as conviction. See also *Tudhope v Stewart*, 1986 S.L.T. 659.

[62] See Walker and Walker, *Law of Evidence in Scotland*, para.12.6.4. See also *Handley v Pirie*, 1976 J.C. 65, *McLeary v Douglas*, 1978 J.C. 57 and *Robertson v Aitchison*, 1981 S.C.C.R. 149. See also Renton and Brown's, *Criminal Procedure*, 6th edn, para.31–09 and Macphail, *Evidence*, para.8.40.

[63] But see *McAvoy v HM Advocate*, 1982 S.C.C.R. 263, in which the failure by the defence to object timeously to the admission of a statement by a witness which revealed that A had a criminal record was taken into account as part of the circumstances surrounding the case, but the appeal finding was that, overall, there had been no "miscarriage of justice". Sheriff Gordon, commenting at p.275, pointed out that, "it is not safe for counsel or solicitor to 'sit back and wait for the Crown to make a mistake' as the professional lore used to have it". In other words, even in solemn cases objections should be made timeously.

evidence may still found an appeal even if the defence did not object at the time.

(2) Evidence heard under reservation as to its admissibility?

16–39 The ruling in *Thompson v Crowe*[64] restored the practice instigated post-*Chalmers v HM Advocate*[65] of hearing objections to the admissibility of evidence as soon as they are raised, and outwith the presence of the jury in solemn cases. In summary cases a judge appears to have a choice—either to hold a trial within a trial to determine admissibility or to permit it under reservation as to competency.[66]

PERSON PRESENT IN COURT DURING PREVIOUS EVIDENCE

16–40 The common law barred a witness from giving testimony if they had previously been in court hearing testimony from other witnesses.[67] Statutory intervention has relaxed the rule and criminal cases are now governed by s.267 of the Criminal Procedure (Scotland) Act 1995. That section permits a party to seek the court's permission, in advance, to be present during the proceedings, or any part of them, before giving evidence. The decision is at the discretion of the court, which must be satisfied that this would not be contrary to the interests of justice.

16–41 If a witness has been in court without permission and a party wishes to call that witness to give evidence then s.267(2) can be invoked. This section gives the court discretion to admit the evidence provided the witness's presence in court was not the result of culpable negligence or criminal intent; and that the witness has not been unduly instructed or influenced by what has taken place; or that there will be no injustice by their being heard. It has been held that where a potential witness has been permitted to sit through trial proceedings because neither the Crown nor the defence knew she had relevant evidence to give, that does not constitute "consent" to be present.[68]

16–42 When a witness is allowed to remain in court after giving testimony, but is then recalled, it seems that current practice is to reject any objection to the recall on the ground that the witness has heard some of the testimony and has almost certainly heard that part of it which has led to the recall.[69] The overarching principle that the court should hear any witness, whether cited or not, but who is available to be examined has been noted in the law reports,[70] appears to reflect the modern view,[71] and is embodied in statute.[72]

---

[64] 2000 J.C. 173.

[65] 1954 J.C. 66.

[66] See *Clark v Stuart*, 1950 J.C. 8 at 11, read in conjunction with *Thomson v Crowe* per Lord Justice-General Rodger at 1415B–E and the discussion in Davidson, *Evidence*, 9.67–9.72.

[67] See Dickson, *Evidence*, para.1599.

[68] *Affleck v HM Advocate* 2005 S.C.C.R. 503.

[69] See *Dyet v N.C.B.*, 1957 S.L.T. (Notes) 18, where the justification for permitting the recall was that it was in the interests of justice to do so. *Macdonald v Mackenzie*, 1947 J.C. 169 at 174. NB also pp.175 and 176, where it was held to be the duty of the judge to question the competence of any witness who has been present in court where this is apparent to him.

[70] *McDonnell v McShane*, 1967 S.L.T. (Sh. Ct) 61.

[71] See, e.g. Macphail, *Evidence*, para.3.31, and Wilkinson, *The Scottish Law of Evidence*.

[72] s.265(1)(d), Criminal Procedure (Scotland) Act 1995.

Therefore in both civil and criminal cases, a person who has appeared in court as a witness, whether cited as such or not,[73] is available as a witness for either side and is compellable to give such evidence in the interests of justice.

THE HOSTILE WITNESS

If a witness does fail to live up to their early promise regarding their **16–43** anticipated testimony the examiner has to make a strategic decision as to whether to abandon the examination or treat the witness as "hostile". If the latter course is adopted then the examiner switches to cross-examine the witness rather than conducting an examination-in-chief.[74] In the course of that subsequent cross-examination the examiner can suggest to the witness that he or she is acting out of bias, intimidation, fear, self-interest, etc.[75] It is for each party to decide how best to use a witness and when and if to change tactic whenever the circumstances warrant.[76] Leave of the court is not required.

FURTHER EVIDENCE

After all the witnesses have been led, further evidence may come to light that **16–44** a party wishes to bring to the attention of the court. For example, if late in the trial a witness gives evidence that seriously challenges the testimony of an earlier witness it may be desirable to put this evidence to the earlier witness. Alternatively, a later witness may open up a fresh line of evidence which a party feels could usefully be explored with a witness who has already testified. Or, it may simply be the case that the agent for the party calling the witness forgot to ask that witness a significant question.

In these circumstances, lawyers can seek leave from the court to recall a **16–45** witness, or to call completely new witnesses who can supply fresh evidence relevant to the case, but which has only emerged during the case. Witnesses may also be recalled by the court. This can be done either before or after the close of the case for the party seeking to adduce the fresh evidence and will be at the discretion of the trial judge.

---

[73] See below under "Recall of a Witness". But note the requirement in solemn criminal cases for both parties to give notice to the other of the witnesses they intend to call—s.67 of the 1995 Act. There are also exceptions in the case of the accused where he or she intends to give evidence, and co-accused who plead guilty during the course of the trial. These are dealt with below.

[74] The term "hostile" is an English term. It is not formally recognised in Scotland but the effect is the same.

[75] See *Frank v HM Advocate*, 1979 S.L.T. 26; *Manson v HM Advocate*, 1951 J.C. 49.

[76] *Avery v Cantilever Shoe Co*, 1942 S.C. 469 at 471.

RECALL OF A WITNESS

16–46 At common law, a witness may only be recalled by the presiding judge *ex proprio motu*, or at the request of one of the parties. The recall may be at any stage of the trial, even after both parties have closed their case,[77] but the recall is limited to clarifying some ambiguity in that witness's evidence.[78] The recalled witness is classed as the judge's witness and must be questioned only by the judge. Both parties have a right to cross-examine a recalled witness on any new evidence elicited by questions from the judge.[79]

16–47 Section 263(5) of the Criminal Procedure (Scotland) Act 1995 extends the common law recall rule in two ways. First, the recalled witness becomes the witness of the party recalling him or her; and, second, questioning is not limited to resolving ambiguities. In addition, the party wishing to invoke the section may do so at any time up to the close of their case. Thus in *Todd v MacDonald*[80] the prosecutor was allowed to recall a witness in order that he might identify the accused when this was vital to a conviction and the question had been overlooked in chief.

16–48 Section 263(5) only applies when a party seeks to recall a witness *before* the close of the case. If further evidence comes to light *after* the close of the case then ss.268 and 269 of the Criminal Procedure (Scotland) Act 1995 Act apply. They deal respectively with additional evidence and evidence in replication.

ADDITIONAL EVIDENCE

16–49 Section 268 permits either party to seek leave to adduce additional evidence, including where necessary the recall of a witness, when the conditions of s.268(2) are satisfied. The Thomson Committee[81] recommended these statutory provisions in the wake of the decision in *Lindie v HM Advocate*[82] which attracted a good deal of criticism due to the very narrow grounds upon which additional evidence could be admitted.[83] The procedure under s.268 is open to either party, who must make a motion to this effect to the judge who may only grant the motion under s.268(2) where, to paraphrase:

(i) the new evidence is material, and either it was not reasonably available at the time or its materiality could not reasonably have been anticipated (s.268(2)(b)(i)); or

---

[77] A case is "closed" in solemn proceedings at the point before the commencement of the speeches to the jury; and in summary proceedings, just before the prosecutor proceeds to address the judge on the evidence (see s.268 of the 1995 Act).

[78] For solemn cases, see *Lindie v HM Advocate*, 1974 J.C. 1 at 6, and for summary cases see *Todd v MacDonald*, 1960 J.C. 93 at 95 and 96.

[79] *McLeod v HM Advocate*, 1939 J.C. 68.

[80] *Todd v Macdonald*, 1960 J.C. 93 at 96.

[81] Cmnd 6218, paras 43.05 to 43.13; Recommendations 120 to 123.

[82] 1974 J.C. 1; a decision based on s.4.

[83] See, G. Gordon, *"Lindie v HM Advocate"* (1974) 19 J.L.S. 5 and Macphail, *Evidence*, Chs 8.56 and 8.58. Ironically, if the facts of *Lindie* were to recur, there would still be no statutory remedy, since in that case the speeches had begun.

(ii) it is accepted that at the time when the party closed their case *either* the additional evidence now being introduced was not available and could not reasonably have been made available, *or* the materiality of such evidence could not reasonably have been foreseen by the party now wishing to introduce it (s.268(2)(b)(ii)).

Evidence in Replication

Separately, under s.269, the Crown may, with the leave of the court: **16–50**

(iii) lead additional evidence for the purpose either of contradicting defence evidence which could not reasonably have been anticipated, or of proving that a witness who has given evidence[84] has in the past made a statement inconsistent with the one given during the trial (s.269(1)(a) and (b)).

The judge may permit the additional evidence to be led notwithstanding that a witness must be recalled,[85] and in a solemn case notwithstanding that a witness or a production will now be introduced who or which was not on the original lists served by the parties, and the requisite notice was not given concerning them. In all cases, if the motion is granted, the judge may adjourn or postpone the trial before allowing the additional evidence to be led.[86]

In the course of hearing an appeal from either solemn or summary proceedings the High Court may hear fresh evidence.[87] The tests for admitting new evidence are strict ones. In addition to having been unavailable at the trial, for which there must be a reasonable explanation,[88] the evidence must be "important and reliable" and "likely to have had a material part to play in the jury's determination of a critical issue at the trial".[89] Two of the most recent and controversial cases are those of *Church v HM Advocate*[90] and *Elliott v HM Advocate*.[91] These two cases were heard within a fortnight of each other. *Church* was heard first and hailed as a breakthrough in the application of the section in allowing additional evidence to be heard. However, it was quickly overturned by *Elliott*, a full bench decision which disapproved the decision in *Church*, rejected the liberal implication of s.228 made there and restated the traditionally strict approach to the question of   **16–51**

---

[84] Not necessarily a defence witness, although presumably the Crown can deal effectively at the time with any such issues as may arise in the course of examining one of their own witnesses.

[85] For a case in which the test of evidence "reasonably available" was applied, see *Salusbury-Hughes v HM Advocate*, 1987 S.C.C.R. 38.

[86] See *Sandlan v HM Advocate*, 1983 S.L.T. 519 for the court's approach to interpretation of these statutory provisions, albeit in their previous statutory form in s.149A of the Criminal Procedure (Scotland) Act 1975.

[87] ss.106 and 175 respectively of the Criminal Procedure (Scotland) Act 1995.

[88] ss.106 and 175 respectively of the Criminal Procedure (Scotland) Act 1995. See *McIntyre v HM Advocate*, 2005 S.L.T. 755.

[89] *Stillie v HM Advocate*, 1992 S.L.T. 279 per the Lord Justice-General at 284c, interpreting the forerunner statutory provision to s.106, namely s.228 of the Criminal Procedure (Scotland) Act 1975, and approving dicta in *Cameron v HM Advocate*, 1988 S.L.T. 169.

[90] 1995 S.L.T. 604.

[91] 1995 S.L.T. 612.

whether additional evidence "was not and could not reasonably have been available at the trial".[92]

EVIDENCE ON APPEAL AND MISCARRIAGE OF JUSTICE

16–52 There is increasing potential for new forensic techniques to shed light on previous evidence and raise the prospect of an appeal based on fresh evidence, for example, techniques emerging relating to the scope to re-analyse real evidence for DNA in ways unavailable at the time of the trial. Police forces regularly conduct "cold case" reviews and, recently, historic forensic evidence that was previously not capable of yielding reliable evidence may now do so thanks to new scientific discoveries. The reliability of DNA test results, particularly on items of clothing or bodily samples that may be decades old, has attracted considerable academic interest and criticism and are always likely to be a site of contest in a trial.

16–53   The Scottish Criminal Cases Review Commission ("SCCRC") was established in April 1999. Its remit is to investigate applications made to it concerning an alleged miscarriage of justice, often based upon evidence excluded at the trial or fresh evidence that has come to light since the conclusion of the trial. The SCCRC reject a very substantial number of the applications they receive and there must be solid substantive grounds for an application to have a chance of success. The SCCRC website provides further details of the application procedure and policy.

---

[92] See the articles by M. Scott, "The Cases of *Church* and *Elliot*", 1995 S.L.T. (News) 189, and P. Ferguson, "Fresh Evidence Appeals", J.L.S.S. 1995, 264.

Chapter 17

THE CIVIL PROOF

INTRODUCTION

In a civil proof the general rule is that the pursuer bears the burden of proof **17–01** and thus is the one who leads evidence first, followed by the defender. Thereafter, the procedure is as described for criminal cases, with each party examining their witnesses in chief, having them cross-examined and then re-examining them where appropriate. Most civil cases are heard before a single judge with civil jury trials (before a jury of 12) reserved for personal injury cases. In a civil jury trial, in contrast to a criminal trial on indictment, before calling witnesses, counsel for each party address the jury concerning what it is hoped to prove.[1]

To enable ease of comparison the remaining sections of this chapter **17–02** follow the format, wherever possible, of the previous chapter concerning criminal trials.

JUDICIAL QUESTIONING

During a proof the judge can intervene to ask questions for clarification or, **17–03** if appropriate, to open up a further line of inquiry. The civil proof is still occurring within an adversarial environment and the human rights considerations mentioned in Ch.8 are equally applicable.[2] However, the burden of proof is less onerous—proof on a balance of probabilities and the presumption of innocence does not dominate the process. Judges may adopt a more inquisitorial approach without objections from the parties or other repercussions. This is especially so where there are broader interests at stake beyond the issues in dispute between the parties. An example of this is in the family justice system in residence and contact disputes where the child's welfare is the paramount consideration, and takes precedence over the parties' claims and counterclaims. The welfare principle thus permits, indeed requires, judges to ensure that the outcome is in a child's best interests and may necessitate judicial intervention to a much greater extent than is usual or acceptable in criminal proceedings.

---

[1] See Hajducki, *Civil Jury Trials*, 4.16–4.23. For a recent discussion of the conduct of civil jury trials see the five bench decision in *Hamilton v Ferguson Transport (Spean Bridge) Ltd*, 2012 S.C. 486.
[2] *CG v United Kingdom* (2002) 34 E.H.R.R. 31.

EXAMINATION OF WITNESSES

17–04 Examination in chief, cross examination and re-examination all function in the same way and serve the same purpose in a civil proof as they do in a criminal trial. These processes are intended to produce testimony on oath or affirmation that supports the parties' pleadings in the closed record, tests the credibility and reliability of the witnesses and satisfies the respective burdens of proof of the pursuer and defender. Lawyers prepare for examination of witnesses based upon the precognitions and statements of their own witnesses and information provided through the disclosure and recovery stages prior to proof when the parties are exchanging their pleadings. The nature of the questioning, for example in terms of the scope for leading questions and refreshing memory, is greater than in trial, largely for the reasons explained above, the absence of a presumption of innocence paradigm. If a witness has a personal interest in the outcome of a case, then that may well affect their credibility but it does not generally disqualify them from testifying.[3]

CROSS-EXAMINATION

17–05 Section 4 of the Evidence (Scotland) Act 1840 established the right to cross-examination. Where there is more than one defender with separate representation, each of the defenders in turn is entitled to cross-examine each of the pursuer's witnesses in the order in which they appear in the instance of the closed record. The first defender's witnesses will be cross-examined first by the remaining defenders in the same order, and then finally by the pursuer. The second defender's witnesses will be cross-examined by the remaining defenders, then the pursuer, and then the first defender and so on,[4] forming a circular order of cross-examination. In *Boyle v Olsen*[5] the Court of Session was faced with an unusual situation in which there was more than one pursuer and it was held that each pursuer might cross-examine, not only the defender's witnesses, but also the witnesses for the other pursuer.

17–06 According to Lord Justice-Clerk Cooper in *McKenzie v McKenzie*,[6] while it should not be necessary for a party to put every fact averred in the case to every witness called for the other party, nevertheless:

> "[The] most obvious principles of fair play dictate that, if it is intended later to contradict a witness upon a specific and important issue to which that witness has deponed, or to prove some critical fact to which

---

[3] Evidence (Scotland) Act 1840, s.1.

[4] As Macphail explained, para.8.25, "[i]n a civil action by P against D1, D2 and D3, where the defenders have conflicting interests and are separately represented, P and his witnesses are cross-examined by D1, D2 and D3; D1 and his witnesses are cross-examined by D2, D3 and P; D2 by D3, P and D1; and D3 by P, D1 and D2". In such cases, it seems from *Ayr Road Trustees v Adams* (1883) 11 R. 326 that all such evidence will be regarded as evidence *in causa*.

[5] 1912 S.C. 1235, a salvage case in which two pursuers conjoined their actions.

[6] 1943 S.C. 108 at 109. See also *Harringon v Milk Marketing Board*, 1985 S.L.T. 342 for an example of a case in which failure to cross-examine was nearly fatal.

that witness ought to have a chance of tendering an explanation or denial, the point ought normally to be put to the witness in cross-examination. If such cross-examination is omitted, the witness may have to be recalled with the leave of the Court, possibly on conditions as to expenses; and in some circumstances the omission may cause fatal damage to the case."

Failure to cross-examine may be strategically damaging in circumstances where the credibility of witnesses is an important factor in the case.

PREVIOUS STATEMENTS

The position with regard to previous statements in civil proceedings is less **17–07** strict than in criminal proceedings. Section 3 of the Civil Evidence (Scotland) Act 1988 provides that a previous statement made by a witness is admissible "in so far as it tends to reflect favourably or unfavourably on that person's credibility". Moreover, since the abolition of the hearsay rule in terms of s.2 of the Civil Evidence (Scotland) Act 1988, it is admissible to lead evidence of the *content* of a witness's previous statement. It had always been possible to lead evidence of the making of the statement. The reason for admitting a previous statement is to show that the witness is a more credible or reliable witness by virtue of being consistent with their story. As indicated above, s.3 permits the use of previous statements, both to support or attack a witness's credibility and to lead evidence of the contents of the statement. As in criminal cases though, statements in precognitions remain inadmissible.[7]

In relation to the admissibility of hearsay evidence in civil proceedings, **17–08** the decision in *MT v DT*[8] ruled that statements made by a child can be admitted into court, notwithstanding that the child is not present or examined in court for competency.

When it is alleged that a witness is now giving fabricated evidence, and in **17–09** particular that it is a recent fabrication, at common law evidence may be led to show that the same witness told the same story much earlier in the history of the case, in order to negative such an allegation.[9] The evidence of a previous consistent statement can be produced in re-examination, by calling additional witnesses either before the party's case is closed or before the final speeches.

A party seeking to prove a witness's previous inconsistent statement must **17–10** first lay a basis for this by putting to the witness the fact that it was made, and to whom, and give them the opportunity to confirm or deny that fact.[10] Only if it is denied, can the evidence of the previous inconsistent statement be led.[11]

---

[7] s.9 of the Civil Evidence (Scotland) Act 1988.

[8] 2000 S.L.T. 1442.

[9] *Barr v Barr*, 1939 S.C. 696, *Gibson v N.C.R.*, 1925 S.C. 500, and, most importantly, *Burns v Colin McAndrew and Partners*, 1963 S.L.T. (Notes) 71, which imposed the prerequisite that the witness's credibility must first be impugned.

[10] See Davidson, *Evidence*, para.12.135.

[11] See *Gall v Gall* (1870) 9 M. 177.

OBJECTIONS TO EVIDENCE

17–11 According to Macphail[12] the practice in the courts in Scotland "is that a pursuer may not found on a ground of liability which has not been averred and has been the subject of evidence to which no timeous objection has been taken". However, Macphail also noted that there was authority[13] for the view that the failure of the other party to object timeously to the admission of evidence, which in effect opened up matters not on record, could amount to its admission. In civil cases, the prudent course for the challenging party is to object to the evidence in question as soon as it is sought to admit it.[14]

17–12 Other than in jury trials, the general rule in civil cases is for the judge to allow the evidence in under reservation of the question of its admissibility. This permits the issue to be debated later and also ensures that the evidence is on record for any subsequent appeal court to consider.[15] A failure to follow such a practice will have the effect in some cases of depriving the court of the evidence for all time and can lead to a successful appeal.[16]

17–13 In jury trials there is a risk that if a decision on admissibility is not made as soon as the point is raised, the jury will be led to rely on the evidence thus admitted and may not be swayed by any subsequent instruction by the presiding judge to ignore what they have heard. Thus, according to *McDonald v Duncan*,[17] the appropriate procedure is that "if an objection is taken to the admissibility of evidence, it is for the judge there and then to decide that question and not to hold it up until the conclusion of the whole proof, and then to give a pronouncement on it".[18]

17–14 In *Avery v Cantilever Shoe Co.*[19] Lord President Normand explained the Scottish procedure as follows:

> "[It] is for the counsel to make up his mind, subject to the Court's seeing that the witness has fair play, how he will examine his witness, and for the counsel at the end of the day to lay his submissions before the Court, having in view his own method of handling the witness, and, if he so chooses, to ask the Court to disbelieve the witness, provided that he has given him a fair opportunity of answering any charge of unreliability or untruthfulness which may emerge from his evidence."

---

[12] Macphail, *Evidence*, para.8.40.

[13] Notably *McGlone v British Railways Board*, 1966 S.C. (H.L.) 1, and *O'Donnell v Murdoch Mackenzie & Co*, 1966 S.C. 58, 1966 S.C. (H.L.) 63. See also *Brown's Exr v North British Steel Foundry Ltd*, 1967 S.L.T. (Notes) 111, and *Gibson v B.I.C.C.*, 1973 S.L.T. 2, in which the House of Lords criticised the Scottish closed record system for its rigidity.

[14] *McDonald v Duncan*, 1933 S.C. 737.

[15] *McDonald v Duncan*, 1933 S.C. 737 and Hajducki, *Civil Jury Trials*, at 4.32–4.35. But see also *McGowan v Mein*, 1976 S.L.T. (Sh. Ct) 29, where the sheriff saw good reason for departing from this practice.

[16] As in *Baretdji v Baretdji*, 1985 S.L.T. 126.

[17] *McDonald v Duncan*, 1933 S.C. 737, per Lord Anderson at 744. See also *McCallum v Paterson*, 1969 S.C. 85.

[18] Hajducki, *Civil Jury Trials*.

[19] 1942 S.C. 469 at 471.

Persons Present in Court During Previous Evidence

At common law in civil proceedings (as well as criminal proceedings) there **17–15** was an absolute bar against hearing testimony from a witness who had been in court prior to giving evidence and had therefore heard some of the previous testimony.[20] The position in civil cases is governed by s.3 of the Evidence (Scotland) Act 1840. This provision gives the court a discretion to admit the evidence of any witness who has been present "without the permission of the court" and "without the consent of the party objecting", provided the witness's presence in court was not the result of "culpable negligence or criminal intent" and that "injustice will not be done by his or her examination". The burden of proof on each of these issues rests with the party seeking to adduce the witness.[21]

In civil cases, s.1 of the Evidence (Scotland) Act 1852 renders competent **17–16** witnesses who appear without citation. It follows from this that a witness cited by one party in a civil case but not examined by that party may be called by the other party. This was the point established in *McDonnell v McShane*,[22] in which the witness in question was the defender in an affiliation and aliment action. It was ruled that he could be called as a witness by the pursuer, even though he had not been cited as a witness, since citation simply serves the purpose of securing the attendance of the witness and thereafter he or she is compellable for either side, provided competent.

Further Evidence

There is no general rule with regard to the admissibility of fresh evidence **17–17** that covers all civil cases. However, certain exceptions have been recognised in which the interests of justice require that evidence in replication of evidence already led should be admitted. In Court of Session cases,[23] the common law position in both Outer House first instance and Inner House reclaiming cases is that fresh evidence may be led after the close of the proof only if it could not have been made available previously by the exercise of reasonable diligence. This normally means that no warning of it could have been gleaned from a careful study of the closed record.[24]

When the Court of Session is hearing appeals from decisions of the sheriff **17–18** court, the Inner House has the power under s.72 of the Court of Session Act 1868 to hear additional evidence if necessary in the interests of justice.[25] In the sheriff court itself, a sheriff conducting a proof has no power to hear fresh evidence after the proof has closed, but the sheriff principal can hear such evidence in any case appealed to him in terms of s.27 of the Sheriff Courts (Scotland) Act 1907. Such examples as arise in practice are normally in the nature of *res noviter*, which, again, could not reasonably have been

---

[20] See Dickson, *Evidence*, para.1599.
[21] *Macdonald v Mackenzie*, 1947 J.C. 169 at 174.; also at 175 and 176, where it was held to be the duty of the judge to question the competence of any witness who has been present in court where this is apparent to him.
[22] *McDonnell v McShane*, 1967 S.L.T. (Sh. Ct) 61.
[23] For which, generally, see Maclaren, *Court of Session Practice*, at 562.
[24] Maxwell, at 559.
[25] See *Gairdner v Macarthur*, 1915 S.C. 589.

anticipated at the time of the original proof.[26] Once new evidence comes to light after a civil jury trial has been concluded, the only way of dealing with it would appear to be with a new trial.[27]

RECALL OF A WITNESS

17–19 At common law, the recall of a witness is limited to clarifying some ambiguity in that witness's evidence.[28] Statute has extended the scope of recall. Section 4 of the Evidence (Scotland) Act 1852 permits a party to recall a witness and put questions to that witness which are not limited simply to those which resolve ambiguities. In addition, the party wishing to invoke the section may do so at any time up to the close of their case. The recall may be at any stage of the proof, even after both parties have closed their case.[29]

---

[26] See, e.g. *McFarlane v Raeburn*, 1946 S.C. 67 (alibi not disclosed in closed record for affiliation and aliment action).

[27] Hajducki, *Civil Jury Trials*, 6.38–6.40.

[28] For examples of the limitations imposed by the common law rules in civil cases, see *Gairdner v Macarthur*, 1915 S.C. 589 and *McFarlane v Raeburn*, 1946 S.C. 67.

[29] i.e. before the summing up speeches.

BIBLIOGRAPHY

Beaumont, McEleavy, and Anton, *Private International Law*, 3rd edn (Edinburgh: SULI, W. Green, 2011).

Brown, Burman and Jamieson, *Sex Crimes on Trial* (Edinburgh: Edinburgh University Press, 1993).

Bruce and Hall, In the eye of the beholder: The Science of Face Perception (Oxford: Oxford University Press, 1998).

Burton, *Judging in Good Faith* (Cambridge, Mass.: Cambridge University Press, 2002).

Chalmers, *Evidence*, 3rd edn, (Dundee: Dundee University Press, 2012).

Cross and Tapper, *Evidence*, 12th edn (Oxford: Oxford University Press, 2010).

Davidson, *Evidence* (Edinburgh SULI, W. Green, 2007).

Dickson, *Evidence*, 3rd edn (Edinburgh T & T Clark, 1887).

Dobash and Dobash, (eds), *Women, Violence and Social Change* (London: Routledge, 1992).

Dobie, *Sheriff Court Practice* (Collieston: Caledonian Books—reprint of 1948 edition, Glasgow: Hodge).

Dent and Flin (eds), *Children as Witnesses* (Chichester: Wiley, 1992).

Du Cann, *The Art of the Advocate*, 2nd edn (Harmondsworth : Penguin, 1993).

Spencer and Flin, *The Evidence of Children*, 2nd edn (London: Blackstone, 1993).

Ellison, *The Adversarial Process and the Vulnerable Witness* (Oxford: Oxford University Press, 2001).

Ferguson and McDiarmid, *Scots Criminal Law: A Critical Analysis* (Dundee: Dundee University Press, 2012).

Gloag and Henderson, *Introduction to the Law of Scotland*, 13th edn (Edinburgh: W. Green, 2012).

Griffiths, *Confessions* (Edinburgh: Butterworths, 1994).

Gudjonsson, *The Psychology of Interrogations, Confessions and Testimony*, (Chichester: Wiley, 1992).

Hajducki, *Civil Jury Trials*, 2nd edn (Edinburgh: Avizandum, 2006).

Hyam, *Advocacy Skills*, London: Blackstone, London 1999).

Jasanoff, *Science at the Bar* (Cambridge, Mass: Harvard University Press, 1995).

Jones, *Expert Evidence: science, medicine and the practice of law* (Oxford: Clarendon Press, 1994).

Lewis, *Delayed Prosecution for Childhood Sexual Abuse* (2006).

McBryde, *Bankruptcy,* 2nd edn (Edinburgh: W. Green 1995).

MacDonald, *Criminal Law of Scotland*, 5th edn (Edinburgh, W. Green, 1948).

McLaren, *Court of Session Practice* (Edinburgh: W. Green, 1916).

Macphail, *Evidence* (Edinburgh: Law Society of Scotland, 1987).

Macphail, Lord, *Sheriff Court Practice*, 3rd edn, T. Welsh (ed) (Edinburgh: W. Green, 2006).

Maxwell, *Practice of the Court of Session*, (Edinburgh, Scottish Courts Administration, 1980).

Mowbray, *The Development of Positive Obligations under the European Convention of Human Rights by the European Court of Human Rights* (2004).

McCluskey, Lord, *Law, Justice and Democracy* (London: Sweet and Maxwell, 1987).

Moody and Tombs, *Constructing Prosecution Decisions: The case of the procurator fiscal* (Edinburgh: Scottish Academic Press, 1982).

Murphy, *Murphy on Evidence*, 8th edn (Oxford: Oxford University Press, 2003).

Nicolson and Webb, *Professional Legal Ethics: Critical Interrogations* (Oxford: Oxford University Press, 1999).

Paterson and Ritchie, Law, *Practice & Conduct for Solicitors* (Edinburgh: W. Green, 2006).

Redmayne, *Expert Evidence and Criminal Justice* (Oxford: Oxford University Press, 2001)

Renton and Brown, *Criminal Procedure*, 6th edn (Edinburgh: W. Green, 1996).

Roberts and Zuckerman, *Criminal Evidence*, 2nd edn (Oxford: Oxford University Press, 2010).

Scott Robinson, *The Law of Interdict*, 2nd edn (Edinburgh: Butterworths, 1994).

Shaw, *Effective Advocacy* (London: Sweet & Maxwell 1996).

Stewart, *Stair Memorial Encyclopaedia*, Evidence Reissue, The Laws of Scotland, (Butterworths, 2006).

Thayer, *A Preliminary Treatise on Evidence at the Common Law* (1898).

Twining, *Theories of Evidence: Bentham and Wigmore* (London: Weidenfeld and Nicolson, 1985).

Walker, *The Battered Woman Syndrome* (New York: Springer, 1984).

Walker and Walker, *The Law of Evidence in Scotland*, 3rd edn, M. Ross (ed.) (Edinburgh and J, Chalmers, T & T Clark, 2000).

Wilkinson, *Scottish Law of Evidence* (Edinburgh: Butterworths, 1986).

Williams, *A Very British Killing—the death of Baha Mousa* (London: Jonathan Cape, 2012).

INDEX